D0986287

ARKANSAS POLITICS AND GOVERNMENT

*State Politics and Government*

General Editor

Daniel J. Elazar
Temple University and Bar-Ilan University

Associate Editors

Ellis Katz
Temple University

John Kincaid
University of North Texas

Advisory Editors

Thad Beyle
University of North Carolina
at Chapel Hill

Diane D. Blair
University of Arkansas

Samuel Gove
University of Illinois,
Urbana–Champaign

Robert Miewald
University of Nebraska–Lincoln

Kenneth Palmer
University of Maine at Orono

Charles Press
Michigan State University

Stephen L. Schechter
Russell Sage College

Published in association with
the Center for
the Study of Federalism.

DIANE D. BLAIR

# Arkansas Politics & Government

DO THE PEOPLE RULE?

UNIVERSITY OF NEBRASKA PRESS

LINCOLN & LONDON

Publication of this book was aided by a grant
from The Andrew W. Mellon Foundation.

Portions of chapter 15 have previously been published, in different form, as "The Study and Teaching
of Arkansas Politics: Political Science as Pioneering," *Arkansas Political Science Journal* 1 (February
1980): 75–92, and "Teaching American State Politics: Arkansas," *American Political Science Association News,* Fall 1980, pp. 10–13.

Copyright © 1988 by the University of Nebraska Press
All rights reserved
Manufactured in the United States of America

The paper in this book meets the minimum requirements of American National Standard for Information Sciences—Permanence of Paper for Printed
Library Materials, ANSI Z39.48–1984.

Library of Congress Cataloging in Publication Data
Blair, Diane D., 1938-
Arkansas politics and government.
(State politics and government)
Includes index.
1. Arkansas – Politics and government.
I. Title.   II. Series.
JK5116.B42    1988      320.9767      87-31423
ISBN 0-8032-1188-0 (alk. paper)
ISBN 0-8032-6073-3 (pbk: alk. paper)

Second printing: 1994

For Jim,
my best teacher about
Arkansas politics, and about
most other things as well

# CONTENTS

DANIEL J. ELAZAR

# Foreword

The more than continental stretch of the American domain is given form and character as a federal union of fifty different states whose institutions order the American landscape. The existence of these states made possible the emergence of a continental nation where liberty, not despotism, reigns and self-government is the first principle of order. The great American republic was born in its states as its very name signifies. America's first founding was repeated on thirteen separate occasions over 125 years, from Virginia in 1607 to Georgia in 1732, each giving birth to a colony that became a self-governing commonwealth. Its revolution and second founding was made by those commonwealths, now states, acting in congress, and its constitution was written together and adopted separately.

As the American tide rolled westward from the Atlantic coast, it absorbed new territories by organizing thirty-seven more states over the next 169 years. Americans, older and newer, transformed the fledgling republic into the leader of the free world by establishing free government at home first and foremost. Nineteenth-century American patriots liked to speak of the American empire, but it was an empire of self-governing states by design. Without those states the American people could not provide for their domestic concerns or maintain their federal government. Other forms of political order could not provide the same combination of order and diversity, liberty and self-government.

Most of the American states are larger and better developed than most of the world's nations. Each has its own story, its own character as a civil society; each is a polity with its own uniqueness. They share a common tradition of governance, but to view them as the same because their institutions resemble one another would be like assuming the nations of continental Europe to be the same because they share a common commitment to parliamentary institutions, or the nations of Africa to be the same because they emphasize presidential rule.

The American states exist because they are civil societies. They were first given political form and then acquired their other characteristics. It is their polities that are crucial to their being. Each of those polities has its own constitution, its own political cultural synthesis, its own relationship to the federal union and to its section.

It is in and through the states, no less than the nation, that the great themes of American life play themselves out. The advancing frontier and the continuing experience of Americans as a frontier people, the drama of American ethnic blending, the tragedy of slavery and racial discrimination, the political struggle for expanding the right to vote—all found, and find, their expression in the states. The changing character of government from an all-embracing concern with every aspect of civil and religious behavior to a limited concern with maintaining law and order to a concern with providing the social benefits of the contemporary welfare state has been felt in the states even more than in the federal government.

*Arkansas Politics and Government: Do the People Rule?* is the third book in the Center for the Study of Federalism/University of Nebraska Press series State Politics and Government. The aim of the series is to provide books on the government and politics of the individual states of the United States that will appeal to three audiences: political scientists, their students, and the wider public in each state. Each volume examines the specific character of one of the fifty states, looking at the state as a polity—its political culture, traditions and practices, constituencies and interest groups, and constitutional and institutional frameworks.

Each book in the series reviews the political development of the state to demonstrate how the state's political institutions and characteristics have evolved from the first settlement to the present, viewing the state in the context of the nation and section of which it is a part, and discussing the state's relations with and roles vis-à-vis its sister states and the federal government. The state's constitutional history is examined and related to the workings of the state's political institutions and processes. Local government and community politics are also considered. Finally, each volume reviews the state's policy concerns and their implementation, from the budgetary process to particular substantive policies. Each book concludes by summarizing the principal themes and findings to draw conclusions about the current state of the state, its continuing traditions and emerging issues. Each volume also contains a guide to existing literature on that state and to state government documents.

Great care has been taken to select authors who can best achieve the numerous goals of the series. The series editors have sought scholars who are thoroughly familiar with the discipline and practice of political science, who know how to write in clear and straightforward prose, and—perhaps most important—who are sensitive to the special character of their states. Diane Blair brings all this and more to *Arkansas Politics and Government*. In addition to being an established scholar of its government, she has been deeply involved in the political activities of Arkansas, witnessing at first hand the give-and-take of campaigning, government decision making, and policy implementation.

Since each book will have a unique match of state and author, the books are not expected to be uniform. However, they do focus on the common themes of federalism, constitutionalism, the continuing American frontier, sectionalism, and political culture, to provide a framework within which to consider the institutions, routines, and processes of state government and politics.

## FEDERALISM

Both the greatest conflicts of American history and the day-to-day operations of American government are closely intertwined with American federalism—the form of American government (in the eighteenth-century sense of the term, which includes both structure and process). In learning about state government and politics we can hardly be surprised that this is the case. Arkansas's relationship to the federal government has been typical of that of other southern states, aggressively self-assertive in matters relating to slavery and civil-rights issues, first to protect the "peculiar institution" and then the "southern way of life," while at the same time actively involved in the search for federal aid in matters of infrastructure and economic development. This uniquely southern pattern of conflict and cooperation has been well documented. Arkansas was one of the first states to open an office in Washington during World War II to secure federal military facilities to bolster the state's twice-depressed sagging economy. It was one of the active beneficiaries of the New Deal. Virtually every part of the state gained from New Deal and other federal programs, whether in the form of welfare and public works projects, soil conservation and river-basin development projects, public health and law enforcement assistance.

As it continued to pursue federal aid, Arkansas also was the scene of some of the most active resistance to the enforcement of the desegregation decisions of the United States Supreme Court. Governor Faubus's attempt to resist the racial integration of Little Rock Central High School in 1957 was the opening battle of the decade-long near civil war that led to the ending of legalized racial discrimination in the South. Although the civil rights revolution is now history, this book vividly illustrates the fact that both cooperation and conflict continue to characterize Arkansas's intergovernmental relationships.

## CONSTITUTIONALISM

The American constitutional tradition grows out of the Whig understanding that civil societies are founded by political covenant entered into by the first founders and reaffirmed by subsequent generations, through which the powers of government are delineated and limited and the rights of the constituting members clearly proclaimed in such a way as to provide moral and practical restraints on governmental institutions. That constitutional tradition was modified by the federalists, who accepted its fundamental principles but strengthened the institutional framework designed to provide energy in government while maintaining the checks and balances they saw as needed to preserve liberty and republican government. At the same time, they turned nonbinding declarations of rights into enforceable constitutional articles.

American state constitutions reflect the melding of these two traditions. Under the U.S. Constitution, each state is free to adopt its own constitution, provided that it establishes a republican form of government. Some states have adopted highly succinct constitutions like the Vermont Constitution of 1793 with 6,600 words that is still in effect with only fifty-two amendments. Others are just the opposite, such as Georgia's Ninth Constitution, adopted in 1976, which has 583,000 words.

State constitutions are potentially—and often have in fact been—far more comprehensive than the federal constitution, which is one of limited, delegated powers. Because states are plenary governments, they automatically possess all powers not specifically denied them by the U.S. Constitution or their citizens. Consequently, a state constitution must be explicit about limiting and defining the scope of governmental powers, especially on behalf of individual liberty. Overall, six different state constitutional patterns have emerged. One is the commonwealth pattern, developed in New England, which emphasizes Whig ideas of the constitution as a philosophic document designed first and foremost to set a direction for civil society and to express and institutionalize a theory of republican government. A second is the constitutional pattern of the commercial republic. The constitutions fitting this pattern reflect a series of compromises required by the conflict of many strong ethnic groups and commercial interests generated by the flow of heterogeneous streams of migrants into particular states and the early development of large commercial and industrial cities in those states.

The third is that found in the South, which can be described as the southern contractual pattern. Southern state constitutions are used as instruments to set explicit terms governing the relationship between polity and society, such as those terms which protected slavery or racial segregation, or those which sought to diffuse the formal allocation of authority in order to accommodate the swings between oligarchy and factionalism characteristic of southern state politics. Of all the southern states, only Louisiana stands somewhat outside this configuration, providing the fourth state constitutional pattern, since its legal system was founded on the French civil code. Its constitutions have been codes—long, highly explicit documents that form a pattern in and of themselves.

A fifth pattern is that found frequently in the less populated states of the Far West, where the state constitution is first and foremost a frame of government explicitly reflecting the republican and democratic principles dominant in the nation in the late nineteenth century, but emphasizing the structure of state government and the distribution of powers within that structure in a direct, businesslike manner. Finally, the two newest states, Alaska and Hawaii, have adopted constitutions following the managerial pattern developed and promoted by twentieth-century constitutional reform movements in the United States. Those constitutions emphasize conciseness, broad grants of power to the executive branch, and relatively few structural restrictions on the legislature. They stress natural-resource conservation and social legislation.

Arkansas shares the southern constitutional tradition. The state's first constitution was adopted in 1836 and subsequently adapted to exigencies of secession and Reconstruction. These constitutions gave way to the constitution of 1874, which brought resegregation and other changes in constitutional approach. It has since been repeatedly amended and otherwise adapted to desegregation and modernization. Arkansas's constitutions can profitably be examined to reflect the changes in the American constitutional tradition because they have had to make explicit what other states, not touched by the Civil War and its aftermath, have been able to leave implicit in their fundamental laws.

## THE CONTINUING AMERICAN FRONTIER

For Americans, the very word *frontier* conjures up the images of the rural-land frontier of yesteryear—of explorers and mountain men, of cowboys and Indians, of brave pioneers pushing their way westward in the face of natural obstacles of one kind or another. Later, Americans' picture of the frontier was expanded to include the inventors, the railroad builders, and the captains of industry who created the urban-industrial frontier. Recently television has begun to celebrate the entrepreneurial ventures of the automobile and oil industries, portraying the captains of those industries and their families in the same larger-than-life frame as the heroes of that first frontier once were portrayed in.

As is so often the case, the media responsible for determining and catering to popular taste tell us a great deal about ourselves. The United States was founded with the opening of its rural-land frontier that persisted until World War I, more or less, spreading farms, ranches, mines, and the towns serving them across the land. Early in the nineteenth century, the rural-land frontier generated an urban frontier that was based on industrial development. The creation of new wealth through industrialization transformed cities from mere regional service centers into generators of wealth in their own right. That frontier persisted for more than one hundred years as a major force in American society as a whole and perhaps another sixty years as a major force in various parts of the country. The population movements and attendant growth on the urban-industrial frontier brought about the effective resettlement of the United States as a nation of freestanding industrial cities from coast to coast.

Between the world wars, the urban-industrial frontier gave birth in turn to a third frontier stage, one based on the new technologies of electronic communication, the internal combustion engine, the airplane, synthetics, and petrochemicals. These new technologies transformed every aspect of American life and turned urbanization into metropolitanization. This third frontier stage produced a third settlement of the United States, this time in metropolitan regions from coast to coast, involving a mass migration of tens of millions of Americans in search of opportunity on the suburban frontier.

In the mid-1970s the first post–World War II generation came to an end. Many Americans were speaking of the "limits of growth." Yet despite that anti-frontier rhetoric, there was every sign that a fourth frontier stage was

beginning in the form of the rurban, or citybelt-cybernetic, frontier generated by the metropolitan-technological frontier just as the latter had been
generated by its predecessor. The new locus of settlement is medium-sized
and small cities and the rural interstices of the megalopolis. The rurban-
cybernetic frontier first emerged in the Northeast, as did its predecessors,
but it is finding its true form in the South and West, where these citybelt
matrices are not being built on the collapse of earlier forms but are developing as an original form. The present sunbelt frontier—strung out along the
Gulf Coast, the southwestern desert, and the fringes of the California
mountains—is classically megalopolitan in citybelt form and cybernetic
with its aerospace-related industries and sunbelt living made possible by air
conditioning and the new telecommunications.

Arkansas has enjoyed an ambiguous relationship with the continuing
American frontier. Even when it was in the path of the original westward
movement, from just after the War of 1812 until the Civil War, its settlement
was in most respects a spillover of the southern stream moving westward.
Settlers created a "backwoods" culture over much of the new state. The
exception was in the southeast, where a "poor man's" version of southern
plantation culture developed. It was bankrupted by the Civil War to re-
emerge as a planter-sharecropper society after the war. As a poor state,
Arkansas retained in many regions, until after World War II, what are
usually called "frontier conditions."

Poor to begin with, Arkansas was hard pressed after the Civil War and
was not significantly touched by industrialization or by the urban-industrial
frontier. It did somewhat better in relation to the metropolitan-technological
frontier, changing insofar as the whole country was changed by its impact.

Arkansas is already doing better on the new rurban-cybernetic frontier,
since several parts of the state—particularly in the central Ozarks and the
northwest corner—have proved attractive to those seeking rurban lifestyles.
The new frontier may reshape settlement patterns in the state; it has already
reshaped the state's politics and infused its government with a new spirit, as
this book demonstrates. Although still outside the sunbelt megalopolis,
Arkansas seems to be developing an attraction of its own for certain populations.

## THE PERSISTENCE OF SECTIONALISM

Sectionalism—the expression of social, economic, and especially political
differences along geographic lines—is part and parcel of American political
life. The more or less permanent political ties that link groups of contiguous

states together as sections reflect the ways in which local conditions and differences in political culture modify the effect of the frontier. This overall sectional pattern reflects the interaction of the three basic factors. The original sections were produced by the variations in the influence of the rural-land frontier on different geographic segments of the country. They, in turn, have been modified by the pressures generated by the first and subsequent frontier stages. As a result, sectionalism is not the same as regionalism. The latter is essentially a phenomenon—often transient—that brings adjacent state, substate, or interstate areas together because of immediate and specific common interests. The sections are not homogeneous socioeconomic units sharing a common character across state lines, but complex entities combining highly diverse states and communities with common political interests that generally complement one another socially and economically.

The nation's sectional alignments are rooted in the three great historical, cultural, and economic spheres into which the country is divided: the greater Northeast, the greater South, and the greater West. Following state lines, the greater Northeast includes all those states north of the Ohio and Potomac rivers and east of Lake Michigan. The greater South includes the states below that line but east of the Mississippi, plus Missouri, Arkansas, Louisiana, Oklahoma, and Texas. All the rest of the states compose the greater West. Within that framework, there are eight sections: New England, Middle Atlantic, Near West, Upper South, Lower South, Western South, Northwest, and Far West. Arkansas is in the Western South.

From the New Deal years through the 1960s, Americans' understanding of sectionalism was submerged by their concern with urban-oriented socioeconomic categories, such as the struggle between labor and management or between the haves and have-nots in the big cities. Even the racial issue, once the hallmark of the greater South, began to be perceived in nonsectional terms as a result of black migration northward. This is not to say that sectionalism ceased to exist as a vital force, only that it was little noted in those years.

Beginning in the 1970s, however, there was a resurgence of sectional feeling as economic social cleavages increasingly came to follow sectional lines. The sunbelt-frostbelt confrontation is the prime example of this new sectionalism. "Sunbelt" is the new code word for the Lower South, Western South, and Far West; "frostbelt" is the code word for the New England, Middle Atlantic, and Great Lakes (Near Western) states. Sectionalism is once again a major force in national politics, closely linked to the rurban-cybernetic frontier.

Arkansas's location on the periphery of the Western South meant that the state was settled originally by white frontiersmen and adventurers seeking to escape civilization, not build it. They settled in the hills and hollows of the Ozarks and were followed by settlements of small farmers. They remained a population of plain folks who sought more than anything else to be left alone, for whatever reasons. Even the relatively rich and powerful who built a very modest plantation economy in the southeast and who brought in black slaves to do its work failed to attain the status of the antebellum planter class, which itself remained an underclass until our own times. This, in turn, led to a society divided into clearly segregated white and black populations until the 1960s. Nevertheless, as this book discusses, the race issue was not as critical to Arkansas as it was in the Lower South. After a surprisingly aggressive and even unexpected resistance to racial desegregation, Arkansas accepted the new reality and has adjusted to it with relative ease. In part, this accommodation was a reflection of the western dimension of Arkansas's character that led to a division of the white population into two distinct groups—the lowlanders in a triangle stretching from the northeast to the southwest, and the highlanders of the northwest and west. The former were part of traditional southern society whereas the latter were more populist in orientation.

## THE VITAL ROLE OF POLITICAL CULTURE

The United States as a whole shares a general political culture that is rooted in two contrasting conceptions of the political order that can be traced back to the earliest settlement of the country. In the first, the polity is conceived as a marketplace in which the primary public relationships are products of bargaining among individuals and groups acting out of self-interest. In the second, the political order is conceived to be a commonwealth—a polity in which the whole people have an undivided interest—in which the citizens cooperate in an effort to create and maintain the best government in order to implement certain shared moral principles. These two conceptions have exercised an influence on government and politics throughout American history, sometimes conflicting with and sometimes complementing each other.

The national political culture is a synthesis of three major political subcultures: individualistic, moralistic, and traditionalistic. All three are of nationwide proportions, having spread, in the course of time, from coast to coast. At the same time each subculture is strongly tied to specific sections of the country, reflecting the streams and currents of migration that have carried people of different origins and backgrounds across the continent in more or less orderly patterns. Each of the three reflects its own particular synthesis of the marketplace and the commonwealth.

The same locational factors place Arkansas within the traditionalistic political culture. The traditionalistic political culture is rooted in an ambivalent attitude toward the marketplace, coupled with a paternalistic and elitist conception of the commonwealth. It reflects an older, precommercial attitude that accepts a substantially hierarchical society as part of the ordered nature of things, authorizing and expecting those at the top of the social structure to take a special and dominant role in government. Like its moralistic counterpart, the traditionalistic political culture accepts government as an actor with a positive role in the community, but it tries to limit that role to maintaining the existing social order. To do so, it functions to confine real political power to a relatively small and self-perpetuating group drawn from an established elite who often inherit their right to govern through family ties or social position. Social and family ties are even more important in a traditionalistic political culture than personal ties in the individualistic. Those who do not have a definite role to play in politics are not expected to be even minimally active as citizens. In many cases, they are not even expected to vote. As in the individualistic political culture, those active in politics are expected to benefit personally from their activity, although not necessarily by direct pecuniary gain.

Political parties are not important in traditionalistic political cultures because they encourage a degree of openness that goes against the grain of an elite-oriented political order. Political competition is expressed through factional alignments, an extension of the personal politics characteristic of the system; hence political systems within the culture tend to have loose one-party systems if they have political parties at all. Political leaders play conservative and custodial rather than initiatory roles unless they are pressed strongly from the outside.

Although Arkansas is rooted in the traditionalistic political subculture of the southern United States, it also has a certain moralistic streak in its mountainous areas that has contributed to a traditionalistic-moralistic synthesis in that part of the state. More recently, an individualistic dimension has been added in the urban areas. Nevertheless, the traditionalistic political culture meant for years that large segments of the population did not see it as their place to participate in politics. In Arkansas, as in the rest of the South, this was exacerbated by the disfranchisement of the black population and, to a lesser extent, through various devices designed to discourage ordinary white people from voting as well. Because of its populist northwest, however, Arkansas did not fall as completely into the hands of a political elite as other southern states. Since the civil rights revolution of the 1960s, disfranchisement of blacks has given way to black participation and with it greater opportunities for white participation as well. Today political participation in Arkansas is governed by a more general openness tempered by the residues of an older political culture.

All told, Arkansas is a much underrated state whose low image in the eyes of other Americans is nominally supported by statistics, folklore, and events—at least those events that capture the public eye. Take the statistics: in most quality-of-life measures, Arkansas ranks near the bottom among the fifty states, not actually at the bottom, but low enough. Thirty years ago, when Harry Ashmore was still the editor of the *Arkansas Gazette*, he wrote in an editorial that Arkansas was ranked at the bottom of the list with regard to per capita expenditures on education. His newspaper received a host of indignant letters pointing out that actually Mississippi was at the bottom and Arkansas ranked second from last. It is not hard to guess Ashmore's retort. And yet the statistics, no matter how formally valid, do not accurately reflect the level of public services in the state even before the great surge forward described in this book.

The folklore image of Arkansas has been much the same since the state was first settled. It is an image of backwoods hillbillies cut off from civilization by choice, their way of life ranging from lazy to degenerate. Yet what looked like the behavior of ne'er-do-well mountaineers could also be understood as rugged independence. Those who took the trouble to get to know the state's citizens found among them the cultivated, the gentle, and the concerned as well as their opposites.

During the civil rights revolution, public events did project an Arkansas with little to be proud of. Ironically, a state previously known for its relative liberalism on the race question in the context of the Jim Crow South suddenly found itself in the headlines as the first-line of massive resistance that had to be countered with federal troops. Yet Governor Faubus's refusal to allow the integration of Little Rock Central High School was more in the nature of a desperate attempt by a politician to extend his own career than a reflection of systematic policy.

Happily, in the past two decades, Arkansas's better reality has begun to surface through the statistics and the folklore. This book describes that better reality and how it manifests itself in the state's government and politics.

# Preface

After fifteen years of thinking, writing, and teaching about Arkansas politics, and even more years of practicing it, I have come to see one particular puzzle as central to any understanding of the state's political past and critical to any evaluation of the political present and future. Briefly, here is the enigma.

For most of Arkansas's history, most of its citizens were hardworking and hard-pressed farmers, struggling for subsistence against formidable odds. For all of its history as a state, Arkansas has had democratic institutions through which this majority of the citizenry should have been able to elect sympathetic officials, demand attention and assistance, and hold the government accountable. Yet this kind of demand and response has been a rare event rather than a routine occurrence. Anyone with even the most superficial acquaintance with Arkansas knows that its people have always been fierce in the protection of what is theirs, quick to take offense against slight or injury. And yet, despite the state's proud motto of "Regnat Populus" (The people rule), there is little evidence in the nineteenth century or for most of the twentieth of either popular assertion of just demands or of government provision of necessary and useful services. Indeed, for most of Arkansas's 150 years, state government's relationship to its people seemed to range from irrelevant to injurious.

Recent decades have brought profound political change. There are obvious light years of difference between a state government that spent virtually nothing on schools or roads or health and one that now spends well over a billion dollars annually on these and other services; between Governor John Roane (1849–52) asserting, "I am convinced, after careful investigation into the history of the common school, that no possible good can come of it or ever can result to the state or any considerable proportion of the people," and Governor Bill Clinton stumping the state in behalf of excellence in education; between Governor Jeff Davis (1901–1907) boasting that "nigger domination will never prevail in this country . . . as long as shotguns and rifles lie around loose and we are able to pull the trigger" and Governor Winthrop Rockefeller (1967–71) leading the singing of "We Shall Overcome" on the capitol steps following the assassination of Martin Luther King, Jr.[1]

If, as one of Arkansas's earliest observers reported, "Arkansas will have longer to struggle with the disadvantages that attend to it . . . than other frontier states," there is abundant evidence that Arkansas has at last begun to struggle, and occasionally to triumph.[2] For the political scientist, however, and for all serious students of politics, these visible, dramatic symbols of change provoke as many questions as they answer: Why did attentive and useful state government take so long to evolve? Are the changes, obvious to even the most casual contemporary observer, fundamental changes in substance, or superficial changes in symbol and style? Have a representative political system and a responsive state government actually been achieved? And if so, have they been secured?

In chapter 1 I explore these questions and also document, through a narrative overview, the extent to which state government was as much an affliction as an aid to most Arkansas citizens for much of the state's history. In chapter 2 I offer some social, economic, and political explanations for the curious acquiescence of Arkansas people in this ineffectual kind of government. The traditional way of doing politics in Arkansas is described in chapter 3, and the various forces that ushered in the contemporary political system are explored. In chapters 4 and 5 I analyze the results of those changes as they are reflected in campaigns, elections, parties, and the increasingly regional nature of voting behavior. Chapter 6 deals with interest groups, which have become an integral part of contemporary politics.

Whether changes in the political system have produced equally significant changes in actual governance is the subject examined in chapters 7 through 10 dealing with the constitution, and the executive, legislative, and judicial branches of government. Since some of the most important state governmental decisions are made in response to, or reaction against, policies emanating from the national government, the cooperative and combative aspects of Arkansas's federal relationships will be explored in chapter 11. While the focus of this study is state politics and governance, a major part of Arkansas public affairs is transacted with equally profound consequences for citizens by counties and cities, the subject of chapter 12. To further test whether political alterations and institutional reforms have had major substantive impact, in Chapter 13 I examine the changing politics of state taxing and spending and the state's long struggle with public education policies.

In chapter 14, an overview is offered of the major characteristics of contemporary politics and government in Arkansas, and of the political future that they seem to indicate. In chapter 15 I suggest some of the best sources for further research. This is a critical chapter because serious examination of Arkansas's political system is in its pioneering stages, and this book is offered as a preliminary analysis rather than a definitive study.

As many will quickly note, it takes a big dose of bravado to offer any generalizations about Arkansas politics to the reading public. Arkansas voters are notorious for quickly confounding any assertions about their expected behavior; and the hundreds of "experts" on Arkansas politics who populate every courthouse, campus, and coffee shop in Arkansas (from many of whom I have learned much and drawn freely) will be swift in exposing the flaws in my analysis.

Since such dialogue is essential to democratic health and further learning, it will be welcome. And when error is exposed, all of us "experts" on Arkansas politics can take refuge in the immortal words of one of Arkansas's past political masters: "Just because I said it doesn't make it so."[3]

ACKNOWLEDGMENTS

I am indebted not only to the scholars cited throughout this book but to many other important sources of ideas, information, and encouragement. Some of Arkansas's busiest people, past and present public officials and political activists, carved time from their crowded schedules to be interviewed, to respond to surveys and inquiries, to visit with and be questioned by me and my students. Their insights were invaluable.

Equally essential was the voluminous information on Arkansas and its politics reported daily in the state press. My appreciation of a free press in general, and of the Arkansas press corps in particular, was confirmed and strengthened as I did the research for and wrote this volume.

I am also grateful to my students, whose enthusiastic interest in my course on Arkansas politics was a major stimulus to this study, and whose questions, criticisms, and observations have constantly challenged and sharpened my own insights. One of these students in particular, my graduate assistant Heather Miles, made indispensable gifts of both time and intellect to this volume. Also, my colleague Robert Savage patiently provided the appropriate mixture of criticism and encouragement.

Finally, my family gave me many hours that rightfully were theirs, along with their comforting assurance that this project was important to them as well as to me.

ARKANSAS POLITICS AND GOVERNMENT

## CHAPTER ONE

# The Past in the Present

*The room was being crowded by incoming ballot boxes. Country-men, most of them sweat-soaked and ragged and old, were bring-ing in boxes from rural precincts; wooden boxes, tin boxes, now and then a cigar box or egg crate. Voice of the people.*

Charles M. Wilson, *Rabble Rouser*, 1936

*I have got my first time to see any of them vote for a measure that truly had the interests of the people at heart.*

State Senator, 1901

On March 29, 1984, fifteen hundred mourners gathered at Little Rock's Central High School to mourn the death of a beloved and valued Arkansan. Led by Governor Bill Clinton, an array of distinguished speakers expressed anguish over the loss of twenty-two-year-old Roosevelt Thompson, Jr., killed in an automobile accident while driving back for what would have been his triumphal last semester at Yale. Tribute was paid to all he had accomplished at Central High (president of his class, editor of the paper, starting lineman, Presidential scholar), to the further glories he had achieved at Yale (Phi Beta Kappa, the Lyman prize for scholarship and character, Rhodes scholar), and to the future many had assumed would be his: governor of Arkansas, perhaps U.S. senator, possibly the first black president. Governor Clinton, his voice breaking with emotion, read the passage from Luke in which a young Jesus preached to his elders at the temple in Jerusalem, and then asked the mourners to "thank God that we are here at Central High, the finest example of all the best in Arkansas, and of the long road we have traveled in our state."[1]

On September 23, 1957, a very different kind of group had gathered at Central High. Hundreds of angry white agitators hurled racial obscenities at and threatened physical violence against the first black students to enroll at Central. Governor Orval Faubus had opposed the Little Rock School Board's desegregation plan and had appeared in chancery court to support a request for an injunction to halt desegregation, which was granted. When this injunction was overturned in federal court, Faubus ordered the Arkansas National Guard to seize the school and stop the "Little Rock Nine" from entering. It was after a further federal court order directed that the National Guard be withdrawn and that integration proceed that the mobs gathered, whereupon President Eisenhower ordered in the 101st Airborne Infantry Division, under whose protection Central High was integrated. While Governor Faubus maintained then, as now, that his actions were necessitated by his obligation to preclude violence, most analysts of this event suggest that Faubus was even more strongly motivated by his desire for reelection to an extraordinary third gubernatorial term.[2]

In this respect alone, the actions were "successful": Faubus in fact went on to an unprecedented six two-year terms. Many of the educational and economic development programs that Faubus had earlier initiated, however, were severely disrupted, and Arkansas acquired an instant global identity as a state characterized by racism, violence, and demagoguery.[3]

Although Arkansas had indeed traveled a long road from 1957 to 1984, neither of these two episodes offers an entirely accurate abstract of the temper of its times. While Arkansas had manifested all the major symbols of southern segregation and white supremacy (Jim Crow laws, a white primary, inferior public services for blacks, occasional lynchings), this racism had always been more tempered than that in some of the states in the deeper South. In 1889 Bishop Henry M. Turner, presiding bishop of the African Methodist Episcopal Church, had predicted, "Arkansas is destined to be the great Negro state of the Country. The rich lands, the healthy regions, the meagre prejudice compared to some states, and the opportunities to acquire wealth, all conspire to make it inviting to the Colored man. The Colored people have a better start there than in any other state in the Union." Similarly, the early twentieth-century Arkansas black politician Mifflin Gibbs wrote favorably in his autobiography of the distinctly nonsouthern tolerance he had encountered.[4]

While these assessments turned out to be excessively optimistic, blatant race-baiting was a relatively rare campaign device; many blacks voted in the general election and even in the "white" primary, where local custom permitted; and in 1950, the national director of the National Association for the Advancement of Colored People (NAACP) had noted, "in all fairness first place for acceptance in the South of the trend toward desegregation must go to Arkansas." By 1957, the time of the crisis at Central High, substantial integration had already taken place in the state's colleges, with no interference from Governor Faubus. In fact, one of Faubus's first acts as governor had been to enlarge the Democratic State Committee to accommodate six black members. Arkansas, then, was an unlikely place and Faubus (raised in the Ozark hills where blacks were nonexistent and in a family with progressive reformist traditions) an unlikely leader for an event that precipitated even more intransigence and violence elsewhere and that stigmatized Arkansas for decades thereafter.[5]

Similarly, while the grief over Roosevelt Thompson's death was heartfelt and universal, in November 1984, Arkansas voters not only elected thoroughly nonracist Bill Clinton to the first third term granted any Arkansas governor since Faubus but in the Second Congressional District simultaneously elected to the U.S. House of Representatives a colorful and controversial sheriff who had referred contemptuously to a black federal judge as a "token judge" and had promised that he would not "coddle prisoners with fried chicken and watermelon" but rather would put them "out on the road-gang cleaning the ditches where there are copperheads and water moccasins." The critical issue that propelled Tommy Robinson ahead of four opponents in the Democratic primary was his outspoken opposition to court-ordered consolidation of all Pulaski County (Little Rock and its environs) public schools; the television commercial that so effectively appealed to the emotions surrounding this issue (a little white girl waiting for a school bus on an ominously dark and empty country road) led Paul Greenberg to note, "Its producers could have based it on a close reading of *The Mind of the South*," with the obvious conclusion that "Arkansas ain't part of the Midwest yet." In January 1985, when the Arkansas Legislative Council got into a heated debate over the costs that might be assessed against state government for the court-ordered consolidation, one senator observed that the emotionalism reminded him of 1957, and the state legislature in regular session overwhelmingly passed a resolution favoring an amendment to the U.S. Constitution restricting federal jurisdiction over public schools.[6]

Arkansas, like the rest of the South, has gone through a remarkable metamorphosis in race relations in recent decades. The black vote, that ominous possibility against which all political institutions were once organized, has become an occasionally decisive electoral bloc, calmly accepted by the white citizenry and eagerly wooed by all candidates. By 1970 only 8.6 percent of Arkansas's black students attended completely segregated schools; by 1976 Central High was one of the most thoroughly integrated high schools in the nation. When the original Little Rock Nine gathered for a twentieth-anniversary celebration in 1977, it was widely noted that while one of their numbers was working in Washington as President Carter's $50,000-a-year assistant labor secretary, Orval Faubus, whose comeback attempts in 1970 and 1974 had failed, was working as a bank teller in Huntsville, Arkansas, to supplement his state pension.

By 1981 black men were chairing the board of trustees at both the University of Arkansas and Arkansas State University; and for a brief period in 1982, Little Rock had both a black mayor and a black city manager. The manager's tenure was ended when Governor Clinton hired him away to hold the state's most prestigious cabinet position, director of the Department of Finance and Administration. Clinton's appointment was not particularly surprising. Mahlon Martin was widely acknowledged to be surpassingly competent, and Clinton's 1982 comeback victory over Frank White (after White's upset defeat of Clinton in 1980) was due in large measure to Clinton's black support.[7]

What was somewhat surprising was the choice of Martin's successor as city manager: Susan Fleming, a thirty-two-year-old mother, then pregnant with her second child. This represents another remarkable turnabout from the days in 1963 when State Representative Paul Van Dalsem of the Arkansas legislature could titillate the Little Rock Optimists Club with his formula for handling politically active women: "We don't have any of these university women in Perry County but I'll tell you what we do up there when one of our women starts poking around in something she doesn't know anything about, we get her an extra milk cow. If that doesn't work, we give her a little more garden to tend. And then if that is not enough, we get her pregnant and keep her barefoot." When reapportionment thrust Van Dalsem into a district combining rural Perry County with urban Pulaski County, he was defeated, in part by women who symbolically shed their shoes before voting; and when further reapportionment permitted Van Dalsem's return to the state legislature, one of his first acts was to cosponsor a resolution ratifying the proposed federal Equal Rights Amendment (ERA).[8]

It is not just for blacks and women, but for all Arkansans, that life has changed dramatically in recent decades. While Arkansas still ranks near the bottom among states in per capita income, that income was 76 percent of the national average in 1985, compared with 48 percent of the national average in 1940 and 60 percent of the national average in 1960. In 1940 most of the working population was engaged in farming; by 1985 only 6.5 percent were employed as farmers, farm managers, and farm laborers, and with increasing urbanization and industrialization, many Arkansans began to experience at least a taste of the prosperity utterly unknown in the past to all but a very privileged elite.

By almost any measure of political well-being—voting participation, honesty of elections, numbers and caliber of candidates, degrees of competition, governmental accountability, quantity and quality of government services—Arkansas politics in the 1980s had taken a long series of giant steps, all in the directions envisioned by classical democratic theory and most contemporary concepts of good government. In the midst of overwhelming evidence of change, however, constant themes and echoes remain from the past.

## SOME RECURRING THEMES

When Governor Clinton urged his program for educational excellence upon the citizens in 1983, arguing in part that better institutions would attract a higher quality of industry and population, there were 150-year-old echoes of Territorial Governor John Pope urging educational improvements upon the legislature in 1833 because "many people with large families had not migrated to Arkansas because of the lack of educational facilities"; and the statewide campaigning done by Clinton and his wife in behalf of educational improvements was in many ways a replica of the Education Caravan that Governor Sidney McMath led through the state in the summer of 1949.[9]

When Governor Clinton announced in 1985 that economic development would be the keystone of his third administration, he was following in the footsteps of numerous gubernatorial predecessors. Governor John Roane (1849–52) proposed that the state advertise Arkansas's natural resources to attract a large population and suggested that a geological survey to advertise the state's mineral wealth, together with his programs for internal improvements and education, would not only attract labor and capital but would solve the state's acute financial problems by increasing the number of taxpayers. A whole series of late-nineteenth-century governors practically turned state governance over to the railroads, all in the name of what the railroads could contribute to economic development. Nineteenth-century boosterism probably reached its peak with Governor William Fishback (1893–95), who concentrated his energies on Arkansas's exhibit at the Columbian Exposition in Chicago, which, he argued, offered a splendid opportunity for Arkansas to attract desirable immigrants and industry. Both as governor (1917–21) and thereafter as president of the Arkansas Advancement Association, Charles Brough was a tireless crusader for Arkansas's economic potential. Among his promotional ideas were catchy mottos, booster buttons, letter-writing campaigns, an automobile map of Arkansas, and "a staff that will devote 24 hours a day to seeking new and varied ways of putting Arkansas before the world in a garb so attractive that it is undoubtedly a hard-hearted person who does not fall a victim to the attractions of this charming young miss." A considerably more sophisticated approach to economic development was made under the governorship of Benjamin ("Business Ben") Laney, Jr. (1945–49). The Arkansas Resources and Development Commission was formed to consolidate agencies dealing with the development and promotion of resources and to encourage industrialization to balance the state's agrarian economy. Working closely with the Arkansas Power and Light Company (AP&L), the commission then formulated the "Arkansas Plan," a proposed cooperative effort by science, business, and government; and virtually every governor from Laney's time on has had some scheme or innovation, some Arkansas Plan, for economic development.[10]

Most of these initiatives, however, were rejected or thwarted or proved to be too superficial to make any significant impact. The legislature's response to Governor Roane's proposal was to lower the tax base, refuse to authorize the geological survey, and to keep for county patronage positions the federal funds intended for internal improvements and education. Governor Fishback threw himself into the Columbian Exposition and other public relations activities for the state largely because he was unable to exercise any substantive leadership over the legislature. Charles Brough was deeply chagrined when the state he had spent a decade boosting as a progressive place for industrial profit closed that decade by becoming the only state to adopt by popular referendum a law prohibiting the teaching of evolution, that is, to forbid the teaching of modern science. He protested vigorously but was ignored. Decades later, however, Governor Frank White (1980–82), who had campaigned for office as the kind of sophisticated businessman who could attract high-tech, high-profit industries to Arkansas, signed into law a bill requiring equal treatment in all public classrooms of evolution science and "scientific creationism."[11]

What virtually all the gubernatorial and other advocates of economic development have discovered is that Arkansas, despite its geographic location close to the center of the continental United States, is virtually unknown outside its boundaries. Cephas Washburn, contemplating a journey to Arkansas territory as a missionary to the Cherokees, noted ruefully in his 1819 journal: "At that time Arkansas was a perfect terra incognita. The way to get there was unknown; and what it was, or was like, if you did get there was still more an unrevealed mystery." Over a century later, H. L. Mencken claimed, "I know New Yorkers who have been to Cochin China, Kafristan, Paraguay, Somaliland and West Virginia, but not one who has ever penetrated the miasmatic jungles of Arkansas." Mencken, of course, deliberately exaggerated, and especially when it came to Arkansas, certain of the satisfying howls of outrage his taunts inevitably provoked. [12]

It is true, nevertheless, that in a national survey conducted in 1982 by the Center for Urban and Governmental Affairs at the University of Arkansas at Little Rock (UALR), scarcely half of the respondents could place Arkansas in its correct geographical location. This general vagueness about Arkansas, its locale and attributes, was even further confirmed in a professional study commissioned in 1984 by Governor Clinton as part of his economic development thrust. Among this study's conclusions: "We believe that Arkansas today is suffering from two heavy burdens. . . . Many of its strengths are not known. . . . The most impressive misperception about the state is its location. . . . There is confusion about how far south, how far west the state is located . . . and what its natural resources are." [13]

There is something decidedly peculiar about the general mystery surrounding Arkansas, a state located in the very heartland of America, a state that has been a state longer than half of its sister states. The causes and consequences of this curious isolation and anonymity (which in turn permitted many false and exaggerated perceptions) will be explored. The major purpose of the preceding overview, however, is to suggest that it is impossible to understand the contemporary political system in Arkansas without understanding the past that produced it. Arkansas politics, like the politics of any state or nation, is the product of population and settlement patterns, social and economic factors, historical trends and episodes, personal values and public opinions, all of which combine into a distinctive pattern of conducting public affairs. Landmark events, generated internally or imposed externally, may dramatically change part of the pattern; energetic leaders, for better or worse, may channel traditional attitudes and values into new dimensions; but the seeds of Arkansas politics in 1986 were planted even before statehood in 1836. Since the assertion that state government only recently became a positive influence in the lives of its citizens is central to this book's thesis, it is first necessary briefly to document this characterization and then to offer some explanations for it.


### THE RECORD OF MISRULE

Even prior to statehood, Arkansas politics came to be dominated by a small group of people whose public "service" seems to have been primarily directed toward personal profits (through inside knowledge of lucrative land deals) and patronage for themselves, their relatives, and favorites. Known as the Family, the Dynasty (and sometimes as Sevier's Hungry Kinfolks), the Johnson-Conway-Sevier-Rector cousinhood accumulated 190 years of public officeholding, including two U.S. senators and three governors in antebellum Arkansas; and other offices went only to their partisans. They did preside over the establishment of the basic institutions of government. In most respects, however, their legacy must be judged a negative one.

At the Family's urging, the first state legislature created two banks, which, through a combination of unrealistic expectations, mismanagement, favoritism, and rascality, were total failures, saddling emerging Arkansas with a debt of $3 million, a poor credit reputation, and a suspicion toward state government, all of which were to last into the twentieth century. Through a series of national acts, the U.S. Congress deeded about one-third of the total acreage in Arkansas to the state for educational and internal improvement purposes, but nearly all of this bounty was squandered away on local patronage: no public educational institutions or roads resulted, and many of the levees built under the national swampland acts were so poorly constructed and located that they soon washed away. The regime failed at even the most fundamental of government responsibilities, that of providing law and order. Throughout the antebellum period, almost every political contest was accompanied by duels, stabbings, pistol-slayings, hangings, and arson, and Family members were among the most prominent participants in these and other acts of violence. Questionable balloting procedures and fraudulent vote counts were other long-lasting traditions originated under the Family's regime.[14]

Donald Stokes, based on an exhaustive review of Arkansas public affairs from 1836 to 1850, came to the following conclusion:

Family rule had not benefited the state: legislature followed legislature without grappling with realities; irresponsible, if not criminal banking programs had ruined state credit; there was no reliable all-weather transportation system, and the state government had done nothing to establish one; the penitentiary had proved very expensive, and none of the several efforts to establish state colleges and a common school had been successful. Whatever benefits the average Arkansan had enjoyed from the society and resources of the state he had gotten from his own efforts, from the local community, or from the federal government, and only rarely from the state. On the other hand, for decades he would be cursed by the faults of the state's banking enterprises and the almost total lack of an internal improvements program.[15]

Two other legacies of this period cast equally dark shadows over the state's political future. First, Arkansas entered the Union as a slave state (paired with Michigan as a free state), with all the pernicious consequences of slavery for black and white citizens alike. Many arguments were advanced in behalf of Arkansas's somewhat premature agitation for admission, but there is no doubt that the most compelling of these reasons was the determination to enter the Union while the legal status of slavery could still be secured. Second, because the Family was personally allied with Andrew Jackson, Arkansas began its political life totally dominated by the Democratic party. The opposing faction, which almost by default became associated with the Whigs, at times generated rather spirited opposition. Between 1836 and 1856 the Whigs never got less than 32.9 percent in presidential elections (including a 44.9 percent showing for Zachary Taylor in 1848), and in 1842 the state senate had fourteen Democrats to seven Whigs and the house of representatives had forty-two Democrats to fourteen Whigs. Still, no one but a Democrat ever won the presidential or gubernatorial election in Arkansas, and the only Whig ever elected to Congress filled the brief time remaining in an unexpired term. Even more important, the elections were solely contests between insiders and outsiders, with state policies or specific measures for public improvements rarely at issue.[16]

In the 1850s Arkansas began to experience its first genuine boom in population growth, urban development, and land values. *Ballou's Pictorial* in Boston asserted, "The future destiny of Arkansas, it is safe to predict, will be a brilliant one"; and this decade of development, culminating with the Family's loss of all major offices in 1860, might have initiated a less elitist, more productive kind of politics.[17] The Dynasty's defeat, however, occurred simultaneously with the presidential victory of Lincoln and the Republicans, which in turn precipitated the southern secessionist movement.

After an initially reluctant response, Arkansas joined the Confederate cause, and whatever political and economic development might have occurred instead became the tragic story of military defeat and occupation, death and deprivation. The major official obligation of the state during the war, of course, was the protection and survival of its citizens, but even here it has been noted that "the state of Arkansas, for whatever reasons, made the poorest showing of any state in the Confederacy in attending to human needs."[18]

While the war itself had devastating personal and economic consequences, Reconstruction, especially Radical Reconstruction (1867–74), had the most lasting political consequences. It is extraordinarily difficult, even today, to obtain a totally objective view of the Reconstructionists (perhaps partially because then, as now, the major state newspaper was the *Arkansas Gazette*, which then, as now, would never give credit to anything tainted by Republican sponsorship). To the Reconstructionists' credit, the first genuine effort to establish common schools was initiated, the University of Arkansas was finally established, civil rights were secured for the freed slaves, and the first significant railroad development was begun. Still, whatever may have been its original ideals and intents, the most lasting effects of this imposed administration included an additional $10 million debt, primarily extended for internal improvements and railroad construction that never materialized; a further corrupted election process; an intensified suspicion of and contempt for strong state government; and a long-lasting belief among most native white Arkansans that a Republican vote was a vote for arrogant, alien, untrained, and dishonest public officials.[19]

When Arkansas's own, the Redeemers, recaptured power in 1874, it was natural that they would reflect the popular view that a passive, low-tax, inactive state government was much to be preferred over an interventionist and expensive one. Foreign control had been ousted and black power diminished. If the Redeemers turned out to be as prone to pocketing funds as the Reconstructionists (three successive state treasurers left office under charges and considerable evidence of embezzlement) and if the decision to repudiate the "unjust" debts of Reconstruction meant the absolute destruction of Arkansas's credit reputation on the national bond market until 1917, it was presumably the necessary price for reversing Reconstructionist extravagance. And to secure these "blessings" for posterity, the Redeemers wrote a Constitution, adopted by the people in 1874, that placed numerous obstacles in the path of any future tendencies toward governmental activism.[20]

Fouse and Granade have summarized Arkansas political developments from 1874 to 1900 as follows: "During the Conservative Era Arkansas faced tremendous changes, and coped mainly by attempting to ignore them." The historian C. Vann Woodward, born in Arkansas and winner of a Pulitzer Prize, has provided a more elegant description of this period: "The Redeemers tried by invoking the past to avert the future. The politics of Redemption belonged to the romantic school, emphasizing race and tradition and deprecating issues of economics and self-interest." By the 1880s, however, for at least some Arkansans, the romance began wearing very thin.[21]

Faced with a perpetual struggle for survival against nearly insurmountable odds, there was finally what Harry Ashmore has termed a "thrust from below."[22] The Patrons of Husbandry, the Agricultural Wheel (begun in Des Arc in 1882 and growing to a membership of 40,000 in Arkansas and 500,000 across the South), the Brothers of Freedom, the Farmers' Alliance, the Union Labor party, and finally the Populists all arose to demand more concern for the common farmers and workers, the "producing" classes, against the favored economic elite. The essence of their complaints is captured in a letter written by an Arkansas farmer to his local paper in 1883:

Our best farmers work hard year after year and after supporting their families in the most economical manner, they have nothing left at the end of the year wherewith to school their children or increase the fertility of their land and the laborer is scarcely able to keep the wolf from the door. While this is the lot of the farmer, the merchant lives comfortably, if not in luxury; builds his brick houses and grows rich; railroads declare large dividends in largely watered stocks; wholesale and commission merchants grow into millionaires; banks and manufacturing companies make fabulous sums of money; lawyers wear fine clothes, and officers of the government live in elegance and ease. This is pre-eminently an agricultural country and the farmer ought to be the most prosperous and independent man in the world; and he and the laborer begin to inquire: Why this condition of things?[23]

Of course, much of the "condition of things" related to national and international factors, such as the disastrous skid in cotton prices from 11.1 cents to 5.8 cents a pound from 1874 to 1894, over which the state government had no control. What was within the appropriate sphere of state government, however, and what numerous and increasingly angry voices began to demand were regulation of railroads and other utilities; decent roads to be paid for by taxes on property owners rather than labor by the landless poor; schools for their children; abolition of the convict lease system; and honest elections.[24]

By contemporary standards, these demands hardly seem unreasonable; but to the wealthy planters and their urban allies they constituted a serious threat to the status quo. Unsurprisingly, then, when the "have-nots" came perilously close to success in the 1888 gubernatorial election, the establishment fought back with the most powerful weapon in its arsenal: fear that Republican victory would bring a return of black political power. Although a few policy bones (establishment of a state railroad commission, for example) were eventually thrown to the dissidents and the political process became somewhat more democratic in form (primary elections replaced the elite-dominated nominating conventions), the great agrarian uprising ultimately produced neither economic betterment nor political power for those at the bottom of the economic heap, whose numbers continued to swell and whose misery deepened for another half-century.

Arkansas, then, began the twentieth century with a state government that had never yet demonstrated its value to or concern for the average citizen. In terms of public education, the Southern Regional Education Board found Arkansas at or next to the bottom of all states in terms of per pupil spending, teacher salaries, length of school terms, and average daily attendance. Indeed, it was estimated that only 43 percent of the school-age population was attending school, with an average school term of sixty-nine days, and in 1910, the first year the State Department of Education kept records of such, only 300 students were graduated from Arkansas high schools and only a small fraction of the school's teachers had anything more than an eighth-grade education themselves.[25]

In terms of health and welfare, other than a home for Confederate veterans and an insane asylum (which an 1895 legislative visiting committee found "well managed" except for an unusually heavy death rate due to lack of proper sewer facilities and inferior meats), state services and funds were nearly nonexistent. This is not because there was no need for such: recently unearthed remains of a cemetery used by black Arkansans in early twentieth-century southwest Arkansas found skeletons more severely affected by malnutrition and disease than those reported for any skeletal population in the prehistoric or modern world. Relief for any kind of indigence, however, was simply not seen as a state (or indeed public) responsibility. Since roads had no demeaning connotations of charity, and since their absence was a major obstacle to economic development, they should have fared better; but attempts to pass legislation providing any state aid for roads were defeated repeatedly, with Governor Little warning in 1907 that any state aid would cause local authorities to slacken their efforts (which were in fact minimal).[26]

What the common folk did achieve at the beginning of the twentieth century was the election of one who claimed to be their champion. Governor Jeff Davis (1901–1907) railed against the trusts and railroads and "high-collared roosters," defeated the patricians and brought the plebeians into (temporary) control of the Democratic party, and forced the enactment of some modestly reformist legislation. He also, however, used racial dema-goguery with a vehemence and skill unprecedented in Arkansas politics, and as even his most sympathetic biographer admits, "Even his antitrust law did little to disturb existing economic structures and basic power relation-ships. Arkansas farmers continued to live in a world of insecurity and economic hardship, and most were no better off in 1913 (when Davis died) than they had been in 1900. Jeff had come and gone, leaving them with a treasure of memories, but little else had changed. The men and women between the plow handles were still scratching out a meager living from the land, and the decisions that controlled their lives were still made else-where."[27]

In fact, in statistical terms, the percentage of farms operated by tenants, a condition described by Leland Duvall as "the nearest approach to medieval serfdom ever achieved on the North American continent," increased from 32.1 percent in 1890 to 51.3 percent in 1920 and 63 percent in 1930. By 1935 about two-thirds of Arkansas farmers did not own the land they farmed, and in some areas of eastern Arkansas, tenancy, with its inevitable implications of hunger, squalor, ignorance, and hopelessness, reached 90 percent.[28]

Under Governor George Donaghey (1909–13) some slight gains were made in public health and education, the state capitol was finally completed, and the notorious convict leasing system was officially abolished. Governor Charles Brough (1917–21) pushed through a whole litany of progressive programs for roads, schools, administrative efficiency, and women's suf-frage. Governor Thomas McRae (1921–25) forced a reluctant legislature to raise some revenues for the schools. Despite these genuine steps forward, however, a study made in 1931, based on an enormous compilation of statistical data from the U.S. Census Bureau and other official sources, vividly illustrates how far Arkansas still lagged behind the nation in at least certain quantifiable measures of human well-being (table 1).

Considering the enormous caution traditionally displayed toward any state expenditures, it is ironic that by 1935 the only factor in which Arkan-sas led the nation was per capita public indebtedness, a debt so high that Arkansas became the only state ever to fall into bankruptcy three times. An orgy of excitement over road building in the second and third decades of the

Table 1: Arkansas and the Nation, 1930

|  | United States | Arkansas | Rank |
|---|---|---|---|
| Taxable property per capita | $2,137.98 | $673.31 | 43 |
| Ratio of farm tenancy | 29.5 | 52.7 | 43 |
| Farms supplied with electricity | (Calif., 1st, 59.5%) | 1.0% | 48 |
| Days of school sessions | 171.5 | 145.5 | 48 |
| Total enrollment in high schools | 15.5% | 8.1% | 48 |
| Salaries of teachers | $1,364.00 | $680.00 | 47 |
| No. of volumes in public libraries per 100 pop. | 126 | 24 | 48 |
| Urban population | 56.2% | 20.6% | 46 |

*Source:* Compiled from Charles Angoff and H. L. Mencken, "The Worst American State," *American Mercury,* September 1931, pp. 1–16; October 1931, pp. 175–88; November 1931, pp. 355–70.

twentieth century led to the creation of hundreds of local improvement districts, but a combination of poor planning, patronage politics, and extensive corruption produced many short roads "leading nowhere," and a long series of scandals. In 1927 the state assumed the debts of the local improvement districts, and by 1935 that sum amounted to more than $166 million.[29]

With the onslaught of the Great Depression, which according to many accounts came to Arkansas earlier, ravaged more deeply, and lasted longer than in the nation generally, the state government became a mere holding operation, simply trying to stay afloat and doing so primarily by severe retrenchments in its already meager public services. Governor Junius Futrell (1933–37), for example, argued that public education was unnecessary beyond the primary grades and asked the legislature to cease funding schools above the eighth grade. He also obstructed rather than facilitated efforts by the national government to alleviate the widespread human suffering in Arkansas. It was only under a threat by the federal government to cut off all funds that the legislature finally, in March 1935, enacted a two-cent sales tax to provide some state contribution to the national relief effort. During the 1930s federal assistance to Arkansas was more generous than it was to any other state, but its programs operated without the cooperation, and often over the opposition, of state political leadership.[30]

According to V. O. Key, reviewing twentieth-century Arkansas politics through the World War II years, "The only recent governor who distinguished himself by suspecting that anything was wrong with Arkansas and that something could be done about it was the late Carl Bailey (1937–41)."[31] But at the very time Key was writing *Southern Politics*, a young war hero returned to the state knowing, as did many other GIs, that there was a very great deal wrong with Arkansas, and that he and his fellow veterans could and would change it. Sidney McMath (1948–52) challenged the political establishment in ways it had not been threatened since the days of Jeff Davis, and under his leadership relative giant steps were taken in highway construction, health care, extension of electricity to rural areas, educational upgrades, and electoral reforms. Furthermore, totally unlike Jeff Davis, McMath set a tolerant tone in race relations, urging repeal of the state poll tax, supporting a state antilynching law, and appointing some blacks to previously all-white boards and commissions. Revelations of serious improprieties in the awarding of highway contracts, however, denied McMath the third term that only Jeff Davis before him had ever succeeded in winning.[32]

After an inconsequential interregnum (Francis Cherry, 1953–55), another product of the GI revolt picked up the fallen mantle of public-service reform. Orval Faubus had gained his earliest political values from the radical sentiments expressed around the campfires of the migratory fruit-pickers with which his family traveled and from the speeches made by his father, secretary of the Madison County Socialist party. Equally important were his experiences during World War II in Germany, where he observed a fine road system: "Germany was a poor country and I wondered what they would think if they knew that when I, a representative of a wealthy country, went back I would have to get a mule to get home." Faubus had served in the McMath administration and thus began his administration with both a genuine concern for the disadvantaged and dispossessed and with the political skills to use state government in their behalf. He fought for and obtained sizable increases in education and welfare expenditures, established a model institution for mentally retarded children, and appointed recently arrived Winthrop Rockefeller to head the revived Industrial Development Commission. After more than 120 years of existence, it seemed that Arkansas state government had finally begun to demonstrate the positive difference it would make in the lives of most Arkansas citizens. In 1957, however, in the events at Little Rock, and in a pattern amply precedented in Arkansas political history, economic progress was sacrificed to political expediency.[33]

I will conclude this brief historical overview by reiterating the original assertion: for most of its 150 years, Arkansas state government did very little to justify its existence. Of course, some important mitigating circumstances should also be entered into the record.

First, it must be kept in mind that our contemporary expansive notions of the legitimate sphere of governmental activity are of relatively recent origin. That government has not just the authority but the obligation to ensure a certain measure of well-being for its citizens is a concept that only began achieving acceptance in America in the 1930s, and it remains controversial. Furthermore, the idea that any of these responsibilities fall within the sphere of state governments is of even more recent vintage. At the beginning of the twentieth century, by far the greatest bulk of governmental activity in America was purely local: local governments accounted for 59 percent of all public expenditures in the United States, compared with 35 percent for the federal government and 6 percent for the states. Furthermore, at least until the aftermath of the "reapportionment revolution" of the 1960s, state governments throughout the United States were often unresponsive, and frequently obstructionist, to the needs and demands of their populations.[34]

It must also be acknowledged that throughout its history, Arkansas seems to have been unusually plagued with adversities over which no state governments could have been expected to exert much ameliorating control. These included natural disasters (drought, crop disease, and floods, including the 1927 disaster that inundated more than four million acres) and, probably of even greater consequence, national and international economic factors, which constantly played havoc with Arkansas's basically agrarian economy.

Once seduced by cotton in the 1850s, Arkansas's economic well-being became perilously tied to fluctuating world markets, and until well into the twentieth century, cotton was Arkansas's only significant cash crop. Arkansas's few nonagricultural pursuits (mostly lumbering and some mining) were also basically extractive endeavors, with the manufacturing and refining value added to these natural products, and the profits thereby collected and enjoyed elsewhere. Considering the overwhelmingly agricultural basis of the economy, which in turn was increasingly characterized by landless, moneyless tenants; considering that in 1900 there were only 31,525 wage-earners in a total population of 1,311,564 (and most of those working under conditions approaching peonage); considering all the implications of what has frequently and accurately been described as essentially a colonial economy, it is clear that even the most visionary and skillful of political leaders would have had extraordinary difficulties in establishing and sustaining an activist and service-oriented state government. As countless studies in recent decades have demonstrated, states with higher levels of economic development spend more on a greater variety of essential services, whereas below a certain minimal level of modernization, lack of economic development has a very direct and negative effect on the quantity and quality of health, education, welfare, transportation, and other services.[35]

Still, while economic conditions set the parameters of what is possible, political and governmental decisions have their own independent, influential impact. And those decisions, in Arkansas, rarely operated to the clear benefit of the vast majority of its citizens. Again we return to the enigma stated at the outset: why did the common people of Arkansas, possessing the power that a large numerical majority is supposed to confer in a representative democracy, tolerate for so long a state government that rarely assisted them, and often obstructed them, in their struggle for survival? A great deal of the answer seems to lie in the people who came to Arkansas and the governmental attitudes and expectations they brought with them.

## CHAPTER TWO

# Some Socioeconomic, Cultural, and Political Explanations

*If the plantation system engendered the habit of command, the Arkansas frontier encouraged the rejection of all authority and an every man for himself attitude.*

Michael B. Dougan, *Confederate Arkansas*, 1982

*One thing that they taught me was that politicians are the source of all disillusionment.*

Shirley Abbott, *Womenfolks*, 1983

## THE SOCIOECONOMIC ENVIRONMENT

When Arkansas was admitted to the Union in 1836, its territory consisted of 53,335 square miles, much of it densely forested, little of it easily accessible. On its eastern border, separated by the Mississippi River from Tennessee and Mississippi, lay a vast flood plain, almost impassable in the rainy season, its swamps a known breeding ground for malaria and other dread diseases. The Ozark Mountains straddled two-thirds of the state's northern border with Missouri, and its entire western border fronted on Indian Territory, legally closed to white migration and settlement. The southern border, coming up the Red and Ouachita rivers from Louisiana, was more easily penetrable, but these rivers were highly unpredictable, ranging from trickle to flood, and the Red River route was further complicated by a hundred-mile logjam known as the Great Raft. The most popular path into the interior was by canoe or raft up the Arkansas River, which transects Arkansas in its flow from the uplands of Colorado to the Mississippi. (See map 1.)

The earliest white inhabitants of Arkansas were hunting and trapping Frenchmen, *coureurs de bois*, who left little mark other than some French place names; nor did Spanish possession (1762–1803) leave any permanent settlements or cultural heritage behind. As late as 1804, army surveyors descending the entire Arkansas River did not see a single white inhabitant. As permanent settlers began arriving in the nineteenth century, most clustered along the Arkansas River, their link to each other and to the outside world.

An imaginary diagonal line drawn from the state's northeast to southwest corners approximates the major geophysical division within Arkansas, with flat plains to the east (Mississippi Alluvial Plain) and south (Gulf Coastal Plain) of the line, and hilly uplands to the north (the Ozarks) and the west (the Ouachitas). At almost the precise geographic center, on the Arkansas River, is Little Rock, Arkansas's second territorial and first state capital, and since the 1830s by far its largest town.

Although the lowland areas had much the deepest, richest soil, much of this land originally lay under dense cane and swampland, and therefore most of the early settlers headed to the elevated sections, where the soil was thin and rocky but the climate far healthier. Originally, sizable plantations developed only along the rivers (especially the Arkansas and Red), because only where relatively good transportation could ensure a profit on cotton exports could a major investment in land and slaves be justified. Later, as the swamplands were slowly cleared and drained, the fertile black soil of the Delta began to grow more populous, and its inhabitants more politically powerful.

It is somewhat presumptuous to ascribe migration motives retrospectively to thousands of people who came through decades of time for what were undoubtedly a variety of purposes, and such retroactive analysis is especially difficult when many of the accounts of early settlers are exaggerated to the extremes of either shining heroism or thoroughgoing degeneracy. Whereas some Arkansas historians have claimed to find in every sturdy forefather a "sterling character," a "strong manhood," transcendent virtues of ability, integrity, industry, and rectitude, accounts written for the titillation of eastern and European readers emphasized the lawless and luckless nature of Arkansas's early inhabitants: "Freebooters, who have been driven out of good society on the other side of the river"; "some of the worst and

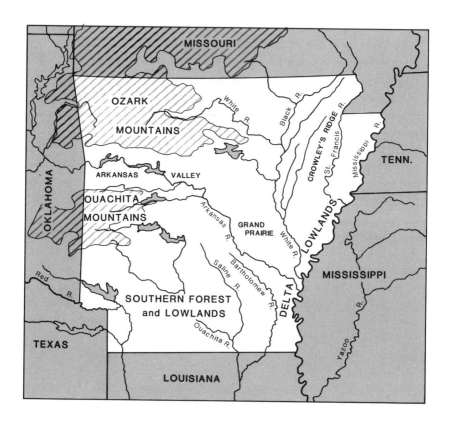

Map 1. Arkansas Regions and Rivers. (*Source:* Prepared by Department of Geography, University of Arkansas at Fayetteville.)

most desperate characters that the country affords"; "homicides, horse-stealers and gamblers"; "bad characters, gamblers, drunkards, thieves, murderers who all thought that the simple-minded backwoodsmen were easier to be cheated than the war settlers of older states"; "the kind of folks that pirates terrorize and merchants cheat and planters impress into peon-age, the wandering sheep that grazed their way into Arkansas to establish there a moron's paradise."[1]

To whatever extent early Arkansas may be thought of as a refuge for outcasts and renegades, however, by the time serious settlement began, and certainly from statehood onward, there was a much more prosaic and encompassing explanation for in-migration, namely, the ease of obtaining cheap, indeed often free, and always fresh and abundant land. The U.S. government, which owned almost all the land in Arkansas after the Loui-siana Purchase and the removal of the Indians, offered 160-acre tracts in Arkansas to enlistees in the War of 1812 and the Mexican War. Other acreage could be purchased directly from the federal government or from the state, to which millions of acres were ceded for disposal. Between 1821 and 1836, more than a million and a half acres of public land were sold in Arkansas at an average price of $1.25 per acre; and additional millions of acres continued to be confirmed to the state in the antebellum period, which land could be obtained under arrangements much more generous than those available elsewhere. Millions of acres of good bottomland became obtain-able at twenty to seventy-five cents per acre with a ten-year exemption from taxation if the settlers constructed levees against overflows, and additional millions of acres were acquired simply by possession. At least through 1850, squatting was still the rule rather than the exception, especially in the upland counties.[2]

These arrangements are worth noting because they undoubtedly had enormous influence in establishing a particular pattern of citizen-state rela-tionships. Assuming that the major objective of antebellum settlers was to obtain and secure land, the national government must have seemed far more consequential than any state institutions. The national government was not only the major source of land but it also provided the essential surveys, saw to the removal of Indians, built the earliest roads (indeed the only real roads in Arkansas until the 1850s), made the rivers navigable, and financed and encouraged most of the major swamp-draining and levee-constructing im-provements.

State government was not totally unimportant to all early Arkansans. Certainly the large landowners would have recognized the advisability of close relationships with the political establishment, for in the establishment's hands was the power to make one's investment even more profitable through additional favorably priced and situated land purchases and advance knowledge of advantageous river and road improvements. Still, for every large landowner there were hundreds of small, self-sufficient farmers and herdsmen, raising enough to provide for their families, trading in pelts and hides and beeswax for their few essential purchases. For these yeoman farmers, many of whom were squatters, state government was irrelevant at best, irritating and intrusive more often, especially in the form of taxes. If, as the Van Buren County tax list of 1850 indicates, only 8,659 of the county's 748,000 acres were subject to property taxation, then there were at least some respects in which the 448 free families were better off than the 64 landowners and anxious to keep at arm's length from an expensive and seemingly unnecessary relationship.[3]

When Arkansas's second territorial governor, George Izard, expressed concern upon arrival that the necessary papers and records for his work were missing, a prominent citizen assured him that there was no cause for concern, since "everyone did as he pleased anyway."[4] And if the officials in turn did as they pleased, challenging each other to duels, securing appointments and contracts for family and friends, cutting themselves in on the most lucrative land deals, the semilegal squatters, if they even noticed this pattern of public affairs, were in a poor position to complain.

Perhaps the most important attribute of those who came seeking land in Arkansas was that they did not travel far to find it. Nearly 90 percent of all who came to Arkansas between 1834 and 1880 were furnished by just ten states: Tennessee (24.7 percent), Missouri (16.3 percent), Mississippi (12.2 percent), Alabama (9.8 percent), Texas (7.9 percent), Georgia (6.6 percent), Illinois (4.2 percent), Kentucky (3.2 percent), Louisiana (1.8 percent), and North Carolina (1.8 percent), with the four states immediately east of Arkansas (Tennessee, Mississippi, Alabama, and Georgia) supplying over half the total. There were some interesting and understandable preferences within these migratory movements. Families from Missouri especially, but also from Tennessee, Illinois, and Indiana, showed a decided preference for the uplands, whereas those from Louisiana and South Carolina preferred the lowlands. What is most important, however, is that Arkansas was not a melting pot of different nationalities or even regions but rather was a state settled primarily by nearby and overwhelmingly southern neighbors.[5]

In terms of ethnic origin, almost all who came to Arkansas were American rather than foreign-born: from June 1834 through May 1880, foreign countries accounted immediately for only 134 ascertained arrivals, or 0.3 percent of the total in-migration. Arkansas settlers drew overwhelmingly from a British heritage, mostly English, Welsh, and Scotch-Irish, with only small numbers of German and Irish descent, and very little else.[6]

Although in the late nineteenth century some efforts were made, primarily by the railroads, to induce foreign in-migration, and a few colonies of Germans, Poles, Bohemians, and Italians responded, their numbers never approached the levels necessary to affect significantly the overwhelmingly Anglo-Saxon culture. In 1900, foreign-born Arkansans constituted only 1.1 percent of the state's population, and by 1914 even such very selective and limited recruitment efforts as existed had become so controversial that "Arkansas all but closed its doors to strangers from abroad." Arkansas's population was equally homogeneous in terms of religion, which was overwhelmingly Protestant. In 1890, 85 percent of all church members were either Methodist or Baptist.[7]

Considering the rudimentary condition of law and law enforcement, it may have been fortunate that the settlers were all so much alike in terms of past residence, national origin, and religion. On the other hand, this near-uniformity probably acted more to retard than to advance political development. The kinds of political debates and divisions that emerged in many other states from ethnic and religious rivalries, from clashes between old and new immigrants fighting to assert or defend their culture, often brought bitterness and ferocity to the political scene; but they also forced a more participatory and meaningful process. If, as W. J. Cash observed, "complexity in man is invariably the child of complexity in the environment," then it is important to remember that Arkansas lacked such complexity. Rather, a totally homogeneous environment tended to produce a narrow-minded and nativistic provincialism, an intense suspicion toward any unfamiliar group, "a terrified truculence toward new ideas from outside."[8]

The one sizable group of "strangers" who were imported, with political consequences even more fateful than the absence of non–Anglo-Saxon white ethnics, were black slaves. While in some respects Arkansas was more attuned to the western frontier culture than to the southern plantation culture, it is the institution of slavery that provides the core of southern distinctiveness; and after a slow start in the establishment of this "peculiar institution," Arkansas ended with a terrible flourish.

The U.S. Census of 1820, taken the year after Arkansas obtained territorial status, indicated the existence of only 1,617 slaves in a total population of 14,274. Later, as the rich, flat lands along the Mississippi were drained and cleared, and as larger plantations became more possible and profitable, each succeeding census through 1860 showed substantial increases both in the number of slaves and in their proportion to the population (table 2).

Despite the rapid increases in the slave population, the number of slaveowners still only constituted 3.5 percent of the white population by 1860, and there is some understandable puzzlement as to why Arkansas finally opted for the Confederate cause. Part of the answer seems to lie in the origins and outlook of the Arkansas pre–Civil War population. By 1860, 96 percent of those living in Arkansas had come to Arkansas from a slaveholding state; and in this respect at least, elected officials were thoroughly representative of their constituents. Of the first six Arkansas pre–Civil War governors, five came from Tennessee and one from Kentucky; and in both 1850 and 1860, 8 percent or less of the state legislators had been born in nonslaveholding states. Furthermore, highly disproportionate numbers of the political leadership were planters, owning twenty or more slaves.[9]

Given these numbers, perhaps the more surprising phenomenon is that Arkansas showed as much reluctance as it did toward the early agitation for secession. When Arkansans were asked to vote in February 1861 on delegates to a special convention to consider the secession issue, candidates who supported the Union drew 23,628 votes to only 17,927 for the secessionists. Furthermore, the convention elected (40–35) an outspokenly antisecessionist chair, and voted 139 to 35 against aligning Arkansas with the Confederacy. After the firing on Fort Sumter, however, when Lincoln called upon state governors to provide armed men to suppress the rebellion, the convention was rapidly called back into session, and this time the vote was 65 to 5 for secession.[10]

In these developments, as well as from the original migration patterns from which they developed, can be found many possible explanations for what appears to be the curious quiescence of Arkansas people in the unproductive state government of the nineteenth century. First, the Civil War swiftly aborted, indeed reversed, the economic boom that Arkansas was just beginning to enjoy and with it whatever political maturation this economic development might have engendered. If, as many political scientists have persuasively argued, a minimum "threshold" of economic development is essential for the establishment of a democratic political process, then the Civil War further delayed Arkansas from crossing that threshold. In the war's aftermath, the state was bankrupt and facing a dearth of taxable objects: the value of real property, set at $153,699,473 in 1860, was

Table 2: Racial Composition of Arkansas's Population, 1830–1860

|      | Total Population | White   | Free Blacks | Slaves  |
|------|------------------|---------|-------------|---------|
| 1830 | 30,388           | 25,671  | 141         | 4,576   |
| 1840 | 97,574           | 77,174  | 465         | 19,935  |
| 1850 | 209,897          | 162,189 | 608         | 47,100  |
| 1860 | 435,450          | 324,191 | 144         | 111,115 |

*Source:* Waddy W. Moore, ed., *Arkansas in the Gilded Age, 1874–1900* (Little Rock: Rose Publishing, 1976), app. 3.

assessed at $30,000,000 in 1864, and the first effort to collect taxes from that base produced only $257.97 in cash and $2,565.80 in warrants. Even more deleterious to democratic development was the increasing entrapment of not only the freed slaves but increasing numbers of once independent yeoman farmers into the degrading and dependent status of tenancy. Those wholly involved in the sheer struggle for survival have more pressing concerns than political contests, and those totally dependent upon "the man" for land, shelter, and work are in absolutely no position to articulate and organize around their needs and demands.[11]

An urban middle class, often in history the vanguard of political change, did not become a significant sector of the population until well into the twentieth century. Arsenault has convincingly argued that the rise of Jeff Davis at the turn of the century was largely the upsurge of rural resentment against the perceived comfort and affluence of town and city dwellers, but these are highly relative concepts. In 1900 Arkansas had an urban population of 6.9 percent (compared with Illinois's 51 percent or Ohio's 45 percent or even Tennessee and Georgia's 14 percent), and only three Arkansas "cities" had a population of more than 10,000: Little Rock, 38,307; Fort Smith, 11,587; and Pine Bluff, 11,496. In short, some of the essential or at least usual components of democratic development—some disposable wealth, an economically self-sufficient population, cities as sources of diversity and dissent, a somewhat heterogeneous population—were simply nonexistent. Nor, due to Arkansas's continued isolation from the outside world, was it likely that many Arkansans would discover that politics was practiced differently, and a bit more usefully, elsewhere.[12]

As geographic barriers had effectively isolated Arkansas from the mainstream of east-to-west migration patterns, so poor transportation and communications continued to isolate Arkansas from the ferments of the external, modernizing world. Both land and river travel within Arkansas remained difficult and dangerous for decades after statehood and beyond. Interest in railroad construction began in the 1850s, but lack of capital, the hazards of construction, and the satisfaction of the planters with river transportation all meant that as late as the 1870s there were virtually no railroads in Arkansas except a short line of forty miles from Little Rock to DeVall's Bluff, from which a connection to Memphis via boat could be made. Newspapers were established early, most important the *Arkansas Gazette* in 1819, and by 1850 there were fourteen newspapers (all but one weeklies) with a total circulation of about 7,250 (in a population of 209,897). For their news, however, the editors depended upon their own partisan sentiments and on the word of passing travelers and lamented, "we have no means of hearing what is doing in the world." Mail service was so slow and unreliable that some of the pioneers who came to Arkansas "never heard from their relatives in the Eastern states again."[13]

Considering the formidable obstacles to transportation and communication in the nineteenth century, Arkansas voter turnout in at least some elections was quite impressive. Brian Walton has estimated percentages of the eligible electorate voting in gubernatorial elections from 1836 to 1860 ranging from 63 to 86 percent. Furthermore, all accounts of antebellum campaign contests indicate that candidates took the electorate seriously enough to hustle around from county to county making impassioned appeals to the citizenry with "bad whiskey and worse oratory." Given the general absence of entertainment in rural, backwoods Arkansas, the occasional political canvass, accompanied by free food and liquor, by verbal and sometimes physical violence, must have been a welcome diversion in otherwise uneventful lives. Popular participation, however, should not be confused with popular influence.[14]

That the candidates of both parties had been picked in very tightly closed conventions, that the debates had more to do with who was and was not a jackal, pimp, hypocrite, or skulking poltroon than with the means for improving state roads and river passages and commercial markets, that the election count itself was frequently and blatantly falsified—all this was part of the entertainment. The highly partisan press certainly boosted its circulation through venemous accounts of the dastardly doings, and newspaper sales were especially brisk when the printed insults solicited by the press resulted in duels and brawls. The aspiring literati who penned lengthy inflammatory letters to the editor must have enjoyed seeing their prose in print under such high-sounding pseudonyms as Aristides, Conservator, Esto Perpetus, and Diodorus Siculus. But to the average Arkansas settler, striving to clear his fields, plant his crops, and feed his family, this could have had little substantive meaning. For most Arkansans, then, whose lives would proceed in the same path regardless of any election outcome, politics was simply a spectator sport. [15]

For some, of course, the political process was a game with extraordinarily high stakes and therefore had to be taken seriously. The politicians wanted their jobs. Those who had invested in extensive land purchases had to exert themselves to obtain the information and improvements that might make these investments more profitable. Above all, those who could imagine no successful way to make their vast holdings profitable without slave labor had to make politics their abiding occupation.

Even when the slaves became freedmen, there was still a hierarchical political and social order that had to be maintained if life was to be tolerable. For farmers in the highlands, where in many counties slaves and later freedmen were sparse or entirely absent, indifference may have been a viable option. For those in Chicot County (where slaves constituted 81 percent of the population in 1860) or in other lowland counties where the black population exceeded the white population, political involvement was not a matter of choice but a compelling necessity, as any relaxation of attention might result in disastrous changes in the status quo. Political involvement has generally accompanied a perception of stakes, and the social and economic environment of traditional Arkansas provided relatively few citizens with a sharp sense of important personal consequences to be gained or feared from a particular political outcome.

## THE POLITICAL CULTURE EXPLANATION

In addition to specific social and economic factors, it is also important to understand, as Daniel Elazar and others have extensively documented, that within the American democratic tradition, three distinctive types of political culture have produced equally distinctive patterns of conducting public affairs. Political culture is rooted, as is all culture, in the cumulative historical experiences of a people; and as settlers came to America, and then moved westward across the nation, they carried with them historical memories and ethnic and religious affiliations that were manifested in different orientations toward politics. Within the familiar American pattern, then, of written constitutions, separation of powers, and campaigns and elections are important variations in perceptions of what politics should be, of what can be expected from the government, of the kinds of people expected to become active in politics, and of the actual ways in which government is practiced by citizens, politicians, and public officials.[16]

According to Elazar, the Moralistic political culture, which developed first in the Congregationalist towns of New England and spread west across the northern parts of the nation, has a commonwealth concept of the community. In this conception, government is seen as a positive instrument through which the general welfare is to be secured, and political participation by all citizens is encouraged as a righteous and important activity through which shared moral principles can be implemented to create a good society for all. The Individualistic political culture, which developed in the Middle Atlantic colonies and spread westward, has a utilitarian concept of government. In this construct, politics is viewed as an extension of the competition of the marketplace, and political participation is encouraged as a valuable process through which citizens can compete to advance their own self-interests.

The Traditionalistic political culture, which developed in the Tidewater colonies of the southern coast and spread westward across the south, developed a paternalistic concept of government, with an obligation on the part of the plantation-owning elite to exercise political as well as economic decision-making responsibilities for the lesser born and less fortunate. Under this conception, political power is often inherited as a family right and obligation, and the major purpose of government is to protect and preserve the status quo.

While all these models developed particular variations in individual states and have become increasingly hybrid with passing decades, at least throughout the nineteenth century, Elazar's formulations place Arkansas squarely within the Traditionalistic pattern. Note, for example, the close fit between Elazar's description of the hallmarks of the Traditionalistic political culture and what have already been described as the salient characteristics of nineteenth-century Arkansas politics:

Government tries to limit (its) role to securing the continued maintenance of the existing social order. To do so, it functions to confine real political power to a relatively small and self-perpetuating group drawn from an established elite who often inherit their "right" to govern through family ties or social position. . . . At the same time, those who do not have a definite role to play in politics are not expected to be even minimally active as citizens . . . those active in politics are expected to benefit personally from their activity. . . . Political parties are of minimal importance . . . because they encourage a degree of openness that goes against the fundamental grain of an elite-oriented political order. . . . the traditionalistic political culture is found only in a society that retains some of the organic characteristics of the preindustrial social order . . . unless political leaders are pressed strongly from the outside they play conservative and custodial rather than initiatory roles.[17]

Both because the landed aristocracy was less numerous in Arkansas (it is estimated that less than one hundred Arkansans ever owned more than one hundred slaves) and because the frontier with its antiaristocratic influences was much nearer, elitism never reached the apogee in Arkansas that it did, for instance, in South Carolina or Virginia. Unquestionably, however, the large landowners, because they had the wealth, the skill, the leisure, and the incentives within a political culture permitting and accepting their natural dominance, had extraordinary weight in setting the political agenda, selecting political leaders, and shaping Arkansas's political character.

According to Elazar's political culture maps, only one small portion of Arkansas, the northwestern Ozarks, does not fall clearly within the Traditionalistic pattern. This area he characterized as Moralistic, and both the fierce individualism of the hill people and their antipathy to Whig elitism suggest that they cannot be fairly placed in the tidewater, paternalistic, Traditionalistic pattern. If, however, the Moralistic culture necessitates a widespread belief that "politics is one of the great activities of man in search for the good society," then the aggressively independent and often fatalistic Ozark uplanders seem to have been more anarchistic than Moralistic, more motivated by a deliberate quest for remoteness than by any search for "the good society."[18]

Roy Reed, only semifacetiously analyzing his upland Arkansas ancestry, has recently written, "we were barbarians, especially after a couple of generations in the woods, cut off from Ireland and Scotland to the back of us and not yet come up against any established authority over here that was big enough and mean enough to whip us into line." Similarly, Orval Faubus recently related that when he was growing up in the Ozarks, the biggest threat that one mountaineer could make to another was not violence but the threat that "I'll law you." And if these uplanders "simply did not elect to have neighbors within the sound of musketshot or the sight of chimney smoke," or "moved on when they could hear a neighbor's rooster crow," how much less must they have desired to see the sheriff or tax collector coming down the road.[19]

These were people who preferred taking care of their own needs, avoiding society and government whenever possible, perhaps letting themselves be courted with whiskey and promises by the occasional campaigner but basically believing that government was an inconsequential nuisance. If the Family, or the Reconstructors, or later the Redeemers, wanted to use government as their private playpen, this simply confirmed their basic belief, pinpointed by Shirley Abbott, that "politicians are the source of all disillusionment."[20]

According to Abbott, whose maternal ancestors were among the thousands of highlanders scratching their living off the stony hillsides, they were "the most independent people who ever lived, and I am convinced they went off into the woods of their own will, gladly, by preference, because they believed chiefly in themselves and wanted no truck with institutions. . . . What they produced was not for society but for themselves, and they took pride in their own dogged self-sufficiency. If they had to do without schools or stores or markets for their produce, they did without. They did without doctors and lawyers and tried every way they could to do without tax collectors. Civic-minded they were not."[21]

It is only when all these elements of nineteenth-century Arkansas are considered together that one can begin to comprehend why the voices of the poor farmers, despite their numerical majority, were so rarely heard. The agrarian economy never provided either the surplus capital or the incentives for an interventionist and activist state government; and the influence of agrarianism was compounded by the effects of a nonparticipatory political culture. The plantation-oriented Traditionalistic political culture of the lowlands prohibited participation by the black population and discouraged political activism except among the elite. The subsistence-style farming of the uplands produced suspicion about and contempt for the political process rather than widespread participation in it. Economics, which is usually at the basis of political competition, provided a powerful incentive for the planters to protect their own interests but no counterincentives around which the yeoman farmers, whose economic self-sufficiency bred an equally fierce political self-sufficiency, could see themselves usefully organizing.

Clearheaded and farsighted political leaders might have educated the common people to their just political demands and aroused their governmental expectations, but the closed political system, dominated first by the Family, then by the Reconstructors, and then by the Redeemers, had no mechanisms for recruiting and powerful means for discouraging this kind of public champion. Arkansas was trapped in its own provincialism, and this provincialism was more often exploited by politicians than seriously addressed as an obstacle to social and economic development. In the short term, it was far more politically profitable to curse the Abolitionists and Yankee interlopers, the railroad trusts and Wall Street interests, and all the other assorted alien enemies "conspiring" against Arkansas and its people than it was to address the basic factors of a cotton-based agrarianism that doomed Arkansas to vulnerability and exploitation. Finally, in the 1880s, the common people did arise, organize, and demand a more responsive and useful state government. The major outcome of this uprising, however, was a politics even less likely to address their basic interests than that which preceded it.

## THE POLITICAL SYSTEM EXPLANATION

The Redeemers, that coalition of Confederate war heroes, planters, and businessmen who had ousted the Reconstructors in 1874, shared a generally noninterventionist view of state government with taxes, appropriations, and regulations kept to a minimum. What this meant in practice was a free ride and beneficial treatment for the railroads, timber, and mining companies but a thoroughgoing neglect of the thousands of small farmers sinking deeper into debt and tenancy and of the nonfarm laborers earning less-than-subsistence wages under totally unregulated conditions of employment. It was the sharpening perception of favoritism for the few and neglect of the many that finally created the beginnings of organization, protest, and demands for change. Why should the railroads and manufacturers be getting every possible kind of assistance from state government when the farmers and workers got none? The railroads and manufacturers paid no taxes, whereas the "producing class" frequently had to surrender their property to the auction block for nonpayment of taxes. While the railroads charged exorbitant freight rates the small farmers could not even get their goods to local markets because of the dearth of decent roads, and the future looked no brighter for their children without adequate education. The oppressive credit system, the regressive tax system, the blatant and frequent misconduct of countless public officials, all finally became intolerable to the point of protest.[22]

While the Redeemers largely ignored the protesters, the Republicans eventually recognized in their growing numbers a possible opportunity for recapturing power. In 1888, therefore, the Republicans nominated no candidate of their own but instead backed C. P. Norwood, gubernatorial candidate of the dissident Union-Labor party, to which Wheelers and Alliance-men also pledged their support. By the standards of states accustomed to closely competitive general elections, the attempt was an abject failure: Democrat James P. Eagle received 99,214 votes to the 84,213 votes cast for C. P. Norwood. For those unaccustomed to genuine competition, however, this election was ominously close, especially because of the amount of fraud that had been necessary to secure even this "narrow" victory.[23]

The 1888 election was a seminal event, producing two very contradictory patterns that strongly shaped Arkansas politics for the next seventy or eighty years. One reaction, the democratic or majoritarian response, was the first, feeble recognition of the legitimacy of at least some of the dissidents' demands. Governor Eagle, for example, urged the legislature to improve the public roads, reform the penal system, support public education, and establish a regulatory railroad commission. The legislature ignored or defeated most of these requests. It was, however, the entering wedge of populism as opposed to patricianism; and the populist impulse periodically surfaced from that time on in gubernatorial elections. Governors Daniel Jones, Jeff Davis, George Donaghey, Charles Brough, Carl Bailey, Sid McMath, and Orval Faubus were all originally elected against the wishes of the economic establishment, and all pushed (with varying degrees of enthusiasm and success) for some programs for the common people. Senators Joseph T. Robinson, William Kirby, Thaddeus and Hattie Caraway, and Congressmen Otis Wingo, Clyde Ellis, and Brooks Hays all reflected, again with various degrees of consistency, a populistic, progressive orientation. It was this impulse that led to adoption of an initiative and referendum amendment to Arkansas's Constitution in 1910, to early support for the election rather than appointment of U.S. senators, and to enfranchisement of women even before the national suffrage amendment was ratified.[24]

There was, however, another reaction to the election of 1888, one that was viciously antidemocratic and that resulted in more paralysis than progress. Alarmed by the vigor of the threat to comfortable Democratic hegemony, the political establishment saw to the enactment of a series of electoral "reforms" that emasculated the opposition and forced the emerging populistic temper to participate within a one-party, issueless, and ultimately unproductive mold.

Especially considering the fraud, thuggery, and violence that had come to characterize the election process, the election reform act of 1891 had some genuinely laudable provisions. One, for example, prohibited the last-minute transfer of polling places. Its two most important provisions, however, were obviously intended to ensure the future electoral fortunes of the Democratic establishment. One effectively turned over all the state's election machinery to the Democratic party, with only token representation for Republicans and populistic parties. The other disfranchised illiterates (over one-fourth of the population at that time) by removing all political symbols from the ballot and providing that only the precinct judges (not a friend or fellow party member) could assist illiterates in preparing their ballots. The legislature also initiated a constitutional amendment placing a one-dollar poll tax on the "privilege" of voting, and in 1892 (by which time the 1891 reforms were in effect) this amendment was ratified. The legislature also gerrymandered the congressional districts to dilute and confine the remaining pockets of Republicanism, a gesture that was probably superfluous, since blacks had constituted at least one-third of the Republican vote, and blacks were hardest hit by the printed ballot and poll-tax requirement. There is still some debate over the extent to which these changes reflected a genuinely reformist impulse in reaction to the flagrant election abuses that had become commonplace, the extent to which they were intended to disfranchise all the "common folk," and the extent to which they were singularly targeted at disfranchising blacks. There can be no dispute, however, over the resulting dramatic decline in voting, from 191,000 participants in the 1890 election to 133,000 in 1900, nor can the escalating racist rhetoric of the period be ignored or mistaken.[25]

The enfranchised freedmen had enjoyed a brief period of being wooed by the Democrats (especially when a threatened black exodus greatly alarmed the planters), some modest officeholding and patronage under Republican auspices, and a tenuous alliance with some of the agrarian organizations. While it is probably true, as Ashmore has observed, that the freedmen were always more "pawns than participants," and it is certainly true that even within the Republican party they were subject to tokenism, even this limited political strength was decimated by the election reforms and by the rising tides of Jim Crowism and outright bigotry. From this time forward, every non-Democratic candidate was successfully pictured as a threat to white control, "a vote for Negro supremacy and bayonet rule." Distracted by racism from the true logic of their circumstances, poor whites, the natural economic ally of the equally poor black sharecroppers and workers, were shamed and stampeded into a belief that a secure future for the white race was totally dependent upon solidarity within the Democratic party, and that a vote for populism in any guise constituted racial treason. By 1906, when the Democratic State Committee at Jeff Davis's urging amended party rules to restrict voting eligibility in the primary to "all legally qualified white electors who paid a poll tax," it was simply formalizing an exclusion that had already become operational.[26]

While some poll-tax-paying blacks continued to vote in the general election, they were voting in contests that had already been decided. Furthermore, their loss of electoral utility to the white Republican establishment gave strength to the lily-white elements in GOP ranks who could argue that their black members not only cut into the available patronage but that their presence made it very difficult to recruit whites, "a costly burden to their struggling party."[27]

In one other important respect, Arkansas politics became more "open" in this period. Beginning statewide in 1902, the selection of party nominees by the voters in primary elections rather than by closed and elite-dominated county and state conventions was another reflection of what David Y. Thomas has termed the "plebian temper" of this period. Before describing the hallmarks of this "new" political system, however, one other observation seems pertinent.

John Gaventa, in a recent prize-winning study of the apparent acquiescence of Appalachian miners and mountaineers in decades of neglect and abuse by their elected institutions, asked many questions similar to those raised at the outset of this study. Why, given their numbers, did they never mount a rebellion against those who systematically exploited them? Why did they never recognize their potential power and use it, or at least argue for an alternative arrangement of the political order? Gaventa's conclusion is that the Appalachians' apparent quiescence was not just the product of a political culture (similar to that in the Arkansas uplands) that was indifferent to and scornful of communal action. Rather, Gaventa suggests, it was a logical, learned response, a knowledge gained from every previous attempt to protest that superior political and economic forces had and would overcome them.[28]

The possible analogy here would be that the populistic uprising in late-nineteenth-century Arkansas, an uprising that achieved a few policy responses but produced no significant betterment in the life of the average Arkansan, was beaten by a clever ploy that precluded a potentially powerful combination of poor blacks and whites from organizing around and acting upon their common interests. With their one major thrust to power effectively thwarted, politics again became the inconsequential pastime of a relative few rather than the arena in which the hopes of the many could be fulfilled. The response, as before the agrarian uprising, appears as acquiescence but actually was now based as much on defeat and disillusionment as on disinterest. With the blacks disfranchised, the agrarians demoralized, and the Republicans reduced to impotence, the Democratic party found the first six decades of the twentieth century again secure in their hands.

## CHAPTER THREE

# Traditional Politics and Its Transformation

*At the origin of the Southern one-party system stood the single figure of the Negro . . . and the Negro must be supplanted by other concerns before one-party supremacy will break down.*

Alexander Heard, *A Two-Party South?*, 1952

*I hope that segregation as a political issue is dead forever. I believe that essentially it is.*

Governor Dale Bumpers, 1971

For the first seventeen presidential elections in the twentieth century, Arkansas went Democratic, and did so by margins far exceeding the national Democratic norm. Elections to the U.S. Congress were just as consistently Democratic, and the Democratic candidate won the governorship in thirty-three successive elections from 1900 to 1964. In fact, the average Republican percentage of the gubernatorial vote from 1900 to 1948 was less than 15 percent and from 1950 to 1960 only 22 percent. Republicans never held more than five seats (and usually only two) out of one hundred in the state house of representatives, and never more than one (and usually none) in the state senate from 1900 until 1982. In short, Arkansas was the most thoroughly and consistently Democratic state of any in the nation. While these figures represent a total triumph for the Democrats, however, they were produced by a political system that was only minimally democratic.[1]

In terms of voting participation, for example, the record was dismal both

in comparison with nineteenth-century Arkansas standards and in contrast
to the rest of the nation. In 1948, while 51 percent of the national voting-age
population was voting for president, only 25 percent of the voting-age
population in Arkansas was doing so; and in 1960 the comparable figures
were 64 percent in the nation and 41 percent in Arkansas. Comparisons with
the national and other state electorates can be somewhat misleading given
the disfranchisement of Arkansas blacks (who constituted one-fourth of
Arkansas's population through 1940) and the inconsequentiality of the
general election in comparison with the Democratic primary. Even using the
fairest possible comparative measures, however, it is clear how nonparticipatory Arkansas politics had become. Between 1920 and 1946, the
average percentage of all adults voting in Democratic gubernatorial primaries was 22.6 percent (compared, say, with 56 percent in New York), and the
average voting turnout of the eligible white electorate was only 30.3 percent
(compared with over 50 percent in North Carolina, Mississippi, and Louisiana).[2]

It is impossible to estimate how much of this nonparticipation was due to
the poll tax (which had to be purchased and the receipt preserved far in
advance of the elections) and how much was due to disinterest and/or
defeatism. If an east Arkansas sharecropper or an Ozark subsistence farmer
ever did get his hands on a dollar of cash money, it is difficult to imagine
why he would choose to spend it in this fashion. And for black Arkansans in
such circumstances to pay this price to vote in a general election contest
previously decided in the primary is to assume a civic virtue that even
Aristotle would have found astonishing.

There are numerous other possible explanations for the low voter turnout. Although women were enabled to vote in the Democratic primaries
beginning in 1918 and in all elections after 1920, female participation rates
have only gradually begun to equal (and occasionally exceed) male voter
turnout, and they still lag somewhat behind men among older people. More
educated people are much more likely to be voters, and in 1940, for
example, only 8.6 percent of Arkansans aged twenty-five and over had
completed high school, an unsurprising statistic, since as late as 1948 only
half of all schoolchildren had a high school to attend. Economic affluence is
also positively associated with voting, and per capita income in Arkansas
was $332 in 1940, or 48 percent of the national average.

Finally, it is important to remember that the choices offered to the
electorate rarely dealt with meaningful issues. Given that the only important
contests took place within the Democratic primary, the electorate was

deprived of those policy distinctions and issue orientations generally associated with Democrats as compared with Republicans and, rather, were offered a choice between competing personalities, all bearing the Democratic label. Furthermore, unlike some southern states where strong and stable rivalries within the Democratic party produced a dualism somewhat approximating two-party competition, the Arkansas system was characterized by totally splintered and discontinuous groupings, arising and fading from one election to the next with no issue salience or consistency whatsoever. V. O. Key, the greatest student of traditional southern Democratic politics, found through 1948 absolutely no statewide faction with cohesion, continuity, or content. Rather he found "a multiplicity of transient and personal factions, not of clear-cut groupings of voters, but of rather sharply defined groups of first, second and third-string lieutenants loyal to the leader for personal reasons—mainly desire for office—and like all such groupings, their life expectancy was short."[3]

Boyce Drummond, in an extensive and thoughtful update of Key's analysis in 1957, concluded similarly that "no candidate or faction in recent years has been successful in building a state organization that lasted longer than one or two campaigns." Drummond went on to observe: "Lacking strong organizational support, which might obligate him to advocate specific policies or programs, a candidate simply attempts to persuade the voter that he is the best qualified candidate. Such persuasion is gained more often than not by negative methods. Constructive discussion of issues or principles of government is spurned in favor of character assassination, mudslinging, and demogogic speeches."[4]

One observer described these primary campaigns as "a sort of legalized knife fight and perpetual stomping contest"; another described campaigns as "dog fights" and nothing more. Occasionally an editor would complain, "just for once we'd like to see a governor's race in Arkansas in which candidates run on their own merits, on specific plans which they have in mind for the betterment of our state," rather than trying to prove, "usually in a last minute verbal blitzkrieg that his leading adversary is a crook and an ignoramus."[5]

Lacking those policy-related distinctions that party labels contribute, the only way in which candidates, all Democrats, could distinguish themselves from each other was with fiery oratory on their own behalf, character assaults on their opponents, and assorted campaign gimmicks. "Was this candidate or that one more showy and satisfying? Did Jack or Jock offer the more thrilling representation of the South in action against the Yankee and the black man?"[6] The system practically guaranteed a campaign of "bucket and bile," and perhaps as was true in the nineteenth century, did provide an entertaining and therefore welcome diversion in a world that offered few others.

The money for these campaigns seems minimal by today's standards: an estimated $20,000 in the 1920s, up to $100,000 in the 1930s, and up to $200,000 by the 1950s for a strongly contested gubernatorial primary. Most of this money seems to have been contributed in very large amounts from those who, either because they did business with the state or were regulated by the state or wanted employment by the state, recognized the clear consequences of state elections on their fortunes and so were willing to invest in the possibility of favored treatment. The major contributors, therefore, were highway contractors and related construction and road machinery firms, printers and textbook publishers, wholesale grocers, bond houses and insurance firms, railroads, the utilities and the liquor dealers, plus state employees, who were routinely "maced" by gubernatorial and other candidates. For a few self-interested individuals, then, politics commanded very close observation and attention.[7]

In addition to low participation and issueless campaigns, two other features of traditional Arkansas politics helped to define its nature and limit its utility as an instrument of popular governance: the importance of local leaders in "delivering" the vote and the widespread existence (and acceptance) of fraud. In the absence of party competition to clarify issue differences and of mass technology for reaching the voters, a statewide contest depended largely upon lining up the support of local leaders who could corral their area vote, and again according to Key, "These local potentates loom larger in Arkansas than in most southern states." The foremost function of any statewide campaign manager was to line up these local bosses, and while in some instances their leadership was based on prominence and respect in the community, and could be secured on the basis of persuasion, in many other instances it was necessary to bargain on the basis of a quid pro quo. One gubernatorial campaign manager of the 1940s recalls, "Some wanted jobs, some wanted roads, some wanted both—but they all wanted something." Many also expected a cash payment, euphemistically entitled "walking around money," and many of these local leaders, understandably, were centered in the county courthouse.[8]

In many counties, jobs working for the county were the only cash-paying jobs available and therefore highly prized. County roads, the lifeblood of farmers and merchants, were built or not built depending upon the grace of the county judge. Furthermore, with the cooperation of the county clerk, it was easy to determine who had voted and for whom. With a very small and therefore highly manageable electorate, with a number of those participants economically dependent upon the goodwill of the courthouse crowd, the power of these local potentates is unsurprising.

The bosses may occasionally have exaggerated their actual power to inflate their self-importance and bargaining position. Based upon Key and Drummond's observations, as well as upon numerous personal experiences and interviews, however, there is little question but what most statewide races depended primarily on local organization and maneuver. A 1940s candidate for the state supreme court recalled for me that in eastern Arkansas it was necessary to see only one or two people in each county: "If they were for you, they delivered; if not, they beat your brains out." As recently as 1966, a political activist seeking support for a young man making his first statewide race asked a friendly hill county leader to give his man a little encouragement, "say like 800 votes," and exactly 800 votes were tallied for him. Brooks Hays recalled that in seeking the Democratic nomination for governor in 1928 he had made all the arrangements necessary for carrying Boone County and asked the local boss to telephone in the results early on election night. That would not be possible, the gentleman said, since there was no telephone. Hays persisted: could the results be wired by telegraph? That would also be difficult, said the county leader, but then added: "Look here, Brooks, if you're that anxious I can tell you what the vote's going to be and we could just write it down now." Hays also ruefully recalled how viciously this system of local control was used against him in the special Democratic primary for Congress in 1933, when he was "counted out" in Yell County (often known as the free state of Yell), which certified a vote of 2,454, although official poll tax lists contained only 1,651 names.[9]

As these and numerous other incidents indicate, the entire elections process in Arkansas was frequently manipulated through an almost infinite variety of techniques made possible by both the voting process and the apparent tolerance of the public. The poll tax itself, the only voter registration system Arkansas possessed until 1965, was an open and frequently accepted invitation to abuse as huge blocks of poll taxes could be purchased and then distributed to "friends" (or simply voted in the desired direction). Liquor stores, anxious to protect their legitimacy in wet localities, would buy large lots of poll taxes and distribute them to their customers, who would presumably vote wet in any future local option elections. Eastern Arkansas planters routinely bought poll taxes for all their tenants and sometimes saved them the bother of even making an appearance at the polls, a "favor" also frequently performed for their womenfolk. Illiterates who did vote were given a notch stick (a stick that could be placed on the ballot with notches coinciding with the "right" choices) to facilitate their voting; any "wrong" choices could be easily detected and corrected, since there was virtually no secrecy of the ballot. The paper ballots contained a carbon duplicate, signed by the voter, both original and duplicate containing identical numbers. And despite a state law requiring such, there were almost no voting booths in Arkansas until the late 1960s.[10]

Should all these measures be insufficient, there remained the infinite possibilities of outright fraud: deliberate defacement and subsequent discarding of ballots in the process of counting them and wholesale destruction (through burning, trashing, and even, in one instance, eating) of ballots if necessary. These kinds of practices were much more widespread and flagrant in some localities than in others, varying with the manageability of the electorate, the perceived stakes (in Garland County, for example, the illegal gambling operations absolutely necessitated a compliant political establishment), the skill and enthusiasm of local leaders, and local mores. In Newton County, for example, it was traditional to wait outside the courthouse on election day until one got the "highest dollar" and then a congratulatory slug of whiskey afterward. In other counties, chicanery was limited to the absentee ballots; any blanks were completed by those counting the vote with the names of machine-favored candidates.[11]

Virtually any statewide contest, however, was somewhat tainted by the tactics necessary to ensure victory in some counties, and despite numerous charges of fraud by the losers and occasional court challenges of consequences, the courts were generally as inclined as the citizenry to look the other way. Drummond, writing in 1957, concluded that "at least three gubernatorial races, two United States Senatorial races, and one Congressional race since 1930 were decided by corrupt practices"; and Key concluded that while "Tennessee has the most consistent and widespread habit of fraud, with Arkansas a close second," Arkansas's first political problem was still "the establishment of the essential mechanisms of democratic government."[12]

In this context Key was referring to the fundamental requirement of honest elections. More broadly, however, he was referring to the fact that democratic nations have found political parties to be indispensable instruments of self-government, an absolutely essential means through which identifiable groups of politicians, anxious to secure control of government, provide for the organization and expression of competing viewpoints on public policies between which voters can choose and through which they can hold government accountable. And this fundamental requirement for self-government was missing in Arkansas.

## THE NO-PARTY SYSTEM

Arkansas's solidly Democratic nature had enormous instrumental value in preserving the segregated status quo. In an unwritten but clearly understood trade-off, any Democratic presidential candidate in the early twentieth century was guaranteed virtually all the electoral votes of the South provided he made no unsettling moves in the direction of racial equality. Furthermore, southern Democrats, once elected to the U.S. Congress, could remain for decades without serious challenge, thereby acquiring powerful committee chairmanships through the seniority system as well as a veto on any presidential programs deemed threatening to the southern way of life. Following the 1964 elections, not a single member of Arkansas's congressional delegation had been in office for less than 20 years: the two senators and four congressmen had 138 years of seniority among themselves, the chairmanships of the U.S. Senate Foreign Relations and Government Operations committees, of the House Ways and Means and Interstate and Foreign Commerce committees, and choice rankings on Senate Appropriations and Finance, House Rules, and Agriculture.

This determination to preserve Democratic dominance, stemming originally from and sustained by its instrumentality in maintaining the subordinate status of the black population, condemned the entire political system to partyless, and therefore in most respects meaningless, politics. As the preceding discussion clearly indicates, the Arkansas Democratic party was not an electoral organization, bound to recruit the most attractive candidates and frame the most beneficial issue appeals in order to ensure victory over their Republican opposites. Rather, it was a very loose holding company under whose name transient and candidate-oriented factions competed for power on the basis of personality appeals and local alliances.[13]

The Arkansas Republican party was no more an electoral organization than was the Democratic party. Rather, it was organized solely as an arrangement for securing federal patronage for its exclusive membership and receiving whatever rewards (appointments, prestige, cash) might be offered by presidential aspirants seeking support at the Republican National Convention. Often termed "post office Republicans" (because postmasterships were the most plentiful patronage prizes), the typical southern state Republican organization was characterized by Alexander Heard: "The most signal characteristic of the party's southern leadership has been a lack of interest in winning elections. They have been big fish in little ponds and they have liked it. They have not sought to disrupt their closed corporation by electing local candidates. . . . They have been patronage referees or palace politicians, but not candidates or campaign managers."[14]

The Arkansas Republicans clearly fit this description. Dominated for years by Powell Clayton and his faithful assistant Harmon Remmel (and thus sometimes called a two-family system), unhappy insurgents occasionally charged that the organization was antielectoral, because so long as the party was small there were fewer of the faithful to reward and no mass following demanding accountability. Certainly no serious effort was made until well after the middle of the twentieth century to build a voting constituency. In fact, the first efforts to do so in the 1960s were vigorously opposed by the established organization, leading Jeannette Rockefeller to recall that, in 1960, "the Republican Party was truthfully about five old men who sat on a porch until there was a Republican President and then held out their hands for some patronage." Confirming this analysis, Thomas Kielhorn concluded: "If by party we mean a political organization that actively seeks votes in the pursuit of office, then with the exception of two hill counties in the Arkansas Ozarks, it can fairly be stated that Arkansas did not have a Republican Party until the early 1960's."[15]

In spite of this nonelectoral Republican party mechanism, there continued to be a small but faithful Republican electorate. The hereditary Republicans of the highlands, especially in Newton, Searcy, and Madison counties, consistently voted for Republican presidential candidates, usually for Republican gubernatorial candidates, sent Republicans to the state legislature, and even held Republican primaries for local offices. Those blacks who voted stayed loyal to the party of the Great Emancipator, and some migrants from northern states brought their Republican affiliations with them.

There was, however, no genuine effort on the part of Republicans to break the Democratic stranglehold and no reliable way for voters to ascertain, within the kaleidoscopic, transitory factionalism of the Democratic party, which of the faces and names would best serve their own interests. Key traced many political and governmental inadequacies to the door of the South's curious brand of one-party and therefore essentially no-party politics: low voter participation; issueless campaigns; a disposition to fraud and favoritism; an emphasis on demagogic personalities; fragmented, timid, and ineffective state governments. His most serious charge, however, was that, given the fact that politics generally comes down to a conflict between those who have and those who have less, this kind of political disorganization consistently favors the haves over the have-nots. In the great ongoing issues of taxation, expenditures, and regulation, Key asserted, the grand objective of those comfortable with the status quo is obstruction—leave us alone to enjoy what we already have—for which little organized action is necessary. For those still aspiring, however, still attempting to climb the ladder and needing such institutional supports as schools and roads to do so, sustained organization is necessary but was nearly impossible. There was no mechanism through which to act, and their wishes found expression in fitful rebellions led by transient demagogues who gained their confidence but often had neither the technical competence nor the stable base of political power to effectuate a program.[16]

Recently, some political scientists have suggested that Key's emphasis on party politics, or the lack thereof, as the major contributing factor in the South's regressive public policies was excessive. They have suggested that certain economic development factors have much more direct causal impact on public policies than do electoral politics, and therefore that Arkansas's retarded school system, inadequate roads, stingy social services, and regressive tax policies can be much more directly attributed to its agrarian economy, to its lack of industrialization and urbanization and wealth, than to its lack of two-party competition. If politics was not the chief enemy of progress, however, neither was politics its instigator and ally.[17]

There had been some steps forward from the nineteenth to the twentieth century. Verbal violence had largely replaced physical violence. The absolute control of a handful of relatives had been replaced with a more pluralistic pattern in which no group controlled more than its own locality. When Arkansas extended the primary suffrage to women in 1918, and became the second southern state (and the twelfth in the nation) to ratify the Nineteenth Amendment in 1920, giving national suffrage to women, the potential white electorate was doubled. A few governors had pressed for progressive change and occasionally had been successful in enacting (though not always implementing and rarely sustaining) programs that acknowledged pressing public problems, but, even the best of these leaders never seriously challenged either the economic or the political status quo.

James MacGregor Burns has provided a provocative distinction between two kinds of democratic leadership, transactional and transformational.

Transactional leadership, according to Burns, is based on an exchange or brokerage relationship between leaders and followers. It can be constructive in negotiating and securing basic needs and interests of followers, but it is also superficial and limited, dominated ultimately by a calculation of political costs and benefits. Transformational leadership, based on a symbiotic or collective relationship that binds leaders and followers together, is much more educative and elevating, because the "leader's task is consciousness-raising on a wide plane," arousing and elevating the hopes and demands of followers to an awareness of their needs and entitlements, and leaving permanent institutions behind that sustain progress after the leader is gone.[18]

Arkansas voters did elect some genuinely distinguished delegates to represent them in Congress. Senator Joseph T. Robinson, who was Alfred E. Smith's vice-presidential runningmate in the 1928 election, was Democratic majority leader from 1932 to 1937 and capably assisted President Franklin D. Roosevelt in securing passage of New Deal legislation. Senator J. W. Fulbright authored the resolution committing the United States to United Nations support and involvement, established the highly successful international scholar-exchange program that bears his name, and as chairman of the Senate Foreign Relations Committee led the challenge to cold war "myths," which, he contended, were crippling rather than strengthening U.S. foreign policy, most notably in Vietnam. Congressman Wilbur D. Mills became known as "the third House of Congress" during his long tenure as chairman of the House Ways and Means Committee, from which all revenue legislation (and at that time all House Democratic Committee assignments) must originate. Congressman Brooks Hays distinguished himself by efforts to meliorate rather than escalate the Central High desegregation crisis, and after his electoral defeat he was honored by presidential assignments and academic appointments. Still, none of these luminaries in Arkansas's national delegation ever challenged the political and economic establishment in Arkansas. In fact, they worked closely and comfortably with it.

At the state level, those few governors who had a reformist bent were either thwarted or co-opted by the establishment, or found the traditional two two-year terms totally inadequate for making or sustaining real change. Using Burns's very broad distinction, the Arkansas political system produced a few capable transactional leaders but no transformational ones.

Admittedly, that kind of leadership would have required extraordinary skill and determination against staggering odds: Arkansas's ruralism and continued isolation from the mainstream of modern ideas; an uneducated and provincial population struggling for economic survival and character-ized by widespread economic dependency; a religious tradition that empha-sized salvation in the next world rather than reform and justice in this one; and what Drummond has summarized as "the general cultural immaturity of the state." What any leader would have had to overcome is what Arsenault, in describing both Governor Jeff Davis and his followers, has termed "the anti-institutionalism of the nineteenth-century frontier," a distrust of all concentrations of power and an ambivalence about governmental activism. "They knew that good politics would make them feel better, but they were not sure what good government would do for them."[19]

And lacking any experience with good government, how could they? For a great variety of reasons, then, politics continued to be an occasionally entertaining but generally irrelevant sideshow, and state government en-tered the last half of the twentieth century having yet to demonstrate its capacity for making a significant and positive difference in the lives of its citizens. Counting from 1888, the highwater mark of the agrarian-Republi-can challenge, until the 1966 gubernatorial election of Republican Winthrop Rockefeller, this one-party, low-participation, issueless politics character-ized Arkansas's political life for over three-fourths of a century, for over half of its existence as a state.

Well before 1966 developments were underway that would challenge and change almost every aspect of this system. Significantly, however, the major stimuli for change were generated by forces totally outside the state. Dissenters within could never generate sufficient sustained force to over-come the countless social, economic, and political supports for the status quo.

## THE TRANSFORMATION OF TRADITIONAL POLITICS

By the 1980s almost every visible feature of traditional Arkansas politics had been transformed. Blacks, against whom the entire edifice was orig-inally established, had become significant participants in, rather than nega-tive objects of, the political system. Elections had become generally honest and much more participatory. Courthouse rings and county bosses were approaching obsolescence. Perhaps most significant, the general election had occasionally become a genuine contest rather than a perfunctory ratifi-cation of the Democratic primary.

Part of this transformation is the story of individual leaders and specific events combining at critical junctures to thrust the political process into unprecedented directions. Senator Huey Long's successful foray into Arkansas in August 1932 in behalf of Senator Hattie Caraway's reelection lasted only one week, but hundreds of thousands heard and remembered his exhortations to the dispossessed to stand up against the economic establishment. Sidney McMath and other leaders of the GI revolt sensitized Arkansans to the shame of widespread, casual election fraud and the desirability of honestly conducted elections. Orval Faubus's escalation of the events at Central High temporarily plunged Arkansas into political turbulence, racial ugliness, and economic decline. These same events, however, galvanized scores of previously apolitical citizens (many of them women) into the political arena, where they remained long after Faubus had departed.[20]

There is no adequate measure for the contributions to change generated by the serendipitous 1953 arrival in Arkansas of Winthrop Rockefeller, but across a very broad spectrum of economic development, race relations, party competition, and governmental reform, it is no exaggeration to say that he "exerted a greater—and more beneficial—influence on a single state than any figure of his generation." This opinion was resoundingly confirmed by the 1980s Big Three of Arkansas Democratic politics, Dale Bumpers, David Pryor, and Bill Clinton, each of whom acknowledged that Rockefeller paved the way for their own political progressivism and had been "the beacon who showed us out of the dark days of Arkansas politics." Hundreds of lesser-known individuals made their own distinctive and essential contributions, and their actions cumulated into an important part of the explanation for change. Fortunately for the student of Arkansas politics, excellent narrative accounts of Arkansas's recent political history have been published and are readily available.[21]

It is also essential to understand, however, that these individual actions were taking place in a political climate that was being radically altered by historic, technological, and economic forces that arose outside the Arkansas political system but touched and transformed the lives of all Arkansans. While the Great Depression ravaged Arkansas for over a decade, the New Deal had more lasting political consequences. By 1939 the federal government had poured over $700 million into the state in grants and loans, much of it for the simple alleviation of human suffering, but also, through the Works Progress Administration (WPA) and other work projects, for 11,471 miles of roads, 467 schools, countless libraries, courthouses, parks, and other public facilities. Severe threats from the federal government had forced the state government into enactment of its first general revenue program and also into assuming a commitment, modest but permanent, toward public welfare for the elderly and the indigent.[22]

While many of these programs encountered enormous hostility and obstructionism from Arkansas's political and economic establishment, the popularity of Roosevelt and the New Deal not only reinforced the commitment of Arkansas's voters to the Democratic party but provided many Arkansans with their first look at the potential benefits of politics and government. Perhaps poverty was not a God-willed infliction to be suffered individually and independently. Perhaps politics could and should be something more than oratory and barbecues and hillbilly bands. One longtime participant in Arkansas politics recently noted the watershed quality of the New Deal as follows: "Before, politics was just a game. It didn't matter who won, because they weren't going to do anything anyway."[23]

World War II was another turning point with profound political consequences in Arkansas, enormously stimulating the economy with defense plants and military installations, quickening urban growth, and revitalizing agriculture with its demands for food and fiber. More than 200,000 Arkansans, over 10 percent of the total population, served in the nation's armed forces, and many returned to Arkansas with a fresher, more critical view. They not only precipitated the GI revolt but now, having some standards of comparison, contributed significantly to what George Tindall has described as "a growing sense of Southern deficiencies." Many took advantage of the GI Bill, creating explosive enrollment increases on the state's college campuses. Others, finding little economic opportunity, left the state, joining the outward streams of Arkansans attracted to economic opportunities elsewhere, and/or displaced by the agricultural revolution.[24]

To label the changes in Arkansas's economy over recent decades as revolutionary is not an exaggeration. Fueled largely by technological developments (mechanization of equipment, pesticides, fertilizers, improved seed and livestock strains), agriculture was transformed into a productive, scientific, and diversified enterprise that employed many fewer Arkansans on much larger farms at far greater profit. In 1940 a majority of the population was employed as farmers, farm managers, and laborers, and cotton still reigned supreme, grown on over three million acres in virtually every county, with total agricultural cash receipts about $100 million for the entire state. By 1980 only 6.5 percent of the population were so employed, soybeans and rice had far outstripped the acreage and cash value of cotton in the Delta, cotton had been totally displaced by profitable poultry and cattle operations in the rest of the state, and net farm income was in the billions of dollars. Leland Duvall and others have told this compelling tale of economic metamorphosis in richness and detail, but one statistic is especially eloquent in its implications: a two-row cotton picker, operated by one person, can do the work of more than 100 fieldhands.[25]

While it is estimated that half of the population still makes its living in ways related to agriculture, in terms of 1980 Census Bureau classifications most Arkansas workers (53 percent) were employed in service industries (the trades, construction, teaching, government, utilities, retail stores, restaurants, etc.), and the second highest number (20 percent) were employed in manufacturing, the number of which establishments increased 143 percent from 1939 to 1972. In short, Arkansas had changed from an agrarian economy, with feudal conditions in the lowlands and patchy, subsistence farms in the uplands, to a more diversified, white-collar, service-oriented economy.[26]

Concomitantly, Arkansas has become more urban than rural, with 51.6 percent of its population living in towns of 2,500 or more by 1984, and 40 percent of its population living within one of six SMSA's (Standard Metropolitan Statistical Areas)—four times the metropolitan dwellers in 1950. Arkansas continues to possess a strong rural flavor: only fourteen of its cities have more than 20,000 inhabitants, sixty-two of its seventy-five counties are more rural than urban, and fourteen counties have no urban population at all. It is still possible to drive for days in Arkansas without seeing any building taller than a county courthouse and no men in coats and ties. Still, the numbers are now in the towns and cities, which are no longer strictly subservient to the rural areas surrounding them but important in their own right and driven by their own varied interests.

While per capita income in Arkansas remained in the very bottom ranks, varying from forty-sixth to forty-ninth of the fifty states, that income had moved from 40 percent of the national average in 1940 to 75 percent of the national average in 1980, a dramatic narrowing of the perennial gap. As will be discussed, this newfound material adequacy for many, and affluence for some, still eludes significant portions of Arkansas's population, especially in those east Arkansas counties where thousands of former cotton pickers and choppers still live with the cruel legacy of the cotton kingdom, and this is especially true for many black Arkansans. However, thousands of Arkansas blacks migrated to better economic opportunities elsewhere, steadily reducing the black percentage of the population from 26.9 percent in 1920 to 22 percent in 1950 and 16.3 percent in 1980. Having migrated northward, they made their contribution to the transformation of the national Democratic party—from an orientation toward rural, small-town, white southern voters to the New Deal coalition of urban, ethnic, labor, and increasingly minority northern voters. And this in turn gradually changed the Democratic party from being the major protector of white supremacy to becoming its most fierce critic and challenger.

By the late 1930s the strains between the southern and nonsouthern wings of the Democratic party began to surface; by 1948 they erupted into open warfare; and by 1964, when President Lyndon B. Johnson campaigned on the promise of eradicating every vestige of racial injustice while the Republicans nominated Barry Goldwater, the only nonsouthern U.S. senator to have voted against the Civil Rights Act of 1964, the entire rationale for the solid one-party Democratic South had evaporated, in fact had been reversed.

Meantime, the U.S. Supreme Court, joined in the 1960s by the U.S. Congress, steadily eliminated virtually all of the legal mechanisms and subterfuges that had sustained the southern social and political system. *Smith v. Allwright* in 1944 put an end to the "white primary," and the Voting Rights Act of 1965 outlawed all racially based voter restrictions. *Brown v. Board of Education* in 1954 and numerous subsequent decisions outlawed separate (and always unequal) school systems, and the 1964 Civil Rights Act outlawed discrimination in all public programs and institutions and accommodations offered to the public. *Baker v. Carr* in 1962 and *Reynolds v. Sims* in 1964 struck down the inequitable apportionment of state legislatures that had sustained rural domination of state legislative politics into the urban age. *Harper v. Virginia Board of Elections* in 1966 ended the legality of a poll tax requirement in state and local elections, thus closing the door left open by passage of the Twenty-fourth Constitutional Amendment prohibiting the poll tax in federal elections.

Arkansas did not submit swiftly or easily to any of these changes. Governor Homer Adkins's reaction to the end of the white primary was to fulminate, "If I cannot be nominated by the white voters of Arkansas, I do not want the office," and the state Democratic party's reaction was to adopt a set of "principles" deliberately repugnant to blacks to which all Democrats were required to affirm allegiance. The furious reaction to court-ordered school desegregation precipitated an immediate round of demagoguery, segregationist laws, constitutional amendments and popular initiatives, and political success for those who rode the tides of resistance.[27]

The fury began subsiding almost as quickly as it had arisen. By 1962 Orval Faubus was using little racist rhetoric; by 1964 he was patching up some of his differences with the N A A C P and appointing some blacks to state boards and commissions. And in 1966 Winthrop Rockefeller, a Republican who had assiduously courted and registered black voters after his unsuccessful gubernatorial race in 1964, got 54 percent of the gubernatorial vote against James D. ("Justice Jim") Johnson, a Democrat who had organized the Arkansas White Citizens Councils, been highly instrumental in forcing Faubus into his segregationist stance, and refused throughout the 1966 campaign to shake black voters' hands.[28]

Since the essence of traditional Arkansas politics was black exclusion and easy Democratic dominance, the black-supported election of the first Republican governor since Reconstruction, and the first ever freely chosen by the native Arkansas electorate, is the single most visible symbol of the political consequences of the sweeping economic and social changes of preceding decades. Before looking further into the contemporary partisan complexion of Arkansas, some additional major modifications in traditional Arkansas politics should be noted.

First, as shown in table 3, Arkansas voters have become much more participatory, now matching, and occasionally exceeding, national levels of voter turnout. Obviously, Arkansas's improved record is due in part to declines in national turnout percentages. Furthermore, Arkansas's two-year gubernatorial term through this period frequently created more "off-year" interest in Arkansas than is characteristic of the nation generally. Nevertheless, average Arkansas voter turnout has escalated sharply, and for a variety of reasons: the elimination of the poll tax and the white primary; the occasional vigorous voter registration efforts by candidates, parties, and interested organizations; the stimulation of spirited close contests replacing predictable outcomes; and, of course, the enfranchisement of black citizens.

It is estimated that in 1940 only 3 percent of black adults had, through payment of poll taxes, qualified themselves to vote. Following abolishment of the white primary (that is, when voting in the more meaningful Democratic primary became possible), this figure increased to 21 percent in 1948 and climbed slowly upward to 33 percent in 1958. In the 1960s the combination of the salience of racial issues in a series of contests (Barry Goldwater versus Lyndon Johnson, George Wallace and Richard Nixon versus Hubert Humphrey, and especially Jim Johnson versus Winthrop Rockefeller), plus the intensive efforts of Rockefeller to recruit black voter support, brought the percentage of the black population registered to vote to 68 percent by 1968 and to 72 percent by 1970. By November 1984 that percentage had slipped slightly to 67.2 percent (compared with 74.4 percent

Table 3: Voter Turnout in Arkansas and the Nation, 1948–1984

| | Percentage of Voting-Age Population Who Voted | |
|---|---|---|
| | Arkansas | United States |
| 1948 | 21.9 | 51.1 |
| 1952 | 36.9 | 61.6 |
| 1956 | 38.0 | 59.3 |
| 1960 | 41.2 | 64.0 |
| 1964 | 53.4 | 63.0 |
| 1968 | 53.9 | 62.8 |
| 1970 | 52.2 | 44.0 |
| 1972 | 48.1 | 55.2 |
| 1976 | 51.1 | 53.5 |
| 1978 | 36.0 | 34.9 |
| 1980 | 51.5 | 52.6 |
| 1982 | 49.0 | 39.0 |
| 1984 | 52.5 | 51.4 |

*Source:* Compiled from U.S. Bureau of the Census, *Census of Population* (Washington, D.C.: Government Printing Office, various years); Richard M. Scammon, ed., *America at the Polls* (Pittsburgh: University of Pennsylvania Press, 1965); Arkansas Secretary of State, *Official Election Returns* (Little Rock: Secretary of State, various years).

of the white population); but even at somewhat lower registration and turnout levels, black voters—as will be discussed—have become a critical factor in swinging close statewide elections and sometimes have been the decisive factor in those counties and localities where black citizens predominate.[29]

The new, more participatory tradition has not spread evenly across the state. As shown in Map 2, there is a considerable range from the exceptionally high turnouts in some of the upland counties to exceptionally low turnouts in some of the lowland counties, a contrast that substantiates Elazar's suggestion of a Moralistic influence in the Ozark uplands amid an otherwise Traditionalistic state. Furthermore, these figures reflect averages in the best possible showings of exciting, visible contests; they can shoot sharply upward in individual counties when a controversial local contest or emotion-arousing ballot issue occurs; they universally scale sharply down-

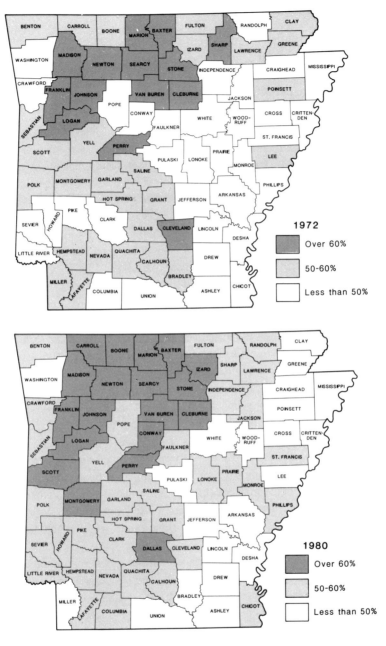

Map 2. Percentage of Voting-Age Population That Voted, by County, 1972 and 1980. (*Source:* Compiled from *Arkansas Votes, 1972* [Conway: Institute of Politics in Arkansas, 1972] and *1980 Arkansas Elections* [Little Rock: Arkansas Secretary of State, 1982].)

ward to only a fraction of the electorate in routine school elections. The fact that state government can no longer routinely conduct itself in an environment relatively immune to mass pressures and desires, however, is a major break with the past.[30]

This "popularization of politics" trend has been reinforced by the decimation of the once all-powerful county rings and leaders, and again the contributing factors are complex. The widespread use of privacy-protecting devices (voting booths and to a lesser extent voting machines) and new expectations of confidentiality have generally freed voters from whatever consequences might once have ensued from bucking the establishment's wishes. Furthermore, relatively few voters now fear the sanctions of the courthouse crowd: county jobs have lost their unique cash-paying luster; the county judge, since 1974 reforms, no longer has total discretionary authority over the placement and repair of county roads; and widespread economic independence has brought a newfound political independence to all of the urban and most of the rural regions.[31]

The major explanation for the crumbling of the courthouse rings is the spectacular rise in the range, power, and influence of the mass media, a development that is transforming politics—and governance—everywhere. The first major media campaign in Arkansas was Francis Cherry's radio talkathon successfully used in his bid for the Democratic gubernatorial nomination in 1952, a year that also brought what has been described as Arkansas's first radio campaign jingle: "Why don't you haul off and vote for Noble Gill, and tell all your friends so they will?" Both the use and the sophistication of mass-media techniques accelerated rapidly in the 1960s with television increasingly becoming the campaign medium of choice. The year 1970 brought the most spectacular demonstration of television's effectiveness in Dale Bumpers's skyrocketing rise from total obscurity to triumphal victory over Faubus in the primary and over Rockefeller in the general gubernatorial election.[32]

By the 1980s virtually all statewide contests and increasing numbers of county and even local elections were depending heavily on television to convey the messages once transmitted by local intermediaries. In fact, as the comparative figures in table 4 demonstrate, the new media techniques (extensive, sophisticated public opinion surveys with television and radio advertising crafted accordingly), have become by far the heaviest weapons in today's campaign arsenals. In 1946 the only broadcast media available was radio, to which only 8.7 percent of the campaign budget was allocated. By 1982 television and radio consumed 59.2 percent of Clinton's primary

Table 4: Democratic Gubernatorial Campaign Expenditures, 1946 and 1982

| 1946 | | 1982 | |
|---|---|---|---|
| Newspaper advertising | $40,000 | Television | $372,201 |
| Radio advertising | 10,000 | Radio | 91,615 |
| Printing | 10,000 | Professional fees (polls and contract services) | 75,507 |
| Salaries | 5,000 | | |
| Postage | 4,000 | Other advertising | 70,356 |
| Travel expenses | 2,500 | Salaries | 32,765 |
| Telephone & telegraph | 2,500 | Headquarters (rent, supplies, equipment) | 30,664 |
| Auto & loudspeaker rental | 2,000 | | |
| Headquarters rent | 1,000 | Direct Mail | 29,453 |
| | | Telephone | 24,082 |
| | $87,000 | Travel | 20,130 |
| | | Newspaper | 19,530 |
| | | Election Day Activities | 10,200 |
| | | Miscellaneous | 6,941 |
| | | | $783,444 |

*Source:* 1946 figures in V. O. Key, Jr., *Southern Politics* (New York: Random House, 1949), p. 465; 1982 figures from Bill Clinton Campaign Committee, "Report of Campaign Expenditures," July 8, 1982, filed with Arkansas Secretary of State.
*Note:* Figures for 1946 are estimated expenses; those for 1982 are reported expenses.

budget, and if professional and consulting fees (many of which relate to what is broadcast and when) are added to this category, the percentage rises to 68.8.

Of course in neither year can these expenses be considered definitive, either as to totals or as to categories of expenditures. While a Campaign Finance Act of 1975 and subsequent amendments have brought much of what was once shrouded in secrecy into the public domain, there are still vast loopholes (discussed in chapter 6) that permit considerable creativity in terms of bona fide reporting of all expenditures. Enough is revealed, however, to suggest the skyrocketing costs of running a statewide competitive campaign, multiplying nine times in this thirty-six-year period. Since the number of voters has also escalated enormously during this time, in part this is the necessary price of reaching a larger and more attentive public.

Nevertheless, many political scientists have strongly suggested that the new media politics has gone a long way toward de-popularizing politics.

Political campaigns, it is argued, were once giant battles between contending armies, with victory going to whichever army could place the most foot soldiers in the field. The new media politics, in contrast, is a battle between advertising agencies, with victory going to the product, or candidate, who can select and afford the most skilled professional talent. The old politics was labor-intensive; the new politics is capital-intensive. The old politics consisted of parades and rallies, of crowds gathered to the town square by the strains of gospel music to be personally touched by lengthy appeals from the candidate himself, assisted by thousands of indispensable dedicated grassroots workers spreading information upward to their candidate about local issues and opinions and personally carrying the word downward to their precincts and neighborhoods about their candidate's virtues. The new politics, it is argued, has made these thousands of human intermediaries between candidate and voter superfluous. Scientifically constructed opinion surveys can reveal much more about, and much more accurately, the likes and dislikes of voters, the range and intensity of their opinions, plus all the correlations with demographic variables, than the old political squires ever dreamed of doing; skilled consultants can precisely tailor media appeals around these documented strengths and weaknesses; and since Little Rock television stations now reach 80 percent of the state's viewers, why spend months touring the small-towns and countryside when a sixty-second prime-time spot can reach infinitely more people?

While much of this is undeniably true, any broad distinction between the participatory glories of the old politics as compared with the technocratic impersonality of the new politics simply does not fit Arkansas reality. First, it must be remembered that traditional Arkansas politics involved very few Arkansans. Crowds did assemble to hear the candidates rail at each other and to eat the free barbecue, but very small percentages of the potential electorate ever got themselves to the polls, and only a handful of Arkansans ever moved from the status of spectator to gladiator. Particularly in the more controlled counties, candidates and their agents did not even go through the pretense of making the rounds. A very few people "did" politics; most did not.

Second, state candidates still ardently seek and prize skilled county coordinators and strong local organizations, who can mobilize volunteers to staff local phone banks, distribute yard signs, manage the candidate's local visits to maximum effectiveness, and provide feedback on issues and appointments especially sensitive to local voters. Local activists do not, cannot, "deliver" an entire county, or even an entire precinct, as once was possible. The difference they make is at the margins; but in an increasingly competitive environment, these margins can be critical. When the Washington County activist Billie "Momma" Schneider died in 1985, Senator David Pryor gave the eulogy and the governor, lieutenant governor, treasurer, land commissioner, and other elected officials were her pallbearers. All had been grateful beneficiaries of the "margins" she could deliver from the young people who worked in her bars and the nursing home residents she fed and feted on holidays.

Betsey Wright, Clinton's campaign manager in 1982 and 1984 (and chief gubernatorial aide in between) is prototypical of the "new breed" of political professionals: young, female, well-educated, supremely comfortable with and competent in today's technological paraphernalia. In analyzing the difference between Clinton's defeat in 1980 and his successful comeback in 1982, however, she ascribed decisive importance to the lethargy of grassroots workers in 1980 and the galvanization in 1982 of thousands of volunteers for whom Clinton's comeback became "a passionate mission." As Clinton himself has observed, "If you have twelve good people who really believe in you, you can still carry a rural county."[33]

Furthermore, for every highly advertised and strongly salient Senate or gubernatorial contest, there are still scores of races where little-known candidates compete for obscure offices, and the preferences of local political leaders can be decisive. On election eve, political activists still receive many calls inquiring "who are we for?" in the less visible races.[34]

Finally, as will be discussed in chapter 14, Arkansas voters still expect, indeed demand, the human supplement to the televised appeals and will punish those who never personally appear in their vicinity (or fail to call them if they do so). David Pryor, the acknowledged master of the personal touch in contemporary Arkansas politics has issued the definitive word: "If you don't like catfish don't run for office." (Pryor has also told his U.S. Senate colleagues that he is "living proof that you can eat catfish nine times a day . . . and survive.") In short, the new politics has not supplanted the old politics in Arkansas campaigns, it has been superimposed upon it; and contemporary Arkansas politics, with all its media gimmickry, is certainly no less participatory than was the traditional Arkansas politics.[35]

Nor has the mass-media age made Arkansas political campaigns more negative and vicious. This was a widely expressed opinion during both the 1980 gubernatorial campaign (when Frank White's television commercials conveyed virtually nothing of his plans for Arkansas's future but concentrated exclusively on excoriating Clinton for rioting Cuban refugees and car-tag increases) and again in the 1982 campaign, when both Clinton and White slammed away at each other in an unending series of negative spots threatening wholesale prisoner releases, massive utility rate increases, devastating harm to the elderly, and even mass gun confiscations should the other be elected. While these spots admittedly do little to enlighten the public, however, they are no more brutal and unenlightening than the "bucket and bile" once spilled by the gallon load on Arkansas's traditional campaign trail.

Furthermore, it must be emphasized that radio and television have probably done more than all the other mentioned factors combined to pierce the physical and intellectual isolation that had shielded so many Arkansans for most of the state's history from any consciousness of broader, and occasionally better, worlds. More than Huey Long and his tirades, more than the New Deal's tangible presence or the returning GI's and their idealism, more than the recent influx of in-migrants, radio and television have made immeasurable inroads into what has been described as "pluralistic ignorance," that isolated and inbred provincialism, which, knowing nothing different, accepted the status quo as the universal and desired condition and viewed the outside (that is, modern) world with hostility and suspicion. Where people once lived in almost total isolation from even nearby neighbors, giant satellite dishes now dot the landscape, and political contests and choices take place within an infinitely broader frame of reference.[36]

Traditional Arkansas politics stemmed from ruralism and agrarianism, from economic dependency and physical isolation, from widespread poverty in material terms and severe malnutrition of mind and spirit. Above all, it stemmed from the encompassing supreme purpose of suppressing the black race. With race substantially removed from the agenda, with the economy transformed and modernized, with material sufficiency widespread and parochial suspicions diminishing, Arkansas could finally practice a new, more participatory, and potentially more useful politics.

Briefly returning once more to the comparative gubernatorial campaign expenditures of 1946 and 1982, the $87,000 estimate for 1946 suggested that an additional $25,000 might be necessary for the primary run-off. No funds were recommended because none would be necessary for the perfunctory general election. In sharp contrast, by 1982, Clinton had to spend not only over $783,000 to secure the Democratic gubernatorial nomination, but then another $884,699 to win the general election. Clearly, Democratic domination of Arkansas politics is giving way to a more competitive model.

## CHAPTER FOUR

# Contemporary Political Patterns

*Despite the still lopsided Democratic contingents in elected offices, it may be time to formally recognize the death of the one-party system in Arkansas, where it has existed in its most undefiled state.*

Ernest Dumas, 1984

*The traditional South does survive, but primarily among whites of relatively low economic status, especially those living in rural areas.*

Michael Mezey, "The Minds of the South," 1983

Reflecting all the social, economic, and legal upheavals just described, the first partisan cracks in the "Solid South" began appearing in presidential contests, specifically in 1948, when four southern states deserted the Democrats for Dixiecrat Strom Thurmond. Other southern states actually bolted into the Republican column for the popular war hero Dwight Eisenhower in 1952 and 1956, and still others departed from the Democratic reservation to support Richard Nixon over John Kennedy in 1960, and Barry Goldwater over Lyndon Johnson in 1964. Finally, in 1968, twenty years after the apostasy had begun elsewhere in the South, Arkansas cast its first non-Democratic electoral votes since Reconstruction; but George Wallace, candidate of the American Independent party, not Richard Nixon the Republican, was the beneficiary of Democratic disenchantment.

It was not until 1972, courtesy of the candidacy of George McGovern, that Arkansas finally lost its Democratic virginity. Four years later, as if in penance for this monstrous act of heresy, Arkansas gave Jimmy Carter his largest majority (65 percent) of any state but Georgia (66.7 percent). In 1980 Arkansas took its second cautious dip into presidential Republicanism, giving Ronald Reagan a very thin plurality (48.13 percent) over Carter (47.52 percent). Finally, in 1984, Arkansas went wholeheartedly for Reagan over Walter Mondale, this time by a margin (60.4 percent) that exceeded the national average.

Arkansas, then, having voted for none but Democratic presidential candidates from statehood until 1968 (with the artificial exceptions of the Civil War and Reconstruction), has voted Democratic only once in the last five presidential elections. The following array shows the average Democratic percentage of the popular presidential vote in the last twenty presidential elections; it depicts a virtual revolution in presidential preferences.[1]

|         |        |
|---------|--------|
| 1908–24 | 59.6%  |
| 1928–44 | 75.4%  |
| 1948–64 | 55.4%  |
| 1968–84 | 42.6%  |

While Arkansas has still never elected a Republican to the U.S. Senate, these races have become distinctly more competitive, and that competition is in the general election. Dale Bumpers, for example, after a fierce primary victory over incumbent Senator Fulbright in 1974, was elected to the Senate that fall with 85 percent of the vote. In 1980 he had no primary opposition but received only 59 percent over a very unimpressive Republican challenger. David Pryor, after a close and bruising Democratic primary in 1978, cruised effortlessly through the general election with a 76 percent victory. Seeking reelection in 1984, however, he was unchallenged in the Democratic primary (as was Bumpers again in 1986) but had to spend over $1.5 million and campaign nonstop for a year to achieve a 57 percent general election victory margin.

John Paul Hammerschmidt, riding Winthrop Rockefeller's 1966 coattails to victory in the northwestern Third Congressional District (see map 3) became Arkansas's first Republican congressman since statehood. Since then, his only close challenge came from Bill Clinton in 1974; by 1980 and again in 1984, the Democrats did not even attempt to oppose him. In 1978 Hammerschmidt was joined by a second Republican congressman from the Second Congressional District (metropolitan Pulaski County and surrounding rural counties). Ed Bethune gave up his seat in 1984 to challenge Pryor unsuccessfully for the Senate, and his seat was recaptured by the Demo-

Map 3. Arkansas Congressional Districts, 1980. (*Source: Congressional Directory* [Washington, D.C.: Government Printing Office, 1984].)

crats. It was a momentous turning point in 1982, however, when for the first time in the twentieth century, all four congressional seats were contested in the general election, a feat repeated in 1986. Arkansas, which had almost specialized in congressional seniority, had only twenty-six years of it following the 1978 elections, and its most senior member was Republican Hammerschmidt.

As elsewhere in the South, fading memories of the Civil War and Reconstruction and the New Deal, the unacceptability of a series of Democratic presidential candidates, and a much more industrialized, urbanized, and generally modernized environment had finally made it possible for Republicans to compete seriously, indeed to become dominant in recent presidential elections. The focus of this study is state politics, however, and Republican development in Arkansas state politics differs not only from the presidential level but also from the general patterns of Republican emergence elsewhere in the South. Whereas in most southern states Republicans had their first victories in presidential contests, Arkansas's first Republican victory came in a gubernatorial contest; and whereas in most southern states the Republican party had its first state successes by offering a more conservative alternative to state Democrats, Winthrop Rockefeller's victories in 1966 and 1968 represented a more progressive alternative to Arkansas voters.

The explanation for the first deviation is complex but essentially threefold. First, the attachment of Arkansas voters to the Democratic party (and their negative view of Republicans) has been unsurpassed by voters in any other state and therefore took longer to change. In proof of this assertion, one public opinion survey of Arkansas voters in 1958 found that "the single most negative concept in the state was the concept of Republicanism." Second, in contrast to other southern states, where prominent Democratic political leaders and officeholders encouraged and led the bolt from the national Democratic party and its candidates, Arkansas's political establishment, especially its congressional delegation, generally defended and supported the national Democratic ticket.[2]

Finally, Arkansas is usually classified as being in the Rim or Peripheral or Border South rather than the Deep South, a distinction partly based on its geographic location at the border of the Old Confederacy but also a demographic distinction. Arkansas, with only a 21.7 percent black population in 1960 and only a 16.9 percent one in 1970 (and with thirty-seven of its seventy-five counties having less than a 5 percent black population) was not so universally touched and threatened by the civil rights revolution as were

Mississippi, Alabama, and other Deep South states. Thus, while Goldwater was sweeping the Deep South in 1964, in Arkansas he carried only a handful of counties with a high black population bordering Louisiana and a few traditional Republican counties in the northwest uplands. In an interesting analysis of presidential voting behavior in the Arkansas-Mississippi Delta, Barry Brown noted the greater predominance of the plantation economy in the Mississippi counties; the focus on racism as an issue in most major twentieth-century Mississippi political campaigns; the greater ease with which blacks, because of their lower numbers, became registered voters in Arkansas; and a great difference in White Citizens Council membership (about 300,000 in Mississippi, never more than 20,000 in Arkansas). As for the other deviation from the southern norm, Arkansas Republicanism emerging at the gubernatorial level as a progressive alternative, the explanation stems from a unique combination of personal choices and political events.[3]

## RECENT STATE POLITICS

Winthrop Rockefeller came to Arkansas in 1953 for personal rather than political reasons, spent his early years immersed in developing his vast agricultural enterprises and only gradually was drawn into civic contributions and public service, most notably as Faubus's appointee to head the newly established Arkansas Industrial Development Commission in 1955. During his nine-year chairmanship, over 600 new industrial plants were built and more than 90,000 new jobs (with an annual payroll of almost $300 million) were created, developments for which Rockefeller personally could claim considerable credit and from which he derived much satisfaction. His involvement in Arkansas public affairs increasingly convinced him that sustained economic progress necessitated a more modern, open, and honest politics that, he decided, only a competitive party system could provide.[4]

By the early 1960s, Rockefeller had begun financing one of the most sophisticated partisan apparatuses in America, complete with professional pollsters, elaborate headquarters, well-paid field-workers, and a public relations campaign specifically designed to discredit state Democrats as the party of bossism and corruption and to persuade voters of the legitimacy and desirability of the Republican party and a two-party system. In 1962 Rockefeller personally financed the race of the Republican gubernatorial candidate and twenty-two state legislative aspirants (only one of whom won), and in

1964 Rockefeller campaigned in his own right for governor, leading a field of 154 Republican state and local candidates. Faubus and other Democrats held their ground, but Rockefeller's margin (43 percent) set a new high for any Republican gubernatorial candidate in the twentieth century. Perhaps equally important, Rockefeller carefully kept his campaign separate from the right-wing appeals of Barry Goldwater and therefore was in an excellent strategic position to appeal strongly to Arkansas's as yet largely unregistered black voters.[5]

Rockefeller spent lavishly on black registration efforts between his defeat in 1964 and his expected rematch against Faubus in 1966, but then events played even further into his hands. In the crowded Democratic gubernatorial primary that suddenly developed when Faubus announced his "retirement," the wildly flamboyant, militantly segregationist "Justice Jim" Johnson was able to distinguish himself from a pack of less colorful contestants and secure the nomination. While Johnson used the fall campaign to accuse Rockefeller of being a plutocrat, a socialist, a cemetery wrecker, and a "prissy sissy," Rockefeller talked of economic development and educational advancement. Given the choice between what Johnson represented (further instability, racial disharmony, possible adverse economic consequences) and what Rockefeller represented (racial peace and economic progress), the voters narrowly (54 percent) gave Rockefeller the governorship.[6]

Rockefeller's appeal was especially strong among black voters (an estimated 71 percent voted for him) and urban voters; and when the Democrats nominated another old-time Democratic establishment candidate in 1968 (the former House Speaker and Faubus ally Marion Crank), the same coalition of blacks, urban voters, and disgusted Democrats gave Rockefeller a slim (52 percent) reelection victory. Rockefeller's second term, however, became increasingly problematic. The overwhelmingly Democratic legislature became even less cooperative, Rockefeller's unwillingness to play even the most basic political games, his increasingly evident drinking problems, and his insistence on a substantial tax increase all eroded his fragile base. In 1970, then, when the Democrats finally nominated Dale Bumpers, a candidate with virtually no ties to the old Faubus machine, with no segregationist or indeed any other kind of political record, an articulate, intelligent, and forward-looking candidate, Rockefeller was doomed, receiving less of the vote in 1970 (32 percent) than he had in 1964 (43 percent).[7]

Following their new and seemingly more successful formula of nominating younger, cleaner, and more progressive candidates (Dale Bumpers again in 1972, David Pryor in 1974 and 1976, Bill Clinton in 1978), Republican gubernatorial candidates averaged only 29 percent of the vote in the five gubernatorial contests after Rockefeller's 1968 victory, a throwback to the traditional margins. Indeed, in the decade of the 1970s it seemed that Rockefeller's most potent contribution to political change in Arkansas was the improvement forced upon the Democrats, who then, in their new progressive mode, could reassume their total domination of state elections. Furthermore, Rockefeller's untimely death from cancer, at age sixty-one in 1973, left the emerging Arkansas Republican party without its most generous benefactor.

Beneath the surface of sweeping Democratic victories, however, two developments of critical importance to future Republican strength were taking place. First, as a result of the Rockefeller years, and most specifically as a result of his carefully crafted "acceptance" strategy and public relations campaign, most Arkansans had come to accept the concept of two-party competition as a positive public good. The pervasive hostility toward the mere concept of Republicanism that Rockefeller had found in the late 1950s had been replaced by 1970 with attitudes going beyond mere acceptance of legitimacy to articulated positive evaluations: that a two-party system meant wider choices, better government, more honesty. In a political environment where any hint of Republicanism was once considered socially unacceptable if not treasonous, this was an attitudinal change of surpassing significance.[8]

A second major development of the 1970s was that the Arkansas Republican party began more and more to resemble ideologically its national counterpart. As long as Rockefeller led the Arkansas Republicans, the party had a progressive, reformist cast, and those whom Rockefeller had brought into the party continued to dominate party offices and shape presidential preferences until 1980. After Reagan's sweeping nomination victory and subsequent election, however, power within the Arkansas GOP switched sharply to the right. In 1976, although Republican voters favored Reagan (62 percent) over Ford (37 percent) in the presidential primary and Arkansas's convention delegates were pledged accordingly, they quickly switched to Ford on the first ballot, publicly criticizing Reagan's right-wing extremism. In 1980, over the objections of Reagan partisans, who wanted another presidential primary, party officials opted for a convention delegate selection process, with the selected delegates dividing as follows: eight for Howard Baker; seven for George Bush; three for Ronald Reagan; one for

John Connally. In the aftermath of Reagan's election in 1980, there was a mild "purge" of remaining Rockefeller moderates.

It was also in 1980 that Republicans achieved their third gubernatorial victory. In one of the most surprising upsets in Arkansas political history, the Republican Frank White defeated the incumbent Democrat, Bill Clinton, making 1980 the first time when Republican candidates for president and governor triumphed simultaneously. Neither Reagan nor White had a very wide victory margin: Reagan's plurality was only six-tenths of a percent more than Carter's, and White won with 52 percent. Nevertheless, White's election was particularly impressive because it defied the Arkansas tradition, broken only twice previously in the twentieth century, of giving an incumbent governor a nearly automatic, sometimes called courtesy, second term.[9]

In 1982 Clinton recaptured the governorship with 55 percent of the vote. In 1984, despite the electorate's increased enthusiasm for Reagan, Clinton became the first governor since Faubus (and only the third in Arkansas history) to win a third two-year term, by 63 percent of the vote.

Given these sharp swings back and forth, and the frequent divisions between national and state partisan preferences, it is understandable that one recent analysis of the state's politics was entitled, "Arkansas: Independent and Unpredictable," and another entitled, "Arkansas: Roller-Coaster Style Partisan Change." Has Arkansas, once so predictably Democratic, become totally unpredictable? Will it continue to whip back and forth between Republican and Democratic choices? Has a genuine basis for two-party competition been established, sufficiently stable this time to last out the century?[10]

It is certainly clear that Arkansas has ceased to be "safe" for any Democratic presidential nominee. Whether the national Democratic party will attempt to accommodate southern voters in future elections (which in turn might necessitate reforming those nominating procedures that almost ensure the nomination of a candidate perceived as too liberal for southern tastes) is a question far beyond the scope of this study. Furthermore, presidential preferences are a very unreliable guide to party identification and voting behavior generally. What is certain is that Arkansans have become extremely adept at splitting their tickets.

The classic example of truly rampant ticket-splitting in Arkansas is the election of 1968, in which Arkansans simultaneously reelected Rockefeller, a Republican, to the governorship; reelected J. W. Fulbright, a Democrat, to the U.S. Senate; and gave a plurality of their presidential votes to George

Wallace, candidate of the American Independent party. The historian C. Vann Woodward, asked to explain this enigma, candidly responded, "Your guess is as good as mine!" The political scientist Jim Ranchino suggested that voters were showing some consistency in choosing three antiestablishment candidates, all known for their independence and individualism on controversial subjects. Perhaps even more fundamental in explaining not just 1968 but countless examples of ticket-splitting since is that Arkansans have been accustomed for decades to voting for whom they consider "the best man," almost without regard to party. Since all significant choices took place within the Democratic primary, where party label was essentially irrelevant, the choice had to be made on the basis of individual appeal. Voters have simply begun using this long-familiar choice mechanism in the general election.[11]

Perhaps even more illustrative of Arkansans' newfound ability to split their tickets is the general election of 1972, in which every one of Arkansas's seventy-five counties gave substantial margins (ranging from 58.1 percent to 81.4 percent) to Nixon, a Republican, and even more substantial margins (ranging from 57.5 percent to 85.7 percent) to Bumpers, a Democrat. In that year, nearly half of all voters split their tickets, and the phenomenon has continued to occur since.[12]

Aided by widespread ticket-splitting, Republicans have moved from a position of utter hopelessness through the 1940s to a somewhat more respectable but still subcompetitive position in the 1950s to an occasional gubernatorial victory and seeming presidential advantage by the 1980s (figure 1). While the phenomenon that Key described as "presidential Republicanism" (Republican gubernatorial and Senate candidates polling less than half the votes of the Republican presidential contender) is still slightly in evidence, the gaps have narrowed considerably and are occasionally reversed. Furthermore, the Republican vote in all major races, once very loosely and occasionally inversely connected, is becoming much more closely correlated; that is, increasing numbers of voters are voting straight Republican tickets.[13]

While the increasing competition in national and gubernatorial contests is an important part of contemporary Arkansas politics, it is equally important to emphasize that below the tip of this highly jagged and irregular iceberg lies a still overwhelmingly and apparently impervious Democratic base. Statewide, Arkansas elects not only the governor but six other executive officials, and only in 1966 and 1968 (when Maurice L. "Footsie" Britt rode into the lieutenant governorship on Rockefeller's coattails) have Re-

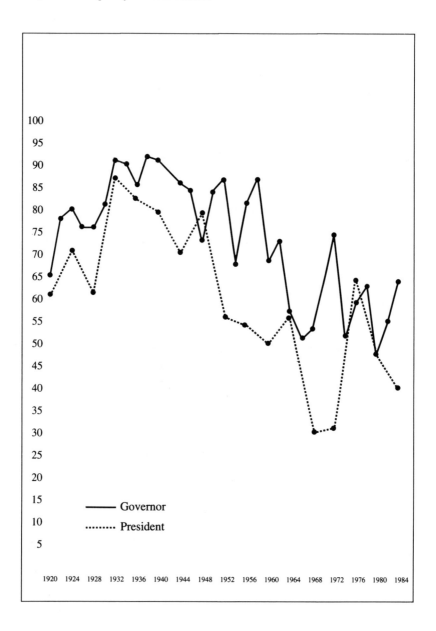

Figure 1. Percentage of Democratic Vote for Governor and President in Arkansas, 1920–1984. (*Source:* Compiled from official election returns.)

publicans ever captured any of these offices. Indeed, in contrast to 1968, for example, when Republicans ran for all these positions, in the 1970s and 1980s they have rarely even been contested in the general election. It is here, and even more revealingly in state legislative and local races, that the lack of depth to emerging Republicanism is most evident and that the observation made in 1966 that Republicanism was "sweeping over Dixie at glacial speeds" seems most apt.[14]

In contrast to some other Rim or Border southern states where Republicans had secured from one-quarter to one-third of state representative bodies by 1980, the growth of Republican representation in the Arkansas legislature has been markedly more measured. By 1980, for example, there were still only seven Republicans (out of one hundred seats) in the house of representatives, one Republican (out of thirty-five) in the senate. By 1982 Republicans had eight seats in the house and two in the senate and in 1984 achieved further increases to nine in the house and four in the senate, figures maintained in 1986. Since for most of the twentieth century the maximum number of Republican senators was one (and usually none), and Republican membership in the house had reached its previous maximum of five in 1918 and declined to a usual two until the 1960s, Republicans have made some progress. Only twice to date, however, has a Republican challenger ousted a Democratic incumbent. More significantly, all the Republican state legislative successes to date have been confined to a few northwestern counties and to one of the more affluent Little Rock districts in Pulaski County. Underscoring the strong regional basis to Republican electoral strength is that in 1980, a year when the Arkansas electorate chose Republicans for both the presidency and the governorship, only one Republican won any countywide contest outside the northwest Ozarks area. Indeed, regional political tendencies have emerged (or reemerged) so strongly in recent decades, that they have become fundamental to any understanding of contemporary Arkansas politics.[15]

REGIONALISM IN CONTEMPORARY ARKANSAS POLITICS

As discussed in chapter 2, the northern and western uplands and the southern and eastern lowlands were originally settled by migrants who came from somewhat different areas (predominantly from Kentucky and Tennessee and later from Missouri in the uplands, predominantly from Deep South states in the lowlands) and practiced very different agricultural pursuits (small subsistence farms in the uplands, large cotton plantations with slave labor in the lowlands). From the 1830s through the 1850s, Democratic support was strongest among the Jacksonian yeoman farmers in the uplands, and Whigs found more favor in the wealthier, lowland areas. As slavery and secession came to dominate political choices, however, these geographic tendencies sharply, and permanently, switched. The slave-owning lowlanders became the staunchest advocates of "the Democracy." The relatively slaveless uplands, where secession was originally opposed and only reluctantly and inconsistently accepted, sent nearly 10,000 troops to fight for the Union and developed some lasting pockets of Republicanism. Newton, Searcy, and Madison counties consistently voted Republican in presidential contests from the Civil War onward and often elected Republican state legislators and local officials as well.

For the first half of the twentieth century, however, sectionalism was for the most part submerged within an overwhelming consensus for Democrats. None but a few highland counties showed any tendencies whatsoever to disrupt Democratic dominance, nor were there any consistent tendencies for any region to support more liberal or conservative candidates within the Democratic primary through the 1950s.

Key did detect, in the 1944 Senate race between Homer Adkins and J. W. Fulbright, "a glimmer of the general tendency of the upland people of the south to be more enthusiastic over candidates who can be considered progressive," and certainly through the 1940s the more liberal members of Arkansas's congressional delegation (Clyde Ellis, Brooks Hays, J. W. Fulbright) had a northwestern base; but Drummond, who also found no persistent regional voting patterns, noted that this northwestern "liberalism" was a "curious mixture of rugged individualism and social conformity compounded with the influence of fundamentalist evangelical churches." Bartley and Graham also concluded that, into the early 1950s "Arkansas voters betrayed few indications that there were any differing interests between lowlands and mountains, countryside and city, affluent and nonaffluent. Whether counties were located in the black belt or mountains or whether they were metropolitan or rural made little consistent difference."[16]

There remained, however, strong demographic, economic, and cultural differences within Arkansas, and in the later 1950s and into the 1960s they began to manifest themselves, first within some Democratic gubernatorial primaries, and increasingly in actual partisan tendencies in the general election. In the most thoroughgoing analysis to date of these regional differences, Robert Savage and Richard Gallagher assembled and analyzed seventy-one social, economic, and political county-level attributes. While emphasizing that Arkansas was still highly homogeneous and that moving from the northwest to the southeast corners was not like moving through separate worlds, Savage and Gallagher still found sizable clusterings or loadings into three distinctive county types, which they labeled Ozark, Delta, and Urban (map 4).[17]

The Ozark counties, centered in the northern and western areas, were most distinctive for their higher voter participation, somewhat older population, somewhat greater expenditures on education and highways, and the fact that Republicans were more likely to find favor here. The Delta counties, centered in the state's southern and eastern portions, had a more youthful and relatively poorer population, which was much more likely to be nonwhite and less educated and showed the greatest commitment to the Democrats. Five counties labeled Urban appeared in separate parts of the state, distinguished by a population more concentrated in the productive years (eighteen to sixty-five), higher measures of modernity (lower birth rate, better housing, larger manufacturing establishments, greater percentage of professional-managerial positions in the labor force), and a support for Republicans not far behind the Ozark counties. Subsequent research broadly confirms and raises some interesting questions about public opinion variations between these regions. Nevertheless, the partisan voting tendencies observed by Savage and Gallagher, who used voting returns from 1970 to 1974, have become even more consistent and pronounced, as shown in map 5 (based on recent elections that were reasonably competitive).[18]

County voting patterns, of course, are very broadly descriptive, subsuming thousands of individual voters who were in the minority (and sometimes a substantial one) in a pattern not of their choosing and suggesting a monolithic quality to "a county vote" that is not there. Even with such caveats against the ecological fallacy, however, these maps offer important insight into strong and significant regional tendencies in contemporary Arkansas politics.

Clearly, in both presidential and gubernatorial contests, northwestern Arkansas, containing the prototypical Ozark counties, has become rather reliably Republican. Republicans have had a base here since the uplanders' opposition to secession. Significantly expanding this base, however, has been extraordinary recent population growth, due in large part to in-migration. Between 1970 and 1980, Arkansas's growth rate (18.9 percent) was one of the fastest in the nation. Nearly two-thirds of that growth was due to in-migration; and, as map 6 illustrates, most of that growth and in-migration was concentrated in these Ozark counties.[19]

 Urban    Ozark    Delta

Map 4. Ozark, Urban, and Delta Counties. (*Source:* Robert L. Savage and Richard J. Gallagher, "Politicocultural Regions in a Southern State: An Empirical Typology of Arkansas Counties," *Publius* 7 [1977]: 97. Reprinted by permission.)

**President**                    **Governor**

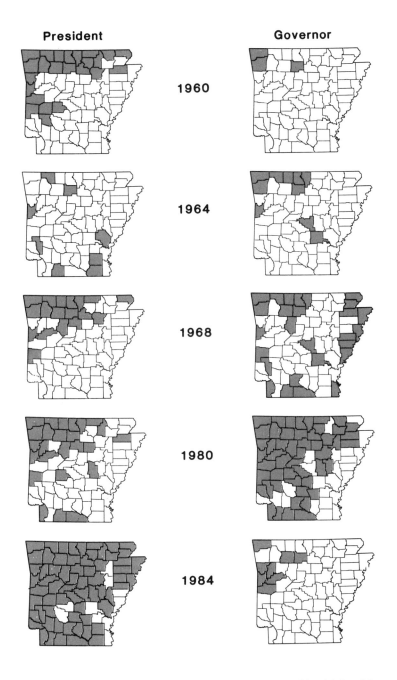

Map 5. Counties Carried by Republican Gubernatorial and Presidential Candidates, 1960, 1964, 1968, 1980, and 1984.

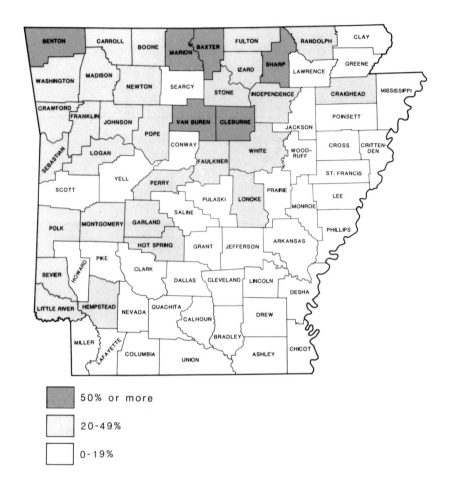

| | 50% or more |
|---|---|
| | 20-49% |
| | 0-19% |

Map 6. Percentage of Population Growth in Arkansas Counties, 1970–1980. (*Source:* Compiled from U.S. Bureau of the Census, *Census of Population, 1970, 1980* [Washington, D.C.: Government Printing Office, 1973, 1982, 1983].)

Many of these in-migrants are associated with the burgeoning economy of northwestern Arkansas; many others are retirees, exchanging the higher taxes and harsher winter climates, especially of the Midwest, for the lower taxes, milder climates, and plentiful natural recreational resources of northern Arkansas. And many of these in-migrants have brought their Republican preferences with them.

This is not to suggest that all newcomers and all retirees are Republicans. The retirees' ranks include former union stewards as well as plant managers, Social Security pensioners as well as coupon clippers, and many of those moving into Arkansas have some previous Arkansas ties. Nevertheless, as a group, they are measurably less Democratic than are long-time natives, as evidenced by both opinion surveys and voting trends. One survey in 1982, for example, found that 34.9 percent of those with residency in Arkansas of ten years or less considered themselves Democrats compared with 54.5 percent of those who had been residents for twenty or more years, and county analysis shows strong correlations between nonnativism and Republicanism.[20]

In addition to Republicans by inheritance and Republicans by in-migration, a third component of rising Republicanism in northwest Arkansas is the "metropolitanization" of those counties, especially the more northern ones, strung together by Highway 71 along Arkansas's western border. Benton, Washington, Crawford, and Sebastian counties have nearly begun to merge into one urban-suburban entity with many along the corridor living in one county, working in another, shopping or "schooling" in another. Sebastian, Benton, and Washington counties are almost prototypical examples of southern urban Republicanism, rarely supporting any Republican nominees until the Eisenhower years but voting almost consistently Republican in every presidential and most gubernatorial elections since. Indeed, Sebastian County, perhaps further influenced by a significant concentration of military retirees, has become Arkansas's most consistently Republican county, and its influence is clearly spreading to the more rural counties (especially Franklin, Scott, Logan, and Crawford) within its metropolitan orbit.[21]

Inheritance, in-migration, and urbanism have uniquely combined in the Ozark counties to produce an environment where the Republican label is not only acceptable but increasingly advantageous. This area, closely coinciding with the Third Congressional District, has kept the Republican John Paul Hammerschmidt in office since 1966, supplies most of the votes in Republican primaries, and is the foundation of recent Republican strength in U.S. Senate and gubernatorial elections. In 1982 Frank White carried seventeen of the twenty counties in the Third Congressional District but only one county outside it. Almost all Republicans thus far elected to the state legislature come from this area. Indeed, in an overwhelmingly Democratic legislature, Republicans now hold a majority in the Third Congressional District state senate caucus. In Benton County in 1986 there was greater voter turnout in the Republican than in the Democratic primaries, a first for Arkansas. In these counties, but almost only in these counties, Republicans are increasingly competing for and being elected to county offices as well.

In the aftermath of the 1980 census and subsequent reapportionment, the northwest section of Arkansas obtained four new seats in the legislature, and future reapportionments are expected to be equally advantageous as a base for potential Republican growth. Also working strongly to the benefit of Republicans is the exceptionally high voter turnout in the Ozark counties: only here does voter turnout occasionally exceed 80 percent of those registered to vote (and only here does voter registration occasionally exceed population). The Republican presence in Arkansas is regionally limited, but its strength within that region has been steadily growing, and the region itself is growing in population and political influence.[22]

At the other extreme, both geographically and politically, lie the Delta counties. The lasting effects of geography upon politics are revealed in map 7, which illustrates the natural regions of Arkansas and the percentage of black population in Arkansas's counties. The Mississippi Alluvial Plain and the West Gulf Coastal Plain have striking topographic differences that are clearly reflected in very different contemporary economic patterns: the Mississippi Alluvial Plain has absolutely level terrain and some of the world's deepest soils; today it is the site of vast soybean, rice, and cotton plantations; the West Gulf Coastal Plain has gently sloping terrain, some rich soils in the fertile river valleys, extensive deposits of sand and gravel and of industrially significant bauxite and petroleum, and very extensive forests occupying 70 percent or more of the land. Today, cattle pastures dominate the agricultural land, more than 120 wood-related industries draw from the forests, and oil companies in Union and Columbia counties produce over 20 million barrels of crude oil per year. During the nineteenth-century settlement period, however, cotton—with its attendant slavery— reigned supreme in both these plains, and the bulk of Arkansas's black population still resides primarily in the old cotton kingdom.[23]

Since Reconstruction, the Delta has been the area of staunchest Democratic strength, but the demographic basis of that strength has totally

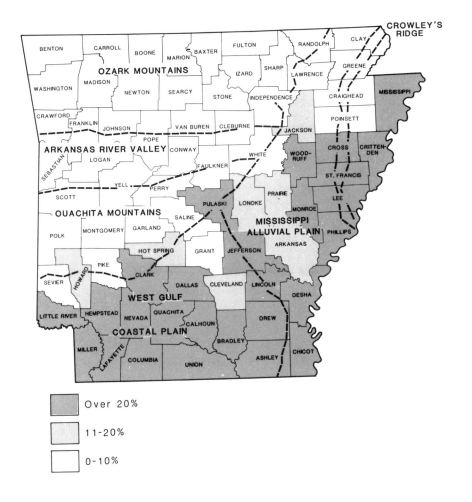

CROWLEY'S RIDGE

OZARK MOUNTAINS

ARKANSAS RIVER VALLEY

OUACHITA MOUNTAINS

MISSISSIPPI ALLUVIAL PLAIN

WEST GULF COASTAL PLAIN

BENTON | CARROLL | BOONE | MARION | BAXTER | FULTON | RANDOLPH | CLAY | GREENE
WASHINGTON | MADISON | NEWTON | SEARCY | STONE | IZARD | SHARP | LAWRENCE | CRAIGHEAD | MISSISSIPPI
CRAWFORD | FRANKLIN | JOHNSON | VAN BUREN | CLEBURNE | INDEPENDENCE | JACKSON | POINSETT
SEBASTIAN | LOGAN | CONWAY | POPE | FAULKNER | WHITE | WOODRUFF | CROSS | CRITTENDEN
SCOTT | YELL | PERRY | PULASKI | LONOKE | PRAIRE | ST. FRANCIS | LEE | MONROE
POLK | MONTGOMERY | GARLAND | SALINE | GRANT | JEFFERSON | ARKANSAS | PHILLIPS
PIKE | HOT SPRING | CLARK | CLEVELAND | LINCOLN | DESHA
SEVIER | HOWARD | DALLAS
LITTLE RIVER | HEMPSTEAD | NEVADA | QUACHITA | CALHOUN | DREW | CHICOT
MILLER | LAFAYETTE | COLUMBIA | UNION | BRADLEY | ASHLEY

Over 20%

11-20%

0-10%

Map 7. Natural Regions of Arkansas and Percentage of Black Population, 1980. (*Source:* Map of natural regions in R. Stroud and G. Hanson, *Arkansas Geography* [Little Rock: Rose Publishing, 1981], p. 27; black population compiled from U.S. Bureau of the Census, *Census of Population, 1980* [Washington, D.C.: Government Printing Office, 1982, 1983].)

changed from that of whites, seeing in Democratic solidarity the most certain security for continued white supremacy, to blacks, responding favorably to the more egalitarian programs of the Democratic party. Arkansas's blacks constitute only 14.6 percent of Arkansas's voting-age population and only an estimated 13.9 percent of its registered voters. This means, however, that with overwhelming support from the black electorate, a candidate can receive little more than a third of the white vote and still win a statewide race (and without any black support, a candidate may need nearly two-thirds of the white vote to win). Clearly, in any closely competitive race, black support can be critical. Black voters kept Arkansas in the Democratic column for Lyndon Johnson in 1964, were essential to Rockefeller's victories in 1966 and 1968, provided Clinton with both his primary and general election winning margins in 1982, and saved Congressman Bill Alexander of the First District from primary defeat in 1986.[24]

Two features of the contemporary black vote in Arkansas are especially noteworthy. First, it tends to be monolithic, giving 90 percent or more margins to candidates who have found favor in black communities. In the 1982 Democratic gubernatorial primary, for example, Clinton beat Purcell by 579 to 7 at the East Little Rock Community Center, and by 724 to 12 at the Townsend Park School in Pine Bluff.

Second, the black vote has tended, since the Rockefeller years, to be thoroughly Democratic. Unlike northern black voters, who made a massive switch from the party of the Great Emancipator to the party of the New Deal between 1928 and 1936, and have generally maintained a firm Democratic loyalty since, for Arkansas black voters the early years of sizable voting participation (more than doubling between 1958 and 1968) were characterized by partisan schizophrenia. The Democratic party was the party of Franklin D. Roosevelt, Lyndon Johnson, and Hubert Humphrey, but it was also the party of Orval Faubus, Jim Johnson, and Marion Crank. The result, for a while, was massive ticket-splitting: it has been estimated that in 1968, for example, over 90 percent of Arkansas black voters chose the Democrat Hubert Humphrey and the Republican Winthrop Rockefeller. In 1970 black voters stayed with Rockefeller against the Bumpers sweep. In 1972, however, with Rockefeller no longer leading the state Republican ticket, and Bumpers having proven that he was not simply a nonsegregationist but a sympathetic friend, black voters left the state Republican ticket in droves and have not yet been tempted to return.[25]

Periodically, black political leaders become angry over what they see as the tendency of the state Democrats to take their support for granted; and periodically, the state Republicans announce new plans for recapturing the black vote that once was theirs. To date, however, the Democratic "sins of omission" have created less furor in the black community than the Republican "sins of commission." For example, in 1980 Governor Frank White infuriated the black community (and stunned many Rockefeller Republicans as well) by bringing their old nemesis Orval Faubus into his administration. In 1984 the Republican nominee for Supreme Court justice was none other than Rockefeller's 1968 opponent, "Justice Jim" Johnson, the man who had once said, "I am opposed to rape and murder and would speak out against them, and the greatest crime, even beyond these, is integration." So long as Faubus and Johnson are welcome in the house that Lincoln built, black voters are unlikely to feel genuinely comfortable there. The nomination of the black businessman Solomon Scaife as the Republican candidate for lieutenant governor in 1984 apparently did nothing to counterbalance the presence of Justice Jim on the Republican ticket: Scaife, in fact, while losing all seventy-five counties, did worse in substantially black counties and precincts than elsewhere.[26]

Black enthusiasm for black candidacies can in fact be generated, as Jesse Jackson's quest for the Democratic presidential nomination in 1984 exemplifies: of the fourteen county caucuses carried by Jackson, all were Delta counties and all but two have more than twice the statewide average black population—and these caucuses drew far greater turnout than caucuses in the rest of the state. When this very visible Jackson turnout did not translate into delegate victories, Arkansas's black political leaders threatened lawsuits and Democratic desertion. Despite this disgruntlement, however, Mondale still fared much better in the Delta counties than he did elsewhere in Arkansas, carrying eight of them against a statewide sweep for Reagan, and other Democratic candidates for major office reaped their usual 90 percent or more margins in black precincts.

The Delta counties, then, together with the urban blacks in Pulaski County (Little Rock) and Jefferson County (Pine Bluff) have become a significant source of Democratic strength, keeping the First and Fourth Congressional Districts securely Democratic, providing hefty majorities and sometimes winning margins to statewide Democratic candidacies, and capturing a small but increasing number of local offices in communities with substantial black populations. If the Delta counties still possessed the preeminent power that was theirs in most of the nineteenth and twentieth centuries, continued Democratic dominance of Arkansas might be assured. Several factors, however, make the Delta counties a less impressive base for the Democrats than the Ozark counties are for the Republicans.

First, as shown in map 6, the Delta counties are generally slow-growth to absolute-loss counties. Second, as indicated in map 2, voter turnout is usually much less in the Delta counties than in the Ozarks. Third, according to campaigners and campaign managers, the black vote is not an "easy" vote. Black voters must be registered, courted, organized, and deliberately turned out for maximum effectiveness, and this is both an exhausting and an expensive undertaking. Candidates expecting large turnouts in many black communities are still expected to foot the bill for "knockers and haulers" (those who knock on doors and drive carloads of voters to the polls) and for other "election-day" expenses. This is the contemporary version of the traditional "walking around money" and at least through 1986 is still considered essential.[27]

What has been changing remarkably is the nature and thrust of black political leadership. Until recently, black ministers (frequently the most educated members of their communities, and certainly those with the most outreach potential) were the intermediaries between white candidates and black voters. While black ministers still provide some political leadership, increasing numbers of black leaders, especially in urban areas, are professional people (lawyers, and especially teachers), businessmen, labor union leaders, and community activists. They are more skilled and competent, much more issue-conscious, much less accommodationist, and more militant than were the traditional black leaders. These qualities have made them more effective and forceful in articulating black voter demands to white candidates and officials. Consensus, however, is much more difficult to achieve as competing issue concerns and personal agendas divide the black leadership, sometimes in open and angry debates. These are healthy signs of political vitality in Arkansas's increasingly diverse and demanding black community, but a divided minority group has less political clout than a unified one.[28]

Nevertheless, the Delta counties, primarily because of the voting tendencies of their black populations, have become almost as essential a support base for most Democratic candidates as the Ozark counties are for the Republicans, as all recent statewide races, especially those for U.S. senator and governor, have demonstrated. Nothing illustrates this rapid emergence of partisan regionalism more dramatically than the changing support base of Dale Bumpers. The Ozark counties, which made his 1970 gubernatorial election possible, had turned against him by 1980, whereas the tenuous support he first received from the Delta counties had become his mainstay.[29]

What about the emerging Urban counties, those five counties (Pulaski, Sebastian, Washington, Craighead, and Garland) with high loadings on "modernity" factors that Savage and Gallagher found to be almost as favorable to Republicans as the Ozark counties? Do they hold the balance of power between the Republican-leaning Ozark counties and the Democratic-dominated Delta counties, and if so will a rising urban Republicanism tilt Arkansas toward a more Republican future? Unfortunately for typological neatness and predictive power, there are no such clear-cut patterns.

While Sebastian and Washington counties, and to a lesser extent Garland County, have shown some strong Republican tendencies, that seems much better explained by their geographic location in the uplands region than by any urbanism per se. Craighead County has been much more tentative in its Republicanism, and Pulaski County, containing the state's largest and third largest cities (Little Rock and North Little Rock) defies any easy characterizations. Little Rock, for example, elected a Republican mayor in 1951 and 1953, voted consistently Republican in congressional elections from 1978 to 1984, and has filled one of its state legislative seats with Republican representatives. In 1968, however, Pulaski County gave Humphrey one of his only county pluralities, and in 1980 it bucked the state tides in both the gubernatorial and presidential contests, voting for both Clinton and Carter.

Little Rock is not only much the largest city in Arkansas, it is also the economic, governmental, and communications center of the state, home of both statewide newspapers and of television stations reaching four-fifths of Arkansas viewers. The cultural, commercial, and medical resources of Little Rock attract huge numbers of businessmen, visitors, and shoppers who enjoy its amenities and appreciate its services, but who also refer darkly to the "black hole syndrome"—that all power, money, jobs, and influence seem to be steadily sucked into the Little Rock orbit.

The dominance of the Little Rock financial and commercial community is unquestionable; its political dominance is much more debatable. Statewide candidates with a Little Rock home base have rarely run well (Frank White is the only significant recent exception), and the Pulaski County delegation in the state legislature is regularly opposed and often bested by non–Little Rock coalitions. Indeed, Pulaski County cannot even dominate the Second Congressional District: the Republican Judy Petty carried Pulaski County in 1984 but lost the congressional race to the Democrat Tommy Robinson.

In the 1960s several political scientists predicted that the urban areas of the South would provide the strongest building blocks in emerging Republicanism as the new industrialists, professionals, entrepreneurs, and affluent suburbanites began to vote their economic interests, that is, Republican, rather than the traditions of their ancestors. Pulaski County, it was assumed, would be "the most fertile territory for the growth of Republicanism in Arkansas." Analysis of election returns by precincts within Little Rock (or Fayetteville, or El Dorado, or other cities) does indeed indicate some of the predicted "class" divisions in presidential and congressional races, where ideological choices are somewhat salient: the more affluent neighborhoods increasingly favor the more conservative Republicans. However, these partisan preferences remain rather weak and have not yet begun spilling over consistently into gubernatorial and other state contests.[30]

One of the factors that has confounded predictions of urban Republicanism in Arkansas is the even stronger regionalism previously described. Of the six Arkansas counties in which more than 65 percent of the population lives in cities of 2,500 or more, four (Crittenden, Jefferson, Chicot, and Mississippi) are Delta counties, have substantial black populations, and are even more Democratic than the state generally. Furthermore, those familiar with Chicot or Mississippi County, or indeed with any Arkansas county other than Pulaski, know that there is a big difference between the Census Bureau classification of "urban" (living in population clusters of 2,500 or more) and urbane, which is what the political prophets of urban Republicanism (thinking of Atlanta, Houston, New Orleans) had in mind. In fact, urbanism itself is still a relative concept in Arkansas. By 1986 there were still only four cities in Arkansas with populations of 50,000 or more, only six other cities topped 25,000, and fourteen counties had no urban population whatsoever.

The urban vote is increasing in Arkansas, and has occasionally demonstrated its power—joining with blacks and disgusted Democrats to give Rockefeller his gubernatorial victories, swinging the Democratic party to more progressive choices in the 1970s. Even if city voters constituted a solid Republican bloc, however, which they decidedly do not, it would take more than the city vote to win a statewide election.

One remaining "region" in Arkansas has not yet been formally identified or typologized in scholarly studies but may be even more decisive to Arkansas's political future than it has occasionally been in the past: the "Rural Swing" counties, those twenty-six counties that remained true to their Democratic traditions in supporting Carter in 1980 but in that year's gubernatorial contest did something most had never done before, that is, voted Republican (map 8). When Clinton recaptured all but four of these counties in 1982, he recaptured the governorship; and by 1984 all but one were back in the Democratic gubernatorial fold. Also by 1984, however, twenty-four of the twenty-six had swung, and swung strongly, to Reagan.[31]

Map 8. "Rural Swing" Counties.

These counties may hold a critical voice in Arkansas's near-term political future. The average percentage of urban areas in these twenty-six counties is 25.7 percent, exactly half of the statewide average of 51.6 percent. Even more graphically, fifteen of these twenty-six counties have no towns with a population of more than 5,000, and none possesses a town with more than 15,000 people. Most of the Rural Swing counties remain dry, another indication of traditional rural values in a state where local option elections have turned most (fifty-two) counties wet.

Politically, the Rural Swing counties have been among the most steadfast in their support of the entire Democratic slate. In presidential elections, for example, most voted Democratic in at least twenty-two of twenty-three presidential contests from 1876 to 1964, attracted neither by Eisenhower's personal popularity in the 1950s nor by Goldwater's anti–civil rights stance in 1964. In 1968, however, twenty-one of these twenty-six counties gave pluralities to George Wallace. In 1972 no Arkansas county supported McGovern. With southern farmer Jimmy Carter heading the ticket in 1976, however, all twenty-six trooped strongly back into the Democratic fold and remained with Carter against the state swing to Reagan in 1980.

The record of the Rural Swing counties in gubernatorial contests has been even more consistently Democratic, with only six of the twenty-six supporting Rockefeller in 1966, and only four in 1968. These, then, have been the most rock-ribbed "yellow dog" Democrats in Arkansas, a generalization confirmed by one opinion survey indicating that Wallace voters in Arkansas were the strongest of all Arkansans in their self-identification as Democrats. Why, then, did they throw Clinton out of office in 1980, why did they return him to office in 1982, and what does this behavior indicate about the possible actions of these critical counties in the future?[32]

The 1980 "rural rebellion" against Clinton was precipitated primarily by Clinton's sponsorship of a hefty increase in motor vehicle registration and license fees in the 1979 legislature. To thousands of rural Arkansans, who from necessity own several vehicles, usually in the classes that were subjected to the biggest increases (the heaviest and oldest), these increases seemed as punitive and insensitive as any governmental action could possibly be. Undoubtedly other factors fed the disgruntlement, factors like thousands of fiercely unwanted Cuban refugees being located by Clinton's good friend President Carter at Fort Chaffee, concerns about an unusual number of "outsiders" (many of them young and bearded) being imported into the first Clinton administration, perhaps even disgust at the "unmanliness" of the governor, reflected in his wife's retaining her maiden name.

None of these factors, however, could have turned the tide had not the angry atmosphere, originally created by the car-tag increases, already existed in these rural counties.

Having decided to attempt a rematch in 1982, Clinton systematically attempted to recapture those whom he had lost, beginning with an unprecedented series of preannouncement television ads to apologize for his insensitivity on the car-tag issue (and also for having been too "soft" in commuting prisoners' sentences). The Rural Swing counties did not capitulate easily; indeed, in the 1982 Democratic primary the rural vote favored longtime Democratic fixture Joe Purcell. Clinton won the nomination, however, and in the general election contest between Clinton and White, the media campaigns of both candidates were clearly targeted at the Rural Swing counties. These appeals, and the views and values of voters in these critical counties, will be discussed in the next chapter. It is evident, however, that not only was Clinton's appeal more effective in 1982, but in everything from appearance to staff to legislative program, he has shown enormous sensitivity to the preferences and potential power of the Rural Swing counties since.[33]

Because the occasional angry upsurges against Democrats in national and statewide contests have not tended to percolate down to state legislative and local contests, it might be concluded that the Rural Swing counties will remain securely Democratic in the foreseeable future. If so, when added to the Delta counties, and to less affluent city voters, Republican victories will continue to be confined to northern and western Arkansas and a few silk-stocking neighborhoods elsewhere. At the very least it seems clear that for Republican candidates to move from occasional localized victory to statewide competitive strength, they must not only enlarge their existing urban appeal but cultivate the countryside.

Rockefeller's winning coalition (Republicans plus blacks, urban voters, and progressive Democrats) is highly unlikely to reoccur in the future; black voters have remained alienated from state Republicans since Rockefeller, and Democrats now run their own progressive candidates. Frank White's winning coalition (Ozark counties, affluent urban voters, plus the rural rebellion) would seem to hold more promise for the future. This is especially true when it is remembered that voters, rather than counties, are the decisive actors in politics, and many Arkansas voters continue to be strongly cross-pressured between their longstanding loyalty to Democrats and the contemporary attractions of Republicanism.

## CHAPTER FIVE

# Voters and Political Parties

*Modern democracy is unthinkable save in terms of parties.*
E. E. Schattschneider, *Party Government*, 1942

*The party platform in Arkansas has been as completely irrelevant to meaningful politics as any such document could conceivably be.*
Patrick F. O'Connor, "Political Party Organization
in Pulaski County, Arkansas," 1967

*An extraordinary characteristic of both party organizations in Arkansas is their sharp separation from the party in office.*
Arthur English and John J. Carroll, "Political
Activists in a Southern County," 1984

Political scientists have suggested that three major mechanisms help to explain declining Democratic voting in the South: migration, generational turnover, and individual conversion. Clearly, all three of these factors have been at work in Arkansas.[1]

The important Republicanizing effects of in-migration have already been noted, its influence enhanced because of its concentration in those very Ozark areas where a Republican base already existed and voting turnout is traditionally high. Confirmation of the in-migration influence is offered by 1984 election returns: whereas the state generally gained 18.9 percent population between 1970 and 1980, Republican victories and Reagan's greatest margins came in counties with an average growth rate of 32.9

percent during this same period. Furthermore, the out-migration of Arkansas's black population, many of whom would have probably been Democrats, has further enhanced Republican chances: between 1940 and 1970, Arkansas's white population increased 7 percent while its black population declined 27 percent.

The generational turnover mechanism suggests that as those who have had the strongest attachment to the Democratic party die, they will slowly be replaced by voters for whom the traditional appeals of history, sectionalism, and racism will become increasingly meaningless. While this factor clearly helps to explain the declining distinctiveness of the southern electorate generally, it is difficult to measure in Arkansas because of the absence of reliable, longitudinal survey data with age or generational breakdowns. Furthermore, as recently as 1970, Kielhorn found that young (age twenty to thirty-five) Arkansans were typical of all other Arkansas age groups in terms of party identification.[2]

Still, more recent Arkansas opinion data suggest that some "generational turnover" has begun, and in the predicted—that is, Republican—direction. In Arkansas, as elsewhere in 1984, Reagan's strongest support came from the younger generations: he was favored by 63.4 percent of those under thirty and by 71.7 percent of those between thirty and forty-four, compared with 59 percent of voters between forty-five and fifty-nine and only 57.1 percent of those over sixty. Indeed, among some of the more affluent and upward-scale young, being a national Democrat had become as socially unacceptable by 1984 as any admitted Republicanism had been in the past.[3]

The third and, according to many political scientists, most important force for change has been and will continue to be individual conversion. This hypothesis begins with the assumption that there have been millions of southerners who have thought Republican, that is conservative, but voted Democratic. Often, of course, there was no choice; but also, since many southern Democratic candidates were as conservative or more so than most northern Republicans, this was not ideologically inconsistent. The gradual estrangement in recent years, however, as the national Democratic party has repeatedly espoused economic and social policies in profound opposition to the views of many native southerners, may lead to a total alienation of affections and eventually to a complete conversion to Republicanism.

In Arkansas, at least through the 1960s, the necessary conditions for such individual conversion simply did not exist. As long as the Democratic party was dominated by the Faubus old guard and represented in Congress by such conservative stalwarts as Senator John L. McClellan, while the state Republican party was a progressive Rockefeller coalition, the ideological lines were not only blurred but reversed. By the end of the 1970s, however, both state parties had assumed the ideological coloration of their national counterparts. The Republicans and Democrats in Arkansas's congressional delegation were splitting along Republican-Conservative–Democratic-Liberal lines, Republican and Democratic contestants in major state races were generally in line with national party philosophy, and the stage was thus theoretically set for the state Republicans to begin collecting their long overdue conservative constituency.[4]

The state Republicans have certainly collected some prominent disaffected Democrats as candidates and candidate supporters, many of whom indicated that they were "converting" to the party that better reflected their own conservatism. As one recent convert, a Republican candidate for county judge observed, "I was a Republican all the time and didn't know it." Similarly, a former Democratic state senator and candidate for attorney general publicly announced that now that he had outlived his grandparents, he "would be coming out of the closet and openly casting his first Republican vote." This latter statement was made at a 1982 campaign breakfast for Frank White, himself a proclaimed Democrat and David Pryor appointee until the day he filed in the Republican primary for governor in 1980. The platform on this occasion numbered several previous and prominent Democrats including a former governor (Orval Faubus), two Democratic gubernatorial candidates (Frank Whitbeck in 1968 and Jim Lindsey in 1976), a Jimmy Carter appointee (Vernon Weaver, head of the Small Business Administration), and a former executive secretary of the state Democratic party (Craig Campbell).[5]

Unlike the situation in most other southern states, to date in Arkansas no major official originally elected as a Democrat has switched and successfully run as a Republican, taking his or her constituency along into the Republican electorate. Even without any stirring role models of "defection," however, there are signs of some dealignment among Arkansas voters generally (table 5).

Since the data for table 5 were collected by a number of different pollsters using different methods and serving different purposes, the results must be treated with considerable caution, especially given the fact that the Arkansas electorate has expanded so enormously since the 1960s. Furthermore, since some of these polls were taken on the eve or immediate aftermath of Reagan's victories, the number of actual Republican party identifications is probably somewhat inflated. Even with these caveats, however, two conclusions seem warranted: Democratic strength has eroded somewhat and Re-

Table 5: Party Identification of Arkansas Voters (in Percent)

|  | Democrats (Including Leaners) | Republicans (Including Leaners) | Independents |
|---|---|---|---|
| 1962 | 66.0 | 11.0 | 23.0 |
| 1966 | 58.0 | 8.0 | 34.0 |
| 1970 | 53.0 | 15.0 | 32.0 |
| October 1970 | 59.0 | 17.0 | 24.0 |
| October 31, 1980 | 59.0 | 13.0 | 28.0 |
| November 9, 1980 | 49.0 | 16.0 | 35.0 |
| November 1982 | 60.0 | 6.7 | 30.0 |
| May 1983 | 59.9 | 16.7 | 23.5 |
| April 1984 | 59.6 | 21.7 | 18.7 |
| September 1984 | 57.0 | 26.5 | 16.5 |
| November 5, 1984 | 53.2 | 28.0 | 18.0 |
| November 1, 1986 | 53.0 | 21.0 | 21.0 |

Source: Figures for 1962, 1966, and 1970 are from Rockefeller polls reported in Kielhorn, "Party Development and Partisan Change: An Analysis of Changing Patterns of Mass Supports for the Parties in Arkansas" (Ph.D. diss., University of Illinois, 1973), p. 108. Figures for October 1970 are from Jim Ranchino, *Faubus to Bumpers* (Arkadelphia, Ark.: Action Research, 1972), p. 11. Figures for 1980 are from polls conducted by Precision Research, Inc., Little Rock, in author's possession. Figures for 1982 are from ABC exit polls, cited in *Journal of Politics* 47 (May 1985): 642. Figures for May 1983 are from "A Report on Public Attitudes toward Arkansas Louisiana Gas Company," Precision Research, Inc. Figures for 1984 are from "Arkansas Senatorial Polls," conducted for Sen. David Pryor. Figures for 1986 are from author interview with Gov. Bill Clinton, November 1, 1986.
Note: All of these polls used a statewide sample of 400 or more. Because survey questions varied, percentages do not always add up to 100.

publican identifiers have increased. Democratic candidates, then, begin contemporary contests with a somewhat smaller and more fragile base than they did in past decades. It remains true, however, as it was for Rockefeller in the 1960s and for Frank White in 1980, that Republican candidates for statewide office must attract some Democratic voters or face defeat.

NATIONAL AND STATE PARTISANS

As early as 1949 V. O. Key pointed to the potential significance of the presidency as an organizing influence in state and local politics. "The issues of the Presidency are dramatic enough to reach down into traditional one-party states and divide the voters," he observed, and data in the Arkansas party identification table suggest that some of that pulling power has indeed occurred.[6] Since from 1986 onward Arkansas gubernatorial contests will take place in presidential off-years, however, any such coat-tails may be less important in the future than they have been in the past.

Furthermore, Arkansas's Democratic candidates have developed a superb capacity for disassociating themselves from any presidential nominee whose aura might have negative consequences. In 1984, for example, when all Democratic candidates knew that Reagan's coat-tails might be strong and Mondale's association damaging, Clinton repeatedly noted that while he was a Democrat by "both heritage and conviction," he had never hesitated to criticize the party when he felt it had gone astray and had in fact done so publicly at the 1980 and 1984 national conventions; Pryor ran an "Arkansas Comes First" campaign and released figures showing that his and his opponent's percentages of support for Reagan's legislative initiatives in 1984 were quite comparable; and Tommy Robinson, advertising himself as "an Independent Voice for Arkansas," actually took out full-page newspaper ads welcoming President Reagan to Arkansas.

Especially in the days of national media dominance of political information, however, important questions remain. Can state Democratic candidates continue to divorce themselves successfully from the image-shaping power of the national parties? How long will Arkansas voters be content to view politics through bifocal lenses, distinguishing between a national Democratic party of Jesse Jackson and Geraldine Ferraro and Tip O'Neill and a state Democratic party of David Pryor and Bill Clinton and all the other familiar state and local officeholders? Continued ticket-splitting and increasing numbers of self-identified Independents offer partial solutions to these cross-pressures, and some Arkansans may even begin to adopt a dual-party identification. To date, however, most Americans and most Arkansans have had a single-party identification that has guided most of their election choices, and in 1984 the national Republican party made a concerted effort in Arkansas, and elsewhere in the South, to make that single-party identification a Republican one.[7]

Throughout 1984, a steady parade of prominent Republican officials came to Arkansas, each reiterating essentially the same message: that the Democratic party had become "a plaything of the left," that it had "the most liberal platform ever adopted by any national party," that it had become "too liberal for most Arkansas voters." Further, the Arkansas Republican party spent $30,000 for sixty showings of an advertisement featuring a father and son fishing on the banks of the Arkansas River, with the father speaking to his son as follows: "Y'know, we've got a lot of good family traditions like fishing, hard work, and voting Democratic. But the old Arkansas Democratic Party of John McClellan's day is gone. It's been taken over by liberals who won't stand up for what's right. But Arkansas still has a few good national leaders. Nowadays, they're mostly Republicans. This year me and Kenny are gonna register and vote for some Republicans, 'cause another Arkansas tradition is doing what's right." Clearly, these and other messages were designed to be the siren song of further Democratic dealignment, and there is evidence that this new southern strategy did obtain converts in the South.[8]

The present two-tiered system, which rests on some shaky foundations, is showing signs of erosion and could well continue to crumble. History provides no completely comparable previous phenomena as a guide. Both history and contemporary political science, however, do suggest caution against any easy assumptions that the South in general is so inherently conservative that inevitably most southerners will come to realize that their true ideological home is in Republicanism. Dewey Grantham and William Havard, for example, have always emphasized the strength of the southern reform tradition and that the South encompassed much greater support for economic liberalism than conventional wisdom might suggest; V. O. Key insisted that southern public opinions were not nearly so conservative as the behavior of southern political leaders would indicate; and these historical insights have been confirmed by findings of some contemporary political scientists.[9]

Perhaps most illuminating for the purposes of predicting Arkansas's future political choices is the recent work of William S. Maddox and Stuart A. Lilie, *Beyond Liberal and Conservative: Reassessing the Political Spectrum*. As the title implies, the authors challenge the traditional division of voters into a dichotomy between liberals, who favor government intervention in the economy and who also favor expansion of civil rights and liberties, and conservatives, who oppose government intervention in the economy and also oppose expanded civil rights and liberties. Maddox and Lilie suggest that the economic dimension should be separated from the social or lifestyle dimension, and when so separated, two ideological types emerge in addition to the traditional Liberals and Conservatives: Populists, who favor economic intervention but oppose expansion of civil rights and liberties; and Libertarians, who oppose government involvement in the economy but support expansion of civil rights and liberties. Populists, for example, strongly favor sufficient governmental intervention to regulate giant corporations and utilities, to balance excessive concentrations of wealth in behalf of the "little guy." In that sense, they are economic activists, or "liberals." On such issues as school prayer or women's liberation or penal reform, however, they tend to be profoundly preservationist, or "conservative," suspicious of and angry about many of the social and moral changes of recent decades.[10]

Using this fourfold typology, Maddox and Lilie found the most numerous national grouping to be the Populists (26.3 percent in 1980, compared with 24.4 percent Liberals, 17.7 percent Libertarians, and 16.5 percent Conservatives, with the rest divided or inattentive). They further found Populists to be especially prevalent in the South (31 percent in 1980, compared with 20 percent Liberals, 16 percent Libertarians, and 16 percent Conservatives). The only test to date of the Maddox-Lilie typology on the Arkansas electorate is inconclusive. Nevertheless, the demographic profile of the typical Populist offered by Maddox and Lilie (New Deal generation and older, high school diploma or less, low to middle income, working class, southern), strongly suggests that many Arkansans may fit most comfortably into the Populist mold.[11]

Indeed, returning to the 1982 rematch between Clinton and White, it is apparent that both candidates were pitching their negative and positive imagery not only to the Rural Swing counties but to the presumed Populists therein. White's advertisements portrayed him as a tough-minded, no-nonsense, execution-eager, good old boy in contrast to the bleeding-heart, East Coast, Ivy League, ACLU-liberal Clinton, who specialized in commuting killers' sentences. Clinton's advertisements portrayed White as an untrustworthy interest-dominated plutocrat who might run with the good-old-boy hounds by day but slept with the utility foxes at night, while Clinton was just a caring and concerned down-home Baptist family man who wanted nothing more than another chance to fight the fat cats in behalf of the little guys.

In 1982 Clinton's pitch to the Populists was more successful than White's, and, as previously noted, the lessons of the 1980 rural rebellion have left a lasting impression upon Clinton. Nevertheless, as the two political parties in Arkansas have increasingly come to resemble their national counterparts, thousands of low- to middle-income small-town and rural Arkansas voters may well be wondering if they have a place in either. Surely they do not belong with the wealthy bankers and businessmen, the feudal landowners, the retired Yankees, the golf-playing country clubbers in the state Republican party. But how can they feel comfortable in a state

Democratic party where power seems to be shifting into the hands of black activists, labor leaders, and women's liberationists?

When economic issues dominate the agenda, Populists are more attracted by the kindhearted Democrats than the hardhearted Republicans. In 1970, for example, most Arkansans still gave high marks to the Democratic party for its record in aiding the common man, assisting the farmers, and protecting the poor and sick and elderly.[12] This point is illustrated in table 5 if one compares the partisan tendencies in November 1980 with those in November 1982, when the economic recession placed pocketbook concerns at the top of most voters' agendas. When economic concerns are less pressing, however, giving social or lifestyle issues the opportunity to predominate, Populists are much more attracted by the puritanical Republican right than by the permissive Democratic left. Sarah Morehouse has described this anomaly in contemporary American state politics:

Outside the South, partisan competition is characterized by rural and small-town Protestant America represented in the conservatism of the Republican party and the liberal coalition of metropolitan minorities and industrial labor supporting the Democrats. In terms of this competition, there is no doubt that the South really belongs to the Republicans in ideological terms, being the most rural, homogeneous, small-town and Protestant section of the country. Partisan politics in the South, however, are the exact mirror of those found elsewhere in the country, and they have shown a remarkable resistance to change.[13]

Nothing illustrates this resistance more vividly than the comparative voter turnout figures in recent Democratic and Republican primaries. It is true that, in a major break with past patterns, only twice since 1962 (in 1974 and 1978) has the number of Democratic primary voters exceeded the number of voters in the general election. Still, an immense difference remains between the usual turnout in Arkansas's Democratic and Republican primaries. In 1982, for example, 567,125 persons voted in the Democratic primary and only 13,147 in the Republican; in most Arkansas counties, fewer than 50 people participated in the Republican primary; and in some counties, no Republican primary votes were cast at all. Another way of illustrating this imbalance is that in 1982 Frank White won the Republican primary with 11,111 votes, exactly 1,796 fewer votes than the last-placed candidate in the five-man Democratic primary. In 1984 an increase in Republican turnout of nearly 50 percent still resulted in only 19,562 Republican primary voters as opposed to 492,595 voters in the Democratic primary.

The major explanation for this disparity is not a matter of formal party identification. Indeed, Arkansas voters thus far have firmly resisted any legal requirement of party registration. Rather, Arkansas voters flock to the Democratic primary because that is still where the action is, where most state contests and nearly all local contests (outside a few Ozark counties) are still decided: in 1986 only five counties had contested county or local races on the Republican primary ballot.[14]

This explanation in turn illustrates what is perhaps the major obstacle to any sudden and sizable improvement in state Republican fortunes. Parties can win offices only when candidates running under their party label seek them, and thus far very few office seekers have chosen to run as Republicans. While Democrats generally contest for all offices, Republicans, since Rockefeller's time, rarely seek more than two of the elected executive positions, very few judicial offices, one-third or less of state legislative seats, and only a handful of local offices. In 1986, for example, of the 106 House and Senate seats held by Democrats and up for re-election, Republicans ran for only 15 (in contrast to 1970, when Rockefeller-assisted Republicans ran in 55 state legislative races).

Given the demonstrated ability of Republicans to poll at least 35 percent of the vote in most major statewide contests, why are there still so few Republican candidates for lesser office? The answer lies partly in mathematical advantage: most offices (state and local) are legislative, which can be won only by achieving a majority within a particular legislative district or locality, and Republican voters predominate in few such districts in Arkansas. While there are an infinite variety of motives for seeking office, presumably one common denominator is the desire to win, and the mathematical odds in most areas of Arkansas still favor Democrats. Furthermore, since aspiring legislators would seemingly want not only to win but to have decision-making power in office, there may be something discouraging about the prospects of serving under a label that is doomed to be in a hopeless minority within that body.[15]

No such qualms need inhibit Arkansas's Republican candidates for the U.S. Congress or for the governorship. Indeed, running as a Republican for these offices has one distinct advantage: a much less expensive and usually much less competitive fight for the nomination. Democratic candidates begin by paying much steeper filing fees than do Republicans. In 1986, for example, the Democratic filing fees for U.S. Senate ($7,800), U.S. Congress ($4,500), governor ($1,500) and lieutenant governor ($1,250) were much higher than what the Republicans assessed ($2,500, $1,000, $1,500, and $300) for the same offices. Furthermore, whereas Democratic candidates for major office must usually survive a fierce primary struggle for the nomination, then raise even more funds for the general election, many Republican candidates can still announce their way to the nomination and save their funds and energies for the fall contest. True, unlike the past, when some Republican stalwart would agree to serve as the party's gubernatorial sacrificial lamb simply to protect the party's legitimate claim to future ballot positions (and a one-third share of three-person county election commissions), seven of the nine Republican gubernatorial nominations from 1970 to 1986 involved a primary contest. In most cases, however, the results were so lopsided as to suggest that only one candidate was viewed as credible.

It is some sign of growing Republican strength that the 1984 gubernatorial nomination had two credible contestants: both Woody Freeman and Irwin Davis were articulate and attractive young men who vigorously sought the nomination. In 1986, for the first time in Arkansas political history, there were more contestants (four) in the Republican gubernatorial primary than in the Democratic (three).

In most cases, however, the Republican nomination is still uncontested or very weakly contested, and the Republicans must still occasionally suffer the embarrassment of a hopelessly unqualified candidate who becomes the Republican nominee simply through the act of filing. In 1986, for example, the lone Republican who filed for attorney general was not a lawyer. Furthermore, when it appeared that the only Republican candidate for lieutenant governor was going to be a dedicated white separatist and former member of the American Nazi party, a Republican stalwart filed against him at the last moment, then resigned the nomination after narrowly winning it. In any event, since the few advantages will rarely outweigh the mathematical and other disadvantages of seeking most offices as a Republican, there will probably continue to be far fewer Republican contestants and therefore far fewer Republican than Democratic officeholders for a considerable time to come.[16]

While the major function of the Arkansas Democratic party remains that of staging the primary elections in which thousands of self-starting candidates will battle for the right to be the Democratic nominee (and thence, usually, the officeholder), the state Republican party must still devote much of its efforts to persuading reluctant individuals to enter the public arena. The Democrats, then, have an enormous farm team through which ambitious individuals with superior political talents will rise to the top, a large statewide following, and a guaranteed take at the gate. The Republicans have a small and regional (but more cohesive and possibly more devoted) following and continuing recruitment problems. Both parties are measurably stronger than they were in recent decades, but both still fall considerably short of what a political party is supposed to be in a competitive political system.

While most political scientists assume and understand the value of political parties, many citizens, most college students, and a surprising number of Arkansas politicians and political activists (judging from my longtime service on the Democratic State Committee and Washington County Democratic Committee) do not. Briefly, then, political parties evolved as an essential means for putting notions of democratic self-government and popular consent into practice. Political parties are sometimes defined as groups of individuals organized for the purpose of gaining control of government, a definition that in itself has little inspirational ring. Since the only legitimate means of capturing control of government in a democracy is by winning elections, however, political parties must perform certain public-serving functions if they are to obtain their goal: they must nominate (and if necessary recruit) candidates better qualified and more attractive than those of the opposition party; they must offer programs that address and fulfill popular needs and wishes; and they must deliver on at least some of their promises or face certain criticism and possible defeat at the next election. Perhaps most important, competing political parties provide citizens with the assurance that if those in office are not performing responsibly and responsively, their shortcomings will be publicized, probably in exaggerated form, and alternative candidates and programs will be offered.

It is possible that revolutions in mass communications, an increasingly educated and issue-conscious electorate, and the rise of thousands of special-interest pressure groups will eventually make parties obsolete. To date, however, despite many dire predictions that parties are withering away, they continue to dominate the paths to political power in America. Certainly no democratic system has yet operated successfully without them.

As should be clear from previous chapters, these great, essential implementors of democracy existed in name only in traditional Arkansas politics. The Democratic party, described as one of the most "moribund and backward in the South," was a mere holding company under whose name all candidates sought office; and the Republican party "wavered somewhat between an esoteric cult on the order of a lodge and a conspiracy for plunder." Arkansas had essentially a no-party system, with two very elitist and ephemeral organizations that called themselves parties but that rarely met, had no significant electoral purposes, and no discernible value to the voters (except that the Democrats did manage, staff, and pay for the primary elections).[17]

For a brief period in the late 1960s and early 1970s, with Rockefeller pouring money and enthusiasm and organizational capacity into the Republicans, and the Democrats smarting from two successive gubernatorial defeats, both state party organizations took their first tentative steps into becoming what parties are supposed to be. Rockefeller's death and the Democrats' return to seemingly easy dominance in the 1970s temporarily thwarted this emerging development, leaving the Republicans with a state headquarters but little else and the Democrats, according to one informed analysis in 1976, "perhaps the weakest in the South."[18]

The 1980s were periods of feast and famine for both state party organizations. Clinton's defeat in 1980 shocked the Democrats into renewed organizational efforts, which received the serious and sustained attention of two party chairmen of unusual devotion and longevity: Herbie Branscum from 1976 to 1982 and "Lib" Carlisle thereafter. In the 1980s the Republicans began adapting to and pursuing the fund-raising and other organizational necessities for which Rockefeller's beneficence had obscured the need; they also became more unambiguously conservative and ideologically cohesive. Both parties, however, continued to be plagued with devastating financial crises and shortfalls, and both entered 1986 deeply in debt. Both parties also continued to be hampered by "neutrality" rules, such as that prohibiting party endorsement of candidates in the primary, which some analysts offer as a major explanation for why both Arkansas parties are "weak and ineffective organizations which lack cohesiveness and clout." The Republican party was further debilitated by constant turnover in leadership involving eight state chairmen from 1980 to 1986. A *Washington Post* assessment described the Arkansas Republicans as the "region's poor relation" and noted, "If you love humility, you've got to love the Republican Party of Arkansas."[19]

Despite these wrenching problems, however, both state parties seem to have at last envisioned, if not fully implemented, what a state political party should be. As one recent overview correctly notes, "both state party organizations have become institutionalized. They have attained a *raison d'être* transcending personalistic leadership within the organization or from the statehouse."[20] Not only do both parties now have the usual formal state

structure (biennial state conventions that elect and authorize interim activities by large state committees and somewhat smaller executive committees), both are building their capacity for offering increasingly sophisticated
electoral assistance (direct mail, phone banks, donor lists, opponent and
issue research) to their nominees. No serious candidate relies very heavily
upon these party organizations; the parties are supplements to rather than
substitutes for the candidate's own campaign apparatus. Nevertheless, the
fact that parties have any useful electoral functions at all is a giant step from
the recent past and a beginning approximation of the organization envisioned by the competitive party model.

Furthermore, both parties have developed much more extensive relationships with their parent national party than was once the case. For the
Republicans, this relationship has been a generally beneficial one involving
polling assistance, generous campaign contributions, campaign workshops
for the candidates, and some presidential candidates attractive to Arkansans
to head the ticket. For the Democrats, the relationship has been much more
problematic, involving national pleas for state and local dollars; constant
changes in the selection process for national convention delegates, neces-
sitating time-consuming and often unpopular revisions in state procedures;
and a series of presidential nominees unattractive to Arkansans (with the
exception of Carter in 1976). This national relationship may help to explain
why state Republican organizations in the South are generally ranked
among the nation's strongest, whereas southern Democratic organizations
are the weakest.[21]

In two fundamental respects, however, both Arkansas parties still fall far
short of the competitive party model: neither has a full complement of
seventy-five vigorous county committees; and neither has a major impact on
state public policy choices. While Republican local organization has come a
long way since the 1940s (when the state chairman estimated that an answer
to an inquiry could be expected from only half the counties), and a few
Republican and Democratic county committees have a fairly full agenda
even in nonelection years, in the vast majority of Arkansas counties these
indispensable engines of democracy rarely come out of the garage.

To be fair, a great gap exists between theory and practice all over
America. Still, even by the most lax of standards (Are all leadership and
most precinct positions filled? Is there a permanent headquarters or at least a
telephone listing? Does any meaningful activity take place in the intervals
between elections?) the county committees of both parties are in the lowest
ranks of local party organizational strength. The Democrats do at least have
a functioning party committee in all seventy-five counties; since it is this

organization that must staff, manage, and pay for the primary, which is still *the* election for most offices, some kind of operating apparatus is necessary. Lacking this functional imperative, there are still some Arkansas counties that have no functioning Republican county committee, and therefore hold no Republican primary even when there is a statewide Republican contest. (In a lingering vestige of the "private" white primary, Arkansas is one of only four states in which party primaries are financed by filing fees rather than government funds. Counties may choose to assume this financial burden, but by 1986 only a few had done so.)[22]

Beyond the mere existence of structure, however, is the question of the energy and enthusiasm those within the structure exert in pursuit of their tasks; and many of the much more numerous Democratic county committeemen are notorious for naming their precinct's judges and clerks in the Democratic primary, then disappearing until the next Democratic primary rolls around. A county chair and a handful of activists may organize an occasional fund-raiser, sponsor a political rally, and mount a booth at the county fair, but year-round efforts to build and sustain the party are exceptional.

One standard measure of the worth of a position is the amount of competition for it, and here too local party positions must be ranked low in terms of their general importance. While delegate positions to the quadrennial national party conventions are highly prized and therefore fiercely contested, most county committee positions can be secured by the simple process of filing for them, and many remain perennially vacant. Only in Pulaski County are contests for Democratic county committee positions commonplace. Elsewhere, it takes a local feud or strong personal or organizational rivalry to produce competition, as happened in Mississippi County in 1982 when a record 118 persons filed for eighty county committee positions. In Washington County, where competition from rising Republicanism has produced one of the more vigorous Democratic committees, an uprising of Young Democrats combined forces with the Arkansas Education Association in 1984 to produce an unusual number of contests. One of the few contests in decades occurred in 1968 when an irate woman whose vacuum cleaner would not work filed against the incumbent committeeman, a vacuum cleaner repairman. When he fixed the machine, she withdrew her candidacy. Contests for delegate status to biennial state conventions are equally rare; most county chairs, in fact, will happily pin a delegate badge on whomever from his or her county gets their welcome body to the state convention.

Again, this organizational laxity at the local level is not unique to

Arkansas, but considering the incentives that Frank Sorauf suggests have traditionally motivated individuals toward partisan activism, it becomes clear why Arkansas's local parties are even weaker than the national norm. The major traditional incentive was patronage; people worked hard for the party because their job, or some relative's job, was part of the spoils system and depended upon an election victory. Others engaged in partisan work as a means to secure preferments, special and advantageous consideration in the awarding of contracts, or sympathetic and tolerant oversight of a state-regulated industry. Another stimulus has been the possibility of advancing one's political career through the visibility, contacts, and skills acquired through partisan activity. Some individuals have traditionally engaged in partisan activity for its social and psychological satisfactions, the camaraderie of a circle of likeminded friends engaged in exciting battles together, and the pleasures of association with the great and near-great, the party offering an "island of excitement in a sea of dull routine." Finally, some have entered partisan politics as a way of promoting their political ideology or of obtaining favorable public policy on pet issues.[23]

Virtually none of these incentives would powerfully motivate many people toward local party activism in Arkansas today. Most government jobs at all levels have been removed from the spoils, or patronage, system, and jobs that do require political influence are more likely to be awarded to those who worked in a particular candidate's campaign than to mere party functionaries. This is equally true for the political non-jobs, or "honoraries," which Arkansas governors name by the hundreds each year. Similarly, most government contracts must now be awarded on the basis of best qualifications and lowest bids rather than party loyalty. The access and influence prized by businessmen and other economic influentials still have a strong political base, but whatever rewards and punishments are available flow from contributions (especially financial) to a particular campaign rather than from mere party committee membership.[24]

As for the "stepping-stone" incentive, partisan involvement is still a valuable environment for making contacts and learning the political ropes, and the state Republican party, because of its smaller recruitment pool, has frequently elevated candidates from among the ranks of party activists. Few major Democratic candidates, however, have climbed the rungs of partisan involvement; in fact, partisan activities are widely perceived to detract from rather than to enhance a future electoral career.[25]

Perhaps in earlier, more arid times in Arkansas, meetings of the local party committee provided a welcome escape from life's dull routine and some excuse for congenial companionship, and the convivial atmosphere of state conventions and the friendship or at least recognition by "notables" may still offer some attractions to partisan involvement. For most people, however, there are diversions far more consistently entertaining than the typical county committee meeting or party fund-raiser. In short, most of the material or solidary reasons for party activism have diminished or disappeared.

Finally, there are the "purposive" incentives, those involving commitments to certain attitudes or policy goals. Many observers suggest that ideological or issue incentives have become the major attractions for today's partisan activists. Undoubtedly many of those attracted to the Republican party under Rockefeller's banner had "good government" or reformist goals; later Republican activists have been attracted by the party's present-day conservative ideology; and both George McGovern's liberalism and Gary Hart's "new ideas" brought many new enthusiasts into local Democratic ranks, some of whom have stayed. True ideologues or issue activists, however, are unlikely to remain for years of devoted endeavor in local party organizations for a number of reasons: a party that wishes to win must be too flexible and pragmatic to accommodate ideological purists; most Arkansans and most Americans with a particular issue axe to grind have found interest-group activity much more directly productive of policy results; and, in Arkansas, there is still only the most tenuous connection between the political parties and public policy.[26]

Both state parties go through the ritual of adopting a party platform at their biennial state conventions. These platforms, however, are neither to run on nor to stand on. The state Democratic Convention, for example, repeatedly endorsed ratification of the national Equal Rights Amendment, but the state legislature, consisting overwhelmingly of Democrats, repeatedly refused—through a variety of imaginative strategems—to ratify. Even on matters affecting the party itself, there is no certain connection between the party officialdom's wishes and the performance of officeholders: the state Democratic party has pushed for a law requiring voters to declare their party affiliation and be limited to voting in the primary of their declared choice, but the Democratic-dominated legislature has refused to enact such legislation.

The supreme value to voters of a competitive party system is supposed to be its beneficial policy consequences. With two coalitions of office seekers, each is forced to promise and deliver public-serving programs or suffer the electoral consequences. But in contemporary Arkansas politics, that model little resembles operational reality. It is true that with a better-organized Republican party ready to exploit any perceived Democratic weaknesses, voters have greater assurance that lapses in leadership or policy blunders will be exposed, debated (with heat if not light), and alternatives offered. Thus, when the old-guard Democratic establishment became distasteful to Arkansas voters, it was rejected in favor of Rockefeller. When Rockefeller's failings became apparent and an attractive alternative was offered, Rockefeller was displaced by Bumpers. When Clinton angered a major segment of the electorate, he was replaced by White; when White disappointed and Clinton did penance, the voters rejected White and restored Clinton. To whatever extent these preferences had a policy base, voters do now have more clearly defined choices than they did in the past and a blunt but decisive mechanism for implementing them. In that broad sense, Arkansas's political system, while becoming slightly more Republican, has become somewhat more democratic.

Still, totally unlike the competitive party model, no elected Arkansas governor can then automatically rely on his fellow partisans in the legislature to fulfill the promises made through their party platform to the electorate. For a number of reasons, which will be discussed, political party has almost no significance in the gubernatorial-legislative relationship.

Equally important, however, is the fact that for every major public policy issue (raising of taxes, tightening of school standards, building of highways) that is in the public domain, hundreds of lesser issues (the question of permitting optometrists as well as ophthalmologists to use eye-drops in diagnostic procedures) are of no general interest whatsoever but are of very intense interest to small, particular groups within the population. A great deal of public policy is never mentioned in party platforms, never debated in gubernatorial contests, indeed rarely discussed in public at all. Much of the state's public policy agenda is generated and resolved in semiprivate arrangements between elected and unelected official decision makers and those with special interests who have cultivated their friendship.

## CHAPTER SIX

# The Influence of Interest Groups

*Measuring the influence that organized interests exert upon the Arkansas General Assembly does not lend itself to precise analysis but the suspicion is that it is quite substantial.*

Arthur English and John J. Carroll, *Citizens Manual to the Arkansas General Assembly*, 1983

*Hell, we wouldn't have a government if there were no interest groups.*

State Legislator, 1973

In the earliest days of state government in Arkansas, interest groups would have been superfluous. State legislators represented individuals (and relatively few of them) whose economic interests, primarily farming, were fairly homogeneous, and state government did little that materially affected their livelihoods. Still, in Arkansas as elsewhere, as populations grew, as the economy diversified, and especially as the powers and activities of state government expanded, increasing numbers of individuals found it advantageous to organize around their specialized interests, especially their economic functions, in order to ensure promotion and protection of their particular views. Interest groups are variously known as pressure groups, lobbies, and special interests. By whatever name, they are associations organized for the purpose of influencing public policy, and they have become an integral part of the representation and policymaking process in every modern democratic system.

While every state has its own unique configuration of interest groups, the same four general types of organized interests exist in Arkansas as elsewhere in state politics. First, there are those interests that are regulated by the state. Broadly, this category includes all people who do business in the state and therefore are affected by labor regulations, tax laws, pollution controls, safety standards, and everything else that touches on the profitability of their enterprises. More specifically this group includes those in certain industries that operate primarily under state regulatory authority (such as insurance companies, liquor dealers, utilities, railroads and truckers, banks and other financial institutions, hospitals and nursing homes) and those in professions and occupations (such as lawyers, doctors, realtors, beauticians, undertakers) operating under state licensure.

Second, there are those interests that do business with the state. Highway and other building contractors, printers and publishers, bond brokers, wholesale food distributors, and others may depend heavily on state contracts and therefore want good working relationships with decision makers. Third, there are those interests that are financially dependent on the state, such as teachers and other public employees wanting better salaries and benefits, counties and cities pressuring for more generous turnback funds and taxing authority, health and welfare services seeking greater appropriations. All of the above three types of groups have a direct economic or vocational stake in favorable public policy decisions.

A fourth type of group is motivated more by philosophy or ideology than by economic benefit. Religious leaders, for example, motivated by moral beliefs, have always been ready to descend upon the state legislature when they feared the passage of laws that would make it easier to drink or to gamble. In recent years they have been joined by groups dedicated to civil rights and liberties, to environmental protection, to government reform, to laws easing or restricting the availability of abortions, and to many other issues and causes.

A number of groups fall into several of these categories. Financial institutions, for example, are both regulated by the state and do business with the state, competing for deposits of governmental funds and for the right to handle bond issues. The Arkansas Farm Bureau keeps a watchful eye on state regulations (sale and use of pesticides, livestock inspections, land use and water rights), presses for greater government support in agricultural areas (research facilities, extension centers, farm-to-market roads), and also takes positions on certain "morality" issues (supporting capital punishment, opposing casino gambling).

These four types of groups use an almost infinite variety of means in their attempts to influence public policy. When schoolteachers march on the Governor's Mansion, when members of FLAG (Family Life America God) distribute loaves of homemade bread to legislators, when the Poultry Federation provides continuous food and beverage service to lawmakers in their building conveniently located just off the capitol grounds, when the utilities and consumer-action groups testify for and against utility rate increases before the Public Service Commission, when the Optometric Association patrols legislative corridors with walkie-talkies, when the Motor Carriers Association contributes to the campaign of every incumbent state legislator—all these are actions designed to elicit favorable public policy decisions. Interest-group pressure can be as mild as a quiet conversation or letter-writing campaign, or as dramatic as an attempted crucifixion on the steps of the state capitol. Broadly, however, the methods of interest groups center on public persuasion, electioneering, lobbying, and government penetration.[1]

Historically, public persuasion (that is, the attempt to create favorable public opinion about a group and its goals) has rarely been employed in Arkansas except when a group was working for or against a ballot issue. With so few Arkansans participating in the political process, costly mass public relations campaigns would have been of dubious worth. It may be a small sign of an increasingly attentive and active public that public persuasion campaigns have occasionally been mounted in recent years: Arkansas Power and Light (AP&L) has done extensive advertising about the "fairness" of its rates; the Arkansas Education Association (AEA) has run television spots designed to enhance the image of teachers as caring and competent professionals; and the Arkansas Poultry Federation ran a series of full-page newspaper advertisements in 1985 pointing out that "the poultry industry directly contributes over $1 billion annually to the Arkansas economy, with important benefits to everyone." Even more direct were full-page advertisements sponsored by the Arkansas Good Roads/Transportation Council in February 1985 (just as the legislature was debating a gasoline tax increase with the resulting revenues to support roads) with a map depicting precisely which roads in every county would be built or improved with the proceeds. As these examples suggest, only those organizations with the biggest budgets can afford this very expensive method of exerting group influence.[2]

Electioneering is a much more common method of attempting to influence public policy. If the "right" people are elected to office, interest groups will have a much easier time advancing and protecting their interests. Therefore, a great deal of contemporary interest-group activity is devoted to electing and maintaining a group's friends and sympathizers and politically punishing its critics and enemies; and this assistance takes a great variety of forms.

Many groups endorse candidates and notify their members as to which candidates have "their" group interests at heart. This endorsement can involve a very formal proceeding (an endorsement from the AFL-CIO, for example, takes a two-thirds vote at the state convention) with assured campaign benefits to follow or can be a very informal process of "spreading the word"; it can be preceded by rigorous personal interviews (for example, those conducted by the AEA) or elaborate questionnaires (FLAG, State Employees' Association, Leadership Roundtable), or it can simply be based on the group leadership's familiarity with a candidate's background and record.

Some groups, especially those with large memberships, such as labor and the AEA, can offer manpower and womanpower for campaign tasks; groups with fewer members but deeper pockets can offer their facilities: use of a company plane for transportation on a tight campaign schedule or use of a financial institution at night for a campaign phone bank. Direct-mail campaigns necessitate targeted, reliable mailing lists, which groups are happy to supply to their candidate friends.

Most essential, as the costs of campaigns continue to escalate, is money, and a very large portion of campaign contributions in all state races comes from those with a stake in the outcome. Under the Campaign Finance Act of 1975 as amended in 1977, cash contributions of more than $100 are prohibited, as is any contribution of more than $1,500 from any individual or group per candidate per election; and candidates must report the names and occupations of any contributors of $250 or more in periodic reports to the Secretary of State's Office. Theoretically, then, there are limits on the amount of "influence" that can be purchased through campaign contributions and the disclosure requirement constrains candidates from relying too heavily upon only a few interested sources.

In practice, however, these formal limits only mildly inhibit "interested" giving, especially in that interest groups themselves have no reporting obligations, and only those with omniscient knowledge of the state can begin to fathom whatever patterns these contribution reports may reveal. The political action committees (PACs) of many groups, for example, are camouflaged behind innocuous or altruistic labels, so that it is not immediately apparent that contributions from Vote, Inc., ENPAC, the Century Club, Arkansans for Good State Government, and Volunteer Contributors for Better Government represent, respectively, contributions from Blue Cross-Blue Shield, Arkansas Power and Light, the Nursing Home Association, the state Chamber of Commerce, and the International Paper Company. A $1,500 contribution from Mary Smith could be a generous gift from a relative or neighbor or friend, or it could be from the wife of a big group giver who has already "maxed out" (contributed the maximum), or from the secretary to a lawyer who owns several liquor stores, or from the daughter of one of a company's twelve corporate executives (half of whom are backing the incumbent, half the opponent). Furthermore, virtually no penalty is imposed on those who miss the deadlines for filing their reports or who file inadequate, inconsistent, or incorrect information. According to the Secretary of State's Office, "The most affirmative action we take is we keep a checklist of who's filed, and the ones that miss a deadline we'll give a call."[3]

Both state newspapers routinely publish the names of major contributors in important state races, and members of the state press corps periodically do analytical pieces on how the major economic interests seem to be lining up in key races. The following items, strongly suggestive of the pervasive influence of interest-group giving in contemporary campaigns, have been gleaned from these and other sources:

– In a 1973 study based on interviews with 55 lobbyists, 72 percent reported giving financial help in campaigns.
– A group of seventy-five highway building contractors, bonding companies, and material suppliers gathered in early 1980 and agreed to contribute to all state legislative candidates who would support increased tax revenues for highway construction purposes.
– Frank White's campaign contribution report in 1980 failed to list the occupations of 125 contributors (who gave nearly $100,000).
– Within a month of taking office, Governor White switched positions from opposing to favoring a tax exemption for farm equipment; immediately, 230 farm equipment dealers received letters suggesting that a $200 campaign contribution in either personal or corporate checks would be an appropriate expression of gratitude.
– In 1982 both Clinton and White received nearly 20 percent of their campaign contributions from the banking, financial, and investment community, sometimes from the same individuals.

– In 1982 the name of James Blair, then Democratic National committeeman and also general counsel for Tyson Foods, turned up on contribution lists as a $500 giver to the Republican congressman John Paul Hammerschmidt. Blair offered the following explanation: "Generally, a request comes in on a federal race. Tyson's cannot make a corporate contribution. It gets down to the point that executives in the corporation kind of have to parcel them out, because no one can afford it all . . . and the question is Whose turn is it? It must have been my turn. I shouldn't be as careless with my money."

– In 1984, twenty unopposed state legislators each received between $5,750 and $25,000 in campaign contributions, much of it from interest groups.

– By late April 1986 the Arkansas Power and Light Action Committee had made $1,000, $500, or $250 contributions to 112 state legislators, most of whom were either unopposed or not up for reelection.[4]

Contributors and candidates alike insist that even the most generous of campaign contributions cannot buy a public policy outcome. Contributions can, however, ensure easy access to policymakers when decisions are being made and when the direct attempt to influence them is under way.

This is a reference to lobbying, the third major technique of interest groups, a term that derives from those who have always been found clustering in the halls of legislative chambers to ply their policy wares. When the legislature goes into session, the normally quiet capitol suddenly becomes crammed with those who have come to protect their turf (the ophthalmologists against the ambitious optometrists), plead for a special tax exemption (Arkansas moviemakers, horse breeders, plane and watch manufacturers, winemakers, and so on), or demand more funds for their sector of the public service. Committee meetingrooms, the long corridors outside the house and senate chambers, the galleries above, even the "quiet rooms" behind (supposedly reserved for legislators) turn into cauldrons of ceaseless pressure-group activity.

Some of the lobbyists are "hired guns," longtime professional agents with several interests to represent. In 1985, for example, Joe Bell (son of the longtime state senator Clarence Bell) was registered as the lobbyist for the Missouri Pacific Railroad Company, the Oaklawn Jockey Club, the Arkansas Bankers Association, and Dow Chemical Company, while the former state representative Kent Rubens was registered as the lobbyist for the Arkansas Greyhound Kennel Association, Little Rock Pregnancy Counseling, Inc., and Mid Continent Truck Stops. Others are paid executive directors of interest groups, the "vice president for governmental relations" of large businesses, volunteers representing various associations and causes, or one-day citizen lobbyists bused in from around the state to show mass strength for or against a pending bill. Since the impact of group pressure (as compared with pressure from ordinary constituents, the governor, and other legislators) will be analyzed extensively in Chapter 9, only a few additional points about legislative lobbying are necessary here.[5]

Lobbying by groups in behalf of their interests is a process firmly protected by the Constitution (freedom of association, of speech and press and assembly, of petitioning the government), hallowed by tradition, and necessitated by legislators' need to know the potential impact of their decisions on specific groups within the general public. Lobbying, then, is both legitimate and valuable. It must also be noted that the appropriate relationships between lobbyists and legislators are, at present, less regulated in Arkansas than in almost any other state. In fact, Act 162 of 1967 requires only that lobbyists must register with either the clerk of the house or the secretary of the senate every two years, indicating the interest(s) they represent; and as with campaign contribution laws, even this most mild of requirements is extensively ignored, there being no apparent penalty for violation and no enforcement agency. By 1984 Arkansas was one of only six states requiring no disclosure of what is spent on lobbying, and repeated attempts to enact such requirements have been unsuccessful, as have been proposals requiring lobbyists to wear identifying badges. Nor does Arkansas have any laws, comparable to those in most states, that either prohibit or place stringent dollar limits on various gifts that lobbyists can provide for legislators (recent examples include watches, cases of wine, eyeglasses, and tickets and transportation to sporting events). In fact, group-sponsored meals and parties are so accepted in Arkansas that the House Affairs Committee assists in scheduling these entertainments to avoid unnecessary conflicts, and both legislative chambers obligingly announce and circulate an abundance of invitations. After the 1987 regular legislative session, during which combinations of interest groups were particularly visible and obstructionist, Governor Bill Clinton appointed nineteen members to a special Code of Ethics Commission and directed them to propose comprehensive laws dealing with conflicts of interest and financial disclosure by public officials, candidates, and lobbyists. The commission's recommendations for stricter disclosure and other requirements for lobbyists were rejected by a special legislative session on ethics called by Governor Clinton in February 1988. However, major features of their recommendations were drafted into an initiated act to be presented to voters on the November 1988 ballot.

Stricter lobbying regulations would seem to stand a stronger chance of adoption by the public than by the legislature, where they have heretofore been successfully opposed on the grounds that they would "keep some timid people from appearing before committees because they wouldn't want to register" (an argument advanced by an Arkansas-Louisiana Gas spokesman), that such regulations would just add "another layer of paper and red tape that creates barriers for people who want to communicate" (suggested by an Arkansas Power and Light spokesman), and that such regulations are unnecessary and would be burdensome (argued by lobbyists for the Arkansas Hospitality Association, Medical Society, Retail Merchant Association, and the railroads). Perhaps the most fundamental reason for opposition to disclosure laws, however, was that candidly expressed by one state legislator: "It could be an embarrassing thing, for instance, if a legislator went to dinner with a lobbyist it would be in the paper the next day." Obviously, both the formal structure and the attitudinal environment provide an extraordinarily accommodating atmosphere for lobbying in Arkansas.[6]

While the semivisible activities of legislative lobbying receive most of the attention, many groups work just as fervently to advance their interests within the executive branch, where thousands of decisions are made annually regarding licensure, interpretation and application of broadly worded laws, and allocation of funds. In fact, as state administrative agencies have acquired greater power to assist or thwart the interests of increasing numbers of citizens, interest-group attention has increasingly turned toward ensuring impact on these administrative decisions as well as on the broad laws authorizing them.

This, the fourth major technique of interest groups, is government penetration, and several political scientists have raised warning signals about the extent to which public policymaking has, in effect, been turned over to private interest groups. Boards or commissions that were established to regulate a particular industry or profession in order to protect the public may instead become captives of the very groups they were established to supervise. In Arkansas, for example, there are nearly two hundred state boards and commissions that license and regulate everything from masseurs and mobile home sales to banks and beekeepers. According to one recent study, 76 percent of the gubernatorial appointments to many of these boards are required by law to be made from lists submitted by the industries and associations to be licensed and regulated. The rationale for such arrangements is that nobody is more conversant with the qualifications, professional procedures, and problems of chiropodists, nursing home operators, and inhalation therapists than are chiropodists, nursing home operators, and inhalation therapists. The danger, of course, is that such boards may equate the public interest with their own industry-biased view and may "tend to ignore their mandate for protecting the public and often place professional interests above the public good."[7]

The four major methods used by interest groups to influence public policy decisions—public persuasion, electioneering, lobbying, and government penetration—have become an integral part of the policymaking process in all of the fifty states. There is a general consensus among political scientists, however, that Arkansas is one of the states where interest groups are most powerful, an unsurprising conclusion in view of those factors generally associated with interest-group strength: the status of political parties; the makeup of the economy; and the degree of government professionalism.[8]

The relationship between political party and interest-group strength is an inverse one. Where political parties dominate the political life of a state, interest groups tend to have less influence. When political parties actively recruit candidates, generously finance their campaigns, and take forceful policy positions to which elected officials are held accountable, interest groups have less opportunity for influence. In Arkansas, however, where political parties perform these functions weakly if at all, the resulting vacuum is filled by interest groups, encouraging "their" candidates into office, providing the bulk of their campaign finances, and exerting enormous leverage in behalf of their particular policy goals with no countervailing discipline from legislative party leadership.

The relationship between economic complexity and interest-group strength is also an inverse one. Where a state's economy is highly diversified and heterogeneous (which in turn has generally been a product of industrialization), there will be a proliferation of interest groups, but none has the strength to dominate the political system because multiple interests are constantly competing against each other. In most southern states, however, characterized until recently by an agrarian economy and widespread economic dependency, a few powerful interests could exploit their economic superiority for political purposes.

Accounts of Arkansas politics into the 1960s repeatedly mention a few, and only a few, powerful economic interests with equally potent political clout: the Delta plantation owners and large lumbering interests, which occasionally combined with financial and business interests in Little Rock through an organization known as the Arkansas Free Enterprise Association to, for example, put a right-to-work amendment into the state constitution, fight off New Deal and other economic reform "foolishness," and oppose civil rights advances; the Baptist church when aroused to battle on morality issues; and above all, the private power utilities.[9]

From the 1930s through the 1950s, the influence of the Arkansas Power and Light Company can only be described as extraordinary. Under the leadership of its founder, Harvey Couch, and his longtime political lieutenant, legal adviser, and eventual successor, Hamilton Moses, the weight of AP&L was felt literally from the county courthouse to the White House, and at all political decision-making levels in between. With Orval Faubus's defeat of Francis Cherry, the influence of AP&L waned somewhat while the presence of the Arkansas-Louisiana Gas Company (ArkLa), under its founder and politically skillful leader, W. R. "Witt" Stephens, loomed ever larger, to the point that when Rockefeller became governor, he discovered to his dismay that seventeen of the thirty-five state senators were on the ArkLa payroll through retainers and other devices. (This is an interesting latter-day confirmation of an earlier observation by both V. O. Key and Boyce Drummond that utilities and other powerful economic interests were even more involved in legislative than in gubernatorial elections, since judicious investment in legislative "friends" could protect the status quo against the efforts of whatever progressive forces an activist governor might generate.) While other interests—the liquor dealers, Farm Bureau, railroads and truckers, county judges—are also mentioned in accounts of the traditional political period as occasionally influential, in an underdeveloped economy with only a few major sources of employment and profit there was certainly no genuine balancing of a multitude of competing interests.[10]

Finally, there is also an inverse relationship between government professionalism and interest-group strength. Where the state legislature is well paid, well staffed, and well informed, and where the executive branch consists of highly trained and secure professionals under the clear administrative authority of a strong governor, interest groups have a much more difficult time exerting influence. As Harmon Ziegler has pointed out, "The relationship between legislator and lobbyists is one in which information is the prime resource. . . . That relationship is not necessary when legislators can learn all they need from their own staffs."[11]

While the Arkansas legislature, as will be discussed, has been significantly upgraded and professionalized over the past decade, the heavy reliance of legislators on lobbyists for information is still very evident. According to Van Driesum's interviews in 1973, under conditions of uncertainty, 41 percent of the legislators consulted lobbyists (as compared with

31 percent consulting constituent leaders, 17 percent turning to administrative specialists, and 11 percent turning to the governor). Even more recently, one state legislator, perhaps unwittingly, described the information imbalance: "I try to read all the legislation that I can. But a lot of times it's quicker and more efficient to run out here and find the lobbyist and find out what it's all about."[12]

The same inadequacy of institutional supports permeates the executive branch. Here, too, there have been significant improvements since the 1950s, until which time each new governor swept the entire executive branch clean, replacing all state employees with his generally inexperienced political cohorts. Still, as one recent insurance commissioner pointed out, the billion-dollar highly sophisticated insurance industry, with nearly 1,400 companies doing business in Arkansas, was being regulated by a department consisting of sixty employees with low salaries, no opportunities for continuing education, no actuary, and no computer capability. Similarly, the Public Service Commission (PSC) is constantly plagued by the loss of employees who work just long enough to become experts on allocation and regulatory problems, then are quickly lured away by the larger salaries and greater perquisites offered by the private power companies. Although the governor's authority over his own executive establishment has been significantly strengthened in recent years, powerful centrifugal forces that prefer a state house divided are still at work; they have managed to preserve a considerable amount of fragmentation that makes access and influence much easier.[13]

While weak parties, a simple economy, and lack of professionalism in government all help to explain the strength of interest groups to date in Arkansas politics, these same factors suggest that interest groups, or at least the traditionally powerful interest groups, may encounter more obstacles in Arkansas's political future than they have in the past. Party strength is the product of party competition, and while neither political party in Arkansas yet performs its functions with sufficient rigor to counterbalance the influence of interest groups, as the parties continue to become more competitive, the incentives for an organized electoral effort and greater legislative cohesion should eventually follow. Similarly, steady improvements in both the legislative and executive branches have already begun to strengthen these institutions against the easy penetration and power of interest groups. Finally, while Arkansas's economy still lags behind much of the rest of the nation in many of the standard indicators of modern, complex, affluent societies, the economy has become decidedly more diversified than it was in the very recent past, and the impact of this diversification has already begun to appear. The pressure-group system no longer involves just a handful of dominant economic forces but a kaleidoscopic array of economic and noneconomic interests. Between 300 and 400 lobbyists now register at each regular legislative session, and many (such as the Air Transport Association, Community Mental Health Centers, Medical Technologists, Black Female Action, Inc.) are of obviously recent origin.[14]

This is not to suggest that all groups compete equally in the political process. First, in terms of sheer quantity, the vast majority of lobbyists represent businesses, industries, the utilities, and the professions rather than those who work in these industries, consume their products, use the utilities, and need professional services. There were 380 individual lobbyists registered at the 1985 regular session of the legislature who identified 459 interests or clients. Of these lobbyists, 125 were associated with utilities and more than 200 with individual businesses or industry or professional associations. Only 9 represented organized labor, 8 spoke for retired or senior citizens, and 3 for environmental concerns.[15]

Second, all lobbyists are definitely not equal. One recent informal survey found a consensus among legislators that the most effective single lobbyists were those representing AP&L, Stephens, Inc., the railroads, the poultry and trucking industries, and the state Chamber of Commerce. Still, it is increasingly rare for the economic dominants to be unified or unchallenged in their policy goals. In the 1985 legislative session, for example, efforts by management (represented by Associated Industries of Arkansas, the state Chamber of Commerce) to restrict workers' eligibility for compensation were strongly challenged not only by organized labor but also by claimants' lawyers (represented by the Bar Association and Trial Lawyers Association), and the controversial bill was referred to an interim committee for further study. When it appeared that organized labor would secure the necessary petition signatures to get their preferred version on the 1986 general election ballot as an initiated act, industry representatives negotiated a compromise, which law was unanimously approved at a special legislative session in April 1986. A proposal favored by the financial giant Stephens, Inc., which would have permitted out-of-state bank holding companies to acquire Arkansas banks, stirred such strong opposition from the Arkansas Bankers Association and Independent Community Bankers Association that it had to be "pulled down." Efforts by the trucking and poultry industry to raise permissible tonnage limits on Arkansas highways were stymied for years by countervailing pressure from the Highway Department lobby in league with the railroads.[16]

Increasingly, even the most powerful of interests have found that it may take a coalition of forces to secure their goals. The banking lobby has exceptional clout in the state legislature, perhaps because so many legislators either have banking ties or need the support of local bankers in their private occupations. Efforts by the financial community to remove the 10 percent usury limit embedded in the state constitution were consistently unsuccessful, however, until they finally changed the position of the 113,000-member Farm Bureau from opposition to support (and submitted an amendment that tied the usury limit to the federal discount rate rather than giving interest-setting power to the legislature). An antiabortion bill sponsored by Pro-Lifers and some fundamentalist religious groups in 1985 was drastically modified by an unusual but effective combination of various feminist organizations and the Arkansas Medical Society. It is impossible to overestimate the ubiquitous influence of the major utilities. Being publicly tagged as the tool of the utilities in a campaign, however, has become as much or more of a stigma than the tag of being labor's candidate used to be, perhaps in part because public confidence in utilities and organized labor was equally low in Arkansas by the 1980s.[17]

In 1957 Drummond noted, "Just as Arkansas politicians have customarily repudiated endorsements by Negro organizations, they now disown connections with labor and seek to place the union stamp on the opposition." He went on to predict, "When Arkansas politicians vie for rather than shy from the support of labor groups, organized labor will have come of age." By the 1980s all candidates were courting the black vote, and though too close a tie to unions can still be the political kiss of death (as David Pryor learned to his dismay in his 1972 race against John McClellan, then used to his advantage in his 1978 race against Jim Guy Tucker), virtually all major candidates (including "Justice Jim" Johnson in 1984) now seek labor's endorsement as a coveted commodity.[18]

Teachers, once the timid and grateful recipients of whatever crumbs were scattered on the table, have now acquired a formidable political presence through a militant organization (the AEA) with a multimillion dollar budget. A survey of state legislators in 1979 gave the AEA most mentions as the "most powerful" interest group, an estimate attested to when twenty-six house members who had supported teacher-testing in 1983 reversed and voted against it under AEA pressure in 1985.[19]

Not only have new groups, such as labor and teachers, moved into the ranks of influentials, but new methods, especially litigation, have given influence to groups that otherwise, through lack of either economic clout or large numbers, could not play power politics. The Arkansas affiliate of the

American Civil Liberties Union has fewer than six hundred members, while Baptist and other antievolutionist church members number in the hundreds of thousands. Nevertheless, after the Creation Science bill was passed by sweeping majorities in 1981, the ACLU took the matter into the judicial arena, where numbers and votes do not count, and a federal judge struck down the law as unconstitutional. The mere knowledge that the ACLU, NOW, the NAACP, environmental, and other watchdog groups may file expensive and embarrassing lawsuits clearly constrains decision makers in ways that they could not have imagined in the very recent past.

It is still true that ordinarily those with greater economic resources, greater numbers, and higher status have far more impact than those who lack these attributes. It is still true, as E. E. Schattschneider once observed, that "the flaw in the pluralist heaven is that the heavenly chorus sings with a strong upper-class accent." Nevertheless, an increasingly complex economy has produced many more actors in the political system, and especially when there is division among the economic elite, some of the lesser voices can be heard. In the most recent analysis of interest-group influence in Arkansas a system of "modified inequality" is described:

In Arkansas there are effectively two worlds within which interest groups move. The first is the world of the utility, the corporation, the trade group and employee organization, where one or more paid lobbyists, providing professional representation operate as insiders within the system. In this world the preferred tactics are a personal chat with the legislator, a campaign contribution, and a lobbying effort which is usually divorced from the immediate awareness of the group's larger membership. The second world is that of the public interest group, the feminist, religious or civil rights group, the patriotic organization which operates through its membership in letter-writing campaigns, political protests and high-intensity presentations.[20]

As the parties become stronger through competition, as both the legislative and executive branches continue to strengthen their institutional capacity, and especially as the economy becomes increasingly pluralistic, interest groups will be forced into a more modest position of strength in Arkansas politics. There are, however, two contrary forces that could sustain, or even enhance, the power that interest groups have traditionally enjoyed.

One of these is the ever-escalating costs of running for public office. As noted earlier, gubernatorial campaigns have gone from multithousand- to multimillion-dollar undertakings in recent years; successful races for other statewide races now all top the $100,000 mark; races for the state legislature, which rarely cost more than $2,500 in the early 1970s, now average more than $32,000 (and occasionally cost nearly $60,000); and elections to county and local office are skyrocketing in cost as well: the candidates for Pulaski County prosecutor each spent more than $80,000 in the Democratic primary in 1984. Lacking more rigorous controls or any kind of public funding mechanisms, increasingly expensive campaigns will inevitably make candidates dependent upon those with the biggest purses and highest stakes, and frequently that means the interest groups who envision substantial profits from their political "investments."[21]

The second major countervailing force is the ongoing search by Arkansas to improve its economic status vis à vis the other states. Because all states are constantly engaged in a fierce battle for jobs for their citizens, existing and potential employers are well situated to threaten, divide, and conquer: if you regulate us too stringently, tax us too heavily, mandate overly generous worker benefits, refuse to grant special tax exemptions for our operations and products, we will simply move to a state with a "friendlier business climate." And the hungrier states, such as Arkansas, are most vulnerable to this economic blackmail. As will be noted, any major employer wanting special consideration will generally find public officials eager to oblige, at whatever cost to a rational tax structure, a cleaner environment, a safer workplace, or the general consuming public.

Two recent incidents make this point with almost poignant clarity. In 1985 it was proposed in the legislature that motor vehicles that had been declared total losses should carry a designation to that effect on the title; the proposal was defeated in the House Public Transportation Committee when several dealers in salvaged automobiles showed up vigorously protesting. Their argument was that the legislation would cut their business 30 percent and therefore flew in the face of the state's efforts to stimulate economic development. Also in 1985, when the state Pollution Control and Ecology Department proposed $11,000 in fines against Tyson Foods for improper handling of their sludge with contaminating effects on local water, local businessmen promptly offered to pay the fine for this welcome employer of more than 1,500 persons in Carroll County.[22]

The political climate in Arkansas has become much more open and participatory, much more clean and competitive, than it ever was in the past, and many new groups and interests have taken a seat at the political table. Still, it is well to stay alert to lingering echoes from the past. It is possible that Arkansas, having never experienced government of, by, and for the people, leapfrogged into an era of government of, by, and for its best organized groups.

## CHAPTER SEVEN

# The Constitution: Provisions and Politics

*A constitution . . . requires that only its great outlines should be marked, its important objects designated.*

Chief Justice John Marshall, 1819

*All affidavits of Registration shall be made and executed in quadruplicate, the original and each copy of a distinctively different color. Each form shall be printed at the top thereof with the word "Original," "Duplicate," "Triplicate," or "Quadruplicate," as the case may be. . . . The forms shall be bound together in books or pads and each set of copies shall be capable of being detached from the book or pad and inserted and locked into the Registration Record Files.*

Arkansas Constitution, Amendment 51

The winds of change that produced so many modifications in Arkansas politics in recent decades also generated an intense period of attempted constitutional reform. On three separate occasions between 1968 and 1980, machinery was established to replace the existing constitution, written in 1874, with a new one that was more appropriate to contemporary circumstances and needs. Since none of these efforts succeeded, Arkansas still operates under a constitution better designed to prevent the recurrence of Reconstruction than to enable a late-twentieth-century government to perform effectively. In that sense, the more things change, the more they seem to remain the same.

Still, the constitutional picture is not a thoroughly bleak one. The constitution itself is one of the most democratic in the nation and is one of the most majoritarian components of Arkansas's political system. Some of the most obstructionist provisions of the 1874 document have recently been removed or revised, and contemporary officeholders have devised means for accommodating themselves to much of what remains.

## WHAT CAUSED THE CONSTITUTION

Like all constitutions, Arkansas's is both a formal, legal document establishing the rights of the people and the basic structure and powers of government and a political document reflecting the particular circumstances that produced it. Arkansas has had five constitutions, each of them "born out of some kind of crisis—statehood, civil war, military occupation, Reconstruction, and the reaction to Reconstruction."[1]

The 1836 constitution was the necessary qualification for statehood. It was fairly brief and straightforward, being modeled after the U.S. Constitution but with provisions tailored to Arkansas's frontier circumstances, and it was amended only three times in its twenty-five years of existence. In fact, it was changed very little by the convention that met in 1861 to frame a second state constitution, one appropriate for admission to the Confederacy. The framers simply substituted Confederate States of America for United States of America and provided additional safeguards to the institution of slavery. The third constitution, adopted in 1864 under military occupation, was another minor revision of the original document, with the significant exceptions that slavery was abolished and renewed allegiance to the United States proclaimed.

The fourth constitution, the so-called Carpetbag Constitution of 1868, deserves a little more attention, since it was in opposition to many of its provisions, and specifically to the regime that operated under its provisions, that the fifth and present constitution was written in 1874. Under the Reconstruction Act of 1867, existing southern state governments were declared illegal and no such state could reenter the Union until a new constitution, conforming to the federal Constitution, was approved by Congress. Hence, a constitutional convention (consisting of only nine native Arkansans, three of whom had been slaves) drew up a document that extended the suffrage to blacks, disfranchised former Confederates, eliminated all distinctions based on race, and established a system of legislative apportionment favoring counties with large black populations. Also, reflecting both the semimilitary character of the government and the absence of cooperative local organizations, power was strongly centralized: the governor's appointive powers were broadened to include all judges (except supreme court justices) and all county tax assessors and prosecuting attorneies.[2]

When the Redeemers returned to power in 1874, one of their first acts was to promulgate a new constitution, much of which, understandably, was devised to prohibit the abuses of power and the waste of funds that characterized the Reconstruction period. Above all, the 1874 constitution was specifically designed to protect citizens from possible oppression by their own state government.

This pervasive distrust of government is expressed in almost every section of the 1874 document. To ensure popular control over officialdom, many offices previously appointive became elective, and terms were almost uniformly reduced from four to two years, giving voters, according to one estimate, forty-four rather than fourteen opportunities to exercise their electoral control in any four-year period. To prevent excessive and unwise lawmaking, the legislature was limited to one sixty-day session every other year. Maximum salaries for all state and county officials were specified and fixed. Elaborate statutory detail on everything from the conduct of elections to the times and places of circuit court meetings and the procedures for letting state printing contracts were included to leave little leeway to any state official tempted to abuse his powers. (The word "his" is used advisedly, since many sections dealing with officeholders specify the male gender.) Above all, the taxing and spending powers were circumscribed with every prohibitive device imaginable. Sixty-nine of the 261 sections of the 1874 constitution deal with financial matters, and most in a restrictive way: local governments were severely limited in their taxing powers, state tax and appropriations measures required extraordinary majorities, and there could be no extension of credit or assumption of debt for any purposes whatsoever.[3]

This negative and restrictive document reflects not only revulsion against the excesses of Reconstruction but also the basic socioeconomic conditions of Arkansas in the 1870s. The state was relatively small (with a population of less than 500,000) and overwhelmingly rural (over 95 percent), and most of the people lived in straitened circumstances. Only five towns (Little Rock, Fort Smith, Pine Bluff, Camden, and Hot Springs) contained more than 1,000 inhabitants, so municipal powers were scarcely mentioned, local government presumably being a function of counties. The state government spent only $320,000 in the fiscal year 1874–75, so a sixty-day biennial session might well have seemed adequate for determining allocation to the few state services offered. Fearing the rising tides of tenancy and economic dependency, it made sense to guarantee the people exemption from seizure of their homesteads and to specify a maximum interest rate of 10 percent on private loans.

Ideally, as Chief Justice John Marshall so eloquently noted in *McCulloch v. Maryland*, a constitution should contain only "the great outlines of government," and obviously the Arkansas Constitution falls far short of that ideal. It is lengthy (more than 46,000 words, compared with the U.S. Constitution's 6,700), has had to be frequently amended (sixty-five amendments by 1986, compared with the U.S. Constitution's twenty-six), restricts more than it enables, and makes permanent much of what should have been left to changing legislative majorities. The establishment of both community colleges and public kindergartens required constitutional amendments, for example, because the original constitution authorized public educational funds only for those aged six to twenty-one. Much of the 1874 minutiae seems foolish to our modern minds, and as will be discussed, it creates some serious impediments to contemporary governance.

For all its faults, however, several important mitigating factors should be kept in mind. First, it was an appropriate and understandable document for its time. Second, the Arkansas Constitution is by no means the most lengthy, detailed, and restrictive of state constitutions. Most existing state constitutions were adopted in the late nineteenth century, when public confidence in state government was at its zenith everywhere, and some of them are many times longer and much more prohibitive than is Arkansas's. Third, unlike so many other components of Arkansas's traditional political system, the 1874 constitution does seem to have genuinely reflected the will of the people. Unlike the first and second constitutions, which were never referred to the people, and the third and fourth, which were voted upon by highly unrepresentative segments of the population, the 1874 constitution was both authorized by the people and resoundingly ratified (76,453 to 24,807).[4]

In many ways, then, it was a thoroughly democratic document and was made even more majoritarian by the addition of an initiative and referendum provision in 1910, which gave citizens the right and the means to initiate amendments in their basic document of governance. Finally, and fortunately, the 1874 constitution has been repeatedly revised through a variety of updating mechanisms.

CONSTITUTIONAL CHANGE

Some of the most significant changes in the Arkansas Constitution have resulted from United States Supreme Court decisions that either directly or indirectly declared certain Arkansas constitutional provisions to be in violation of the national Constitution or of federal law. Such voided provisions include those regarding apportionment of the state legislature, the requirement of a poll tax and lengthy residence requirements as voting prerequisites, and the "interposition" amendment adopted in 1956 at the peak of segregationist sentiment. Some other provisions, such as that prohibiting anyone "who denies the being of a God" from holding office, undoubtedly would fall if there were any attempt to enforce them.

The Arkansas Supreme Court has also been an agent of change, occasionally permitting some governmental action that a more literal interpretation of the constitution might seem to preclude but more often through interpretations so unacceptable in contemporary circumstances that a constitutional amendment is precipitated. A series of court decisions in the 1970s literally interpreting the property tax provisions in the constitution would have resulted in dramatic increases in taxation, had not Amendments 57 and 59 been quickly added (in 1976 and 1980) to keep such increases from occurring.

The state legislature has also added to the constitution by filling in details left to its discretion. The legislators were empowered, for example, to establish separate courts of chancery "when deemed expedient," which they subsequently did, and the original judicial circuits were established in the constitution "until otherwise provided by the General Assembly," which has modified them frequently over the years. The executive department, consisting originally of "a Governor, Secretary of State, Treasurer of State, Auditor of State and Attorney General" has been enormously expanded by statutory establishment of offices and departments over the years.

Custom and usage have also modified constitutional practice. The constitution, for example, requires the outgoing governor to give information by message concerning the condition of the government "at the close of his official term to the next General Assembly." In fact, however, it is the incoming governor's "State of the State" speech, nowhere mentioned in the constitution, that has become a traditional opening highlight of the regular legislative session.

Finally, the constitution has been changed by formal amendment. From 1874 to 1986 more than 150 amendments were submitted to the people for ratification, and of these proposals, 65 have been adopted and are now printed as part of the official constitutional document. Most (37) of these were initiated by the legislature, which is authorized to select up to three proposed amendments at each regular session for submission to the voters at the next general election. The other 28 were initiated by the voters themselves by acquiring sufficient numbers (at least 10 percent of those who voted in the last gubernatorial election) of valid signatures (that is, those of qualified and registered voters) on initiative petitions to get their proposed amendment on the general election ballot.[5]

In this amendment process is further evidence of the distinctly democratic nature of the Arkansas Constitution. In many states, amendments initiated by the legislature require extraordinary legislative majorities and/or approval at two regular legislative sessions; in Arkansas, a simple majority of both houses at a single session is sufficient. Only sixteen other states permit the voters to initiate constitutional amendments, and some states require ratification by a majority of those voting in that election rather than, as is now the case in Arkansas, a majority of those voting on that particular amendment. In fact, it has been estimated that only five other states have constitutions that are as easy to amend as Arkansas's. (It should also be noted that the Arkansas Constitution provides for popular initiation of ordinary statutes and for popular referenda on measures already enacted by the legislature, and these devices of direct democracy are available to local as well as statewide electorates.)[6]

In the accessibility of its constitution to popular majorities, Arkansas is much more in the midwestern populist and progressive tradition than in the southern elitist and traditionalistic pattern. Furthermore, the use of these devices offers some evidence in support of V. O. Key's suggestion that the citizenry of the South was not so conservative as the behavior of its political leaders might suggest. The adoption of the initiative and referendum amendment in and of itself was a triumph, led by organized labor, over the conservative establishment, led by lawyers and judges, who argued that only a few people were qualified to vote intelligently on legislation—an argument that prompted a state Farmers Union official to complain that the opposition "must think we farmers and common people are a set of fools and anarchists." Despite the dire warnings of the opposition, Amendment 10 was resoundingly ratified (91,367 to 39,111), and in the succeeding general election of 1912 it was used to defeat a suffrage amendment that included a grandfather clause and to defeat a proposed statewide prohibition act. In that same election, voters approved a constitutional amendment permitting the recall of elected officials and another amendment permitting cities to issue bonds for public improvements (both of which were later invalidated by the supreme court as not having been among the first three amendments submitted). In 1914 an initiated act prohibiting child labor was approved by a vote of nearly three to one.[7]

These and other examples of the occasional progressivism of the Arkansas electorate must be weighed against many examples to the contrary. Voters over the decades also used their lawmaking powers to prohibit the teaching of evolution (1928) and to require compulsory Bible reading in the schools (1930), to place a right-to-work amendment in the constitution (Amendment 34 in 1944), to defeat proposed repeal of the poll tax (1956), and to order all state officials to "oppose in every Constitutional manner the unconstitutional desegregation decisions of May 17, 1954" (Amendment 44 in 1956).

Especially considering that such voting takes place in the general election, which meant until recent decades that only a fraction of the potential electorate was ordinarily participating, it is perhaps best not to assign any particular "public opinion" measurement significance to these hundreds of popular referenda. Indeed, the three most thorough studies to date of Arkansas's uses of the devices of direct democracy all concluded that there were no persistent patterns of liberalism or conservatism, urbanism or ruralism. This contrariness was confirmed by my unsuccessful attempts to find consistent correlations between constitutional revision voting and either demographic attributes or candidate voting patterns.[8]

In the most extensive of these studies, Walter Nunn analyzed voting on twenty-seven statewide ballot issues between 1964 and 1976 and reached the following conclusions: ballot issues fail about one and a half times as often as they pass, but the success rate increased markedly in recent elections; the approval rate for legislature-initiated measures is about the same as that for popularly initiated measures; there is considerable dropoff on ballot issues (that is, many of those voting for major offices do not vote on ballot issues) but that dropoff rate is decreasing; counties above the state average in income, in education, and in black and urban populations sometimes tend to vote for ballot issues more strongly than other counties—but only sometimes; and county population corresponds strongly with the extremes of issue approval (that is, the most highly populated counties are strongest for ballot issues, the least populated counties are strongest against) but with little correlation in the middle ranges. Nunn's general conclusion was that voters do seem to pick and choose quite deliberately among ballot issues but that "voting patterns provide only hazy evidence of their choices."[9]

Federal and state judicial decisions, statutory enactments, custom and usage, and the formal amendment process have all provided essential mechanisms for occasionally updating some of the most restrictive and timebound constitutional provisions. The amendment process, however, also added further length, complexity, and statutory detail to the original document. By the 1960s, dissatisfaction with the piecemeal amendment process began coalescing into a movement for thoroughgoing constitutional reform.

### RECENT REFORM EFFORTS

Since the recent constitutional revision efforts—their origins, proposals, ratification campaigns, and ultimate defeats—have been exhaustively described and analyzed elsewhere, only a brief overview is necessary here. Although sporadic interest in constitutional revision was demonstrated by several governors and legislators in the post–World War II period, steady attention to constitutional reform began with a group of reformist state legislators, labeled the Young Turks, who made repeated attempts in the 1960s to persuade their colleagues and the public of the necessity for a new constitution. Winthrop Rockefeller adopted constitutional reform as a campaign theme, and subsequent to his 1966 election, worked with the Young Turks for legislative approval in 1967 of an appointed, blue-ribbon, Constitutional Revision Study Commission. The work of the commission received sufficiently widespread and favorable publicity to persuade a somewhat reluctant legislature to place on the general ballot in 1968 the question of whether to elect a constitutional convention. In the same curious election that produced the Rockefeller-Fulbright-Wallace victories, the people narrowly (51.5 percent) said yes and elected one hundred delegates to fashion a proposed new constitution.[10]

The delegates' ultimate product, the proposed 1970 Arkansas Constitution, eventually obtained endorsements from an impressive number of groups ranging across the entire political spectrum: the Democratic and Republican parties as well as both parties' gubernatorial nominees; all major business, agricultural, and "good government" organizations; everyone from the conservative Young Americans for Freedom and Associated Industries of Arkansas to the liberal National Conference of Christians and Jews and the NAACP. In fact, the ratification campaign featured the endorsements of many prominent Arkansans, and proclaimed, "Everybody is supporting the new Constitution for one basic reason: It is a much better document than our old 1874 charter." In November 1970, however, the voters rejected the proposed new document that "everybody" favored by a margin of 57.5 percent to 42.5 percent, with favorable majorities in only eleven counties. It was an unexpected and highly demoralizing defeat.[11]

With the 1974 gubernatorial election of David Pryor, who had been one of the Young Turks, constitutional revision took a fresh tack. Pryor pushed for and the legislature enacted another constitutional convention, this time to consist of thirty-five appointed delegates who were prohibited from tinkering with some of what were thought to be the most hallowed and potentially controversial provisions, such as the right-to-work amendment and the independent Highway Commission. This convention was about to begin its work when the state supreme court invalidated its legitimacy, ruling that such prohibitions constituted an unconstitutional limitation on the people's right to change their government.

Somewhat surprisingly, the next legislature passed another call for a popular vote on the question of holding another elected constitutional convention, and to general amazement, once more in 1976 the people voted yes, by a 56 percent majority. Delegates were elected in 1978 who worked with equal diligence and even greater political sensitivity than their predecessors. Again, there seemed to be widespread support for the proposed new document, and it was promoted through a somewhat more sophisticated ratification campaign. But in 1980 the voters again rejected the outcome, and this time by an even larger margin of defeat: 62.7 percent to 37.3 percent, with favorable margins in only nine counties. Continuing their tradition of unpredictability on ballot issues, Arkansas voters had twice within a decade expressed their support for constitutional revision by approving constitutional convention calls, then twice rejected the proposed new documents submitted for their approval.

The rejected documents were broadly similar in what they would have accomplished. Both would have shortened, streamlined, and simplified the 1874 document through the pruning of much deadwood: eliminating obsolescent provisions such as boundary descriptions and archaic references to canals, turnpikes, and public abattoirs, and removing provisions and amendments long since superseded. Both would have maintained all the traditional guarantees of personal and political rights (speech, press, religion, and so on) while adding some new ones (freedom of information, the right to privacy and to a clean and healthful environment). In both the 1970 and 1980 constitutions, all three branches of government would have been revised in accordance with contemporary notions of institutional strength and effectiveness. The legislature, to consist entirely of single-member districts, would have been able to opt for annual rather than biennial regular sessions and to call itself into special session by a three-fifths vote. In the executive branch, the number of elected executive officials would have been reduced (from seven to four in 1970, to five in 1980) and given four-year rather than two-year terms. A newly elected governor was to be given more time to prepare a budget and greater reorganization authority over an executive establishment, to consist of no more than twenty major departments. Both constitutions would have created a more administratively integrated judicial branch with the supreme court's supervisory powers over other courts strengthened, the separate systems of circuit and chancery courts combined into district courts with separate divisions, and numerous existing courts of limited jurisdiction combined into one county trial court.

Instead of existing constitutional specification of particular allowable millage rates for local government (one mill for policemen's retirement, one mill for firemen's retirement, and so on), both new constitutions would have substituted a property tax of five mills for general operations of cities and counties with any additional millage rates subject to voter approval. In fact, the thrust of both documents was to avoid statutory specificity, such as dollar limits on officials' salaries, and, rather, to give the state and local governments the decision-making power to cope with changing needs and circumstances, subject always to the scrutiny of the electorate.

These and other revisions were closely comparable to the proposals advanced by constitutional reformers in the majority of American states that attempted thoroughgoing constitutional revision in the 1960s and 1970s. Like reformers elsewhere, however, those in Arkansas discovered that constitutional revision is one of politics' most complicated and hazardous thickets, much more likely to fail than to succeed.

One of the most serious obstacles to constitutional reform is general citizen indifference. It is extraordinarily difficult to excite most citizens about and give them a sense of stake in the composition of the State Board of Apportionment or the constitutional status of legislative interim committees. Structural and procedural matters have little glamour, especially when they are buried at the bottom of the ballot in a general election in which live, contesting candidates are spending enormous sums to capture voter attention. In both 1970 and 1980, polls showed that a majority of potential voters were undecided close to the eve of the election, and one 1970 preelection survey showed that 59 percent of the respondents had read or heard nothing about the new constitution. In a special election devoted exclusively to constitutional revision, one in which only those interested in that issue will turn out to vote, adoption of a new constitution is more likely. Those unenthusiastic about reform, however, managed to engineer a vote in a general rather than special election, which setting in and of itself was probably fatal in both instances.[12]

While many citizens are indifferent to constitutional reform, some individuals and groups are always intensely interested, fearful of the harmful consequences a particular change will make in their advantageous status quo. In 1970, for example, county judges feared loss of power to a newly strengthened county legislature, chancery judges resisted their potential consolidation with courts of law, realtors feared potential increases in property taxes, and various professional associations opposed the rumored consolidation of their separate licensing boards into one administrative authority. In 1980 organized labor opposed removal of the 10 percent usury limit, the Arkansas Education Association feared the loss of the Education Department's independent status to greater gubernatorial direction, some legislators resented the redistricting that mandated single-member districts would necessitate, and fundamentalists suspected a backdoor attempt to get an equal rights amendment into the constitution through the reference to "sex" in the revised equal protection clause.

In both instances, then, as is generally the case with proposed constitutional reform, many separate groups opposed to different particular provisions cumulated into a negative majority. And in both years, the most effective battlecry of the opponents was the threat that the new constitution would permit an orgy of tax increases. In 1970 opponents ran advertisements warning, "Danger! The Proposed New Constitution Provides 22 *New* Ways to Increase Your Taxes"; in 1980 similar threats of higher taxes were broadcast, together with a last-minute report from the Legislative Council that the new constitution would cost between $35 million and $48 million to implement. The combination of popular caution and indifference, the cumulative negativism of opposed interests, the perceived threat of higher taxes, along with the disadvantageous setting in a general election, defeated the proposed new constitutions and left the Arkansas government still operating within its restrictive and often obsolete 1874 framework.[13]

The continuation of "bedsheet" ballots (seven separately elected state executive officials, nine county executive officials, plus all state and local legislators and judges) constantly asks voters to fill offices whose functions are obscure with individuals whose qualifications are unknown—an open invitation to mischief. "Chief" executives find their administrative authority diminished by a host of separately elected executive officials, and occasional political rivals. The time restrictions on legislative sessions inevitably produce some grievous errors, and the requirement of a three-fourths majority for passage of appropriations measures gives obstructionist minorities golden opportunities for legislative blackmail. Important revenue decisions may be based not on what is the fairest or most productive tax but on which tax (usually the sales tax) requires the least majority for passage.

These and other governing problems are often frustrating to today's officials, themselves more likely to be activists and to be surrounded with expectations of accomplishment. Nevertheless, the adverse impacts of the 1874 constitution are probably more comparable to a nagging headache than to a malignant tumor of the brain. This is true both because contemporary officeholders have learned to cope with some of the most confining constitutional provisions and because the voters have been demonstrating a new-found willingness to amend others.

## CONTINUING CONSTITUTIONAL ADAPTATION

A variety of devices have evolved over the decades whereby Arkansas government can function within the restrictive 1874 document. One such mechanism is simply to ignore it: Amendment 42 mandates that no more than one of the five highway commissioners may be appointed from a single congressional district; now that there are only four districts (compared with the six that existed when the amendment was adopted in 1952), it is impossible to have a legally constituted Highway Commission, so the requirement is simply ignored.

More frequent are a number of expedients for making an end-run around the constitution while still technically complying with its mandates. Although the constitution states that General Assembly sessions are not to exceed sixty calendar days every other year (and the resulting sense of time limits still permeates each regular session), only once since 1965 has the legislature concluded its business so expeditiously. Rather, members vote, by a two-thirds majority, to "extend" the session, which they can apparently do ad infinitum, and they have also begun to "recess" rather than adjourn, so that they can call themselves back into session without awaiting the governor's call. The Arkansas legislature has rarely resorted to the device, popular in some other states, of literally covering the clock on the wall to "stop time," but when a deadline was approaching in 1985, one senator simply moved back the hands of the clock.[14]

Constitutionally imposed salary limits are guaranteed to become obsolete, and those adopted in 1976 (Amendment 56) have already done so. In addition to their official salaries, however ($35,000 for the governor, $14,000 for the lieutenant governor, $26,500 for the attorney general, $7,500 for legislators), additional amounts are appropriated for numerous office-related expenses such as travel, entertainment, and public relations. Despite article 5, section 22, bills are no longer read aloud in their entirety on three separate days; rather, the bill's title and first few words are read, and the Speaker quickly moves to the second "reading."

These and other semilegal gimmicks have some definite drawbacks. They are potential time bombs to be used in challenging the legitimacy of governmental actions; expense allowances as opposed to salaries are an invitation to abuse; and disregard for some clearly outdated constitutional provisions probably encourages disrespect for others. The legislature, for example, refused to reapportion itself from 1890 to 1937 despite a clear constitutional requirement to do so every ten years; and despite an unmistakable requirement that all property be assessed equally at 20 percent of value, the state supreme court found in 1979 that county assessments in fact ranged from only 2.7 percent to 13.9 percent of value.

The major point, however, is that despite the antigovernmentalism of the 1874 constitution, Arkansas's governing apparatus has managed to expand from a handful of employees to more than forty thousand, from an annual state budget of $320,000 to one of over a billion dollars annually, and both the state and local governments are providing a range of public services unimaginable in the 1870s.

Furthermore, while the recent constitutional revision efforts did not produce a new constitution, the years of debate and discussion do seem to have produced a political climate much more amenable to gradual constitutional reform. One of the reasons constitutional reformers pushed so strongly for total revision was that, from the 1958 election until the 1974 election, voters had approved only one of the numerous constitutional amendment proposals submitted by the legislature.[15]

From 1974 to 1986, however, twelve additional amendments were added, some of them bringing about changes that the defeated new constitutions had proposed: Amendment 55 (1974) thoroughly revised and updated county government structure and gave counties a healthy measure of home rule; Amendment 58 (1978) established an intermediate court of appeals; Amendment 60 (1982) removed the 10 percent usury limit from the constitution and tied allowable interest to the federal discount rate; Amendment 61 (1982) removed the requirement that the county road tax be submitted for voter approval at each general election; Amendment 62 (1984) repealed four earlier provisions restricting local governments' ability to issue capital improvement bonds; and Amendment 63 (1984) finally gave Arkansas governors the same four-year term that forty-six other states had previously found advisable. Additional changes proposed in the new constitutions have been adopted by simple statutory action: a statewide code of ethics; a measure of municipal home rule; extensive executive reorganization. In short, of the twenty-seven major changes recommended by the 1968 Constitutional Revision Study Commission, ten have been accomplished by constitutional amendment or by legislative or administrative action, and additional modernizing amendments have also been added.[16]

AN ASSESSMENT

This overview of the provisions and politics of the Arkansas Constitution seems to suggest several conclusions. First, recent constitutional revision efforts offer another example of the ways in which Arkansas political history tends to repeat itself. A proposed new constitution sponsored by Governor Charles Brough was resoundingly defeated by Arkansas voters in 1918. Still, of the twenty-four significant changes recommended in that constitution, twenty were eventually enacted in the form of constitutional amendment or statute. Another period of constitutional updates, prompted in part by wholesale revision efforts, seems to be in progress.[17]

Second, the piecemeal approach to reform, while valuable, is still a less satisfactory approach to modernization than is thoroughgoing revision. The legislature is limited to the submission of three constitutional amendments in any election, and these submissions are just as likely to reflect a powerful legislator's pet proposal as to address a fundamental flaw in the constitution. (In fact, in 1985, house-senate rivalries resulted in only one proposed amendment, to enlarge the jurisdiction of municipal courts.) The popular initiative, of course, is wholly uncoordinated by any comprehensive scheme of constitutional improvement. Furthermore, while it is theoretically equally accessible to all citizens, it is much more accessible to those with strong organizational networks, ideological appeal, and/or economic resources than it is to those simply motivated by "good government" concepts. In 1986, for example, county officials, the Right to Life movement, and the business and financial community easily secured more than enough petition signatures to get their respective proposals on the ballot for four-year terms for county officials, restrictions on abortion, and nonelection status for certain types of revenue bond issues. Common Cause's efforts to rationalize the legislative majorities required for various kinds of tax increases fell by the wayside. Furthermore, additional amendments, even while accomplishing worthy purposes, nevertheless add to the length and complexity of an already verbose and convoluted document.[18]

While Arkansas voters have shown an increased willingness in recent years to remove the shackles from their governing institutions, they still seem to reserve their greatest enthusiasm for constitutional amendments that keep their taxes low (the Property Tax Relief and Rollback Amendment of 1980 was adopted by an 81 percent majority) and their greatest disapprobation for perceived threats to public morality (a proposed casino gambling amendment in 1984 was defeated by 70 percent). It is much more difficult to attract voter interest in measures dealing with governing structure and procedures, and such measures often require repeated submissions before passage: the four-year gubernatorial term had been rejected six times before its ultimate adoption.[19]

In the immediate aftermath of the defeat of constitutional revision in 1970, the political scientist Robert Meriwether, executive director of Arkansans for the Constitution of 1970, offered the following grim explanation: "Another thing seems obvious: state constitutional revision—from the inception of the idea, through study commissions, legislative enactments, constitutional conventions, educational programs, ratification campaigns, or what have you—requires more political sophistication and maturity than any other type of political endeavor. Arkansas, in 1967–1970, just didn't have it." To the extent that diagnosis was accurate, and it was certainly a widely expressed one, the fact that Arkansans reacted even more negatively to constitutional revision in 1980 than they did in 1970 might suggest that the political climate, though somewhat more forward-looking than in the traditional period, is still more easily tilted to reaction than to reform.[20]

That judgment, however, must be tempered by other considerations. First, the electorates in many states other than Arkansas have shown immense caution and conservatism when presented with proposed new constitutions. Second, 1980 was an atypically conservative year in recent Arkansas politics, the only time in eleven gubernatorial elections between 1966 and 1986 when voters opted for the less progressive candidate. Finally, Arkansas voters have been demonstrating an increased willingness to revise some of the 1874 constitution's most archaic provisions. The pervasive antigovernmentalism that so strongly shaped the 1874 constitution is beginning to be replaced with a recognition that state government can be beneficial as well as mischievous and therefore needs the constitutional authority to service increased public needs and expectations.

## CHAPTER EIGHT

# The Power and Politics of the Executive Branch

*The multitude of responsibilities and duties carried out by an Arkansas governor places him at the center of the state's policy-making process.*

Robert Johnston and Dan Durning, "The Arkansas Governor's Role in the Policy Process, 1965–79," 1981

*In fact, the Arkansas Constitution may so severely limit the governor that the likelihood of one of them having a significant impact on history and events is greatly reduced.*

Cal Ledbetter, Jr., and C. Fred Williams, "Arkansas Governors in the Twentieth Century," 1982

The Arkansas governorship has been alternately described as an office of feeble incapacity and of towering strength. Since the framers of the 1874 constitution were not only antigovernmental but fiercely antigubernatorial, they deliberately designed a governorship of strictly limited powers: a two-year term; a meager salary specified in the constitution itself; executive power divided between the governor and other separately elected executives; and a veto that could be overridden by a simple majority of the legislature.

The two-year term became a four-year term beginning with the 1986 elections, and since the brief term has frequently been identified as the most debilitating feature of the Arkansas governorship, the extension potentially represents the single greatest enhancement of formal gubernatorial power. Still, the four-year term also applies to the other elected executives (who have increased from four to six since 1874); the constitutionally specified salary (though increased from $10,000 to $35,000 in 1976 and supplemented with a public relations allowance) remains the lowest in the United States; and the veto override majority remains unchanged. These and other factors have made the governorship a special object of constitutional reformers and have led to Arkansas's relatively low rankings in comparative studies of formal gubernatorial powers.[1]

Yet, as political scientists often acknowledge, and as any Arkansas citizen could substantiate, there is often, and there is in this instance, a great gap between formal power and actual influence. The governor is the central figure in the state's political system. Certainly he (to date all Arkansas governors have been male) is by far the most visible figure on the state's political scene. Louis Harris and other pollsters have repeatedly demonstrated that over 90 percent of a state's citizens can correctly identify their governor (as compared with 60 percent who can name one of their U.S. senators and even smaller percentages who can identify their congressman). Beyond simple name recognition is a tendency for many citizens to identify state government wholly with the incumbent governor. The results of a "consciousness-raising" quiz I administered for more than a decade to thousands of beginning state-and-local government students confirm this point. All students, always, have been able correctly to supply the governor's name; but beyond that most fundamental fact, there is absolute ignorance. No more than 5 percent have ever been able correctly to identify the lieutenant governor, the secretary of state, or any of the other elected executive officials, and certainly not to describe their duties. No more than 10 percent can name their own state senators or representatives. Only a handful of students—who attend a state university, drive automobiles licensed by the state over state-built roads, picnic in state parks, and ingeniously evade state liquor laws—have ever been able to specify three functions of Arkansas's state government. Their working knowledge of state government is almost exclusively limited to the identity of the governor, about whom most have strong evaluative sentiments.[2]

As will be emphasized, this singular visibility makes the governor both extremely influential and very vulnerable: there is no other likely object on whom to confer credit or cast blame for much of what happens within the state's borders, whether the governor was instrumental or not in the reaction-generating events. In terms of public familiarity, media focus, political clout, and policy imprint, the governor is the sun around which many lesser planets revolve.

Nevertheless, the portrait of gubernatorial impotence also has considerable legitimacy. Governors must convince an often indifferent public, critical press, and reluctant legislature of the correctness of gubernatorial initiatives; none may be ordered into submission or even acceptance. State agencies, especially those with independent constitutional status and/or powerful interest-group clientele, can remain supremely indifferent to the governor's alleged administrative authority. The governor's political base must be constantly nourished and courted or it will evaporate or migrate elsewhere. Furthermore, much of the gubernatorial agenda is set by forces—everything from natural disasters to international economics—far beyond his control.

The Arkansas governor has more influence than any other single actor in the state's political system, and both his formal and informal powers have been significantly strengthened in recent decades. The central questions, however, are whether the governor's actual powers are equal to the expectations surrounding this office and whether this institution has become a reliable and responsive mechanism through which citizens can effectuate their public service preferences. These questions can best be addressed after a review of contemporary gubernatorial functions, and of the powers and limitations inherent in each.

Most scholars who have analyzed the American governorship have found it useful to specify the various roles performed by governors, and there is considerable agreement in the literature on the parts today's governors are expected to play: chief administrator or manager; legislative leader; ceremonial chief of state; leader of public opinion; head of political party; chief crisis manager; and, increasingly, manager of intergovernmental relationships. This standard array differs somewhat from those recently articulated, in a very impromptu fashion, by Governor Bill Clinton after his first two years in office. Since the focus here is Arkansas, it seems best to employ those categories and titles that a contemporary Arkansas governor has identified.[3]


SUPER LEGISLATOR

Two months after a gubernatorial election, the state legislature meets for its biennial regular session. This session lasts no more than ninety days, but it may set the tone for the entire gubernatorial term, and governors-elect therefore must spend most of their transition time preparing for it. Unlike the situation in traditional Arkansas politics, when the winner of the Democratic gubernatorial primary, certain of his November election, had leisurely months to prepare for the session, such planning must now await the general election outcome, giving a frantic aura to the brief transition period. Also unlike the past, when a governor's winning coalition was largely held together by patronage promises, which then preoccupied the transition, today's governors-elect turn first attention to policy rather than personnel considerations.[4]

Most specifically, a governor-elect must give first attention to the budget that the legislature will shortly be adopting and that will guide state spending for the next two years. By the time of the general election, the Legislative Council has already begun reviewing agency requests and making its recommendations, and if a governor wants to have any impact on spending priorities, he must quickly inject his preferences into the process. The process and politics of state budget making will be analyzed extensively in chapter 13, so it is sufficient to note here that, although the public may be more interested in the first demonstrations of gubernatorial style, and nervous administrators and ambitious aspirants are more interested in personnel decisions, to most serious state attentives, and to the governor, budgetary decisions are those with the greatest substantive impact.

Aside from the budget, and probably chief among all of today's gubernatorial roles, is that of policy leadership. Theoretically, under the classic concept of separation of powers, it is up to legislative bodies to initiate and create public policy, the executive's job being simply to apply and administer whatever statutes are enacted. By mid-twentieth century, however, at every level of government, policy formulation had largely passed into the executive domain, which possesses superior resources of expertise, unity, popularity, and media focus. Executive policy formulation is especially likely in a state such as Arkansas, where the legislature, despite some dramatic improvements, remains a part-time and unprofessional institution.

The legislature is, of course, a critical obstacle between gubernatorial advocacy and official adoption, and the governor's legislative proposals must often be revised and trimmed to meet legislative objections. Since confrontation makes good copy, the clashes between the governor and the legislature claim much of the media's attention. In fact, however, Arkansas governors have become both more active and more successful in their legislative leadership role. One recent analysis of the Arkansas governor's role in the policy process concluded that, especially since 1965, governors have initiated more legislation over a broader range of subjects than did their predecessors, and that from 1957 to 1979 all governors except Winthrop Rockefeller steered at least three-fourths of their major policy proposals successfully through the legislature. Evaluations since 1979 report equal or greater batting averages.[5]

Success rates are even higher at special sessions, sometimes aptly called governor's sessions, since they may be convened only upon the governor's call. Only after the legislature has dealt with the items listed by the governor, and then only upon a two-thirds vote of both houses, may they deal with other matters for a period not to exceed fifteen days. Special sessions were once a rarity (only one was called between 1880 and 1907) but have recently become commonplace, averaging at least one per gubernatorial term for the past quarter century. With many legislators inconvenienced by this unplanned interruption in their income-producing occupations, governors usually find an assembly anxious to deal quickly with the gubernatorial agenda and return to their private pursuits.

Even in regular sessions, however, gubernatorial preferences tend to prevail, and that is somewhat surprising. Unlike their counterparts in many other states, Arkansas governors no longer have any voice in selection of legislative leadership or in making committee assignments. Unlike governors in competitive-party states, who can muster the automatic support of most of their fellow partisans on major policy thrusts, political party is almost meaningless in terms of gubernatorial-legislative relationships in Arkansas. (Rockefeller's failures with the Democratic-dominated legislature had much more to do with the perceived liberality of his proposals to an as-yet unreformed legislature and the ineptness of his personal dealings with legislators than with partisan differences per se, as Frank White's general success with a very modest legislative package in an equally Democratic-dominated legislature tends to confirm.) Governors cannot introduce bills; that can be done only by representatives and senators. Gubernatorial bills receive no priority treatment in the senate, and the priority scheduling they have enjoyed in the house for the last twenty years was canceled by a change in house rules in 1985. Furthermore, the simple majority (unlike the extraordinary majority of two-thirds or three-fourths in forty-four states) required to override a gubernatorial veto might logically weaken the governor's legislative leadership.[6]

In fact, however, the veto power is a strong one, and governors have a host of informal powers that more than compensate for their modest arsenal of formal powers. The strength of the gubernatorial veto is suggested by the infrequency with which it has been overridden. From 1958 to 1983 there were only fourteen overrides, an average of less than 1 percent. Eleven occurred during Rockefeller's tempestuous legislative sessions, and of the remaining three overrides, two occurred with explicit or tacit gubernatorial consent. Of course, at least some bills are introduced by legislators simply to placate constituents or organized interests; the sponsoring legislator knows (and even hopes) they will be vetoed, thereby protecting the public from bad policy while giving the legislator credit for having tried. Conversely, governors customarily notify sponsoring legislators of their intent to veto, thereby giving legislators the opportunity to withdraw bills in instances where the veto would be genuinely embarrassing. Despite the simple majority requirement for overrides, then, the veto power is a strong one, so formidable in fact that usually the mere threat of its exercise is sufficient to stop a bill's progress.[7]

Much of the strength of the gubernatorial veto relates to timing. During the session, the governor has five days to sign or to veto legislation presented to him, and if he does neither, the bill becomes law. On bills presented during the last five days of the session, as many are, the governor has twenty days from the date of adjournment to act, by which time legislators have returned to their respective homes. Furthermore, Arkansas's governor (like most governors but unlike the president) has the item veto on appropriations bills, that is, he can selectively negate particular expenditures within a general spending measure. The veto power, then, does enhance the governor's capacity for legislative leadership. Still, it is something of a penultimate weapon, which works more by its mere existence than by actual usage.

Far more useful in the ordinary course of exerting legislative influence is the governor's capacity to strengthen or weaken a legislator's relationship with his or her constituency. In the past, this largely revolved around how many jobs and how many roads a legislator could secure for the district; with most state jobs now removed from the spoils system, and roads built where the Highway Commission determines, these are no longer such significant coins of exchange in the legislative-gubernatorial relationship. Nevertheless, governors still make more than 500 appointments annually to a multitude of boards and commissions, and legislators are anxious to secure a "fair share" of these prestigious prizes for their district. Also, gubernatorial recommendations can be critical in securing funding for or deciding on the placement of state facilities, and these material testaments to a legislator's influence are a much larger component of constituent evaluations of legislative effectiveness than are voting records. Additionally, the governor's discretionary authority over the awarding of some federal funds, especially community development grants, has augmented the persuasive devices in the gubernatorial arsenal. During the legislative session, a cadre of temporary gubernatorial aides vigorously works the legislature, ascertaining what the particular price for legislative cooperation might be, and distributing the gubernatorial loaves and fishes accordingly. The following account of one 1985 gubernatorial-legislative exchange is indicative of many others:

> The sources said Mr. Clinton told Hogue he'd "done everything for Jonesboro except move the state Capitol up there," and he expected more support from Jonesboro-area legislators in return. Mr. Clinton has appointed Hogue to be his House representative on the Legislative Council, a key appointment, as well as keeping a campaign commitment to Craighead County by appointing Dalton Farmer of Jonesboro to the powerful Highway Commission. The source said Mr. Clinton also reminded Hogue that he'd appointed a Jonesboro man, Fred Carter, to be adjutant general of the Arkansas National Guard and had promised to provide funding for construction of a convocation center–gymnasium at Arkansas State University in Jonesboro.[8]

Unique to Arkansas is another addition to gubernatorial strength: his "gift" from the State Racing Commission of 10,000 free passes to the Oaklawn Park race track at Hot Springs. With such a pass, the regular admission fee of one dollar is waived, a cost that might seem inconsequential for anyone planning a day at the races. This, however, is a matter of pride rather than pocketbook. Anyone who cannot casually display these coveted demonstrations of "insider" status at the local coffee shop risks public disgrace. Legislators, who receive less than 100 of these magic markers, can secure additional supplies from the governor if they are in his good graces, thereby enhancing their own prestige with clamoring constituents. Both the state press and bemused aides have speculated, only semifacetiously, that racing passes may have passed more gubernatorial bills than any other factor (and they are *the* most frequent cause for calls to the gubernatorial transition office).[9]

Finally tipping the balance in the executive's favor are his political clout and public stature. Unlike many legislators, no contemporary Arkansas governor merely walks into office. He gets there only after a campaign trial by fire that severely tests and hones his abilities to assemble an effective organizational apparatus, to employ the media effectively, and to shape an attractive and appealing leadership image. Governors, if they wish, can share their political resources with legislators who find themselves cross-pressured between interest group or other demands and gubernatorial preferences. This was Governor Bumpers sales pitch, for example, in persuading reluctant legislators to vote for a substantial income tax increase in 1971: "I doubt that a vote for this tax will cause you opposition because it will likely be forgotten by next year's election. Should it cause problems, however, I personally will call my friends in your district (many of whom are not presently your friends) and see that they give you all possible assistance in your re-election campaign."[10]

As has been aptly observed, "When it comes to getting support for policies in the legislature, a governor who has the support of public opinion is tough to beat on the important issues"; and Arkansas governors have proven themselves adept at bringing that public opinion to bear on legislators. This is not a new development. Governor Faubus, for example, in building the legislative majority for a sales tax increase in 1957, made personal phone calls to supporters in wavering legislators' districts to ensure that the first few people a legislator encountered on weekend trips home from the session would be prominent local personages who would express their strong support for the tax. Today's governors use today's technology: computers, fed with campaign lists of donors and workers, address and print letters to tens of thousands of gubernatorial "friends" urging immediate contact with legislators in behalf of the governor's legislative program; and legislators are quickly inundated with calls and letters or see blue ribbons (a gimmick promoting Clinton's "blue-ribbon" education program) suddenly sprouting in constituents' lapels. Legislators know that these displays of public support are orchestrated but are reluctant to flout that relatively small portion of the population that is attentive to legislative decisions and that is politically active.[11]

Success in the superlegislator role is also due to a more receptive legislature than traditional governors usually encountered. The "reapportionment revolution" of the 1960s meant that governors and legislators now share somewhat common constituencies. Together with many of the previously described changes in the state's political environment, these developments have produced more of a "new breed" of legislator, motivated by many of the same policy concerns that fuel today's governors. Another example from the Bumpers's years is illustrative in this respect. A freshman senator complained to Bumpers that he had consistently supported every administration bill but had received nothing tangible for his constituents in return. "True," Bumpers replied, "but did you ever vote for anything you didn't think was right?" That kind of exchange is still rare, but it would have been unthinkable in the past, when the gubernatorial-legislative relationship was based exclusively on material quid pro quo's.[12]

Most recent Arkansas governors have chosen to be policy activists, and they have ample powers to effectuate their role as superlegislators. Ironically, governors are much more limited in their executive functions.

### CHIEF ADMINISTRATOR

The 1874 constitution assigned to the governor the responsibility for "seeing that the laws are faithfully executed" and also established that the "supreme executive power shall be vested in a Governor." Other and later provisions, however, divided the executive power among other elected officials, took away the word "supreme," gave constitutionally independent status to two major state agencies (the Game and Fish Commission in 1944, the Highway Commission in 1952), and established appointive "buffer" boards with lengthy, staggered terms in between the governor and all educational, penal, and charitable institutions.[13] This fragile formal base for the governor's administrative authority might have been inconsequential when a few hundred employees, all working in the state capitol, provided some basic state services. By the 1980s, however, with more than 40,000 employees scattered throughout the capital city and around the state, providing a wide range of services out of a multibillion dollar budget, the governor's responsibilities as supervisor of the executive establishment had become much more complicated and compelling.

Arkansas, like most other states, has responded to the challenge of enlarged budgets and payrolls by somewhat strengthening the governor's managerial capacity. According to most analysts and most governors, however, here—where public expectations may be highest—powers are weakest. Governors, because they are identified as the "chief executive" and are also the public personification of state government, will be held accountable for the efficiency, courtesy, integrity, and competence of anyone working for the state. The governor's ability to influence the actions of state agencies and the behavior of state personnel, however, is considerably less than is commonly supposed.

An authoritative chief administrator requires adequate powers of fiscal management, supervisory control, and appointment and removal. With respect to fiscal or budgetary powers, timing, incrementalism, debt prohibitions, and constitutionally earmarked revenues all constrain the gubernatorial impact on state spending. Nevertheless, Arkansas has moved from a strictly legislative budget to one in which the governor's recommendations are weighty ones. It is with respect to supervisory control and appointment and removal that Arkansas governors are weaker than many other state's chief executives and less authoritative than the title of chief executive suggests.[14]

Supervisory control means the governor's ability to direct and oversee the operations of state agencies, to make his policies and priorities known throughout the bureaucracy, and to secure acquiescence to them. Since any administrator's span of effective control is limited, this process works best when related functions (everything regarding health or energy or the environment) are integrated into a limited number of departments, each with a single director who reports to the governor and is accountable to him. A giant step from complete chaos toward this administrative ideal was taken in 1971, when Act 38 consolidated sixty separate state agencies into thirteen major departments, each with a single director reporting to (though not in all cases solely selected by) the governor. Theoretically, this reversed the proliferation of separate state agencies, increased the governor's effective span of control, and provided the governor with a cabinet (the thirteen department heads) to be his accurate informants and loyal lieutenants in overseeing state government. Judging by the fury with which this plan was opposed by interest groups (who prefer administrative separatism, where they can directly influence agencies, bypassing the governor) and the regularity with which legislators (whose agency influence is also enhanced by administrative separatism) have attempted to dismantle the original consolidation, the governor's administrative authority was increased by this reorganization.

Still, the 1971 reorganization was in fact a very modest and limited one. Only two of the then-existing 180-plus state agencies were abolished; the consolidations that did take place were primarily in terms of "housekeeping" functions (centralized purchasing, personnel, and budgeting) rather than rule making or policy authority; the plan left hundreds of boards and commissions of varying stature and authority running around loose; and the original thirteen major departments had escalated up to eighteen by 1985. These factors, plus the separate election of six other executive officials, give Arkansas governors one of the lowest comparative rankings in terms of formal administrative powers. Unsurprisingly, in a 1977 survey of state agency heads, only 21 percent of Arkansas respondents (compared with 38 percent nationally and up to 91 percent in some states) ranked the governor as having the greatest influence among state political actors on departmental programs and objectives.[15]

Probably the greatest administrative insufficiency stems from the powers of appointment and removal. To be a forceful administrator one must have the authority to assemble one's own administrative team of top subordinates, people who share the governor's policy preferences, will be responsive to his managerial directives, and will be political allies rather than adversaries. Such powers are universally granted to corporate chief executives, to football coaches, and to some state governors; but Arkansas governors find themselves surrounded by many important "subordinates" who are not of their choosing or whose choice is surrounded by compromising complications.

The other six executives are directly elected by the voters: the lieutenant governor, secretary of state, attorney general, auditor, treasurer, and land commissioner run their own separate campaigns and manage their own operations absolutely distinct from the governor afterward. Unlike twenty-two other states, where the governor and lieutenant governor run as a team, there is no team-ticketing of the governor with the one who will take his place when he is out of the state or leaves the office. Also unlike many other states where the lieutenant governorship is a prime stepping-stone to the governorship, and therefore a potentially dangerous rival, only one elected Arkansas governor to date was a previously elected lieutenant governor. A far greater likelihood of division and rivalry is that between the governor and the attorney general: of the last five attorneys general, four have made a bid for the governorship, and they are understandably more interested in their own political visibility than in assisting the governor in running his ship of state.[16]

Of those who do constitute the governor's "cabinet," most are selected by the governor (or nominated by a board to the governor) and can be dismissed by him. They, however, like all appointees, require senate confirmation, which may require extensive lobbying and consideration of powerful senators' preferred choices. Furthermore, because of the longstanding practice of statutorily specifying certain qualifications for many administrative positions, governors must either narrow their choices to those with the requisite residence or occupational backgrounds or try to change the requirement. In 1979 Clinton had first to get the law changed requiring the state health director to have practiced medicine in Arkansas for seven years before he could hire the West Virginian with special expertise in rural health care whom he desired.

Most frustrating of all are the numerous "buffer boards" and the constitutionally independent agencies. Shielded from the governor by their own sources of revenue, and headed by directors selected by their governing commissions, the Game and Fish Commission and the State Highway and Transportation Department, which receive about 20 percent of all state revenues, march to their own drummers. Despite gubernatorial opposition, the Game and Fish Commission has gone directly to the people with special requests for more revenues, and the independence and power of the long-time director of Highways are legendary. Because in the minds of many Arkansans roads are the most important benefit the state provides, many legislators are much more anxious to please the Highway Commission than the governor. As one legislator recently observed, "I'd rather have a high-way commissioner than a governor from Craighead County."[17]

The buffer boards, consisting of five, seven, or ten members with staggered five, seven, or ten-year terms, were deliberately designed to keep governors (most of whom have served two two-year terms) from ever capturing a majority on the board and therefore from ever being able to dominate any of the institutions so governed. The device has generally protected these institutions from what were once the unsettling ravages of the spoils system. They have also meant, however, that a governor who wishes to make innovations and improvements in nursing home operations or educational television or the prisons may have to overcome the wishes of hundreds of individuals appointed by his gubernatorial predecessors to do so. Governor Pryor, in a moment of deep frustration, once mused, "What this state needs most is a few good funerals." In the absence of such divine intervention, members of boards and commissions can be removed only for a criminal offense involving moral turpitude, gross dereliction of duty, or gross abuse of authority, in substantiating which the governor has the burden of proof (Act 160 of 1979).[18]

In practice, of course, many administrators offer their resignations to incoming governors, or finally find themselves so frozen out from gubernatorial access that they get the message and step down. In practice also, however, many administrators chosen as the governor's own people soon "go native," that is, become increasingly more responsive to pressures from their agency employees and clientele groups than to the governor. For these and other reasons, the cabinet has not been extensively used by recent governors, who rely instead on gubernatorial staff members with specific agency liaison assignments to keep them informed of problems and to convey gubernatorial directives.[19]

The once absolute authority of incoming governors to fire all state employees and replace them with their own people has gradually been modified by both law and custom. Technically, only about one-fourth of all state employees (compared with three-fourths nationally) are fully covered by a merit system. In practice, however, most state jobs have been removed from the realm of easy patronage. Permanent expectations began under Governor Faubus's extraordinarily long twelve-year tenure; Governor Rockefeller's promise to the people was one of state professionalism, which precluded any massive firings; Governor Bumpers's election took place without the assistance and often over the opposition of those who traditionally demanded jobs in return for support. By the time Governor Pryor took office in 1975, new expectations of permanence and professionalism had set in, and despite occasional charges that Governor Clinton had engaged in more blatantly political hiring and firing than any of his immediate predecessors, at the middle and lower echelons, most state jobs are now immune from gubernatorial turnover. Since the policy consequences of such positions are often negligible, and governors have many more consequential demands on their time, this is probably a net plus for gubernatorial power.[20]

Governors must still devote an extraordinary amount of time (Bumpers and Pryor estimated as much as one-fourth of their working hours) to making more than five hundred appointments annually to hundreds of boards and commissions. At the level of the Highway Commission or State Board of Education, careful selections are critical to a governor's administration and well worth the time expended. For every such major appointment, however, there are scores to be made to such entities as the Oil Museum Advisory Commission, the State Capitol Cafeteria Commission, and the Committee for Purchases of Workshop-Made Products. Since for even the most obscure position there are always more aspirants than openings, one recent study, based on extensive interviews with governors and their aides, concluded that these appointments were so excessive as to be counterproductive: "At the lower levels, where the vast majority of appointments are made, the decision-making process is elaborate and exhausting, the policy consequences may be negligible, and the political consequences are frequently a net minus."[21]

Because the four-year term, and particularly election to more than one four-year term, will give future Arkansas governors the opportunity to secure a majority of "their" people on all boards and commissions, some have predicted a significant strengthening of gubernatorial administrative authority: "A governor will no longer be in a position where it is necessary to spend one year learning the job and the next year campaigning for reelection. With a four-year term and the freedom from constant campaigning that this brings, a governor can be a full time executive for three years instead of one and can spend at least part of that time managing the state."[22]

Perhaps so, but it would take more than a strengthened appointive power and a more leisurely schedule to make the governor's administrative authority equal to popular expectations surrounding it, as those governors long endowed with four-year terms would substantiate. A study made in 1948 of the Arkansas governor's agenda suggested that only 10 percent of his time was spent on being chief administrator. Contemporary governors give more of their time to administrative matters, but they are still more likely to engage in "sporadic intervention" and "crisis management" than continuous direction and control. Enormous political credit and energy must be expended to make even the slightest changes in the bureaucratic establishment, and there are few political rewards for simply being a more competent manager. Few contemporary governors, then, are willing to give the chief administrator role their foremost attention.[23]

HANDLER OF EMERGENCIES

Willingly or not, most governors will find their time and attention intermittently consumed by the eruption of crises. The constitution makes the Arkansas governor commander-in-chief of the state militia and gives him the power to call out the national guard to "execute laws, repel invasion, repress insurrection and preserve the public peace."

By the late twentieth century, invasions and insurrections were unlikely. On numerous occasions, however, governors have used the National Guard to assist citizens during and after natural disasters and to preserve order in potentially explosive situations. Most memorably, Governor Faubus mobilized the Guard at the onset of Central High School's integration in 1957, arguing that riots were imminent. More recently, Governor Pryor used National Guardsmen to take the place of striking firemen in Pine Bluff, and Governor Clinton used them to reinforce federal security measures when a thousand Cuban refugees stormed past the barricades at Fort Chaffee and to preclude violence from erupting at a Ku Klux Klan meeting in Little Rock in 1979.

In one sense, emergencies are empowering situations. Administrative agencies respond most expeditiously in life-threatening circumstances, strengthening the concept of chief executive; and extensive media coverage of the governor directing the troops, hovering in a helicopter to inspect crop damage, or wading into floods to comfort victims reinforces the governor's leadership image. Furthermore, governors now have a $500,000 emergency fund at their disposal, subject only to a usually routine legislative advice procedure.

Emergencies are also potentially emasculating situations, as Governor Clinton learned when a cumulation of crises (tornadoes, drought, a national recession, a Nuclear One plant spill, a Titan II missile explosion, and especially the influx of Cuban refugees) ultimately enervated his leadership image. Who lives by the sword dies by the sword. A governor who overplays his role as hero, constantly riding out to protect "his" people against the forces of evil, can appear ineffectual when the problems are intractable. As modern technology multiplies the list of life-threatening hazards, so the Handler of Emergencies role becomes more potent and more risky, especially because many of today's crises precipitate extensive and often frustrating relationships with the federal government.[24]

### NATIONAL INTERMEDIARY

Governors have always been the focal point in the various horizontal (state-to-state) and vertical (nation-state, state-local) relationships necessitated by the American federal system. Until recently, however, this role was a rather limited one involving requests for extradition (the return of fugitives from justice who have fled a state's jurisdiction), handling occasional border disputes with neighboring states, and an annual trip to the National Governor's Conference. National government concerns were largely left to the state's delegation in the U.S. Congress, and state-local relationships revolved around providing sufficient jobs and roads to satisfy the courthouse crowd.

Now, especially with the explosive growth of federal aid to state and local governments in recent decades, the governor's responsibilities as chief lobbyist and negotiator for the state have multiplied astronomically. The nature and politics of Arkansas's contemporary federal relationships will be explored at length in chapter 11. What is important to note here is the extent to which these relationships are primarily the governor's responsibility. As with the chief executive role, public expectations are high: get our state's fair share of federal funds, get quick federal disaster aid in an emergency, make us look good to the world outside. They are also somewhat contradictory: pay first attention to Arkansas; don't go gallivanting around beyond our borders; don't let the federal government tell us how to manage our affairs; don't shine too much in the national press or we'll suspect you're more interested in promoting your political ambitions than in the state's well-being.

Since decisions made in Washington or Detroit or Taiwan or Tokyo can have enormous economic consequences in Arkansas, governors no longer have the option of remaining insular. Many of the governor's chief staff members have intergovernmental responsibilities, and governors must frequently exert themselves personally to capture the sympathetic attention of other actors (White House aides, congressional committee chairmen, federal power commissioners) in the federal system. Probably the only time when their extra-state efforts are safe from potential political criticism, however, is when they are explicitly devoted to seeking more jobs for Arkansans.

### PROMOTER OF ECONOMIC HEALTH

According to one recent study, southern governors have become "the de facto executive directors of the state chambers of commerce," and the behavior of recent Arkansas governors confirms this observation. In fact, Governor Clinton has estimated that this is his single most time-consuming task.[25]

As noted in earlier chapters, this role has long historical precedent. What is new, however, is the intensity with which economic development is pursued, and the extent to which gubernatorial campaigns now revolve around the job-creation theme, with all candidates spewing statistics on what has and has not been accomplished and which of their efforts will finally elevate Arkansas from its perenially low rankings into full-fledged economic prosperity. The emphasis is understandable: "more jobs and bigger payrolls" is a language everybody understands and applauds (with only a few cautionary objections from no-growth environmentalists chorusing in the background). Governors are never more popular than when they are announcing the coming of a major new industry or cutting the ribbon at a plant-opening ceremony, and legislators are especially cooperative in responding to governors' economic development initiatives.[26]

The problem, of course, is that as the campaign rhetoric has escalated, so have public expectations, and many—perhaps most—of the forces determining Arkansas's economic prosperity are far beyond the governor's sphere of influence. In 1982 a Winthrop Rockefeller Foundation report identified the two-year term as one of the twelve chief obstacles to Arkansas's economic development, arguing that any marked improvements required the time to plan and implement long-term economic policy, whereas the incentive under a two-year term was to go for quick fixes that looked good before the ever-looming next election. In a similar vein, one 1984 observer noted that it was tough to pursue a sensible industrial development policy when Arkansas had changed its director of industrial development seven times in the previous ten years.[27]

Even the lengthiest of gubernatorial terms and the most experienced of industrial development directors, however, cannot preclude competition from cheaper foreign imports (which cost Arkansas 49 percent of its total employment in textiles when three plants closed on one weekend in 1984) or other adverse by-products of complex international markets. Governors who promise too much can be hoist by their own rhetoric, but the exigencies of elections make this role an increasingly essential and tempting one.

## SYMBOL OF STATE

In contrast to the previous roles, in each of which the governor must share power with many others, when it comes to public attention, the governor reigns supreme. Whereas other participants in state politics and government must fight for whatever scraps of popular and media attention they receive, a gubernatorial press conference is an automatic draw, and the gubernatorial presence at any event elevates it to a major media happening. Because of the reflected glory a governor's presence presumably sheds upon events, he is bombarded with invitations to speak, preside, dedicate, inspect, and merely attend thousands of benefits, conventions, openings, rallies, commencements, and so on. Adept schedulers, then, may pick and choose those appearances that will best suit gubernatorial needs.

Some of these events take place out in and around the state. Others are constantly orchestrated in the resplendent gubernatorial conference room as the governor solemnly declares that it is Turnip Planting Week, or Registered Land Surveyors Week, or Gospel Music Month, or American Adopt-a-Grandparent Day, followed by much handshaking and picturetaking. The Governor's Mansion is not only the state-provided residence of the governor and his family but also a quasi-public place, where many charitable organizations hold their benefits and galas. These unceasing ceremonies mean that it is a rare day when the newspapers and nightly television broadcasts do not portray Arkansas's governor in some appealing pose: in a hardhat turning the first symbolic shovel of earth; in shirtsleeves welcoming workers to the mansion on Labor Day; handcuffed to a state trooper on law enforcement day; or cuddling a bunny during Rabbit Breeder's Week. Governor Clinton, for example, issued more than four hundred proclamations in 1985, most of them involving sheer ceremony.[28]

All of this constitutes much more than fun and foolishness. These "pics and procs" are a constant reminder to citizens of their governor's identity and symbolic association with the state, and they offer boundless opportunities for the governor to cement his relationships with the citizenry while pressing for and propagandizing his priorities and policies. The governors of all states employ their ceremonial obligations to create favorable public images and opinions, but according to one study, an activist approach is especially characteristic of governors with weak or moderate formal powers, who can "use their public role to overcome the lack of other more formal powers at their command."[29]

While most nineteenth-century Arkansas governors followed what has been described as the Whig tradition of a dignified and somewhat passive chief of state, by the early twentieth century Jeff Davis refused to "refrain from stirring up emotion in politics. He saw the possibilities which the office offered for dramatizing if not achieving reform." It remained for contemporary governors, however, to use the office systematically and deliberately for dramatizing and publicizing and to employ today's technology to do so.[30]

Public opinion polls and television commercials had become part of the Arkansas election scene by the 1960s. By the 1980s, they were being employed in governance as well. Governor Clinton used television commercials to remind people of his accomplishments after the 1983 and 1985 legislative sessions and radio commercials to urge people to call their legislators and express support for teacher testing during the 1985 session. Furthermore, again reaching a climax with Governor Clinton, polling is now done throughout a gubernatorial term, and those surveys are at least one influential factor in deciding the political tactics if not the substance of policy development.

There is something deeply disturbing about the concept of a professional pollster in Texas or New Jersey having any influence in public policy decisions for the state of Arkansas. The practice seems faintly Machiavellian, with ominous overtones of Orwellianism; and quite naturally governors deny that their decisions are ever governed by polling results.

There is, however, a curious irony here. To the extent that contemporary governors do in fact "look to the polls as the Greeks consulted the oracle at Delphi," they may know more about, and hence give more weight to, public sentiments and preferences than was ever true in Arkansas's political past. If that information is used to shape what has previously been described as transformational or educative leadership, it could prove beneficial. On the other hand, if polls are used to avoid the controversial and unpopular, to refine the gubernatorial capacity only for clever transactional leadership, then extensive reliance upon them could clearly have a chilling effect upon democratic dialogue and competition.[31]

For better or worse, then, contemporary Arkansas governors are the chief symbol of the state and have unparalleled opportunities, enhanced by modern technology, for influencing popular opinion on public issues. There are no rivals for this role, nor any formal restraints upon it. There are, however, some very practical restraints and limits.

First, as suggested at the outset, to be visible is to be vulnerable, as typified in the commonly heard "and four cents for the governor" as the cash register rings up the sales tax. Since few citizens know more about state government than the name of the governor and the size of their state tax bill, the more noticeable the governor becomes, the more exposed he becomes to blame for taxes, spending, or other essential but unpopular state government activities.[32]

Second, because the governor is the state's personification, and because of what has been described as the profoundly personalized nature of Arkansas politics, the governor cannot possibly give of his personal time to all those who feel entitled to it. This is where a skilled gubernatorial staff is critical, which leads to the last major gubernatorial role.

## RUNNING THE GOVERNOR'S OFFICE

As the range and complexity of gubernatorial functions have increased, so have the size and intricacy of the governor's staff. Through the early 1960s, the staff consisted of seven to ten persons, mostly clerical and stenographic assistants. By 1985 there were nearly fifty persons on the governor's staff, most with professional responsibilities for policy development, agency liaison, constituent and intergovernmental relations. Because these are considered uniquely the governor's own employees, incoming governors, even when the transition is intraparty, sweep out the old staff and bring in an entirely new crew, whose only loyalty and accountability is to that particular incumbent. Under the chief of staff's management, thousands of calls and letters (invitations, recommendations, requests for jobs and honorary appointments, policy views, complaints about state agencies, questionnaires) receive responses, while other staff members initiate and generate policy, administrative suggestions, press coverage, and constituency contacts. Whatever the assorted professional responsibilities of individual staff members, all have specifically political functions as well.

Unquestionably, the growth in the governor's staff apparatus has been an empowering influence. No longer need the governor spend 75 percent of his time, as Governor Charles Brough complained was necessary, on decisions regarding pardons and paroles. Special aides can handle the most time-consuming aspects of this function. The author of a study made in 1948 of the Arkansas governor's schedule concluded that over 60 percent of a governor's visitors came to request jobs and other special favors, for social reasons, or as representatives of civic, church, and school organizations, a reflection not only of the time-consuming aspects of the old spoils system but of the absence of staff who could handle many of these matters in the governor's name. A routine function performed by a staff member, or at least adequately prepared by staff for gubernatorial decision, saves the governor's time for more useful matters, and is therefore a net plus.[33]

As always, however, every plus has its minuses. First, the expansion of the gubernatorial staff has created something of a minibureaucracy with personnel and supervisory problems of its own. Governor Pryor alluded to this problem in a postgubernatorial interview: "And a lot of times a public official will spend almost as much time keeping his staff and cabinet and the people he has around him happy as he does keeping his constituency happy."[34]

More important is a problem that may be unique to Arkansas, or at least to states like Arkansas still in transition between the old, small-scale, slow-paced, personalized atmosphere of traditional state government and the new, bigger, bureaucratized and more complex era. Tens of thousands of people in Arkansas feel that they have a personal claim to the governor's time, and cannot be satisfied by any staff aide, no matter how efficiently the aide performs the requested function or favor. Surely in most other states a local road dispute, a county committee contest, a rumored divorce, a child's school problems, do not necessitate a chat with the governor—but they often do in Arkansas. Surely in most other states those who find themselves in the state capital on business or pleasure do not feel compelled or entitled to drop by the governor's office for an impromptu visit—but that frequently occurs in Arkansas. Surely in other states a power failure does not precipitate midnight calls to the Governor's Mansion for assistance in getting the electricity turned back on—but that is still the pattern in Arkansas. And staff aides who are overly protective of the governor's time and schedule can create sticky political backlash as word spreads that "you can't get through to the governor."

Gubernatorial staff members must not only make thousands of politically sensitive decisions about the most appropriate use of the governor's time but must also deal with a fervent belief in gubernatorial omnipotence. One of the most frequently heard phrases is, "If the governor would just pick up the phone," the assumption being that then his will would be done. It is up to the governor's staff, who helped create these heightened expectations of gubernatorial forcefulness during the campaign, to explain the limits of the office to disbelieving action seekers after the campaign is over.

In identifying and describing this role, Clinton also candidly admitted how thoroughly he mishandled it in his first administration. In assembling an effective staff, he learned, it was most important to find people "who are not only good at government, but good at making people feel good." Managing the governor's office does not appear in political science literature as a major gubernatorial role, but in Arkansas it is a critical one.[35]

AN ANALYSIS

Having reviewed contemporary gubernatorial functions, and the powers and limitations encountered in each of these roles, we can now return to the questions raised at the outset. Are the Arkansas governor's powers equal to the demands of modern governance? Has the governorship become a reliable and responsive link between citizen preferences and governmental action?

First, regarding gubernatorial power it seems fair to conclude that while the formal strengths of an Arkansas governor are comparatively modest, the actual power and influence of that office are far greater than those of any other single actor in the state's political system. The most serious incapacities are those involving what was intended to be the governor's preeminent role as chief executive. The governor's role as legislative leader has expanded far beyond original expectations, however, and additional functions regarding economic development, intergovernmental relationships, crisis management, and policy and opinion leadership have all combined to give the governor unrivaled centrality in both politics and governance. This review also suggests that much of the governor's power is somewhat fragile and illusory, based as much or more on the political skills, personal energy, staff competence, and perceived popularity of the incumbent as on constitutional provisions and legal authority. A person of modest talents, average vigor, and little charisma might well find the insufficiency of formal power incapacitating.

Since much of state government's vitality depends upon the governorship, and this in turn depends heavily upon the personal aptitudes of those who hold the office, it is important to understand which individuals are most likely to seek and to obtain the office. Thus far, all of Arkansas's forty-one governors have been white male Protestants, and most (thirty-one) have been lawyers. From 1948 to 1984 the average age of the governor at first election was 44, a younger age than the national norm of 47.4, and if the two Republican governors who were both in their 50s are excluded from this analysis, the average age is a very youthful 40. In fact, when Bill Clinton (33), Steve Clark (31), and Paul Reviere (30) were elected in 1978 to the positions of governor, attorney general, and secretary of state, there was much talk about a baby brigade taking over at the state capitol.[36]

In part what this relative youthfulness reflects is the fact that, unlike the situation in many other states, where aspiring politicians are expected to slowly ascend the political ladder, paying their dues and proving themselves at each rung, Arkansas politics—especially because of the traditional weakness of political parties—is highly porous, accessible to anyone with the ambition to enter it at any level. While in most states governors are usually chosen from the ranks of those with previous state legislative experience (52.4 percent nationally) or in statewide elective office (27.3 percent nationally) only one of Arkansas's last ten governors served in the state legislature (David Pryor, a state representative from 1961 to 1966), and only one held a previous statewide elective office (Bill Clinton, attorney general from 1977 to 1978). Governors Faubus and Bumpers were defeated in earlier attempts for the state legislature, and Pryor's state legislative background was dimmed by six intervening years in the U.S. Congress.[37]

In fact, looking at those who have governed Arkansas for the last thirty years, one is struck by what seems to be the dissimilarity of their backgrounds and career paths to the governorship: a hill county newspaper publisher, a transplanted New York multimillionaire businessman, a small-town trial lawyer and cattle rancher, a former state legislator and congressman, a law professor, and a savings and loan executive. If there is no standard career path to the governorship, is there some common attraction that the office offers to a variety of potential candidates?

Certainly none was attracted, as in earlier times in Arkansas some were, by the salary. (In 1923, when the office paid $4,000 annually, one gubernatorial hopeful bemoaned the estimated cost of a race in his diary as follows: "It is a sad day for civic righteousness when one has to spend more than 4 years salary to get into office." What might he have thought of spending more than twenty-five times what the office paid to obtain it?) Nor has the governorship been a particularly reliable stepping-stone to higher office. Of eight twentieth-century governors who attempted to move up to the U.S. Senate, four were successful and four were not.[38]

Rather, what seems to have attracted most of Arkansas's recent governors to the office was the unparalleled opportunities it offers for making things happen, for being at the political center, for making a difference in the capacities and image of the state and in the lives of its citizens. California Speaker Jesse Unruh once attempted to explain political ambition as follows: "Until you've been in politics you've never really been alive. It's the only sport for grownups, all other games are for kids." In the Arkansas context, all but gubernatorial politics are essentially games for kids. If, as has been suggested, political change and progress depends uniquely on gubernatorial initiatives, and if gubernatorial effectiveness in turn depends heavily upon the personal drive and forcefulness that individual incumbents bring to that office, there may be some comfort in the likelihood that only those individuals with the strongest ambitions are likely to seek and obtain the office. That such individuals always offer potential dangers to the body politic should also be obvious.[39]

There remains the question of the extent to which the office has become an effective mechanism through which Arkansas citizens, for whom little such linkage existed in the past, can express and implement their will. Because of the vigorous competition involved in gubernatorial elections, a competition that now involves partisan and broad policy differences as well as personality contests, there does seem to be the opportunity for an increasingly participatory citizenry with heightened expectations about state services to articulate their general political values in choosing one candidate over others. Furthermore, if the modern techniques of opinion research are used for public-regarding purposes, today's governors have the opportunity to serve as a critical catalyst between public preferences and policy results.

In one recent comprehensive study of Arkansas governors from 1900 to 1970, the conclusion was reached that none had been "great," that six of the sixteen could be classified as "good," that most had been "average." It is too early to determine whether Arkansas's more recent governors will skew such evaluations upward. It is clear, however, that this office that was once strong only by default, strong simply because it was less weak than any other position in a totally fragmented political system, has now become the potential source of transformational as well as transactional leadership. Whether it will be consistently or even occasionally used for those purposes is, of course, unpredictable.[40]

Furthermore, although the governorship is the mightiest force in state politics, the executive remains only one of three branches of government. Both the legislative and judicial branches have also strengthened their capacity to deal with contemporary issues, but they have not embraced the late twentieth century so enthusiastically or comprehensively as has the executive.

## CHAPTER NINE

# The Power and Politics of the Legislative Branch

*These observations . . . provide the basis for concluding that the Arkansas General Assembly does display adequate conditions for legislative accountability. In light of Arkansas' recent past this is certainly a source of satisfaction to those of us committed to democratic practices.*

Donald E. Whistler and Charles DeWitt Dunn, "Institutional Accountability in the Arkansas General Assembly," 1983

*It is hard for a legislator to look past his or her constituency. It takes a very special legislator to do anything but worry about himself and there aren't very many who do.*

Dennis Robertson, Arkansas Farm Bureau Association, 1983

State historians have not attempted to rank Arkansas legislatures as they have governors, but it seems fair to say that if few governors achieved very impressive records of achievement, their efforts still shine in contrast to those of the legislatures with which they dealt. Indeed, the institutional ineffectiveness of the legislative branch is a constant thread in Arkansas political history from the 1830s through the 1960s.[1]

Unlike the governorship, which began the twentieth century in the straitjacket imposed by the 1874 constitution, the legislature brought at least some of its institutional disabilities upon itself. The constitution did establish a biennial session not to exceed sixty days but permitted the legislature to extend the session by a two-thirds vote in both chambers and to set their own compensation. By 1901 the legislature had extended its meeting to 107 days, by 1907 to 117 days, and by 1909 to 145 days, all at a per diem expense rate. Especially because much of their time was spent on purely local legislation (for example, regulating the number and place of train stops) and also because of constant exposés of bribery and coercion by railroad, insurance, liquor, and other lobbyists, the patience of the people snapped, and they used their new power of the constitutional initiative to slap on the handcuffs. Amendment 5, ratified by a 78 percent majority in 1912, provided a payment of six dollars per diem for the first sixty days of a session, three dollars per diem for the first fifteen days of extraordinary sessions, and nothing thereafter.

Four subsequent amendments over the decades have raised legislative salaries, additional statutes have provided supplementary compensation and benefits, and few sessions in recent decades have concluded their work within the sixty-day limit. Nevertheless, the concept of a limited legislature with part-time pay for part-time work still prevails. Indeed, until 1973, the legislature simply ceased to exist at the close of the brief biennial session: no professional staff, no ongoing committees, and no permanent legislative leaders maintained the institutional presence of the legislature in the interim. And, again until recent reforms, the sessions were destined to be nonproductive. Each new term brought a large proportion of newcomers who wandered in bewilderment through a raucous and undisciplined atmosphere in which lobbyists swarmed on the chamber floors (and frequently joined in the voting), bills were scheduled or buried at whim through mysterious manipulations, committees and committee assignments were so numerous as to be meaningless, and whatever real business the legislature accomplished was worked out in late-night (and frequently liquorish) sessions in downtown hotel rooms.[2]

The state press occasionally fulminated against the boodle and booze, and a few citizen reform groups sometimes protested, but there is little to suggest that legislators themselves were embarrassed by their ineffectiveness or that citizens really expected the legislature to do much more than it did. Nor was this situation unique to Arkansas. As the Citizens' Conference on State Legislatures aptly observed in 1973, "We have never really wanted our state legislatures to amount to much, and they have obliged us." Furthermore, there were at least some in Arkansas who greatly preferred and deliberately perpetuated a passive rather than interventionist assembly. As V. O. Key pointed out, Arkansas's atomized politics made it possible "to elect a fire-eating governor who promises great accomplishments and simultaneously to elect a legislature a majority of whose members are committed to inaction," a situation that "gives great negative power to those with a few dollars to invest in legislative candidates . . . and redounds to the benefit of the upper brackets."[3]

The aura of inaction was further guaranteed by apportionment schemes that overweighted the votes and influence of rural areas at the expense of a slowly urbanizing and more action-oriented citizenry. The constitutional guarantee (Article 8) of one representative to each of seventy-five counties, with the other twenty-five to be apportioned on the basis of population after each decennial census, as were to be all thirty-five senate districts, ensured a slight rural bias; but this bias was enhanced by the legislature's refusal to reapportion itself at all from 1890 to 1936 (when a citizen-initiated constitutional amendment gave the apportionment power to a nonlegislative Board of Apportionment) and by the continued guarantee of at least one representative to each county in that and a subsequent 1956 amendment, which also froze existing senate districts permanently in place. Until federal court-ordered reapportionment in 1965, state legislators represented from 4,927 to 31,641 persons, with the result that 35.7 percent of the population could elect a majority of the lower house.[4]

By the 1970s and into the 1980s, all representatives and senators were elected by approximately equal numbers of citizens (22,000 in the average house district, 64,000 in senate districts), and all senators and 74 of the 100 representatives are now elected from single-member districts. In the strictly numerical sense, then, today's legislature is much more representative than it was in the past. Of equal or greater importance is that equitable apportionment, plus the rising power in the 1960s of the dissident backbenchers known as the Young Turks, buoyed by an increasingly reformist atmosphere as reflected in Winthrop Rockefeller's and Dale Bumpers's elections over old guard opposition, finally led to structural and procedural reforms. In 1971 the General Assembly created a special committee to make a comprehensive study of the legislature and report its findings to the 1973 session. The Committee on Legislative Organization employed the Eagleton Institute of Politics to assist with the study, and the subsequent adoption of most of its major recommendations has contributed to a dramatically upgraded legislative operation.[5]

The atmosphere in which the legislature conducts its business has become much more dignified and disciplined. Both lobbyists and liquor have been officially banished from the chamber floors, and the occasional hog calling or fiddle playing is a rare tension-reliever rather than a routine occurrence. Committees have been drastically reduced from more than sixty to ten standing subject committees in each chamber, with the five A committees and five B committees meeting on alternate mornings so that legislators can attend all meetings of the two major committees to which they are assigned and still attend all afternoon chamber sessions. Furthermore, these committees are now authorized to meet during the interim between sessions to study problems and shape legislation before the hectic session begins. The Legislative Council, established in 1949 both as a legislative committee for presession review of budget requests and as a legislative reference bureau, now offers a fifty-person Bureau of Legislative Research, providing professional staff assistance to the interim committees and to individual legislators. The legislators themselves are markedly more devoted to their responsibilities, and most are more likely to spend their evenings poring through the contents of bulging briefcases than pouring down drinks in hotel bars.

THE LEGISLATORS

The only formal requirements for seeking a two-year term in the house or a four-year term in the senate are those of age (twenty-one for the house, twenty-five for the senate) and residence (at least two years in the state, one year in the legislative district). Informally, however, judging by those actually elected to the General Assembly, citizens prefer middle-aged legislators (in their mid-forties to early fifties) who have been longtime residents of the area they represent. In the 1983 assembly, over 80 percent of the lawmakers were born in Arkansas, and of those few who were not, all but eight had been born in a neighboring state. Furthermore, two-thirds of the legislators were representing either the county in which they were born (55 percent) or a contiguous county (12 percent). In the sense of having roots deep in the particular areas that they serve, Arkansas legislators are highly representative of their constituents.[6]

Legislators also reflect the predominant Protestant preferences of the state. From 1957 to 1965, for example, only 11 Catholics and 2 Jews were elected, compared with 650 Protestants. Unlike some turn-of-the-century legislatures where ministers comprised one-fifth of the membership, ministers have become very rare, never more than 2 in recent sessions. Nevertheless, religiosity is still an important qualification: never do more than 2 legislators fail to specify their religious affiliation, which two-thirds of the time is either Baptist or Methodist.[7]

Legislators are much less representative of race and sex than they are of religion. No blacks had served in the twentieth-century Arkansas legislature until 1972, when 3 black representatives and 1 black senator were elected. By 1986 there were still only 5 black members (4 representatives and 1 senator), all from urban districts with predominantly black populations. Women, while gaining numerical strength faster than blacks, still held only 8 of the 100 house seats and 1 of the 35 senate seats after the 1984 elections, far less than the 14 percent of house seats and 7 percent of senate seats women averaged nationwide by 1985; and the number of women seeking legislative positions declined to 12 in 1986, including the 8 house incumbents.

In an unrepresentative sense that many would deem fortunate, most legislators are considerably better educated than the general population. Whereas only 10 percent of Arkansas citizens were college graduates in 1980, three-fourths of all lawmakers had at least a college degree, and over 40 percent had a graduate or professional degree. As the education data suggest, and as the part-time nature of the legislature practically compels, the legislature is also markedly unrepresentative in terms of occupation. A realtor or banker or lawyer, the owner of a furniture store or car dealership, may have the time flexibility and financial security to adjust his or her schedule to a regular session of two months or more, increasingly frequent special sessions, and countless committee meetings and constituent obligations in between. The realtor's or lawyer's secretary, a bank teller, the furniture and car salespersons who must be at work if they are to receive an income, simply cannot serve. Understandably, then, the great majority of Arkansas legislators are self-employed, mostly owners or proprietors of business or agribusiness establishments; real estate, investment, or insurance brokers; or professionals. The number of farmer-legislators has sharply declined in the twentieth century, and the percentage of lawyer-legislators has dropped steeply in recent decades: from 58 percent of the senate and 39 percent of the house in 1949, to 22 percent of the senate and 14 percent of the house by 1979. What has always been true and remains, so, however, is that only a handful of Arkansas legislators, as compared with most Arkansas citizens, work for wages as the employee of somebody else.[8]

The compensation for Arkansas legislators has become much more generous than it was in the recent past. A 1976 constitutional amendment raised the annual salary from $1,200 to $7,500 a year, which together with various per diem payments, expense and travel allowances, can amount to about $15,000 annually. For someone otherwise profitably employed that is enough to break even and for a retiree a nice supplemental income. It is not, however, and is not designed to be, a full-time income on which to support a family.[9]

Obviously, most of those in the informal pool of eligibles (middle-aged white males with long residence, an acceptable religion, a good education, and occupational flexibility) do not seek a legislative seat. What might motivate those relative few who are attracted to the legislative arena? One of the most thorough investigations of state legislators' ambitions was done in the 1960s by James Barber, who concluded that there were four basic types of legislators, distinguished in terms of personal motivation: Reluctants, who are pressed into service by the local elite to keep some wholly un-qualified and undesirable individual from winning an open seat by default; Advertisers, who see legislative service as a means to economic self-advancement (especially true of fledgling lawyers in past times when they could not legally advertise); Spectators, possessing modest ambition and limited skills, who nevertheless enjoy the ego-building fellowship of their colleagues and attention from their constituents; and, least numerous, the Lawmakers, who devote an exceptional amount of time, energy, and leader-ship to the actual formulation of legislation and management of the legisla-tive process. More recent analyses of state legislators nationally suggest that Reluctants and Advertisers are rapidly disappearing, that Spectators are diminishing, and that serious Lawmakers are increasing, a generalization that seems applicable, with some qualifications, to Arkansas as well.[10]

When Arkansas legislators are asked to identify what drew them to the legislature and what they like about serving there, they most frequently respond in terms of community service and helping people. They also, however, mention their general enjoyment of and interest in the political process, and the prestige and influence associated with the office. Like state legislators elsewhere, then, some combination of altruism and ambition, of public-regardingness and private desire, stimulates those with an existing predisposition toward politics to make a try for the legislature when an inviting opportunity (especially the resignation of an incumbent or a new seat created by reapportionment) arises.[11]

Still, several aspects of the Arkansas legislative recruitment process are somewhat distinctive. First, unlike those states where close party competi-tion forces active party recruitment of capable candidates, parties have been uniquely uninvolved in encouraging legislative candidacies in Arkansas. While the Republican party has recently begun some systematic persuasion, and in northwest Arkansas Republican competition has stimulated Democrats to some informal recruitment, only one of fifty-five Democratic legislators interviewed in a 1978 survey had been approached and asked to run by the local Democratic organization. In contrast, many legislators (up to one-half when a seat is vacant, one-third when an incumbent is being challenged) are "sponsored" by some interest or group. Second, while state legislators are usually more pragmatic than philosophical, the very minute portion (3 percent in one 1980 study) of Arkansas legislators who are motivated to service by any strong issue beliefs or ideology is even less than the national average. Finally, Arkansas legislators are most notable for the limited nature of their officeholding ambitions. Whereas two-thirds of state legislators surveyed nationwide harbored ambitions for higher office, almost 80 percent of a 1981 survey of eighty-four representatives and thirty senators in Arkansas envisioned their political career as staying in the legislature. Indeed, Alan Rosenthal cites the Arkansas legislature as an unparalleled example of "static"—that is, nonprogressive—ambitions: "Not many legislators in Arkansas, for instance, have any hope of higher office. In the past decade or so those who have run for higher office have been unsuccessful. . . . Indeed, if an individual were interested in higher office, he or she would probably not have run for the legislature in the first place. Thus, the ultimate ambition of those in Arkansas who run for the legislature is to serve in the legislature."[12]

Given the predominance of static ambitions and also the unique value of seniority (only in Arkansas and Virginia is length of service the determining factor in securing committee assignments and committee chairmanships), it is unsurprising that membership in the Arkansas legislature turns over much more slowly than is true elsewhere. Between 1972 and 1982, the senate and house averaged, respectively, only 20 percent and 19 percent turnover rates. This is not only a dramatic decline from the turn of the century, when 80 percent and 90 percent turnover rates were common, but is in marked contrast to contemporary state legislative turnover rates generally. In the mid-1970s, only one other senate and two state houses had less turnover than did Arkansas; and in 1986 an extraordinary 98 of 100 representatives and 15 of the 17 senators whose terms were expiring sought reelection.[13]

This unusual stability and tenure yields several important benefits. Arkansas legislators have a strong institutional commitment to their assembly, and, through lengthy tenure, have ample opportunity to acquire the procedural and substantive knowledge prerequisite for thoughtful lawmaking. Because they value their legislative position and want to prolong it, they are sensitive to their perceptions of constituent opinions. Finally, while the actual sessions are intermittent events, the fact that most members of the legislature will return for future sessions gives the legislative branch a continuity that strengthens its stance in dealing with the governor and administrative agencies. There was poignance as well as humor at a 1978 roast of the then seven-term veteran senator Max Howell when Governor-elect Clinton noted that Howell had offered the following advice: "Son, I've been in politics since you were born; I'll probably be here when you die; I'll sure enough be here when you're governor and then you'll WISH you were dead!"[14]

The unusual stability of legislative membership, especially when combined with the demographic and motivational traits of its members, also has some less salutary consequences. The remarkably homogeneous nature of the membership replicates on a much smaller scale the provincialism, parochialism, and limited vision that have long plagued Arkansas politics and policymaking. Arkansas legislators, for example, having none but Arkansas experiences, simply cannot tolerate the kinds of state salaries that might attract more qualified people into public service. The strict adherence to a seniority system in the award of committee chairmanships and other perquisites rewards legislators for simply being there, regardless of any programmatic knowledge acquired or leadership skills displayed along the way. Finally, because so few legislators have higher aspirations, there is little incentive other than personal satisfaction for creative policy activism or risk taking. As long as no powerful interests are antagonized or constituent mores defied, most legislators can easily stay in office: over 90 percent of those seeking reelection have been reelected in recent decades, frequently with no opposition (table 6). In that sense, while Arkansas legislators have ample opportunity to become serious and forceful Lawmakers, they are equally free safely to indulge themselves in the less demanding role of Spectator.

THE LEGISLATIVE PROCESS

The fundamental steps in the legislative process are summarized in the list below.

1. *Introduction.* Any member may introduce a bill by filing ten copies with the clerk of the house or secretary of the senate. Bills may be pre-filed, but less than 5 percent usually are. Appropriation bills must be introduced by the fiftieth day, other bills by the fifty-fifth day.

Table 6: Competitiveness of Arkansas Legislative Elections, 1974–1984

| | 1974 | 1976 | 1978 | 1980 | 1982[a] | 1984 |
|---|---|---|---|---|---|---|
| | | | Senate | | | |
| Primary election | | | | | | |
| Number of contests | 5 | 7 | 8 | 5 | 19 | 1 |
| Incumbent challenges | 2 | 5 | 6 | 5 | 15 | 0 |
| Incumbent defeats | 0 | 0 | 2 | 2 | 5 | 0 |
| General election | | | | | | |
| Number of contests | 2 | 2 | 2 | 2 | 11 | 4 |
| Incumbent challenges | 1 | 1 | 1 | 1 | 9 | 1 |
| Incumbent defeats | 0 | 0 | 0 | 0 | 1 | 1 |
| | | | House | | | |
| Primary election | | | | | | |
| Number of contests | 29 | 31 | 38 | 30 | 33 | 25 |
| Incumbent challenges | 17 | 20 | 18 | 18 | 22 | 16 |
| Incumbent defeats | 2 | 5 | 6 | 3 | 5 | 4 |
| General election | | | | | | |
| Number of contests | 11 | 10 | 15 | 16 | 20 | 11 |
| Incumbent challenges | 6 | 8 | 5 | 7 | 17 | 7 |
| Incumbent defeats | 1 | 2 | 0 | 1 | 1 | 0 |
| Total incumbents challenged | 26 | 34 | 30 | 31 | 63 | 24 |
| Total incumbents defeated | 3 | 7 | 8 | 6 | 12 | 5 |

Source: Compiled from Arkansas election returns, 1974–84.
[a]In elections subsequent to the decennial census and reapportionment, all thirty-five senators must run for reelection and redrawn districts characteristically provoke increased challenges.

2. *First and Second Readings.* Usually only the title is read. Amendments can be proposed only on second reading.
3. *Committee Referral.* The Speaker of the house and the chairman of the senate Rules Committee refer bills to standing committees with relevant jurisdiction.
4. *Committee Consideration.* Public hearings may be held. Usual committee recommendations are Do Pass, Do Pass as Amended, or Do Not Pass. Discharge from committee is possible in both chambers by a two-thirds vote of the chamber quorum within ten days of referral, a majority of the chamber quorum after ten days of referral.
5. *Calendar.* Placed on calendar for third reading. Scheduling is done by house and senate Rules Committees.
6. *Debate and Amendments.* Bill must be placed back on second reading for amendment.

7. *Vote.* Constitution requires roll-call votes on final passage. House uses electronic voting; ayes and nays are called in the senate. Most bills require simple majority, but most tax and appropriations bills require a three-fourths majority.

8. *Other Chamber.* If bill passes one chamber, it is sent to other chamber, where steps 2 through 7 are repeated.

9. *Chamber Disagreement.* If amended in second chamber, bill must be returned to originating chamber for a vote as amended. If the two chambers disagree, a rare conference committee is appointed by Speaker of house and president pro tempore of the senate to reconcile differences, followed by both chambers voting.

10. *Governor.* If governor takes no action, bill becomes law within five days; if vetoed, returned to chambers where a simple majority of both houses can override the veto. Bills presented during the last five days of session must be signed or vetoed within twenty days of adjournment.[15]

These steps suggest that the legislative journey must be an arduous one, especially given the time constraints within which hundreds of bills must overcome each of these potential pitfalls. To some extent that is true. Those opposed to legislation, especially if they have the cooperation of some skilled colleagues, have numerous opportunities to prevent passage: arranging referral to a hostile committee; persuading a sufficient number of legislators to be absent to preclude a committee quorum; adding deliberately offensive amendments; objecting to action on obscure procedural grounds; delaying consideration until the bill is lost in the last-minute crush. Especially on tax and appropriations measures that require extraordinary majorities, an obstructionist minority can easily become the tail that wags the dog. Obstructionism is especially apparent when legislators do not wish to take a stand on a highly controversial issue. In four successive sessions from 1973 to 1979, for example, neither the house nor the senate ever took a straightforward roll-call vote on the proposed national Equal Rights Amendment, thereby incurring the contempt but never the electoral wrath of dedicated proponents and opponents.

Despite these pitfalls, however, the legislative process in Arkansas more closely resembles an assembly line than an obstacle course. Whereas only 4 percent to 6 percent of introductions usually become enactments in the U.S. Congress, and only 20 percent to 30 percent of all state legislative introductions become law, the Arkansas legislature passes between 50 percent and 60 percent of all bills proposed. Indeed, in 1985 the legislature passed nearly two-thirds (64.2 percent) of all introductions. Furthermore, the sheer number of laws enacted each year in Arkansas is extraordinary: in 1983

Arkansas, with 932 new laws, trailed only California, Texas, Illinois, New York, and Louisiana in absolute number of enactments; and 1,097 bills were enacted in 1985. Especially considering what has been described as a fairly cautious and antiregulatory political culture and a generally noninventive legislature, what can account for this abundant output?[16]

One part of the explanation is Arkansas's unique budget process, described in detail in chapter 13. Because of the atypical constitutional requirement that "appropriations shall be made by separate bills, each embracing but one subject," (article 5, section 30) the biennial budget is broken down into hundreds of separate measures (336 in 1981), some of which create controversy but few of which are ever defeated. Beyond budgets, however, and of signal importance in understanding the Arkansas legislative process is that the dominant attitude is one of acquiescence to and accommodation of one's colleagues' wishes. Amendment 14, initiated by the people and enacted in 1926, states, "The General Assembly shall not pass any local or special act." Many are passed, however, and are enforced unless successfully contested in the courts. Many other bills are highly particularistic and personal, falling into the category that Frank Triplett once described (and denounced) as "microphilia."[17]

The positive view of this mass-production process is that it signifies a highly accessible and responsive legislature, that "if a citizen . . . can get a bill introduced and cultivated, it will have a fair chance of passing." Also, since time is short and all legislators have an understandable relish for their own measures, this accommodational attitude helps to keep the process running without excessively bruised egos or short tempers. The less benign view is that a chamber in which bills are rarely given a Do Not Pass recommendation by committee and are rarely defeated on the chamber floor has only a dubious claim to being a genuinely deliberative body. Anyone who has witnessed the closing days of a legislative session when an endless parade of legislators stands briefly in the well uttering the traditional incantation ("My bill, my amendment, I'd appreciate a good vote"), or has seen fifty bills rushed simultaneously through the senate (to be later recorded as separate roll calls) as Senator Knox Nelson urges "Vote 'em," inevitably questions whether all proposals thus moved onto the statute books are worthy ones.[18]

The answer, of course, is that some are not. Special sessions are often necessitated by the sins of omission (neglecting to fund kindergartens in 1977) or commission (open-ended tax credits for contributions to colleges and for construction of water impoundment devices in 1985) of the regular sessions. Most notably, but by no means uniquely, the "scientific creationism" law (Act 590 of 1981) was passed with virtually no committee hearings or debate in the senate (where it originated) and perfunctory committee hearings and little debate in the house, and it was never read by the governor, all at an eventual cost of $430,000 in legal fees to the state.[19]

The most egregious examples of lawmaking by accommodation are those measures known as "merely" or "do nothing" bills, because they merely provide some exemption from state retirement law requirements for the deserving clerk of one legislator's circuit judge, a "little old bill that don't do nothing" (except to apply to all those in a similar situation for all time to come). According to the chief legislative aide of one recent governor, the governor's most solemn responsibility in the legislative process is that of sifting out and vetoing the "do nothing" bills.[20]

Much of the microphilia (for example, establishing milk as the state's official drink in 1985) is fortunately free of major import. The ease and frequency with which legislators enact their colleagues' constituency-oriented tax exemption bills, however, has cumulated into very consequential and costly public policy. Each legislative session in recent years has responded to particular pleas for tax relief for interests as varied as Falcon Jet, farm equipment dealers, horsebreeders, moviemakers, Alcoa and Reynolds aluminum companies, International Paper, and The Poets Roundtable. By 1982 a legislative report estimated that the state was losing $217.6 million a year from sales and use tax exemptions and $116.8 million from personal income tax exemptions, and a 1984 report by the Winthrop Rockefeller Foundation estimated that the state "exempts from the sales tax twice the amount that the tax generates in revenues." Nevertheless, the 1985 legislature obligingly accommodated their colleagues' further proposed exemptions.[21]

Fortunately, there are some institutional limits to this legislative leniency. Committees will ignore bills unless the sponsor specifically requests action thereon, and members of the other chamber are not quite so indulgent as members of the originating chamber, which underscores the virtues of a bicameral legislature. Nevertheless, today's legislature must make rapid decisions on hundreds of often obscure legislative propositions. Assuming that these are public-spirited individuals who wish to remain in office, what pressures and factors are most influential as they attempt to arrive at rational voting decisions?

PRESSURES ON DECISION MAKING

The standard technique by which political scientists attempt to assess patterns of legislative decision making is through roll-call analysis. Votes on which there is a significant division of opinion are analyzed through various scaling and correlation techniques, with the usual conclusion that in the U.S. Congress and in most state legislatures, political party is the most important variable in explaining voting divisions on major policy issues. For several reasons, roll-call analysis is not a particularly useful technique for illuminating voting patterns in the Arkansas legislature.

First, despite the fact that the constitutional requirement of a recorded vote on final passage of any bill produces an extraordinary number of roll calls, most of them produce little or no division of opinion. In 1985, of 1,200 bills voted upon by the house, only 17 created a minority position of 20 percent or more on final passage, and only 28 created a minority position of 10 percent or more. Such is not the stuff of which rigorous roll-call analyses can be made.[22]

The most ambitious and extensive assessment of Arkansas legislative voting patterns is Patrick O'Connor's 1973 doctoral dissertation, which examined voting in the house over five sessions, from 1959 to 1969. While O'Connor did find that voting was not quite so random as anticipated, and that regional and economic development differences plus some old guard versus reform factionalism was occasionally evident, he also found that less than 18 percent of even the small number of contested votes could be scaled at all, and certainly not in terms of party affiliation. Until the Republican presence in the legislature reaches a much more critical mass than is presently the case (four Republican senators, nine Republican representatives following the 1986 elections), political party will constitute the least of all pressures on legislative decision making.[23]

Another method of exploring the effective pressures on voting is by surveying the legislators themselves. When eighty Arkansas legislators were recently asked about the relative weight of various influences, they responded that the most influential voting cues came from constituents (especially friends and supporters in their districts) and from fellow legislators; that the bill's sponsor, county and local officials, and lobbyists were moderately influential; and that the governor and his staff, newspapers, and legislative staff and leadership were of only moderate or negligible influence.[24]

Since the previous chapter suggests that the governor is in fact a powerful force in the policy process, the governor's low ranking requires some clarification. In part it reflects the institutional rivalry that has existed since the first kings battled the earliest parliaments and has been compounded by the constant publicity and popularity that most recent governors but few legislators enjoy. Legislators very much want to be independent of executive influence, and often the wish colors the fact. It also reflects the fact that governors use a coterie of likeminded, supportive legislators to sponsor their bills and to do much of their legislative legwork for them, so that the "other legislators" who are acknowledged to be influential are sometimes operating as the governor's surrogates. Most important is the fact that the governor's bills, in numerical terms, constitute a small part of the legislative agenda, a package of fifty or so bills out of the thousand or more introductions. The governor's bills usually give the legislature their most comprehensive and often most controversial items, but on most bills requiring legislative decision making, the governor has no stated position and therefore exerts no influence.

On most matters, then, legislators are most likely to be affected by constituents, lobbyists, and/or their colleagues; and according to most Arkansas legislators, constituents come first. This is no mere lip service to the democratic ideal. Most lawmakers were born and raised in their district, continue to live and work among their constituents, have numerous organizational affiliations there, and even during legislative sessions are home on weekends. Furthermore, unlike contemporary congressional districts, most state legislative districts are sufficiently small and economically homogeneous that prevailing opinion on matters of great concern to the district or in the district should be self-evident. A representative from Springdale is as unlikely to vote against the best interests of the poultry industry as is a Stuttgart representative to vote against rice farming or a Fayetteville representative against the university. A legislator representing many small, rural school districts will of course work for a different school funding formula than will a legislator representing large, urban school districts.

Surveyed legislators in 1981 and 1983 placed much greater weight on "looking after the needs and interests of his own district" than "looking after the needs and interests of the state as a whole," and, in contrast to state legislators generally, are strikingly disinclined to follow their own consciences when in conflict with constituent opinion. As this survey also points out, "While actual competition is low (less than 30% in primaries and less than 10% in General Elections), Arkansas legislators are very fearful of electoral competition." All of these factors combine to ensure that most legislators, if they hear the voice of their people, will attempt to obey its commands.[25]

There is, however, an intervening twist, which Malcolm E. Jewell and Samuel C. Patterson have succinctly stated: "Legislators in the United States are deeply concerned, sometimes even obsessed, with their image among their constituents; but constituents do not, on the whole, reciprocate with commensurate concern about their legislators." A 1967 Gallup poll indicated that only 28 percent of Americans knew who their state senator was and only 24 percent could name their state representative. This invisibility is strongly confirmed by my unsuccessful attempts to elicit the names of their state legislators from thousands of students over the years, and by a 1985 statewide survey indicating that 45.2 percent of the population was totally unaware that the legislature was then in session. For Arkansas legislators as for French revolutionists, it may well be true that *vox populi, vox Dei* (the voice of the people is the voice of God), but on most issues requiring a vote, that voice is silent.[26]

On a few highly salient issues, such as tax increases or teacher testing, the people may have strong and vocal feelings; but how do they feel about a bill establishing conditions under which a member of the Cosmetology Board who also runs a beauty school can participate in the preparation and giving of exams, or a bill transferring regulation of the State Burial Association to the Insurance Department? Hundreds of detailed budget bills, bills sponsored by state agencies, and bills such as those cited above, which are of no concern to most citizens but of vital concern to those who got them sponsored and initiated, constitute much of the legislative agenda.

The critical and often legitimate and useful role that interest groups have come to play in Arkansas state politics was discussed in chapter 6. To assess their impact in the legislative process, several of those observations are worth reiterating here: hundreds of lobbyists, predominantly representing business and industry, are an active and forceful part of contemporary legislative sessions; because of the traditional weakness of Arkansas political parties, the low level of legislative professionalism (brief sessions, modest salaries, little staff), and the extraordinary power of a few dominant economic interests, interest groups have been generally adjudged to have greater strength in Arkansas than elsewhere; and the appropriate relationships between legislators and lobbyists have been less regulated than in any other state. It was also suggested that while some recent developments (especially increased legislative professionalism and increased economic diversification) may have weakened what was once the unchallenged ability of a few dominant interests to work their legislative will, the rising costs of political campaigns have given interest groups an important new avenue of influence.

The General Assembly's working environment has been significantly professionalized in recent decades. In 1927 the two-year appropriation to operate the assembly amounted to $149,169 (including $82.32 for telephones, $301.40 for typewriter rental, $547 for fountain pens, $447 for pocket knives, and $132 for drinking water). By 1951 the biennial appropriation for legislative operations had little more than doubled, to $369,000. By 1983–84 the legislative appropriation was $11,619,258, with most of those expenditures supporting the full-time staff of the Legislative Council and of the Legislative Joint Auditing Committee (established in 1955 to ensure that appropriated funds are honestly and efficiently spent). Unlike past times, when the total absence of professional staff meant that most bills were drafted by lobbyists, the fifty staff members of the Legislative Council now provide professional assistance to legislators in their lawmaking responsibilities. The sharp reduction in the number of standing committees, their provision with some staff, and their authorization to operate in the interim between sessions are all significant steps in the direction of a professionalism that, by providing legislators with objective information, diminishes their total dependence on the self-interested information supplied by interest groups.[27]

There are lingering limits, however, to the degree of legislative professionalism in Arkansas. Political scientists generally agree that "no single factor has a greater effect on the legislative environment than the constitutional restriction on the length of legislative sessions," and by the mid-1980s Arkansas was one of only ten states that still precluded regular annual sessions. Most standing committees have only one professional staff person; only a few interim committees have actually wrestled with complex policy issues; and the recommendations of those that have are often ignored. There are no transcripts of committee hearings that noncommittee members might read for voting guidance. A Do Not Pass recommendation from a committee means that it can reach the calendar only through suspension of rules, which extraordinary means alerts legislators to suspicions somewhere about a bill's worth. A Do Pass recommendation, however, while carrying the assuring imprimatur of committee support, is not accompanied by any committee report explaining what a bill would accomplish and why it is passage-worthy. Especially since those with particular occupational and economic interests typically self-select themselves onto committees dealing with their particular concerns, what is accepted as the recommendation of specialists may in fact represent special-interest advocacy.[28]

The problem of conflicting public and private interests is an inherent one for all part-time state legislatures. One certainly cannot expect part-time legislators on part-time salaries to sever their ties permanently with the occupation that provides their primary income, nor is it reasonable to expect that farmer-legislators should excuse themselves from voting on agricultural legislation or that lawyer-legislators should excuse themselves from voting on the laws under which they will practice. Still, whereas some states have laws and/or strong traditions that preclude the outright use of one's legislative position for personal gain, Arkansas has neither. In fact, nothing prohibits legislators from simultaneously serving as the paid representatives of interest groups, and some do. Senator Knox Nelson retired from his twenty-year executive directorship of the Arkansas Contractors Association in 1984, but still serving as legislator-lobbyists in 1985 were Representative L. L. ("Doc") Bryan (Arkansas Poulty Federation), Representative Jack McCoy (Arkansas Chiropractic Association), and Representative Bob ("Sody") Arnold (Arkansas Oil Marketers Association). Others have equally dubious ties and openly sponsor bills of great economic value to their occupations or their professional clients. It is ironic that, according to a recent survey of the Arkansas senate, while senators rank being self-interested or representing a special interest as the *least* desirable attribute of a state legislator, 27 percent estimated that 21–50 percent of their colleagues had such conflicts, and 17 percent estimated that 65–98 percent of their colleagues did.[29]

In 1979, after years of debate and previous defeat, a state code of ethics law was enacted (Act 570 of 1979), requiring legislators and other officials to disclose their financial interests annually on a form filed with the secretary of state. From these forms, which the state press regularly uses as the bases of stories, it is possible to ascertain which potential conflicts of interest exist. The law, however, does not define a conflict of interest and imposes penalties only for concealing such conflicts, not for having them or for acting in pursuit of them. The special Code of Ethics Commission appointed by Governor Bill Clinton on June 9, 1987, was directed to develop a strong, comprehensive state code of ethics. At present, however, there is still much truth in Harry Ashmore's observation that the Arkansas relationship between legislators and lobbyists "is a sort of unholy meshing of public and private interests without any effective restraint from an electorate bemused by other, perhaps in fact more important, matters."[30]

The methods of lobbyists are much less crude than in decades past, and most of those who have systematically studied the legislator-lobbyist relationship in Arkansas have concluded that most legislators are fairly sophisticated in their dealings with lobbyists and fairly effective at weighing and balancing their pressures. One recent study concluded rather optimistically, in fact, that while lobbyists have very extensive and successful relationships with Arkansas legislators, access to the decision-making process is not restricted to professional insiders but extends to marginal and amateur citizen lobbyists as well. In another study, however, the same authors acknowledge that the attention given to constituents "readily becomes translated into attention to interest groups," because of low citizen participation and a relatively homogeneous economy. When legislative matters vital to an interest group are being considered, that group will ensure that its point of view is conveyed and considered; other points of view may or may not be heard.[31]

What happens to the harried lawmaker when, as is frequently the case, the signals from constituents, the governor's office, and interest groups are either absent or conflicting? During a legislative session, most of a legislator's transactions are with his or her fellow legislators, and these constant interpersonal relationships, enhanced by a feeling that those outside the legislature do not fully understand or appreciate the hard work and sacrifices of those within it, tend to produce remarkable affection, respect, and concern for other legislators' needs and wishes. Hence, as Representative David Matthews recently noted, "Much more important than party, profession, or philosophy is friendship."[32]

In part this is a sensible technique of reciprocity, as the advice of one Arkansas legislator clearly expresses: "Don't oppose anyone else's bills unless there is strong reason to, because it hurts the chances of your bill's passing." At times, however, this spirit goes far beyond the usual legislative norms of mutual expediency to something bordering on sentimentality. Consider, for example, Representative Mack Thompson's persuading the House State Agencies Committee in 1979 to give a Do Pass to Representative Arlo Tyer's bill making it a crime to show X-rated pictures on the grounds that Tyer had been a faithful committee member, had attended all meetings, and "this is the only bill he's had and it's important to him."[33]

Camaraderie aside, unless a bill directly affects his or her district, has produced substantial public debate, or has come before one of his or her committees, a legislator is unlikely to know anything about a bill's contents (what does it really do?) and impact (will it help or hurt me?). This substantive and political knowledge is most readily and reliably obtainable from one's colleagues. Depending upon time constraints, a quick conference with the bill's sponsor or with one's seatmates may suffice. Over time, however, a few legislators are most consistently the cue givers and therefore have the most influence on their colleague's voting behavior.

In neither house nor senate does a formal leadership position necessarily coincide with influence, in part because (similar only to North Dakota and Florida), every two years a new Speaker of the house and president pro tempore of the senate are elected by their colleagues. The Speaker was a formidable figure through the early 1960s, making committee assignments, naming committee chairs, assigning bills to friendly or hostile committees at will, and totally controlling the calendar. Similarly, until 1967 in the senate, the twenty-year service of Nathan Gordon as lieutenant governor, and hence president of the senate, cumulated into an enormous concentration of power in that office (making committee assignments, referring bills, establishing the calendar). During Faubus's twelve-year governorship, these leaders were Faubus men as well and worked closely with him in producing the desired outcomes.[34]

Faubus's and Gordon's retirements in 1966, the election of Republican "Footsie" Britt as lieutenant governor in 1966 and 1968, adoption of legislative reforms, and an unusual influx of newcomers in the early 1970s changed leadership patterns and prerogatives. The house Speaker still "makes" committee assignments and "refers" bills to committees, but committee assignments and chairmanships are strictly governed by seniority, and bill referrals are strictly governed by subject matter. Furthermore, any attempt to end-run the established calendar in the house produces such strong procedural objections that it is rarely worth the effort.

The Speaker may be influential, but only when additional power stems from other sources. When Representative John Miller, who is chairman of the house Revenue and Taxation Committee and cochairman of the legislature's most prestigious and powerful Joint Budget Committee, served as Speaker (1979–80), the Speakership seemed formidable; but his successor as Speaker was not even named as one of the ten most influential leaders in a 1980 survey of the house. Because budget bills are intrinsically important to all legislators and also because they are privileged (that is, have priority on the calendar), Miller comes as close to being a comprehensive chamber leader as the house offers. For the most part, however, leadership in the house is widely dispersed. A committee chairmanship provides the opportunity to exert major influence on bills in that subject area, and those chairmen with strong preferences and forceful personalities can be major cue givers in their respective fields. Subject-matter expertise, oratorical skills, comprehensive knowledge of the rules, popularity, and sheer determination are also sources of influence in the house.[35]

In contrast to the dispersed leadership pattern in the house, power is highly centralized in the senate. When the lieutenant governor's power was first stripped from that office, it was dispersed. By the late 1970s and into the 1980s, however, two of the senate's most senior members had accumulated sufficient seniority, standing and select committee chairmanships, and legislative skill to reconcentrate the power that had been separated. Senator Max Howell, elected to the senate in 1950, is cochairman of the Joint Budget Committee (which not only means control over colleagues' spending projects but because of the privileged status of budget bills the power to speed or slow the entire voting process); chairman of the Judiciary Committee (from which all legislators at times must solicit special bills for "their" judges and court personnel); and chairman of the Efficiency Committee (which hires and fires all senate personnel). Furthermore, "He not only chairs committees, he rules them. It would be an understatement to say he has a strong personality. He is forceful, domineering and intimidating."[36]

Senator Knox Nelson, elected to the senate in 1960, was by 1985 ranking member of the Joint Budget Committee, chaired the Public Health, Welfare, and Labor Committee; chaired the Committee on Committees (which makes committee assignments); and most notably chaired the Rules Committee, which refers bills to committees and establishes the order of business. Nelson's style is that of helping rather than terrifying his colleagues: soliciting their preferences on bill referral; letting them substitute one bill for another on the calendar; expediting their priority projects. When Nelson wants something in return, however, there is an understood quid pro quo. Unlike the house, where the calendar governs the legislative flow, the flow in the senate is governed by Nelson with whatever rule suspensions are momentarily useful; and when his usually quiet voice is suddenly raised in the senate chamber with "Now I want you'all to pay close attention to this bill," it is as effective as a Roman emperor's thumbs down.[37]

When these two work in tandem, which they usually do, their influence is overpowering and there is an occasional uprising in the ranks. In 1981 insurgents were able to enlarge Joint Budget Committee membership from fifteen to twenty-five members, thereby broadening the base of those who have the knowledge and status that Budget Committee membership confers. The Joint Performance Review Committee under Senator Nick Wilson's chairmanship has made recent efforts to become a rival source of influence for more junior members. Especially in the senate, however, there are relatively few cue givers and many who go along with their more influential colleagues, and there is some dissatisfaction with this arrangement. One recent analysis of the senate, for example, concluded, "Senior senators have become very dominant within the Senate's institutional structure and they exercise power from these positions in a self-serving manner, penalizing those who do not go along." It is also widely acknowledged, however, that those with the greatest influence (for example, Representative John Miller and Senators Nelson and Howell), are influential primarily because of the time and energy they devote to their theoretically part-time positions. Nelson, for example, estimates that he spends 80 percent of his time on lawmaking, Howell "works at it year round," and it is a rare day when Miller is not in his capitol office. It is somewhat ironic that Nelson and Howell came into public service as part of the GI revolt, whose battle-cry was that of overthrowing the political establishment, and that Miller is one of the most outspoken opponents of a full-time professional legislature.[38]

Arkansas legislators, like state legislators everywhere, are subject to a variety of pressures in the decision-making process. In a permissive atmosphere that suggests that all bills are good bills unless significant opposition emerges, they are most eager to follow their constituents' wishes, which frequently means the wishes of the best organized and most predominant economic interests in their districts. For a variety of reasons outlined in chapter 8, and because contemporary legislators know that contemporary governors have the benefit of extensive survey research, the governor's legislative program, which constitutes the bulk of major public policy proposals, is generally accepted. The special interests that account for most items on the legislative agenda, especially those groups with skilled lobbyists and the reputation of funding opponents for noncooperative legislators, are able to exert significant pressure in an institutional and attitudinal environment that enhances their influence. Above all, Arkansas legislators seek and follow the advice of their colleagues, among whom some are more equal than others.

## LEGISLATIVE FUNCTIONS AND FUTURE

By the 1980s state legislatures were expected to perform three major functions in state governance: providing services for constituents; overseeing the administration; and making public policy. The questions now remain, how effectively does the Arkansas legislature perform these functions? And are they performed in a fashion consistent with popular expectations and preferences?

Arkansas legislators are quick to identify the first of these functions, constituent service, as one of their most important and time-consuming responsibilities, and most observers would agree with their self-assessment that they perform this function superbly. Whether the matter benefits the entire district (a community development grant, a four-lane highway, more employees in the local branch of the State Revenue Office) or a single constituent (locating misplaced documents, straightening out a computer snarl in driver's license renewal), most legislators are energetic and effective in their response to constituent requests. These activities have much more to do with the legislator's visibility and popularity in the district than does the generally unknown voting record, and even among the attentive public, a reputation for "getting things done" may count for more than the legislator's policy positions. While some lawmakers carry the practice to extremes, spending the whole time in session phoning home to wish constituents a happy birthday, most simply perform in response to constituent requests. Constituents get someone to run errands and interference for them in the state capital, legislators get visibility and credit: a beneficial exchange at bargain rates.[39]

The second function, administrative oversight, is more problematic. The most important instrument through which the legislature supervises the executive branch is through extensive review of budget requests by the Legislative Council and through continuous postauditing by the Legislative Joint Auditing Committee. The details and politics of this fiscal review process are discussed in chapter 13, but it is important to note here that there is no more effective means of ensuring administrative discipline than the threat of reducing or denying funds. Since the legislative branch is intended to be the guardian of the public purse, there is no question of its right to grill agency heads during budget hearings, or to ensure that appropriated funds are being spent according to legislative intent.

Beginning in 1969, however, the legislature began requiring state agencies to obtain the "advice" of the Legislative Council before taking certain actions (granting exceptions to the uniform classification and compensation plan for state employees, for example, or on professional service contracts involving more than $5,000, or on federal grant applications), which has raised constant questions about the appropriate line between legitimate legislative oversight and unlawful interference with executive authority.

The Legislative Council has insisted that there is an important distinction between legislative "advice" and legislative "approval," but as an opinion by the attorney general in 1982 aptly noted, "Only the intrepid will refuse to follow the legislative 'advice,' knowing that future appropriations may well depend on whether the advice is followed."[40]

Aside from fiscal review, the legislature is ill-equipped to oversee the operations of state agencies in any systematic manner. A "sunset" law enacted with great fanfare in 1977 that would have abolished 283 state agencies over a six-year period unless each agency was found worthy of being continued was effectively repealed in 1983; the Joint Performance Review Committee had neither the time nor the staff to do continuous, effective performance evaluations on that many agencies. This committee has become something of a permanent oversight and investigative arm of the state legislature, but its targets and tactics have also been a constant subject of criticism and controversy.[41]

As a practical matter, the most pervasive form of legislative oversight is stimulated neither by laws nor by committee mandates but by constituent or interest-group complaints that stir legislators into investigatory and sometimes punitive action. When the Pollution Control and Ecology Department tried to close a cotton gin on the grounds that its emissions were health threatening, the representative from that district proposed legislation exempting cotton gins from state air pollution control regulations. When the Livestock and Poultry Commission filed suit against a livestock sale barn, alleging failure to comply with state brucellosis regulations, the senator from that district (who was also the attorney for the sale barn) attached an amendment to the commission's appropriations bill to weaken the regulations, prompting the commission director to resign. When the speaker at a conference sponsored by the Governor's Commission on the Status of Women offended the sensibilities of a woman in the audience, she complained to her representative, who tried to get the commission abolished. These and countless other examples underscore the Arkansas legislature's extreme responsiveness to constituency demands. They also suggest that oversight is episodic and punitive rather than systematic and constructive and that it is prompted more by parochial pressures than by general public policy concerns.[42]

Similar criticisms are justified with respect to the legislature's third and presumably most fundamental lawmaking function. The contemporary Arkansas legislature is meeting longer, passing more bills, and appropriating much more money than would have seemed possible in the recent past.

The interim committees plus the ceaseless exertions of a few lawmakers have given the General Assembly a more constant and consequential role in state governance, and the institutional reforms of the 1970s produced a much more orderly, serious, and impressive legislative operation. The legislature also gets high marks for its wholehearted desire to please and represent those with expressed or ascertainable preferences. Because of a strong district orientation, legislators are especially successful at commanding attention to local interests and objections when state policy is being made. According to legislators themselves, however, "Statewide policy decisions are largely the governor's responsibility." And one recent characterization of the General Assembly as "an extremely neutral processing system of constituency-originated policy preferences with very little decision-making regarding the contents of constituents demands," suggests that genuine deliberation is as rare as policy formulation.[43]

The legislature is the most significantly improved and upgraded institution from the traditional period to the present, but its persisting disabilities are apparent in the following remarks made by one of the disappointed participants in the 1985 session: "During the recent session of the legislature, our poorly functioning committee system, time constraints, deal making on less important legislation and personal power playing of a few kept us from dealing in an adequate way with the state's crying need for a comprehensive water code, subverted passage of any meaningful trespass law, and reduced our analysis of the state's budget to a cursory two-day review resulting in a rubber stamp of the plans of a half-dozen members of the Joint Budget Committee and the governor."[44]

The General Assembly is trapped in some of the same dilemmas that hobble other part-time state legislatures. There is unanimous agreement in Arkansas that a full-time professional legislature is neither necessary nor desirable; but it is unrealistic to expect thoughtful and constructive decisions on multibillion dollar budgets and on hundreds of other proposed statutes by a part-time unprofessional assembly. In consequence, some of the most respected and serious legislators have been dropping out, pinpointing the disruptive impact of existing arrangements (a long regular session, inevitably followed by one or more lengthy special sessions called at the governor's convenience, plus scores of interim committee and subcommittee meetings) as the major reason for their retirement.[45]

Such losses of legislative talent, but especially the establishment of a four-year gubernatorial term, have stimulated renewed legislative interest in regular annual sessions and in longer terms for house and senate leaders, to guard against further loss of legislative stature vis-à-vis a newly strengthened governor. Additional institutional reforms, then, are probably part of the near future.[46]

Equally important changes in the electoral environment may be much slower in coming. Over the past two decades, sharply contested and extensively publicized gubernatorial races have become a forum in which some issues of importance to the state's electorate have been debated, and in which Arkansas voters with near consistency have voted for the candidate promising the more forceful leadership and the more progressive platform. In sharp contrast, most state legislative contests remain weakly contested or uncontested, with incumbents who have avoided controversial issues and have created a hard-working image through constituent service subject to little serious challenge. Until a more observant and critical public gives the same searching and demanding attention to legislative contests that it has begun giving to gubernatorial contests, the governor will continue to be the major source of public policy, attentive interest groups will continue to have better legislative fortunes than the average citizen, and those few legislators who can and care to exert extraordinary influence will dominate those content with the satisfactions of simply being there.

## CHAPTER TEN

# The Power and Politics of the Judicial Branch

*Why not cut out the hypocrisy of letting the people elect the judges?*
*The people don't know who he is, or what kind of judge he is.*
David Solomon, Helena lawyer, 1979

*Who says politics should be totally removed? You want judges who*
*care about people. Otherwise, how can you make laws that every-*
*body can abide by?*
Justice Darrell Hickman, Arkansas Supreme Court, 1977

In the past, state judicial systems were considered to be above the ordinary pulls and pressures of politics, and therefore beyond the legitimate concern of political scientists. In recent decades, that antiseptic approach has been almost entirely displaced by a more realistic recognition that judges and courts are deeply rooted in a state's political system and have many strong linkages to it. Some of these linkages have already been mentioned. In chapter 7 it was noted that opposition to judicial reforms in the proposed new 1970 and 1980 constitutions ran deep among some judges, who were among the most articulate and effective opponents of the documents. The "do nothing" bills described in chapter 9 are often those that particular legislators sponsor in behalf of "their" judges or for other court personnel in their constituencies.[1]

Assuredly, and fortunately, there are laws, canons of ethics, and general proprieties that preclude judges from some of the more overtly political activities commonplace in the executive and legislative branches. Judges do not postpone decisions on controversial issues until they have taken public opinion surveys, nor do they let lobbyists swarm through their chambers. They do, however, because they must, maintain good political rapport with the local governments that provide the operating funds for all but the appellate courts in Arkansas and with the legislators who establish their salaries and expense allowances. As one state senator advised some judges, "If you want a pay raise you should come to see us and remember, we are like teenagers—every once in awhile we have to be stroked." Not all judges follow the practice of one Washington County judge who sent Christmas cards to his past jurors in the years preceding elections, but all judges must cultivate sufficiently strong ties to their constituents and clientele groups, especially the bar, to ensure their survival in the electoral system.[2]

State courts also are political in the impact they have on public policy. It is true, as one 1961 study of the Arkansas Supreme Court noted, that "basically, the Supreme Court of Arkansas is a private law court. . . . It is not a court before which many of the great political issues of the day are paraded and whose decisions arouse the interest and passions of the citizenry." Of their 285 civil decisions in 1983–84, only 16 dealt with the constitutionality of state statutes as compared with 63 dealing with contracts or other debt and 46 dealing with automobile or other negligence.[3]

Nevertheless, an occasional decision by the state supreme court has catalytic public policy impact. As I will discuss in chapter 13, a series of decisions challenging the constitutionality of property tax assessment practices and school funding formulas forced these items to the top of the gubernatorial and legislative agenda and indicated the constitutional parameters within which acceptable solutions would have to be drawn. The supreme court's narrow interpretation of the 1982 "Interest Rate Control Amendment" brought enormous distress to the financial community, as did its 1986 decision that no bond issues by local governments were legal without a vote of the people. Decisions to strike proposed constitutional amendments from the ballot because of complex, faulty, and misleading language outraged those who wanted an elective Public Service Commission in 1982 and those who wanted to prohibit abortions in 1984. Clearly, state judicial decisions do have policy consequences, do work to the advantage of some interests and groups and to the disadvantage of others, all of which is the essence of politics.

Arkansas's courts are much less politicized than they were in the 1920s and the 1930s, when many supreme court justices obtained their seats as rewards for successfully managing gubernatorial campaigns and, in the case of C. E. Johnson, continued to act as the governor's chief patronage dispenser and political adviser while on the bench. Today's judges are much less political and infinitely better behaved than those in the nineteenth century, who were among the most enthusiastic participants in the family favoritism, blatant partisanship, and occasional violence that characterized the early Arkansas political tradition. In 1824 one superior court justice mortally wounded another in a duel delayed for six weeks until they could clear their dockets; and in 1827 an employee of the *Arkansas Gazette* wrote to his brother, "The Secretary of the Territory and the Judges of the Supreme Court drink whiskey out of the same cup as the lowest born, and roll together in the gutter." Like politics in general, trials may have provided an entertaining distraction from ordinary routine, but the quality of justice was far from even. Few citizens would exchange the judges and courts of today with their distant predecessors.[4]

Still, the state judiciary is not apart from, but part of, the Arkansas political system, and an examination of Arkansas politics must include the distinctive politics of the bench. The judicial "system" largely consists of many individual judges operating with relative autonomy in their individual courtrooms, and therefore, as Robert A. Leflar has noted, "The quality of our judges is the quality of our justice."[5]

## JUDICIAL STRUCTURE

The judicial functions in Arkansas are performed by hundreds of courts, which, in their broad structure, resemble the general patterns of state courts elsewhere. There are courts of limited jurisdiction, limited both in terms of geographic area and in the minor nature of most of their business, and courts of general jurisdiction, where most major civil and criminal cases are tried and decided. There are also two appellate courts: a supreme court and, since 1979, an intermediate court of appeals, which functions primarily to review decisions of the lower courts on appeal (figure 2).[6]

Until the 1960s, very little was known about the precise number of courts in Arkansas or how many cases they were handling. Since 1965, however, when the legislature officially created the State Judicial Department with the chief justice of the supreme court designated as its administrative director, considerable data on filings and dispositions have been systematically collected and periodically published. What these statistics indicate is that, in fiscal year 1983–84, there were over 640,000 filings in the various courts of Arkansas, a somewhat astonishing figure in a state with an adult population

# THE ARKANSAS COURT SYSTEM

## SUPREME COURT
1 Chief Justice, 6 Associate Justices

Jurisdiction:
—Appellate jurisdiction over lower court cases involving constitutional issues, Acts, Municipal or County ordinances, rules of courts or administrative agencies, appeals from Public Service, Transportation, and Pollution Control Commission, criminal convictions of death, life imprisonment, or more than 30 years, post-conviction relief petitions, writs of quo warranto, prohibition, injunction, mandamus, or certiorari, election cases, attorney discipline, usury cases, products liability cases, questions of oil, gas or mineral rights, the law of torts, or the construction of deeds or wills, or cases in which there is a prior decision by the Supreme Court.
—Appellate jurisdiction over those appeals certified for review from the Court of Appeals.

## COURT OF APPEALS
6 Judges

Jurisdiction:
—Appellate jurisdiction over lower court cases except those appealed directly to the Supreme Court.

## 8 COMBINED CIRCUIT & CHANCERY JUDGES

## CIRCUIT COURT
24 Courts, 31 Judges

Jurisdiction:
—Civil cases over $100.
—Original jurisdiction in felony.
—Juvenile.
—Hears appeal de novo.
—Jury trials.

## CHANCERY & PROBATE COURTS
24 Courts, 29 Judges

Jurisdiction:
—Courts of equity (land disputes, domestic relations, etc.) Hears probate matters and adoptions.
No jury trial.

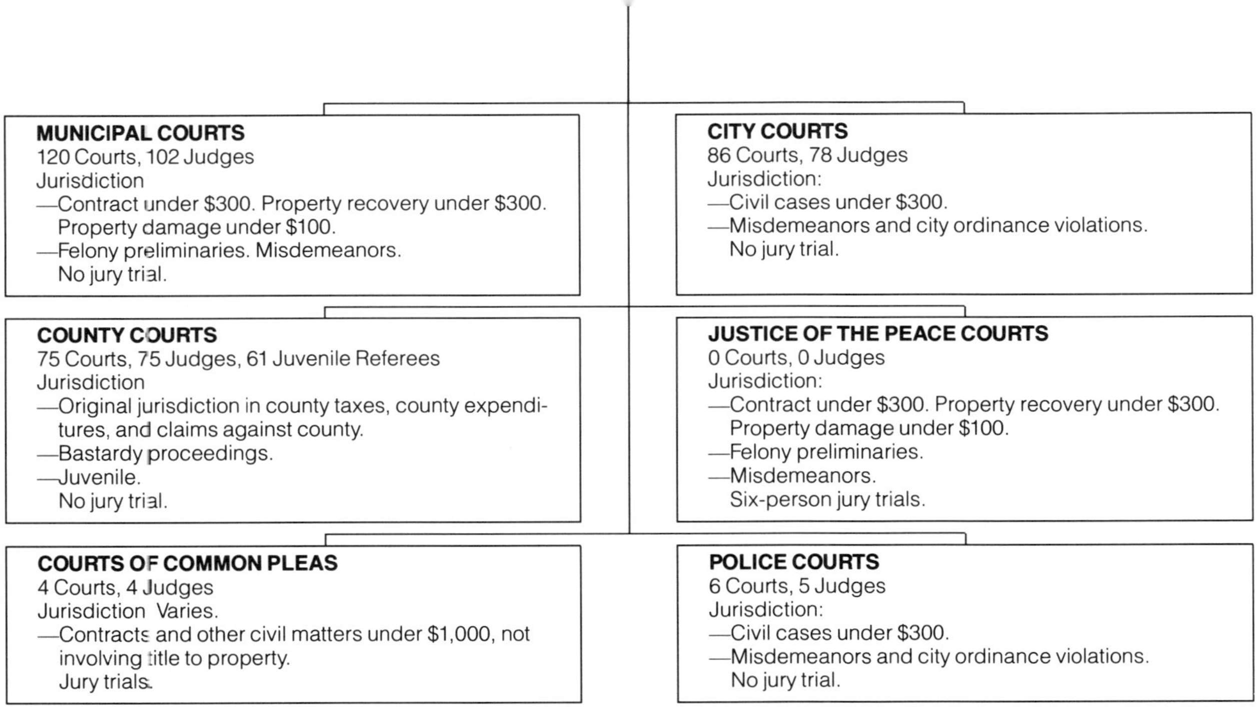

**MUNICIPAL COURTS**
120 Courts, 102 Judges
Jurisdiction
—Contract under $300. Property recovery under $300. Property damage under $100.
—Felony preliminaries. Misdemeanors.
No jury trial.

**COUNTY COURTS**
75 Courts, 75 Judges, 61 Juvenile Referees
Jurisdiction
—Original jurisdiction in county taxes, county expenditures, and claims against county.
—Bastardy proceedings.
—Juvenile.
No jury trial.

**COURTS OF COMMON PLEAS**
4 Courts, 4 Judges
Jurisdiction Varies.
—Contracts and other civil matters under $1,000, not involving title to property.
Jury trials.

**CITY COURTS**
86 Courts, 78 Judges
Jurisdiction:
—Civil cases under $300.
—Misdemeanors and city ordinance violations.
No jury trial.

**JUSTICE OF THE PEACE COURTS**
0 Courts, 0 Judges
Jurisdiction:
—Contract under $300. Property recovery under $300. Property damage under $100.
—Felony preliminaries.
—Misdemeanors.
Six-person jury trials.

**POLICE COURTS**
6 Courts, 5 Judges
Jurisdiction:
—Civil cases under $300.
—Misdemeanors and city ordinance violations.
No jury trial.

Figure 2. Arkansas Court System. (*Source: Annual Report of the Judiciary of Arkansas, FY 1984–85* [Little Rock: Arkansas Judicial Department, 1986], p. 65. Reprinted by permission of Chief Justice Jack Holt, Jr.)

of 1,615,000. The statistics also indicate that over 80 percent of these filings were in courts of limited jurisdiction, primarily in the municipal courts.

Fortunately for the litigants, municipal court judges must be lawyers; but since few cities have had a sufficient volume of cases to warrant a full-time municipal judge, most of the state's municipal judges spend only part of their time on the bench, where they may occasionally be faced with sentencing those who are their clients in their private professional life. Voter approval in 1986 of a constitutional amendment increasing the dollar limit on cases in courts of limited jurisdiction from $300 to $3,000 could substantially increase municipal court activity. Through 1986, however, only Little Rock, Pine Bluff, and Hot Springs prohibited their municipal judges from maintaining a private law practice. In other jurisdictions, where state-set (but locally paid) salaries range from $2,400 to $43,000 a year, municipal judges may be retired lawyers earning some supplemental income or inexperienced young lawyers who need a guaranteed income as their private practice gets established or who are positioning themselves for a future judicial race. Dean Morley, who retired in 1986 after sixteen years as North Little Rock municipal traffic judge, served simultaneously as the attorney and lobbyist for the Arkansas Wholesale Liquor Dealers Association.[7]

The "judges" in the other courts of limited jurisdiction need not be and rarely are trained in the law. City courts (called mayor's courts until 1971) handle the same kinds of minor civil and criminal matters as do the municipal courts in larger towns but are presided over by the mayor or by his or her designee. County courts and courts of common pleas are presided over by the county judge, who is not actually either a judge or a lawyer but rather the elected county chief executive. Until a January 1987 state supreme court ruling that the system was unconstitutional, the major twentieth-century responsibility of county courts had been to handle juvenile justice. This decision, however, did not affect the continuing responsibilities of county courts to resolve questions of disputed paternity (4,652 bastardy cases were filed in FY 1983–84). Only twelve counties have been authorized by special statute to maintain courts of common pleas, and only four of these reported any activity (a total of 102 cases) in FY 1983–84. There is an automatic right of appeal from all these courts of limited jurisdiction to circuit courts, but since limited jurisdiction courts are not courts of record (that is, there is no formal transcript of proceedings from which to appeal), such cases are in fact tried anew.[8]

Most major civil and criminal cases are handled by the courts of general jurisdiction, which are courts of record and whose judges must be lawyers.

The circuit courts hear major civil and criminal cases, and juries are used unless waived. Chancery courts handle cases involving domestic relations, land, and other disputes in which equitable relief is sought: chancellors may order the performance of an act or issue injunctions and restraining orders to command an activity to cease. Chancellors also serve as judges of the probate courts, in which capacity they hear cases involving adoptions, wills and estates, and related matters. Only in rare instances do chancellors employ a jury. In FY 1983–84 there were 108,696 filings in the general jurisdiction courts; 59,280 in the circuit courts; and 49,416 in the chancery and probate courts.[9]

Only Mississippi and Tennessee persist, as does Arkansas, in maintaining this dual system of courts of law and courts of equity, and the origins of the dual system in Arkansas had much more to do with politics than with justice. Although efforts to combine these courts through constitutional reform have been unsuccessful, in 1979 the general jurisdiction courts were realigned into circuits with the same boundaries for circuit and chancery courts, and by 1985, eight of these circuits had only one judge, who acts as both chancellor and circuit court judge.[10]

Until 1979 individual justices of the Arkansas Supreme Court had one of the heaviest workloads in America. Spurred by arguments that an intermediate appellate court would reduce the supreme court's workload, save the justices' attention for more consequential cases, allow judges more time to consider cases and write opinions, and make the appellate process speedier and more efficient, a court of appeals was authorized by constitutional amendment in 1978 and began operation in mid-1979. According to one recent scholarly analysis, "Most of the benefits which were projected by the court's proponents have, in fact, resulted."[11]

With this cursory review of the state's courts as background, two points with respect to the judicial branch of government require emphasis. First, although in general outline this system is comparable to that in other states, and Arkansas courts like courts elsewhere have made important improvements in recent years, Arkansas courts seem to have been less touched by modern court reform movements than those in almost any other state in the country. Second, while Arkansas's numerous courts are often described as part of a state judicial system, this "system" is characterized by considerable decentralization and autonomy.

There have, of course, been remarkable strides since the days when a handful of self-trained or untrained judges together with a pack of equally dubious lawyers rode circuit under difficult and often hazardous circumstances. Court was then held in whatever rude shelter was available, including barns or stables, or outdoors if weather permitted, with whatever local bystanders could be lured (sometimes with promises of free whiskey) into jury service. While some judges still "ride circuit," they do so with relative ease and in the certainty that courtroom facilities, a docket, and some supporting personnel await them. It is also true, however, that while many states, stimulated by ideas generated by such organizations as the American Judicature Society, the American Bar Association and the National Center for State Courts, have extensively rationalized, modernized, and professionalized their state courts in recent decades, Arkansas has taken only modest steps in the directions suggested by court reformers. Such at least is suggested by the following brief list of contemporary concepts of a strong state judiciary when compared with the existing system in Arkansas.[12]

The first reform goal is that of consolidation and simplification of court structure. The idea is that the state courts should be streamlined into only a few basic types of courts (a supreme court, an intermediate court of appeals, one type of trial court of general jurisdiction, one or two types of trial courts of limited jurisdiction), thereby eliminating overlapping jurisdiction, enhancing the prestige of the court, and making the courts easier to understand, use, and supervise. While some of Arkansas's least professional courts (justice of the peace courts and courts of common pleas) have been withering away, the 1970 and 1980 constitutions, which would have consolidated the chancery and circuit courts and provided for only one county trial court of limited jurisdiction in each county, were defeated. This leaves Arkansas with two types of general jurisdiction courts and five different courts of limited jurisdiction. In 1982 Arkansas was ranked fiftieth of the fifty states in terms of court consolidation and simplification.[13]

The second reform goal is that of centralized management and budgeting. The reform view is that state supreme courts, with the assistance of trained court administrators, should have sufficient staff support, funds, and authority to scrutinize the work of lower courts, conduct research on their problems, and provide information and advice to local judges, all to ensure one efficient and uniform standard of justice. To avoid excessive entanglement with legislative favoritism, a judicial compensation commission should recommend salaries for all state judges, and the supreme court should be empowered to make a single budget for the entire judicial system. The logic here is that courts dependent on a crazy quilt of state funding, local funding, court fines and fees, must necessarily traffic extensively in state and local politics to obtain sufficient funds, and local funding means that the caliber of courts varies from jurisdiction to jurisdiction.

As noted, the 1965 legislature did officially designate the supreme court chief justice as administrative director of the Judicial Department, and his administrative staff has begun compiling data on courts and caseloads that had never been systematically collected before. The constitution gives the supreme court "general superintending control over all inferior courts of law and equity" and also authorizes the supreme court to "make rules regulating the practice of law and professional conduct of attorneys." These, however, represent very partial steps toward centralized management and budgeting.

In 1985 a proposed bill to establish a judicial compensation commission was withdrawn when it was rumored that other Bar Association bills might be in trouble with Senator Max Howell, chairman of the senate Judiciary Committee, unless the "offensive" compensation commission measure was pulled down. The supreme court has no power to appoint lower-court personnel or to determine their budgets; and even the power to prescribe procedures is very tenuous, as the chief justice tacitly acknowledged in the following recent response to a concerned circuit clerk whose judge was flaunting procedural requirements: "Some of them, we may just have to let them die off."[14]

No more than fifteen of the general jurisdiction courts presently employ professional case coordinators or administrators. While the state pays all the expenses of the two appellate courts and the salaries of circuit and chancery judges and their court reporters, much of the cost of general jurisdiction court operations is borne by increasingly resentful counties, and all efforts to bring the limited jurisdiction courts within the management orbit of the state Judicial Department have been firmly resisted by many local governments, for whom these courts provide welcome revenue. Municipal courts alone in FY 1983–84 collected almost $19 million in fines and costs, to the delight of many municipalities. While most states now have prestigious Judicial Councils, small committees of judges, lawyers, and laymen who continuously study problems, propose legislative reforms, and lobby for them, the Arkansas Judicial Council consists of all appellate and general jurisdiction judges who, in the terms of one impatient participant, "get together twice a year for meetings and golf games."[15]

In 1986 Governor Clinton finally announced his appointments to the Cost of the Judiciary Study Commission, created by the legislature in 1983; the

Pulaski County Judge vowed to renew efforts to secure state management and funding of general jurisdiction courts, and the Arkansas Judicial Council for the first time voted to endorse this concept. Some changes, then, could be coming. At present, however, Arkansas ranks thirty-first of the fifty states in centralized management and budgeting.[16]

The third reform goal involves judicial education and qualifications. The central ideas here are that, at minimum, all judges should be lawyers; that extensive, ongoing, in-service training programs are necessary to keep judges and court personnel abreast of substantive, procedural, and administrative developments; and that judicial removal commissions should exist through which complaints about inappropriate judicial conduct can be heard and unsatisfactory judges removed from the bench.

While the great bulk of cases in contemporary Arkansas are handled by judges who are lawyers, some "judges" of limited jurisdiction courts are not. Many appellate, circuit, and chancery judges have attended out-of-state seminars and workshops sponsored by national foundations, but such training is neither required nor provided by the state. A $100,000 appropriation in 1985 for beginning an in-state judicial college promises some attention to professional development in the future.

Prompted by a highly publicized example of a circuit judge's misconduct in 1976, the 1977 legislature authorized both a Judicial Qualifications Committee (with jurisdiction over local judges) and a Judicial Ethics Committee (with jurisdiction over appellate, general jurisdiction, and municipal court judges.) The former has never been implemented; members have never been appointed to it nor have funds been appropriated for its operation. The Judicial Ethics Committee does exist and has an investigator to pursue complaints. Because so many questions of constitutionality have been raised about both committees, however, it appears that the only certain means at present for removing a judge from the bench is through the cumbersome, costly, and highly unlikely (because the legislature is so rarely in session) process of impeachment or legislative address. In the exasperated words of the chief justice himself, "You can have a judge who eats valiums like popcorn and a delegation comes and asks me to do something about it and I can't."[17]

The indictment of two successive Little Rock municipal traffic judges on criminal charges, in 1981 and 1985, together with felony charges in 1985 against a supreme court justice (who was later acquitted), stimulated renewed interest in judicial reforms. All the supreme court justices appeared before the 1987 General Assembly requesting a constitutional amendment to establish an effective procedure for disciplining and removing errant judges; and the legislature overwhelmingly selected this proposal as one of its submissions to the electorate for possible ratification in 1988. At present, however, Arkansas ranks thirty-seventh of the fifty states in the area of judicial qualifications and education. [18]

Although Arkansas has been ranked forty-ninth of the fifty states in one overall measure of judicial professionalism, it should also be noted that the crushing case backlogs and repeated serious scandals that have disgraced some other state judicial systems with much higher "professionalism" scores have not yet widely plagued Arkansas courts. It should also be clear from this review, however, that Arkansas does not actually have a judicial "system" in the sense of an integrated hierarchy of courts operating under the scrutinizing managerial eye of the state judicial department. In fact, there is considerable question as to whether the courts of limited jurisdiction are part of the state system at all. [19]

Because courts of limited jurisdiction are not courts of record, municipal and other judges have extensive leeway in their courtrooms, restrained only by the judgment and mores of their attentive constituency and by the local government's need for revenues. Justice, therefore, in the courts where most citizens have their only encounter with the judicial system, can range widely from the arbitrary and heavy-handed to the genial and lenient. On the heavy-handed side, one novice lawyer was reminded by a municipal judge, when he attempted to invoke a law in his client's behalf, "Young man, that may be the law of the state of Arkansas but it is not the law in my courtroom. Guilty." On the lenient side, here is an account of a very "popular" municipal judge in one small town: "Judge K. visits with everyone and buys people coffee and cokes wherever he goes. Many times my friends and I may be eating and when we go to pay, Judge K. has already paid for our meal. He is very nice and really popular with younger people. People can come to him and get their tickets dismissed. I paid for a ticket that I got for tailgating. When my ticket came up in court, he told the secretary to dismiss it. She informed him that I had already paid the ticket. He saw my mother in town and gave her my money back." [20]

Judges in courts of general jurisdiction are somewhat constrained by their desire to avoid reversal of their findings on appeal, and circuit judges must work with jurors who are registered voters and whose impressions of the judge may circulate in the community. Still, only 1 percent of the decisions of general jurisdiction courts are appealed, and generally only the most aberrant judicial conduct, such as open drunkenness on the bench or an outrageously lenient sentence for drug dealers, will rouse a community to closer scrutiny of what is transpiring in their local courtroom.[21]

In theory, concern about the conduct and caliber of Arkansas judges is unnecessary. Since all judgeships are elective in Arkansas, they are constantly under the most powerful potential sanction of all: the right of the people to select qualified jurists and to remove unsatisfactory judges from the bench when they seek reelection. The actual operation of the selection system, however, raises some serious questions about the effectiveness of elections as a device for ensuring popular accountability.

## JUDICIAL SELECTION

Although Arkansas judges were originally appointed, first by the legislature, later by the governor, by 1864 Arkansas had opted for popular election, a method modified during Reconstruction years but resoundingly reconfirmed in the 1874 constitution and sustained since. In a slight tempering of the Jacksonian spirit, elective terms for some judges are lengthier than those of most other elected officials: eight years for supreme court and court of appeals justices; six years for chancellors; four years for circuit judges. Unlike many other states, however, where the trend in recent decades has been toward "merit selection," usually gubernatorial appointment from a committee-recommended list followed by a "retention" election, Arkansas has retained a totally elective judiciary.

Arkansas, in fact, has the most elected judiciary in the nation, that is, the highest percentage (94 percent) of judges who first reach the bench through election rather than appointment. Although twenty-one states still elect most of their judges (ten in partisan, eleven in nonpartisan elections), in many of these states, political custom promotes the practice of judges resigning shortly before their terms expire so that the governor may appont a successor, who then runs for reelection with all the advantages of incumbency. In California, for example, 88 percent of all judges initially reached the bench through gubernatorial selection rather than through the "normal" process of nonpartisan election, and in Texas, 66 percent of all judges were initially appointed despite the established process of partisan election.[22]

What makes this ruse impossible in Arkansas (and only Louisiana has a similar prohibition) is a constitutional amendment prohibiting a judicial appointee from running for election for that office to which he or she was appointed. Amendment 29, proposed by popular initiative and adopted by 52 percent of the voters in 1938, contains several provisions designed to prevent a variety of political abuses that had become commonplace and was not aimed exclusively, or even primarily, at the judicial branch. Still, because it clearly prohibits any person appointed to the U.S. Senate or to any "elective state, district, circuit, county and township office" from being eligible "to appointment or election to succeed himself," it has given Arkansas the most "democratic" judiciary of any in the nation.[23]

The rationale for an elective judiciary is anchored in arguments that it is a more popular and participatory process than the allegedly more closed, secretive, and elitist appointive method. Since judges make decisions with profound consequences for citizens' well-being, it is asserted, citizens should be able—as they are universally deemed entitled to and capable of selecting governors and legislators—to select judges who are sensitive to popular preferences and values. Furthermore, elections make it possible for citizens to hold judges accountable for the quality of their performance and their fidelity to the public trust.

The problem with these and similar arguments is that they presume a number of conditions that would in fact give the electorate a meaningful choice: a vigorous contest for first election to the bench in which the qualifications, values, and views of all contestants were highly publicized; and an equally vigorous challenge when a judge sought reelection, so that his or her performance could be evaluated. Whatever the abstract merits of the arguments for an elective judiciary (arguments that, parenthetically, do not acknowledge the traditional role of the judiciary in protecting unpopular minorities and controversial freedoms), the conditions that would in fact make such elections an instrument of popular choice and accountability are rarely operative in Arkansas.

To begin with, while many open seats produce a genuine contest, many draw only one "contestant," who is then "elected" by acclamation. Elections to the recently established court of appeals, for example, were held for the first time in 1980; in only four of the six districts did more than one candidate file, and there were no contests for the two seats to be filled in 1986. Similarly, responses to a recent survey of circuit and chancery judges indicate that nearly half (twenty-eight of fifty-nine) were first "elected" to their position without a contest.[24]

The chances of a contest are even more dramatically reduced when an incumbent judge seeks reelection. It is very uncommon for a sitting judge to draw an opponent, and defeat of an incumbent judge is the rarest occurrence in Arkansas politics. Incumbent supreme court justices have been defeated only three times in the twentieth century, all in highly unusual circumstances, and successful challenges are equally infrequent at lower levels. From 1972 to 1984, there could have been at least 150 challenges to circuit and chancery judges seeking reelection; there were, however, only 27, and 11 of these came in the aftermath of extensive reapportionment of judicial districts in 1977. In a typical year, only one or two judges of general jurisdiction courts will be opposed, and none will be defeated. From 1972 through 1984, only two sitting chancellors and four circuit judges lost their seats to challengers.[25]

This nearly routine reelection of most judges may well reflect popular satisfaction with incumbents, but it also reflects the hesitancy of practicing lawyers to challenge an incumbent judge. The chance of victory is slim, and the penalty for a lawyer who must continue practicing in the court of a judge he or she attempted to remove from the bench can be severe. Even supporting the losing candidate in a judicial contest is risky business for a lawyer. As one attorney recently noted, "I've heard horror stories about judges who win tacking their defeated opponent's ads up on the wall, and those who signed it being on a 'hit list' (for unfavorable treatment)." As another lawyer noted, "If you strike at the king, you must strike to kill."[26]

Because the electorate is so likely to support the incumbent against a challenger, judges seeking reelection always use "Judge" before their name on the ballot and, in the rare event of challenge, emphasize their incumbency in all advertisements: for example, "Circuit Judge Paul Jameson IS A TRIAL JUDGE NOW. Keep a proven, working trial judge at work on the job. Let the work of the court proceed without interruption. Re-elect Judge Paul Jameson." The insistent, almost frantic tone of this particular pitch was due to the fact that the challenger in this instance, having served as an appointed judge on the court of appeals, was also entitled to run with "Judge" before his name on the ballot, thus creating potential confusion for the electorate.[27]

Because polling research indicates that using "Judge" before a candidate's name is worth an automatic 20 percent of the votes, any candidates who can legitimately attach this appellation do so and feature pictures of their robed selves in all advertising. It is certainly no accident that the single office most frequently held by circuit and chancery judges preceding their election to the general jurisdiction bench is that of municipal judge. Furthermore, nearly half of all general jurisdiction judges (twenty-six of fifty-nine) had received some kind of judicial appointment prior to their first successful race for the circuit or chancery bench. What this suggests is that even in

Arkansas's "purely elective" system, appointments are extensively parlayed into electoral success.[28]

The utility of elections as an instrument of popular influence on the judiciary, then, is at least somewhat stifled by the frequency with which only one candidate seeks the office, the infrequency with which incumbent judges are challenged, and the fact that many candidates, who are not in fact incumbents, by using "Judge" before their name on the ballot appear to be such to the electorate. Of course, where all candidates run as "Judge" (as in the three-man race for the open supreme court chief justiceship in 1980) or where none uses that label (the two-man race for an open associate supreme court justiceship in 1978), the electorate must rely on other clues. What other factors enter into the judicial selection process, and do they enhance or further weaken the "popular accountability" rationale for an elective judiciary?

Since all judicial contests in Arkansas are partisan, the party label might seem to offer some useful guidance to the electorate, especially because studies have demonstrated that there are in fact measurable policy differences between Democratic and Republican state judges and that those differences are in the direction that party affiliation might logically predict (that is, Democratic judges are more likely to find for the tenant in landlord-tenant cases, for the employee in employee injury cases, for the administrative agency in business regulation cases, and so on). Whatever clarifying utility the party label may have in a competitive two-party state, however, totally evaporates in Arkansas in the face of the fact that almost every judicial contest that does take place does so within the Democratic primary. Through the 1984 elections, only one Republican had sought a supreme court position in the twentieth century (the same Jim Johnson who had run six times previously for office as a Democrat and once as a candidate of the White Citizens Council), and at the general jurisdiction level, there were only six general election contests (compared with forty-four primary contests) between 1972 and 1984.[29]

The party label would be superfluous if judicial races gave voters a clear picture of the political and social views and values that accompany the assorted candidates to the bench and inform their actions there. Canon 7B of the official Code of Judicial Conduct states, however, that a candidate for judicial office "should not make pledges or promises of conduct in office other than the faithful and impartial performance of the duties of the office; and should not announce his views on disputed legal or political issues."

Occasionally, this canon is ignored. In 1984, for example, in two races for the supreme court the candidates who were trailing demanded that the frontrunners take stands on such issues as pornography, school consolidation, and capital punishment, challenged them to issue debates, and advertised their own issue positions. In neither instance, however, were the frontrunners goaded into discussing more than their qualifications for office or their views on judicial reform. This canon undoubtedly is an important and valuable assurance of impartiality on the bench. It is somewhat contradictory, however, to the rationale for an elective judiciary.[30]

"Qualifications" for judicial office, then, become the only legitimate campaign issue: which candidate has the greatest measure of knowledge, experience, and integrity. A potentially useful guide to such qualifications, at least for incumbent judges seeking reelection or for judges seeking a higher judicial office, is the survey conducted in election years by the Arkansas Bar Association, in which the state's lawyers evaluate judges on such measures as temperament, quality of written opinions, character and integrity, impartiality, and understanding of complex issues. In 1977, however, the Judicial Council passed a resolution, expressing the collective sense of the appellate and general jurisdiction judges who comprise it, that judges should keep their evaluations confidential; and only a few judges have released their ratings to the public since that time.[31]

With party label inconsequential, debates on issues prohibited, and systematic evaluations of performance somewhat suppressed, on what basis does the electorate choose between competing candidates? One hypothesis is that "name recognition is all, and the candidate with a short, comfortable-sounding name, easily remembered, has a decisive advantage." Certainly the historical rosters of supreme court justices display an exceptional number of names such as Smith, Brown, and Jones, and few names of more than two syllables. Robert A. Leflar, for example, remains convinced that the more familiar, American-sounding name of his 1942 opponent (R. W. Robins) was highly advantageous to the latter. The short-name theory has no explanatory value, however, when all candidates have equally succinct ones (for example, Hays or Brown; Purtle or Harmon; Newbern, Bentley, or Sanders).[32]

Perhaps more important than a short name is a familiar name, especially one with judicial connotations. The name recognition value that comes from previous officeholding is clearly important for election to the general jurisdiction bench: only eleven of the fifty-nine incumbent judges surveyed had never held previous public office, while most had been a municipal or other judge, prosecuting attorney, deputy prosecutor, city attorney, state representative or senator, and many had served in several positions. Interestingly, over one-fourth had a close relative who had served on the bench. Chief Justice Jack Holt, Jr., elected in 1984, followed both an uncle and a cousin to the supreme court bench. Family ties did not assist the race of Griffin Smith, Jr. (son of Chief Justice Griffin Smith, who served from 1937 to 1955), against an incumbent justice in 1958, nor Eugene Harris's attempt in 1980 to secure the chief justiceship that his father had held from 1957 to 1969. The unsuccessful Harris race challenges another generalization, that an eye-catching nickname has strong voter appeal. Eugene ("Kayo") Harris was not a winner, nor was Charles A. ("Charlie") Brown or W. H. ("Sonny") Dillahunty in 1980, nor Wilbur C. ("Dub") Bentley in 1984.[33]

The familiar phenomenon of "friends and neighbors" is obviously influential in judicial races. Candidates in statewide races will generally get the strongest support in their home counties or areas. Harris's major strength came from his chancery district in 1980, for example, and John Harmon's came from those counties where his father-in-law, a former state senator, had political influence. Familiarity, however, can also breed displeasure: the Pulaski County prosecutor "Dub" Bentley got only 23 percent of the Pulaski County vote in his supreme court bid in 1984.

Generally, interest-group endorsements are most influential in less visible races. Thus the AFL-CIO endorsement is eagerly sought in races for land commissioner or lieutenant governor, or for the state supreme court. Labor-endorsed candidates for the supreme court have been much more successful than not in recent years, and at least one victory (John Purtle's in 1978 over Otis Turner, who had the backing of the bar) has been largely attributed to labor's active exertions. Perhaps for this reason, organized labor has staunchly supported the elective method.[34]

The most consequential organized interest is assumed to be the state's lawyers. The most frequently employed newspaper advertisement is that featuring long lists of lawyers' names or signatures endorsing the candidate, for example, "Over 100 Area Lawyers Support the Re-election of Charles Williams, Fayetteville Municipal Judge." Jack Holt, Jr., ran full-page newspaper advertisements on election eve in 1984 listing the names of nearly seven hundred lawyers and bearing a simple message: "Those of us who are members of the legal community believe that there's only one candidate who has the skills, determination, experience and temperament to be our Chief Justice."[35]

As was the case in decades past, candidates for statewide office begin their campaigns by attempting to secure commitments of support and activity from lawyers in each county, hoping that they will spread the word to their clients and others with whom they have influence. Often they begin with their cadre of classmates from law school, a communication system enhanced by the fact that, until recently, Arkansas had only one law school, in which relatively small classes promoted close association among the students. Of the present seven supreme court justices, six graduated from the University of Arkansas Law School at Fayetteville, and the one exception was an undergraduate there. Nearly 80 percent of the general jurisdiction judges have law degrees from the Fayetteville campus as well. Furthermore, most (forty-three of fifty-nine) indicate that they were very or moderately active in the state bar and especially (fifty-two of fifty-nine) active in local bar association activities prior to their elections.[36]

What has changed over the decades is the cost of seeking judicial office, from $10,000 or $15,000 in a contested statewide race in the 1940s to at least $100,000 in the 1980s; and most circuit and chancery judges with contested elections had to spend at least $10,000 in their first race. Here, perhaps, is where support from the legal community is most consequential. With rare exceptions, most of the money in judicial races comes from lawyers, and since large sums are necessary to run a competitive race, judicial candidates who cannot get financial backing from the bar face something of a silent veto. Here also may be the most disturbing aspect of an elective judiciary. The sight during an election year of judicial candidates scurrying from one law office to another in search of support and contributions inevitably diminishes the ideal image of a totally independent, unobligated, and uncompromised judiciary.

Although the judicial canons state, "A candidate, including an incumbent judge, for a judicial office that is filled by public election between competing candidates should not himself solicit or accept campaign funds," there is no secrecy about who has (and has not) contributed. Contributions of more than $250 must be reported and are then published in newspaper accounts. More important, judicial candidates quickly learn that their contributors *want* to give their check directly to the candidate, not to some intermediary, and even the most principled of candidates soon bends to this reality.[37]

If, as most judges and lawyers assume, the bar's influence is the critical factor in judicial elections, another doubt has been raised about the extent to which judicial elections actually represent the voice of the people. This is an especially intriguing question, since one of the major arguments against an appointive judiciary is that it simply replaces the politics of the electoral arena with the politics of the legal community. As a former circuit judge noted, "There is nothing more political than appointments. The only problem is that you're not talking politics that involves the people any more. You're talking politics between the governor and a law firm."[38]

It should also be noted, however, that the actual influence of the legal community may be less than is commonly assumed. Judicial elections are held simultaneously with all other contests, and usually 90 percent or more of those voting for the top of the ticket express their preferences in judicial contests as well. It is difficult to imagine that any sizable proportion of the 434,919 Arkansans who voted in the 1984 Democratic primary for supreme court associate justice have a lawyer, or sought a lawyer's guidance, before marking the ballot. In the most thorough test to date of bar influence in judicial elections, a survey of voters leaving the polls in a highly controversial election to the Texas Supreme Court found that only 7.6 percent of those who had voted had received information from an attorney. The survey also revealed that 85.8 percent of those leaving the polls could not remember the name of the judicial candidate for whom they had just voted! While this test has not been replicated in Arkansas, one poll did indicate that less than 1 percent of Arkansas voters could recognize the names of their supreme court justices. One scholar of state judicial systems has noted, "As long as he remains largely invisible to the public, his chances of remaining in office are excellent." If this is true, Arkansas judges should be invincible.[39]

Perhaps because there is some doubt as to the decisive nature of bar endorsements and support, candidates for judicial office use a wide variety of campaign devices (billboards, yard signs, appearances before civic groups and political rallies, and newspaper, radio, and television advertisements) containing an astonishing array of biographical information: that they chopped cotton, coached Little League, taught Sunday School, belong to a Masonic Lodge, developed shopping centers, and married a Tri Delt. One enterprising (and successful!) candidate for the supreme court chief justiceship ran an advertisement proclaiming his endorsement by twenty-seven Ex-Razorback (University of Arkansas) Lettermen, complete with the rampaging razorback hog logo.[40]

The effective clues to which a judicial electorate responds in Arkansas remain something of a mystery. What is known, however, is that in an elective judicial system, those who reach the bench must ordinarily have some political skills and some measure of name recognition in addition to whatever legal skills they may possess. In the most thorough analysis of the Arkansas Supreme Court to date, Cal Ledbetter, Jr., concluded, "Political activity and influence rather than legal ability or success as a practitioner is the decisive factor in helping one to reach the Supreme Court."[41]

This is not to suggest that appointive methods inevitably produce a more distinguished bench. In fact, some of the most exhaustive research on this subject has concluded that "neither the method of selection nor the term of office seems to correlate very highly or consistently with technical competence, honesty, wisdom and other non-ideological virtues." Still, it is clear that, in Arkansas at least, the elective method has not yet produced a very "representative" judiciary. Through 1986, no woman or black had sought or been elected to a seat on an appellate court, and only two women (and no blacks) have been elected to any of the circuit or chancery judgeships. In contrast, the allegedly more "elitist" appointive method had placed one woman and three blacks on the supreme court to fill vacancies.[42]

Despite the fact, as the previous discussion suggests, that there is little evidence in the Arkansas system that the elective method is a very effective expression of the popular will, there seems little likelihood that the system will be changed. One recent opinion survey suggests the difficulty that would-be reformers of the process would confront. While 56 percent of those surveyed thought justice would be better served by an appointive system, 64 percent wanted to retain judicial accountability to the electorate. According to those who conducted and analyzed this survey, "efforts made to improve problems in the present system of selection such as campaign costs, financing, advertising and enforcement of the Code of Judicial Ethics will be more productive than the efforts expended to change to a different system of judicial selection." The problem, of course, is that the attentive constituency for judicial reform is a very small one, and again, public attitudes are ambiguous. While 59 percent of those surveyed thought the judicial system needed major reform to achieve its goals, 67 percent thought the Arkansas judicial system works reasonably well to provide a fair trial and a measure of justice.[43]

THE FUTURE

The Arkansas judicial branch presents a number of interesting paradoxes. In one respect, it is the most "democratic" judiciary in the nation, but the conditions that would make judicial elections a meaningful statement of popular choice are absent more often than they are present. Although almost all Arkansas judges are "elected" in partisan elections, actual party influence and involvement is minimal, certainly far less than in those states where judges and judicial system personnel are the prime remaining prizes in party patronage networks. Although ranked very low in terms of judicial professionalism, there is little evidence of the extensive backlogs that have clogged the judicial process and made a mockery of justice in some states with highly professionalized systems. In fact, the Arkansas Supreme Court is considered to be one of the most efficient in the nation.[44]

Some close observers see the need for profound changes and improvements. They are concerned that the elective system discourages many potentially excellent judges from the bench because of their distaste for the money-raising and occasional name-calling that election contests entail. They are concerned that the recent dramatic increase in the number of general jurisdiction judges, while providing swifter justice for plaintiffs, has also produced some detrimental effects: judges much more sensitive to the local politics of their one- or two-county constituency than a judge with six or seven counties in his district had to be and a drastic shrinking of the pool of competent eligibles. Many are concerned with the "autonomy" of municipal judges and their capacity to do mischief instead of justice at a level where most citizens have their only encounters with the judicial system. The increasing costs of judicial races have begun to attract the participation of political action committees and could well lead to increased numbers of judges who assume office under a heavy and potentially compromising burden of campaign debts. According to some observers, the relative absence of judicial scandal is not so much due to the caliber of Arkansas judges and the quality of the Arkansas judicial system as it is to the absence of the scrutiny and controls that would bring unjudicial behavior into the open and apply appropriate remedies.

As an increasingly litigious society creates a much larger, more costly, and more visible judicial branch, citizen demands for a more sensibly administered judiciary and a more selective recruitment process should increase as well. The proposed constitutional amendment for a judicial disciplinary and removal process is just such a sign. To date, however, judicial reform has been high on very few agendas.

## CHAPTER ELEVEN

# Arkansas in the Federal System: Cooperation and Conflict

*In a small town where we choked on dust in the summer and bogged down in mud in the winter, where sewage ran down the ditches from overflowing outhouses . . . it was a caring Government in the 30's that gave us loans and grants to pave our streets and build a waste treatment facility. . . . And when Betty and I returned to our little hometown to . . . raise our beautiful children, we raised them free of the fear of polio and other childhood diseases that had been conquered because of vaccines developed with Government grants.*

Senator Dale Bumpers, 1984

*All we're trying to do is get states' rights back. . . . The power of the* FERC *to impose these kinds of burdens arbitrarily, capriciously, and without us having any input, is the power to destroy our respective states.*

Senator Dale Bumpers, 1986

If Arkansas government and politics operated in complete isolation, this chapter would be unnecessary. The consequences of absolute autonomy, however, would be much more momentous than the absence of a chapter. That very sizable portion of Arkansas schools, highways, bridges, dams, courthouses, clinics, jails, levees, sewer systems, and parks constructed wholly or partially with federal funds would be nonexistent. The $1.2 billion Arkansas River navigation project, the largest civil works project ever undertaken by the U.S. Corps of Engineers, would not exist, nor would

Beaver Lake or Greers Ferry Lake, around which prosperous retirement and resort communities now flourish. Without the federal government, those 437,000 Arkansans accustomed to receiving a monthly Social Security check would be severely disadvantaged, if not ruined, and there could be equally disastrous consequences for farmers, military retirees, health workers, welfare recipients, college students, and others whose fortunes are wholly or partially dependent upon direct payments from the federal government.[1]

The absence of sister states would also have major impact on an autonomous Arkansas. Arkansas students who presently pursue dental and optometry studies in Tennessee and prepare to become veterinarians in Louisiana under reciprocity arrangements worked out by the Southern Regional Education Board would be forced into other callings. Of less material but nonetheless major consequence, without the colleges of Texas, the University of Arkansas Razorbacks would have no adversaries in the Southwest Conference.

The imagined consequences of an absolutely autonomous Arkansas, ranging from inconvenience to calamity, could be expanded, but the exercise would be purely hypothetical and preposterous. Arkansas is firmly enmeshed in a complex web of intergovernmental relationships, and this has been true from before it had even territorial status through 150 years of statehood. In Arkansas's earliest years the national government provided all of the few roads and river improvements that were constructed, and early General Assemblies spent much of their time memorializing Congress for more. During the Civil War, of course, federal aid became federal arms. By the late nineteenth and early twentieth centuries, however, southern congressmen were often leading the efforts in securing federal aid for public purposes: road building, farm loans, boll-weevil control, health programs, flood control, agricultural extension services, and vocational education. The extensive and indispensable aid offered to Arkansas by the federal government during the Great Depression has already been noted, as well as the stimulating effect this assistance had in promoting the state's own responsibility for welfare programs and the revenue to sustain them. Indeed, federal funds were the major source of financing for Arkansas's centennial celebration in 1936.[2]

Numerous additional federal aid programs were established in the 1960s, so that, according to one recent study, federal aid as a percentage of Arkansas's total revenue ranged from 27 percent to 36 percent from 1966 to 1980. In 1982, 34.6 percent of Arkansas's general revenues came from federal funds; in the four areas that constituted 70 percent of Arkansas's expenditures that year, federal aid was distributed as follows: public welfare (71 percent), education (18 percent), highways (34 percent), health and hospitals (25 percent).[3]

Another way of describing the salutary effects of federal spending in Arkansas is to note that from 1982 to 1984 the estimated amount of federal spending in Arkansas for each $1.00 in federal taxes paid by Arkansas residents was $1.27. Arkansas assumed only 0.71 percent of the total federal tax burden in 1984, but received 0.84 percent of total federal expenditures, and 0.97 percent of all grants to state and local governments. In fiscal year 1985 the federal government spent $6.9 billion in Arkansas, making Arkansas thirty-first among the fifty states in per capita spending, with $2,913 spent per resident.[4]

In dollar terms, being part of the federal system has been and remains unarguably advantageous for Arkansas. Throughout Arkansas history, however, there has been and there remains a dark undercurrent of suspicion and hostility toward the national government, which has occasionally erupted into angry conflict. Given the material benefits that Arkansas's place in a federal system produces, what accounts for the perceived political advantageousness of "fighting the feds"? Has this kind of political posturing lost its popularity or simply changed its character? Will Arkansas's intergovernmental relationships become more or less problematic in the future?

## COOPERATIVE FEDERALISM

In one of the first and still finest examinations of cooperative federalism, Morton Grodzins used the sanitarian of Benton, in Saline County, Arkansas, to exemplify the fact that most functions of government had become shared ones, with federal-state-local collaboration the characteristic mode of action:

Consider the health officer, styled "sanitarian," of a rural county in a border state. He embodies the whole idea of the marble cake of government. The sanitarian is appointed by the state under merit standards established by the federal government. His base salary comes jointly from state and federal funds, the county provides him with an office and office amenities and pays a portion of his expenses, and the largest city in the county also contributes to his salary and office by virtue of his appointment as a city plumbing inspector. It is impossible from moment to moment to tell under which governmental hat the sanitarian operates. His work of inspecting the purity of food is carried out under federal standards; but he is enforcing state laws when inspecting commodities that have not been in interstate commerce; and somewhat perversely, he also acts under state authority when inspecting milk coming into the county from producing areas across the state border. He is a federal officer when impounding impure drugs shipped from a neighboring state; a federal-state officer when distributing typhoid immunization serum; a state officer when enforcing standards of industrial hygiene; a state local officer when inspecting the city's water supply; and (to complete the circle) a local officer when insisting that the city butchers adopt more hygienic methods of handling their garbage. But he cannot and does not think of himself as acting in these separate capacities. All business in the county that concerns public health and sanitation he considers his business. Paid largely from federal funds, he does not find it strange to attend meetings of the city council to give expert advice on matters ranging from rotten apples to rabies control. He is even deputized as a member of both the city and county police forces.[5]

Grodzins's study, published in 1966, documented other extensive evidence of cooperative federalism in Benton: the aluminum companies that provided the major source of employment were built under authority of the War Production Board and financed by the Reconstruction Finance Corporation; the city's only high school was largely paid for by $506,000 of federal funds, and all the local schools participated in the school lunch and milk programs and received federal aid for vocational and agricultural education; the city's dam and reservoir, used for both water supply and recreational purposes, were constructed with federal funds from the Community Facilities Program, utilizing data gathered by the Corps of Engineers; special censuses contracted for with the U.S. Census Bureau had gained Benton additional income from the state under a state-aid formula based on a city's population; the county welfare program that serviced Benton's needy residents distributed U.S. Department of Agriculture surplus commodities to those deemed eligible by the State Welfare Department. Interviews conducted for Grodzins by Daniel J. Elazar with more than forty Benton officials and civic leaders revealed a unanimous sentiment that federal officers were "fine, friendly and cooperative," that federal rules were not considered onerous, and that the federal-state-local relationship had been and would be a necessity for community development.[6]

Although many of the specific types and amounts of aid have changed over the last twenty years, the essence of what Grodzins discovered and demonstrated in the "hard case" of one small town in one small county in Arkansas is still true today. No official is absolutely autonomous and no government is an island. Extensive intergovernmental relationships have become commonplace.

## CONTEMPORARY INTERGOVERNMENTALISM

One way of illustrating the extent to which contemporary "Arkansas" politics is in fact intergovernmental politics is simply to note some of the major political stories featured by the press in 1985:

- In September 1985 the state Public Service Commission reluctantly approved a settlement making Arkansas ratepayers responsible for about 80 percent of Arkansas Power and Light's share of the $3.5 billion Grand Gulf nuclear power plant in Mississippi. Although Arkansas never requested and would not receive any power from Grand Gulf, the Federal Energy Regulatory Commission (FERC) ruled in June 1985 that AP&L would have to pay for 36 percent of Middle South Energy's 90 percent share of Grand Gulf, an allocation bitterly protested by Arkansas officials but upheld in federal court. Every major political figure in Arkansas angrily denounced the FERC, some were equally abusive of the federal judiciary, and all scrambled to distance themselves from and blame others for the resulting sharp rate increases, which enraged Arkansas customers.
- Arkansas truckers awaited the final outcome of lawsuits filed in Maine, New Jersey, and Oklahoma challenging the constitutionality of taxes assessed by those and other states on Arkansas trucks in retaliation against a 1983 Arkansas law that taxes trucks weighing more than 73,280 pounds $175 a year. A superior court in Maine ruled that retaliatory taxes violated the interstate commerce clause of the U.S. Constitution, but an appeal to the U.S. Supreme Court was expected.
- All Arkansas cities and counties and the state Corrections Department struggled throughout 1985 with the fiscal consequences of *Garcia v. San Antonio Metropolitan Transit Authority* in which the U.S. Supreme Court ruled that fire and police protection employees, and others with unusual work weeks, would have to be paid overtime and receive compensatory time off. Arkansas cities and counties adjusted schedules and rearranged budgets, the Corrections Board approved cutting $1.8 million from other areas to pay overtime, and all of these entities worked with their counterparts in other states successfully to persuade Congress to rectify the situation with amendments to the Fair Labor Standards Act.
- State and local officials also worked to meliorate the effects of "Reaganomics" and to anticipate and affect the final shape of proposed tax reforms: city and county officials discussed various strategies, including requests for a larger percentage of state revenues, to offset an anticipated loss of nearly $50 million in

revenue sharing; Governor Clinton, in his capacity as Chairman of the Southern Growth Policies Board, sent a report to the president and to the governors of other southern states predicting a "significant destructive impact" should Reagan's proposed elimination of the federal income tax deduction for state and local taxes be enacted; Senator Bumpers warned the Arkansas Municipal League of the difficulty they would have financing improvements through sale of tax-exempt bonds if that tax exemption were eliminated.

– Governor Clinton's original refusal to extradite a nineteen-year-old Arkansas girl charged by New York with cocaine-dealing created considerable controversy and criticism. Following Clinton's suggestion that a fifteen-year minimum jail sentence for a first offender was excessive, New York submitted a request specifying a lighter sentence, and the girl was extradited to stand trial.

– Operation Delta 9, a federally coordinated effort to curb the domestic cultivation of marijuana, was personally kicked off in Harrison, Arkansas, by U.S. Attorney General Edwin Meese. Two Arkansas National Guard helicopters were loaned for the purpose, the commanders of the seven State Police Criminal Investigation companies helped coordinate, and a few county sheriffs complained that they learned of the raids only through the national news media.

– The long, legal odyssey of the Little Rock school district in the federal courts on desegregation issues continued, and continued to create harsh feelings, supply grist for political campaigns, and provoke verbal attacks on the federal judiciary.

– After seven years of construction and numerous setbacks caused by inflation, strikes, and the collapse of the federal Law Enforcement Administration, which was to be its major funding source, the Bi-State Criminal Justice Center was finally completed and officially dedicated. It houses the city police departments of Texarkana, Arkansas, and Texarkana, Texas, and the Miller County, Arkansas, and Bowie County, Texas, sheriffs' offices as well as other courts, prosecuting attorneys, probationary officers, and work-release inmates from the Arkansas Corrections Department, who perform custodial services.

– A longstanding dispute over Fayetteville's plans to dump treated sewage into the Illinois River (designated a state scenic river by Oklahoma) continued to provoke charges and countercharges by both states' congressional delegations, governors, attorneys general, the federal Environmental Protection Agency, the Arkansas-Oklahoma Compact Commission, environmentalists in both states, the Arkansas Soil and Water Conservation Commission, the Oklahoma Water Resources Board, and city and county officials on both sides of the border.

– Congressman Tommy Robinson and Governor Clinton asked the Environmental Protection Agency to consider moving about 20,000 barrels of highly toxic wastes from the Vertac plant in Jacksonville to the Pine Bluff Arsenal for safe disposal, but the EPA suggested on-site incineration, and a Pentagon spokesman said they had never taken responsibility for wastes produced by defense contractors. A Jacksonville alderman warned that if an incinerator were moved in, Governor Clinton would need the National Guard to quell citizen riots.

Revelations that the Economic Opportunity Agency (EOA) of Pulaski County was $427,000 in debt and could meet neither its clientele obligations nor its payroll provoked a series of meetings and exchanges between the EOA Board, the Little Rock mayor, the director of the State Human Services Department, the governor's office, the federal Health and Human Services Department, and the Review and Advice Subcommittee of the state Legislative Council. As a temporary measure, most EOA programs were transferred to the Central Arkansas Development Council, in nearby Benton.

Somewhat serendipitously, this brief review brings us back full circle to Benton, home of the Saline County sanitarian who became the personal embodiment, the scholarly folk hero, of cooperative federalism. Other than coincidence, what does this list—itself an extract from numerous other 1985 Arkansas political stories with intergovernmental implications—suggest about contemporary federalism?

First, it underscores the fact that while one may still technically distinguish between the local, state, and national arenas of government, the officials of all these governments operate continuously in the spheres of all the others. Under the U.S. Constitution, Arkansas's two U.S. senators and four congressmen are officials of the national government, but they and their staffs spend most of their time "on matters specifically and directly involving the constituents back home." Reducing the national deficit, eliminating tax loopholes, and sustaining free world trade may be fine in principle, but the bottom line is what is best for the folks at home. Hence, the entire House delegation voted for a bill limiting shoe and textile imports. Both U.S. senators, while voting for drastic deficit reduction methods, also exerted extraordinary efforts to strengthen agricultural export subsidies and retain subsidies for rice and cotton, to halt planned termination of the Farmers Home Administration water and sewer facilities program, and secure additional funding for the Arkansas Educational Television Network, bathhouse renovations at Hot Springs, and a railroad relocation project at Pine Bluff. Congressman Beryl Anthony, from his seat on the House Ways and Means Committee, worked to protect the capital gains treatment for timber income so crucial to his constituency. As Senator Pryor's 1984 reelection theme so succinctly stated: Arkansas Comes First.[7]

The governor is formally responsible only for the state's management and well-being, but in order to advance these goals, he and his staff must frequently telephone the White House, testify before Congress, negotiate with neighboring states, assist local governments in their search for federal grants, meet with the National Governors' Association, even go abroad in search of expanded export markets and increased foreign investments in Arkansas. Technically, only one gubernatorial staff member is designated as Aide for Intergovernmental Relations, but as she herself notes, "Everybody is involved in intergovernmental relations because it is rare to encounter something that is strictly a state problem."[8]

Mayors and county judges are elected by local constituencies to hold local offices, but contemporary mayors, county judges, and other local officials consult frequently with their congressmen about expediting federal grant requests, work with the governor's office on developing Community Development Bloc Grant proposals, lobby the state legislature for greater turnback funds, and meet with their counterparts from other states at national meetings of city and county officials. In Arkansas, as elsewhere in America, extensive intergovernmental contacts and collaboration have become the rule rather than the exception.[9]

While jurisdictional squabbles inevitably arise from overlapping areas of responsibility, they are generally treated as practical and political issues rather than legal ones. The extensive administrative and fiscal rearrangements necessitated by the New Federalism in 1981–82 produced very little dialogue on the merits of the concept. Rather, state and local officials practically accommodated themselves to new decision-making patterns and lessened aid. As one recent analysis of intergovernmentalism concluded, "Pragmatism characterizes operations under the federal arrangement in the U.S. The approach is a problem-solving one without any special effort to work out solutions in accordance with any particular philosophic view of federal, state or local responsibilities."[10]

Although practicality has substantially replaced legality or philosophy as a framework for federal arrangements, conflicts and tension remain. In fact, the review of Arkansas's 1985 intergovernmental politics suggests a great deal more discord than harmony. How can this predominance of conflict be reconciled with the notion of cooperative, mutually beneficial federalism?

First, the discordant tone to many of the intergovernmental stories of 1985 may partially reflect the sheer volume and variety of programs that now involve numerous governments and officials. While intergovernmentalism has enormously expanded the resources, functions, and services of smaller and poorer governments, it has also multiplied the opportunities for misunderstandings, bureaucratic breakdowns, and jurisdictional rivalries. Hence, the increasing interdependence of federal, state, and local governments "creates higher tension levels in the political arena at the same time that shared administrative and program activities are on the rise."[11]

A second important explanation for the combative emphasis in the stories of 1985 is simply a reflection of what is deemed to constitute "news." When the gears of intergovernmentalism mesh, there is no story; when the gears clash, usually unnoted programs and procedures become newsworthy; and when a state or local official shakes a fist in the face of the federal government, it becomes headlines.

Elazar's interviews with county and city officials, all of whom described the various federal officials with whom they dealt as "fine, friendly and cooperative," were conducted in 1958, the year after federal troops had been sent to Little Rock Central High (twenty-four miles from Benton), the year when Orval Faubus was riding public outrage against an intrusive federal presence into an unusual third term. Grodzins noted the irony: "At a time when federal troops were guarding the nearby Little Rock high school, the school superintendent of Benton chose not to speak at all about segregation and described in terms of high praise the entire range of federal services to the schools."[12]

While Faubus captured national and international attention, the everyday workings of federal-state-local cooperation were nonnewsworthy, and the same principle still prevails. The governor's office routinely processes about one hundred requests for extradition annually, with no publicity; it was the one temporary refusal that made the headlines. Thousands of truckers enter and cross the state of Arkansas daily, using Arkansas highways and other facilities without incident; the retaliatory truck taxes made news because they seemed to endanger the usual free flow of interstate commerce. Congressman Robinson and his constituents were irate over the Defense Department's refusal to take responsibility for the disposal of toxic wastes, and vocal citizen concerns kept the Vertac dump constantly and prominently in the news; there was only one small story in 1985 pointing out that the military (including the Little Rock and Blytheville Air Force bases, Army and Navy recruiters, the Army Reserve, the Arkansas National Guard, Army engineers, and military and civilian employees at the Pine Bluff Arsenal) brings a beneficial economic impact to Arkansas of more than a half-billion dollars annually, and that an additional 100,000 Arkansans receive military retirement incomes. The Pulaski County EOA received enormous publicity for its mismanagement of public funds; the other eigh-teen community action agencies in the state received little attention as they continued to operate Head Start, elderly nutrition centers, youth counseling and employment programs, weatherization and recreation programs. Mis-takes and scandal make headlines; routine success does not.[13]

A third explanation for the often contentious and emotional tone to Arkansas's intergovernmental relations has long historical roots. With Arkansas's early decision to be a slave state, it became part of the South; and as John Shelton Reed has noted, the South was essentially "defined in opposition to a powerful, external threat," that threat being embodied in the national government. Sheldon Hackney has captured this defensiveness and sense of grievance as follows: "The South was created by the need to protect a peculiar institution from threats originating outside the region. Conse-quently, the Southern identity has been linked from the first to a siege mentality . . . defending their region against attack from outside forces: abolitionists, the Union Army, carpetbaggers, Wall Street and Pittsburgh, civil rights agitators, the Federal Government, feminism, socialism, trade unionism, Darwinism, communism, atheism, daylight savings time, and other by-products of modernity."[14]

Arkansas, as noted earlier, opted for the Confederate cause with consid-erable reluctance. Once in, however, the state was destined to experience equally with other southern states the cycle of destruction and defeat, military occupation and Reconstruction. Having constructed an entire polit-ical, economic, and social structure around the subordinate position of the black race, the escalating twentieth-century insistence of the national gov-ernment on the primacy of human rights over states' rights inevitably placed severe strains on the national-state relationship. The general sense of per-secution and suspicion toward meddlesome and intrusive outsiders may have been further exacerbated in Arkansas by its physical and social isola-tion, its cultural homogeneity, and resentment against its perennially bottom rankings in all state-by-state measures of social and economic well-being.

Two popular pieces of Arkansas folklore illustrate and support this analysis. One is a boast, commonly heard, told, and taught in earlier times, that Arkansas was the only state that could survive even if a fence were built around it to prevent anything from coming in or going out. This proverbial bit of "wisdom" may have "given Arkansas something to brag about when they desperately needed something to be proud of," but it also reinforced the imagined virtues and viability of autonomy and self-sufficiency.[15]

The second bit of folklore is Arkansas's most famous contribution to

American mythology, the tale of the Arkansas Traveler. This fiddle-tune and dialogue, which briefly became a popular New York skit, tells of a hapless traveler who encounters an Arkansas backwoodsman squatter. The traveler's requests for directions, food, and shelter are at first responded to with incivility, seeming ignorance, and deliberate deception. After an increasingly infuriating exchange, the traveler offers to play the balance of a fiddle tune that the native has played throughout the dialogue. Enchanted with the traveler's talent, the backwoodsman showers upon him all the hospitality his humble circumstances afford. The tale symbolizes the natural suspicion and defensiveness of Arkansans toward "outsiders" and also the warmth and welcome for those who patiently pierce this superficial shell of hostility.[16]

The ambivalence toward the outside world suggested in both bits of folklore has been equally characteristic of Arkansas's relations with the federal government. No state has been more swift to respond to the call for soldiers when the nation has been threatened. Due both to need as defined by federal aid formulae and to a historically powerful congressional delegation, Arkansas has been one of the nation's major beneficiaries of federal programs and projects. When President Franklin D. Roosevelt proclaimed that the South was the nation's Number One Economic problem, however, the response of Senator John Miller of Arkansas was that "what the South really needed from the federal government was a good letting alone."[17]

Tony Freyer, in his recent study, *The Little Rock Crisis*, points out some of the contradictory elements in southern attitudes toward the federal government:

Where federal legislation brought economic benefit, as with the creation of the social security system, the development of the Tennessee Valley Authority, or aid for education or highways, southerners enthusiastically supported national authority. But the use of federal power to enfranchise women or to strengthen organized labor engendered resistance among southerners based on solemn appeals to states' rights. Reflecting this inconsistency, southern politicians could not escape a certain ambivalence: at times they appealed fervently to the Constitution as the touchstone of benign national strength, but on other occasions they attacked the evil of the federal octopus with all the resolution of demagogues.[18]

Some of Freyer's specifics are not particularly appropriate for Arkansas: Arkansas women were enfranchised in the all-important Democratic primary even before a national suffrage amendment was ratified; and the great public power experiment that became the Tennessee Valley Authority was deliberately deflected away from Arkansas by the opposition of U.S. Senator Joseph T. Robinson, who, "reflecting the wishes of his law firm's main client, the Arkansas Power and Light Company, informed Roosevelt that the state was not interested in such a project." The essence of Freyer's observations, however, that Arkansas's attitudes toward the federal government contain many contradictions, is historically accurate and still valid.[19]

Nothing illustrates the ambivalence of contemporary intergovernmentalism better than the first administration of Governor Bill Clinton (1979–80). Clinton, who had moved in and was comfortable with larger worlds, prepared for his first administration by consulting extensively with the Center for Policy Research and the Council of State Planning Agencies on the development of new policy initiatives. He recruited some of his top aides from other states; an Arkansas office was established in Washington to pursue vigorously all possibilities of securing federal aid for the state; and seven of Clinton's original twenty-six staff appointments were specifically given intergovernmental responsibilities. When major tornados struck the state in both 1979 and 1980, federal disaster-assistance centers provided housing; long-term, low-interest loans; farm loss relief; income tax casualty advice; legal services; disaster unemployment compensation; and millions of dollars in loans and grants to individuals, business, and local governments. In 1980, in response to the devastating damage caused by heat and drought, the federal Health and Human Services Department, Community Services Administration, and Small Business Administration came to the rescue with hundreds of thousands of dollars for utility bill assistance to the needy and disaster loans to the severely damaged poultry industry. Governor Clinton, even more than any of his predecessors, turned repeatedly to the federal government for ideas, action, and assistance and successfully obtained them.[20]

Also like many of his predecessors, however, Clinton encountered the iron fist in the helping hand. In May 1980, the White House informed Clinton that the federal installation at Sebastian County's Fort Chaffee had been selected as a resettlement site for some of the estimated 120,000 "Freedom Flotilla" Cuban refugees. Clinton's initial response was correct and restrained: "I know that everyone in this state sympathizes and identifies with them in their desire for freedom. I will do all I can to fulfill whatever responsibilities the President imposes upon Arkansas to facilitate the refugees' resettlement in this country." When the White House repeatedly ignored Clinton's requests for sufficient federal security forces to keep the rioting refugees within the fort, however, and repeatedly reneged on promises not to send additional refugees, and especially when Clinton had to mobilize the National Guard and state police to protect citizens from escapees, his cordiality turned to disgust and fury. The Carter administration, with whom Clinton had close political and personal ties, became an albatross around his neck. Orval Faubus's defiance of the federal government ensured his reelection victory; Frank White's televised charges that Clinton had failed to "stand up" to the president and to keep the Cubans out of Arkansas was an important element in Clinton's 1980 defeat. Furthermore, in a repetition of charges used against Governor Francis Cherry in the 1950s and Governor Winthrop Rockefeller in the 1960s, Clinton's employment of "outsiders" to head state agencies and serve on his staff became part of the critical charges used against him.[21]

When Clinton recaptured the governorship in 1982, his intergovernmentalism was initially much more restrained. He did not attempt to reestablish the Arkansas office in Washington that Governor Frank White had abolished, only one of Clinton's staff members was a nonnative and only one had formal intergovernmental responsibilities, and his relationships with both the federal government and with his fellow governors and the National Governors' Association were much less frequent and aggressive. The word among NGA staffers was that Clinton had "gone native."[22]

By the time of his third and fourth administrations, however, Clinton apparently felt sufficiently secure with his Arkansas constituency to assume again a number of extrastate responsibilities. In 1985 he served as chairman of the Southern Growth Policies Board, and by 1986 he accepted election as chairman of both the National Governors' Association and the Education Commission of the States. Furthermore, unlike some other politicians, who ranted and raved against the Eighth Circuit Court's controversial decision in the Little Rock schools desegregation case, Clinton did nothing to agitate the issue. On the other hand, within hours after the rate settlement decision of the Public Service Commission in the Grand Gulf case, Clinton was airing radio commercials blaming this costly decision directly, and somewhat incorrectly, on federal judges.[23]

## FEDERALISM IN ARKANSAS'S FUTURE

What Governor Clinton's intergovernmental odyssey suggests, and Senator Bumpers's remarks quoted at this chapter's beginning confirm, is that for most Arkansans, and for their leaders, being part of a federal system is neither an unalloyed good nor an unmitigated evil. Through 150 years of statehood, Arkansas's angriest clashes with the federal government were produced by conflicting national and state views of black equality, and it is apparent from the ongoing emotionalism surrounding school consolidation and busing questions that some of the old sensitivities remain. With the basic legal issues of racial equality resolved, or at least reduced to differing concepts of implementation, however, the most longstanding and inflammatory source of Arkansas's state-federal conflicts has been lessened. In fact, by 1985 the respective roles of the federal and state governments in racial equality conflicts had actually switched. When the Civil Rights Division of President Reagan's federal Justice Department asked the Arkansas State Police to drop its affirmative action program for hiring blacks and women, the Arkansas attorney general's office refused: "We feel that we have a fair and workable hiring procedure in place at this point and see no reason to alter it. The State Police has worked hard to eliminate every vestige of racial discrimination and will continue to work to that end."[24] That the national government could be requesting a halt to egalitarian measures and the Arkansas state government be pushing forward is a scenario that would have been unthinkable twenty years previously.

While the federal government in general and federal judges in particular continue to provide convenient scapegoats for unpopular policy decisions, the federal government is not generally viewed as an adversary. In November 1985, a statewide survey found that 66 percent of Arkansans expressed either a great deal or a fair amount of trust and confidence in the national government, and only 8 percent expressed no confidence at all. (The comparable figures for state government were 78 percent and 4 percent.)[25]

Other changes have crept into Arkansas's external relations as well. The isolation and provincialism that bred suspicion and fear of outsiders have been dissipated by extensive communications from and contacts with the outside world. The Arkansas tourism industry now actively woos and cultivates travelers, and distinguished visitors, from Japanese businessmen to Norwegian foreign students, are proudly presented with an "Arkansas Traveler" certificate.

Xenophobia has been largely replaced by curiosity. When Raymond Ho, a native of Hong Kong, arrived in Arkansas in 1983 to head the state's educational television network, A E T N, he was often asked, by waitresses, filling station attendants, and others, if he was a "kung fu" instructor. Ho's radical changes at A E T N and his flamboyant personality predictably produced some tempestuous relationships within the state education establishment and with some longtime legislators, one of whom was heard gloating over "getting some Chink blood" at a legislative committee meeting where Ho was being grilled. On the other hand, the citizens of Arkansas responded to Ho's innovations with massive increases in viewership and contributions.[26]

Some of the state's politicians still speak in foreboding terms of the federal government: "A government big enough to give you things can take away everything you have"; "Our people have felt the burden of the federal government for too long"; "The federal government is our child but now they've got it where the federal government is supreme and we're the children. . . . And it's going to cause the destruction of this system." The politicians making such pronouncements, respectively Jim Johnson, Frank White, and Orval Faubus, have been repeatedly rejected by voters in recent years. The more successful Arkansas politicians are those who occasionally and sometimes vehemently protest a particular action by the federal government but do not operate from a generalized grievance against it.[27]

Indeed, by 1986, four of Arkansas's most successful politicians tacitly acknowledged both the importance and the political acceptability of strong intergovernmental relations by becoming heads of their respective national associations: Governor Bill Clinton, chairman of the National Governors' Association; Lieutenant Governor Winston Bryant, chairman of the National Conference of Lieutenant Governors; Attorney General Steve Clark, president of the National Association of Attorneys General; and Representative John Miller, chairman of the Council of State Governments. In an address in 1984 in Little Rock to the Israel Public Affairs Committee (itself an interesting sign of emerging cosmopolitanism in a state whose Jewish population has historically been minuscule), Governor Clinton urged better understanding among Arkansans of global affairs and the world economy: "The old notion that Arkansas was the only state that could produce all it needed to survive was probably never true, but it was never more untrue than it is today." Arkansas, and its politicians, are becoming more aware of and more comfortable with the world outside its borders.[28]

The sheer number and complexity of contemporary intergovernmental contacts guarantee occasional squabbles with the federal government and with other states. Arkansas citizens can still be "riled up" by federal actions perceived as intrusive and insensitive, or by rumors that Texas is plotting to take their water away, and the cry of "Thank God for Mississippi" (which has historically saved Arkansas from absolute last place in various fifty-state rankings) is still heard in the land. Because they are newsworthy, the controversial and combative aspects of intergovernmentalism will continue to be those most publicized, but the occasional states' rights posturing is more ritual than reality. Reality continues to be the principles embodied in the sanitarian of Saline County: that most relationships in the federal system are cooperative, pragmatic, and broadly beneficial.

## CHAPTER TWELVE

# Politics at the Grassroots: How Democratic?

*For the ordinary citizen, what happens in Washington, or even the state Capitol . . . he doesn't get to make much of a difference. But he can go to the city council, the members are his neighbors, he can talk on every issue.*

William J. Fleming, General Counsel
for Arkansas Municipal League, 1985

*The small towns are a purer sense of what democracy is about.*

Jackie Dillard, Mayor of Alexander, Arkansas, 1985

*Every two years, on schedule, democracy demands a fight. But precisely because of the nature of social relations in the small community, political conflict is threatening. . . . the small community must find other ways to satisfy the formal requirement of democracy.*

James D. Barber, *The Lawmakers*, 1965

Local politics is both more and less consequential in contemporary Arkansas than it was in the past. Counties were originally established as mere field offices of the state government, convenient administrative outposts through which the state could ensure the enforcement of state laws, the conduct of state elections, the collection of state taxes, and the provision of such services as the state deemed necessary.

While counties still perform many of their functions, especially those related to courts, corrections, and law enforcement, under state mandate, they have become much more than mere creatures of the state. They are also, indeed they are primarily, agents of the citizens in their own jurisdiction, providing whatever array of services (roads, hospitals, libraries, nursing homes, airports) that particular constituency desires and is willing to tax themselves to support.

Unlike earlier times when all Arkansas counties were rural and sparsely populated, by the 1980s county populations ranged from Pulaski's 350,000 to Calhoun's 6,000. The larger counties provide a richer menu of services, including everything from recreational facilities to battered women's shelters, while the small, rural counties stick to the basics of road building, law enforcement, and record keeping. Because rural residents have no other local government, however, county government is more visible and important to them than it is to urban residents with their city streets and municipal police departments.

In 1974, Amendment 55 to the constitution gave "home rule" to Arkansas counties; that is, it enabled counties to "exercise local legislative authority not denied by the Constitution or by law"; and in 1981 the state legislature conferred even further discretion upon counties by authorizing a local-option one-cent sales tax. According to one recent study, Arkansas ranks sixth of the fifty states in terms of county discretionary authority regarding finances, functions, personnel, and structure.[1]

Arkansas cities were constitutionally conceived in much more negative and restrictive terms than were county governments: "The General Assembly shall provide, by general laws, for the organization of cities (which may be classified) and incorporated towns, *and restrict their power of taxation, assessment, borrowing money and contracting debts, so as to prevent the abuse of such power."* Cities have also now been given the local-option one-cent sales tax, but they have never been given full home rule. In terms of the discretionary authority granted to municipalities, Arkansas ranks thirty-fourth of the fifty states.[2]

Despite this seeming straitjacket, however, municipal governments have grown in both political prominence and governing power. In 1940 there were nearly 400 incorporated towns in cities in Arkansas, but only 9 contained 10,000 or more people, and those living within municipal boundaries made up only 32 percent of the population. By 1986 there were 480 incorporated towns and cities, 29 of them contained 10,000 or more people, and the municipal population of Arkansas was 60 percent of the state's total population.[3]

As with counties, there is a very wide population range (from 43 to 178,134) and an equally broad spectrum of services, from the most rudimentary (police and fire protection, streets and sanitation) to the most complex (public housing, museums and performing arts centers, diverse recreational facilities). One small sign of the changing times is that by 1984, the $378,000 monthly payroll for the city of Fayetteville (population, 36,608) exceeded the annual expenditures of the entire state of Arkansas in 1874.

In terms, then, of powers and functions, expenditures and services, local governments play a much more material part in delivering a greater variety of services to Arkansas citizens than they ever did in the past. Nonetheless, there are some ways in which the import of local governments and politics has diminished.

First, the local bosses and their "machines," which often meant the county judge and his courthouse crowd, have nearly disappeared. Candidates for statewide office rely more on mass-media appeals than on local leaders to convey their message and mobilize their votes; a less patronage-hungry and more educated electorate is less dependent upon and therefore less manageable by the favors and guidance of county officials; a more regularized election process has lessened the opportunities for either intimidation of the electorate or management of the outcome; and major reforms of county government have lessened and divided the power once concentrated in the office of county judge.

Although these reforms have been broadly beneficial, they have cut deeply into the bargaining power that county officials once had in dealing with governors and the legislature—namely, be good to my county and I'll deliver you a nice vote. Legislators still try to cooperate with "their" county officials, and candidates for statewide office still make an obligatory campaign call at the courthouse; but the alpha and omega of political power no longer resides there except in a few of the smallest counties.

The Arkansas Association of Counties and the Arkansas Municipal League, representing the generalized interests, respectively, of county and city governments, are among the more significant lobbies at the state capitol. Their most frequent programmatic pleas, however—a fixed percentage of the state's general revenue, more state "turnback" funds for local governments, automatic state reimbursement for all state-mandated functions, genuine home rule for cities—have been systematically denied or ignored.

The fact that local governments now spend much of their time and energy organizing assaults on the state treasury symbolizes the second major way in which local politics has lost some of its luster. In Arkansas, as elsewhere in America, local governments have become increasingly trapped in a severe financial bind, the combined consequence of state restrictions on their taxing, spending, and borrowing powers; the effects of inflation on labor-intensive budgets; increased citizen expectations of more and better services; and a traditional reliance on the ever-unpopular and highly inelastic property tax. The major "solution" has been an increased dependence upon intergovernmental transfers, that is, on funds collected by the national or state government but spent by counties, cities, and school districts.

In 1982–83, 43.9 percent of everything spent by local governments in Arkansas consisted of taxes collected by either the national government (7.4 percent) or state government (36.5 percent) and transferred to local governments for expenditure. By the early 1980s, in other words, local governments in Arkansas were actually raising little more than half of what they were spending.[4]

Some of this "dependency" reflects the increased reliance of local school districts upon state funds. For counties and cities as well, however, which respectively received 25.1 percent and 29 percent of their income from intergovernmental transfers in 1982–83, it had become somewhat more difficult to call the tune when someone else was paying the piper. By the 1970s many mayors reported spending most of their time searching for federal funds, a situation that the attorney for the Arkansas Municipal League described in 1976 as "shameful" because it "did not strengthen democracy."[5]

Later that year, however, when Governor David Pryor proposed a dramatic restructuring of this dependency relationship, county and city officials vehemently rejected the so-called Arkansas Plan, apparently preferring stingy but secure state handouts to the much riskier prospects of an enhanced capacity for proposing taxes to (but not imposing taxes on) their own citizens. State and federal aids have empowered local governments to provide many services that would otherwise have been unthinkable, but with the deeper dependency on state and national governments there has been some narrowing of local decision-making prerogatives.[6]

A third reason for the diminished salience of local politics is that individuals as well as governments have become increasingly tied to state and national networks. The intense sense of community, of one's life and fate being closely linked to that of the people and politics of a particular town or county, has been abated by Arkansans' easier association with larger worlds. Roland Warren was one of the first to note the "increasing association of people on the basis of common occupational or other interests, rather than on the basis of locality alone (as among neighbors)" as one of the great changes of modern times.[7]

Throughout Arkansas, especially in the smaller towns, there is still a powerful sense of place and of home, and "neighboring" is still a very common pastime. Even in the community columns in the state's weekly newspapers, however, along with the news of who visited whom are frequent reports of trips to California and Canada, of phone calls from children in Formosa or Saudi Arabia, of shopping expeditions to Tulsa or Dallas, of elderly relatives being taken by helicopter to Little Rock or St. Louis for medical treatment. And many of the "local" meetings listed are those of local affiliates of a state or national organization: the Retired Teachers Association, the Farm Bureau, the Jaycees. Returning to Warren's astute observations:

True, the local office of the state welfare department, the local post office, the local unit of the multibranch bank, the local plant of the national manufacturing company, the local unit of the labor union, and the local branch of the grocery chain are all located within the community and are largely staffed by community people. But the continuation of their very existence in the community, the formulation of their policies, and the determination of their specific behavior is not as subject to local control as was the case in earlier decades.[8]

Despite some loss of community identification and community autonomy, however, there is undeniably still something that can be clearly identified as local politics. The State Education Department may supply most of the funds and many of the standards for local school districts, but it is locally elected homefolk who must answer to their neighbors for decisions that have the capacity to be highly divisive and controversial: whom to hire as school superintendent, whether there shall be school dances, the drawing of attendance zones, disciplinary policies, and so on.

As O. P. Williams and C. R. Adrian have accurately observed, local politics rarely results in "grinding hardships on any large number of citizens," it does not "obviously affect the income of most people," and in this sense it is peripheral; it "floats along the edges of the mainstream of domestic issues." On the other hand, if the school bus is unsafe, if one's children must board it by 5:30 A.M., if the trash goes uncollected, if land transactions are improperly recorded, if local water is inadequate or unsanitary, if the fire department is incompetent—these problems immediately and intensely affect the safety, health, comfort, and convenience of the citizenry.[9]

Since the decisions that result in these outcomes are made by locally elected officials who must live with the consequences and experience the frontline wrath or regard of their neighbors, local politics should be the most thoroughly democratic kind of politics in contemporary Arkansas. Here, if anywhere, the people should in fact rule. In practice, however, local politics both does and does not fulfill the democratic ideal.

THE DEMOCRATIC NATURE OF LOCAL POLITICS

In 1982, when the U.S. Census Bureau last counted, there were 1,424 local governments in Arkansas, that is, 1,424 entities that were governed by elected officials and that could levy taxes and incur bonded indebtedness. This sum included 75 county governments, 472 municipal governments, 372 school districts, and 505 special districts, mostly for drainage and flood control but also for housing and community development, water supply, soil and water conservation, and other single or multiple purposes. In terms of the sheer number of local governments, Arkansas ranks twenty-second of the fifty states.[10]

I shall confine this analysis to general-purpose local governments, that is, to city and county governments, but that still provides 547 local governments, each of them run by at least five and in some cases by more than twenty locally elected officials. If one measure of democracy is an abundance of governing institutions and officials, Arkansas easily meets that standard. The number of county officials elected biennially was sharply reduced from nearly 3,500 to 1,365 in 1974 as part of a radical restructuring of county government that has provided a much more visible and accountable handling of county affairs.

In the finest traditions of Jacksonian democracy and post-Reconstruction suspicion, the executive functions of county government were divided by the 1874 constitution among eight separately elected executive officials: county judge, county clerk, sheriff, assessor, collector, treasurer, surveyor, and coroner. None of these was specifically designated as chief executive, but the county judge was clearly chief among equals. His responsibilities included both executive functions (county business manager, road administrator, purchasing agent) and minor judicial functions. Most important was the county judge's responsibility of authorizing and approving the disbursement of appropriated county funds, most of which went for roads.[11]

Formally, the judge's spending required the approval of the quorum court, a body composed of elected justices of the peace, who, meeting as a group, were charged to "sit with and assist the County judge in levying the county taxes and in making appropriations." As a legislature, however, this institution's powers were notoriously nonexistent. They met only once a year. Equally important, with one justice of the peace mandated for each 200 voters, the justices when assembled were literally strangled by their own size. Even the smallest quorum court had 28 members, most counties had 30 to 60 members, and Pulaski County's 467-member quorum court may have been the world's largest legislative body. Annually the court members would assemble, answer the roll, give their unanimous consent to the judge's approximation of county expenditures for the coming year (which he frequently read aloud from a single sheet of paper), collect their ten-dollar fee, and retreat again to anonymity. Some justices, in between these annual exercises, used their semijudicial status to perform marriages, notarize documents, and collect traffic fines, thereby earning some extra income. At no time, however, in any county, did any quorum court exercise any real restraint over any county judge. In effect, then, the county judge exercised not only executive and judicial powers but legislative powers as well.[12]

The county judge's powers were not absolute: the other elected executives, especially those compensated by fees assessed through their offices rather than through appropriated county funds, certainly did not consider themselves to be subject to the judge's administrative authority. Nonetheless, in terms of county projects, property, employees, and funds, the county judge became the closest thing to an uncrowned king that the American political system had to offer. With no real check on the hiring and firing of county employees, with no internal checks on purchasing and contracts, it was inevitable that power would be abused. The most frequent abuses were kickbacks from road builders, questionable awards of contracts, and use of county employees and machinery for private purposes. This concentration and abuse of power was the main stimulus toward county reform in Arkansas, and a major impetus behind the constitutional revision effort in 1970. Not surprisingly, considering their statewide as well as local political power, the county judges and their allies managed to defeat a county reform constitutional amendment in 1968 and contributed significantly to the defeat of the new constitution proposed in 1970.[13]

There was, however, one serious flaw in the county judges' free-wheeling paradise: a constitutionally limited salary of no more than $5,000 per year. Most judges actually took home much more than that through the semilegal device of also being paid as county road commissioner, but it was the lure of larger lawful salaries that finally turned implacable opposition to county reform to official endorsement of it.[14]

Amendment 55, added to the constitution by a narrow 51.5 percent of the voters in 1974, removed the $5,000 constitutional salary limit on county officials, providing instead that the compensation of each county officer would be fixed by the quorum court within minimums and maximums set by the state legislature for population-categorized counties. Virtually all of the county judge's executive and administrative powers remained intact; in fact, subsequent legislation clearly made the judge the county's "chief executive officer."

Simultaneously with some strengthening of the county judge's formal powers, the amendment mandated a drastic reduction in the size, and a dramatic enlargement in the powers, of the previously superfluous quorum court. They were reduced by Amendment 55 to nine, eleven, thirteen, or fifteen members. As categorized by county population, this now means nine-member courts in forty of Arkansas's seventy-five counties, eleven members in twenty-six counties, thirteen members in eight counties, and fifteen only in Pulaski County. Further assuring their prominence and accountability, these justices are now elected from equitably apportioned single-member districts and must meet monthly. To their existing responsibilities of levying taxes and making appropriations, Amendment 55 added the following: to cooperate with any other political subdivision for public purposes; to create, consolidate, separate, revise, or abandon (with popular consent) any elective county office; to fix the salaries of county officials within minimums and maximums established by state law; to fix the number and compensation of county employees; to fill vacancies in elective county offices; to adopt ordinances necessary for the government of the county. The amendment also enabled them to override the county judge's veto with a three-fifths vote. The clear intent of Amendment 55 was a check and balance system, along the familiar national model. At least it offered the opportunity for a somewhat more active legislative body operating as a somewhat more vigorous check on a strengthened chief executive.

In some of the smaller, rural counties, little has been changed by reform; the county judge still dominates with the passive acquiescence of a smaller but behaviorally similar quorum court. In most counties, however, the judge has become more of a manager and less a political tyrant. Perhaps most important, the required public monthly reporting on the county's financial status has, for the first time in more than a century, placed county finances in the public domain. The structural reforms have had profound political as well as governmental consequences, but before examining these, the fundamentals of municipal structure in Arkansas should be noted.

All but twelve of Arkansas's incorporated towns and cities use the traditional mayor-council form of government. Incorporated towns (those with populations of less than 500) elect a mayor, a recorder, and five aldermen, all of whom comprise the city council. Second-class cities (with populations of 500 to 2,500) elect a mayor, a recorder, and two aldermen from each ward who together constitute the city council. First-class cities (those of 2,500 or more people) also elect a mayor, recorder, and aldermen, but only the aldermen serve on the council. In all these cities, the mayor presides over monthly council meetings, may vote in case of a tie, and has the veto power. Depending upon size, classification, and local ordinance, a city attorney, treasurer, marshal, and collector may also be elected or appointed. While more than 90 percent of mayor-council municipal elections are nonpartisan, in some cities candidates seek municipal office under a party label.[15]

First-class cities may also, by vote of the people, choose other structural arrangements: the city manager form (now used by Arkadelphia, Brinkley, Camden, DeQueen, Fayetteville, Hope, Hot Springs, Little Rock, Maumelle, and Texarkana) or the city administrator form (now used by Barling, Fort Smith, and Siloam Springs). In both forms, nonpartisan elections determine a seven-member board of directors whose members serve without pay and whose major responsibility is to hire and hold accountable a competent administrator to manage the city. In the city manager form of government directors usually run at large, though in some cities part of the board may be required to be residents of different wards. In the city administrator form, four directors are elected by the wards in which they reside while three run at large. In the city manager form, the board usually selects one of its own number to perform largely ceremonial functions as mayor; in the city administrator form, a mayor is elected at large and has the veto power. In both, however, the hired manager or administrator supervises all administrative departments, their operations, and employees.[16]

In theory, there are sharp distinctions between the mayor-council form and the manager and administrator forms of government, distinctions that are hotly debated in scholarly circles and occasionally by citizens when referenda on changing the form of government are under way. Proponents of the mayor-council form of government assert that it is less costly (no high-priced manager), more responsive and sensitive to public wishes (ward elections of aldermen, who provide their constituents with direct, personal access to city departments), and more reflective of popular values than if an outsider with no personal stake in a city's growth or well-being were hired. Advocates of the manager and administrator systems argue to the contrary: that a trained administrator is more efficient and more likely to save money; that "ward-heeling" promotes favoritism and invites scandal; and that managers have as much or more of a professional stake in successful municipal operations as nativism could possible engender.

In practice, however, most of the operational differences among municipal governments in Arkansas seem to be more a function of size than of structure. The differences between Little Rock (population, 178,134; 1,400 city employees) and Little Flock (population, 663; 1 employee) are not due to the fact that the former uses the manager system and the latter does not. All of the larger cities in Arkansas employ some managerial assistance, whether that individual is a city manager or administrator or is an administrative or financial aide to the mayor. And even in the supposedly apolitical, antiseptic managerial form, there is plenty of personal and political maneuvering over policies and personnel.

There are other notable gaps between theory and reality. On paper, Arkansas mayors are classified as "weak" by standard public administration measures: their executive power is fragmented by the existence of other separately elected executive officials and further constrained by municipal civil service commissions and other mandated boards and commissions with lengthy, overlapping terms. In practice, however, depending upon the personal energy and proclivities of the incumbent, upon longevity in office, and also upon local custom, mayors in Arkansas range from the dominating and dictatorial to the self-effacing and forceless. On paper, the commission form of government (under which a small group of elected co-equals acts as legislative authority while simultaneously taking executive responsibility for a selected area of administration) no longer exists in Arkansas since its abandonment by Fort Smith and Eureka Springs. In practice, however, in many small Arkansas cities, one council member becomes in effect the "streets" person, another the "fire and police department" man, another the one to deal with on "budgets." Structural distinctions are important, but they are not as great in practice as formal organization charts might suggest.[17]

More important to an analysis of the "democratic" content of local politics in Arkansas are other nonstructural questions: How representative are local officials of their populations generally and are they equally accessible to all views and interests? How participatory and pluralistic is local politics? Are the contests for office real rather than rigged, and are there a sufficient number of candidates to give voters a meaningful choice? What are the stakes in local elections, and do the campaigns illuminate or obscure the issues involved?

In some respects local politics is extremely egalitarian. For anyone who has any desire for public service, thousands of local offices are at stake every two years, and with very few exceptions the qualifications for seeking those offices are absolutely minimal: to be a resident and a registered voter. One need not be trained in road building to be a county judge, in law enforcement to be a sheriff, in public administration to be a major, or in medicine to be a coroner, and so these positions can be and are filled by farmers and salesclerks, merchants and housewives, pharmacists and florists. That candidates often seek office under such nicknames as Junior and Bubba, Junebug and Jughead, nicely conveys the nonelitist nature of most local contests. Since county offices are partisan, becoming a candidate for county office may necessitate winning a primary election. Still, most municipal and all school-board contests are nonpartisan, and one becomes a candidate simply by filing a petition signed by as few as ten and never more than fifty resident electors. [18]

Local politics is also decidedly democratic in the easy availability and frequent use of the initiative and referendum. Some local policy decisions can be enacted only after approval by local voters, for example, a school millage increase, a county or municipal sales tax, a local bond issue, a change in liquor laws, annexations, any abolishment or consolidation of county offices, or any change in form of city government. City and county legislative bodies (unlike the state legislature) may voluntarily submit issues to their citizens for resolution (as Fort Smith recently did regarding controversial Sunday closing laws), and citizens may invoke a protest referendum against enacted city and county ordinances that they find objectionable (as Fayetteville citizens unsuccessfully did against the city's decision to fluoridate the water). Because signature requirements on the petitions to initiate county and city ordinances are modest (15 percent of those who voted for, respectively, county clerk or city clerk), it is relatively simple to force almost any issue into the electoral arena. Indeed, in 1982, three county electorates considered, and two adopted, local initiatives "requesting the President to Propose a Mutual Verifiable Nuclear Weapons Freeze between the U.S. and the Soviet Union."

## THE UNDEMOCRATIC NATURE OF LOCAL POLITICS

In all the above respects, local government and politics offer abundant opportunities for genuine grassroots democracy. In other respects, however, these "schoolrooms of democracy," as de Tocqueville once described them, fall far short of the democratic ideal. To begin with, only a small fraction of local offices are ever contested. Since most county executive positions provide a livelihood, any open seat will usually attract more than one aspirant, and the county judge and sheriff are sufficiently visible that from one-third to one-half of these incumbents are likely to be challenged in any given year. Most other county executive offices are relatively safe for the incumbent, however, as are most quorum court positions. In 1984, for example, 765 quorum court positions could have been challenged in both the primary and the general election. Instead of 1,530 contests, however, there were 273, over 80 percent of which were for open positions.[19]

In the immediate aftermath of the Amendment 55 reforms (that is, in the 1976 elections), there was a vigorous race for almost every county elective office; and justice of the peace positions remain somewhat more contentious than they were in prereform days, when many positions went unfilled. A spirited race for the quorum court, however, or indeed for any county office other than judge or sheriff, is exceptional.[20]

Municipal races are even less competitive than county elections, and often more closely resemble the determined draft of any willing volunteer than a genuine contest. Resignations from city office are common, and since, unlike any other office in Arkansas, appointees to municipal office may run to succeed themselves, many mayors and aldermen reach office through appointment, then stay in power as long as they choose to do so. Indeed, some very small towns simply dispense with the "nuisance" of holding elections at all. The town of Sherrill, for example, having found some folks willing to serve as city officials in 1978, simply dispensed with municipal elections in 1980, 1982, and 1984. According to the city council's appointed secretary, since the mayor and aldermen want to remain in their positions, "the town has not seen a need for elections." The mayor added, "It's not the way it's supposed to go, but it's the way we do it."[21]

There are, of course, some notable exceptions to this general noncompetitiveness at the grassroots. In some of the larger cities, especially Little Rock, a seat on the city board confers enough prestige, publicity, and potential stepping-stone value that most positions, even those occupied by incumbents, draw competition. And even in the smallest towns, there is an occasional outburst of electoral engagements. Sometimes all or most municipal officeholders will be challenged in angry response to a highly unpopular and/or costly official action: a stiff increase in water rates, a flagrant display of nepotism, some perceived extravagance or abuse of privilege. Most often, however, such races as occur at the local level are personality contests more than policy debates, which again raises questions about the accountability value of the election mechanism.

According to many political scientists, recruitment practices are an excellent guide to the relative openness of a political system. If this is so, then local politics in Arkansas is much more egalitarian than exclusive, because only in a few cities and circumstances are nominations for office highly structured. In Little Rock, the Good Government Committee, composed of prominent businessmen, has recruited and endorsed candidates for the city board of directors since the change to city manager form in 1957, and they have had considerable success. In mid-sized cities, such as Fayetteville and Springdale, the Chamber of Commerce often acts as an informal recruiting mechanism, attempting to encourage the "responsible" sort to take their turn in office when an incumbent signals an intent to step down. In every community, whatever exists by way of a power structure will mobilize and find an acceptable candidate if it appears that the village idiot is about to become mayor by default. At the county level, a few of the more powerful county judges recruit quorum court candidates who will comply with the judge's leadership; and in that minority of counties in northwest Arkansas where Republicans have begun encouraging local office seeking, Democrats have begun some defensive recruiting of their own.[22]

In most city and county contests, however, most candidates are pure self-starters who seek and hold office, often at considerable expense in time and energy, out of a sense of civic interest and public service. With little or no remuneration for most of these positions, this kind of "volunteerism" is an absolutely indispensable element in Arkansas local politics. When asked for the single most important reason they decided to seek office, most city council and quorum court members speak in terms of "serving the community," "returning something to my town," "offering my knowledge and expertise," "meeting the challenge of civic responsibility and volunteering."[23]

Nothing could be more patriotic and praiseworthy than these motives; however, this "volunteerism" also creates severe problems of political accountability. The infrequency of competitive contests and incumbent challenges, combined with the frequency of voluntary retirements, makes local officials relatively immune from constituency pressure and control. As Joseph A. Schlesinger once wisely observed, "No more irresponsible government is imaginable than one of high-minded men unconcerned for their political futures." Even more to the point are the words of W. B. Holliday, announcing his decision to resign the office of mayor of Nashville, Arkansas: "I guess you could say I've gotten tired of the fringe benefits, and by fringe benefits I mean the cussings I've gotten and the 24-hour-a-day complaints. I'm going to let someone else have it. Four years ago, I shut down a pretty successful grocery store so I could do this full time. There has to be something wrong with somebody who'd do that, don't you think?" In such circumstances, it is hard to imagine the effectiveness of threats of electoral opposition and ouster.[24]

Another respect in which Arkansas politics falls short of the democratic ideal relates to the representativeness of local officials. It is true that local offices are much more obtainable than state offices by those with ordinary incomes and occupations, and also by blacks and women. By 1985, Arkansas had the second highest number of black mayors in the nation (twenty-four, compared with Alabama's thirty-one), and there were thirty-five women mayors. While most of the black mayors were elected by towns with majority black populations and most of the women presided over relatively small communities, there were some stunning exceptions. There were, for example, black mayors in Arkadelphia (10,200 pop., 14 percent black), West Memphis (28,138 pop., 33 percent black), and DeQueen (4,594 pop., 8 percent black). While women were 7.3 percent of Arkansas's 478 mayors in 1984, they represented a total population of only 27,265, or 2 percent of the municipal population. In 1984, however, a woman was elected mayor of Arkansas's fourth largest city, Pine Bluff, after a primary contest, a general election, and a runoff. Women and blacks also serve on many of Arkansas's quorum courts and city councils.[25]

This seeming openness of opportunity, however, should be put in perspective. No black has been elected to any of the numerous executive offices in any of Arkansas's seventy-five counties since Reconstruction. While women frequently compete successfully for some of these county offices, especially the circuit and county clerkships, the more visible, vigorously contested and remunerative offices—that is, county judge and sheriff— have unofficially but effectively been closed to female aspirants. Women have secured these positions *only* over their husband's dead (or indicted) bodies, and usually temporarily. Furthermore, reforms that sharply reduced the number of justices of the peace, and thereby made these offices more prestigious and desirable, also reduced the number of "political marginals" holding them. Blacks and women were, respectively, an estimated 8.5 percent and 21.5 percent of prereform quorum courts but only 4.3 percent and 7.5 percent of postreform quorum courts. Even in the state's educational system, in which 78 percent of the classroom teachers in 1983–84 were women, only 2 of the 360 school district superintendents were women. Lingering attitudes that the county judge is primarily a road builder, the sheriff primarily a posse leader, and the school superintendent primarily a disciplinarian, and that males are best suited for such macho tasks, are dying a very slow death in Arkansas.[26]

Few would seriously contend that black and female citizens can be represented only by black and female officeholders. There seems, however, to be something amiss when the Little Rock school district, which had 70 percent black enrollment by 1986, had only two (of six) black school-board members, and when North Little Rock, with 40 percent black enrollment, had none. Theoretically, the minimal qualifications and self-starting, volunteer nature of local offices make them equally obtainable by all. In practice, however, a combination of structural, electoral, and attitudinal factors have erected major barriers to some potential public servants, especially for those offices that are seriously coveted and assumed to be consequential.[27]

The city politics of Little Rock is illustrative. Under the managerial format adopted in 1957, members of the city board of directors have received no pay for their services, a factor pointed to as discouraging by those with modest incomes. Also, whereas some cities with the city manager system have compromised the original at-large electoral system to ensure that four of the seven directors must reside in separate wards even though the entire electorate votes, Little Rock maintained its original at-large "purity." Partially in consequence, since only those with the high visibility that comes from business prominence and/or costly campaigns are usually successful in citywide elections, almost everyone elected to the board since 1957 has been a white male from affluent western Little Rock. Since 1957, that is, in twenty-eight years of elections for seven positions on the board, only two white women, two black men, and one black woman have been elected. And when the black woman, who by 1985 had acquired seven years' experience on the board made a bid for selection by her fellow board members as mayor, she was passed over in favor of a white man attending his first board meeting.[28]

When the board organized in January 1987, after the 1986 elections, Lottie Shackelford became the first woman and second black mayor of Little

Rock. Also by this time, however, citizen groups and state legislators were advancing a variety of proposals to ensure greater representation of and access for black and lower-income neighborhoods in city governance.

Lawsuits challenging the constitutionality of Little Rock's election system have not been successful, the courts finding that there was no racially discriminatory intent behind the at-large system. In several east Arkansas cases, however, the federal courts have been finding otherwise, with dramatic results. Under West Helena's at-large system, only three blacks in a city with 40 percent black population had been elected to the city council from 1917 to 1982. In the ward elections mandated by federal court order in 1983, a city council consisting of four blacks and four whites was elected. In 1986 a federal judge agreed with black plaintiffs that Marianna's wards had been drawn in a racially discriminatory pattern and ordered them redrawn, Pine Bluff "voluntarily" changed from an at-large to a ward election system, and challenges to allegedly discriminatory quorum court districts in Lee and Mississippi counties were in process. To whatever extent at-large elections and gerrymandered districts have artificially suppressed black candidates, then, these obstacles are being systematically removed.[29]

Another recent change in election laws, however, may militate against successful black candidacies. In 1982, a black man won the mayorship of West Memphis by gaining a plurality in a six-candidate field. In the subsequent legislative session, over the vehement objections of the N A A C P, a law was enacted requiring that henceforth, in all county and mayor-council elections, a majority rather than a plurality is essential for election, secured if necessary by a run-off election two weeks after the general election.[30]

Blacks and women have been more successful in obtaining local than state office, and their likelihood of both candidacy and election is increasing. Nevertheless, local governments still severely underrepresent some groups in proportion to their numbers in the population.

There is one last respect in which local politics is considerably less democratic in practice than it could be, and that is in terms of voter and citizen participation. Attendance at regular city, county, and school board meetings usually involves only the governing council, the local press, and individuals involved in a particular agenda item (who quickly depart when their business is resolved). A meeting held in Fayetteville in August 1983 is illustrative: in preparation for an election concerning a one-cent city sales tax to finance sewer improvements, the city board scheduled and widely publicized an informational session that produced precisely eleven attendants—seven board members, two reporters, the principal of the school where the meeting was held, and the principal's wife. Nor are citizens much more likely to express themselves through letters and phone calls than they are to attend meetings. While most local legislators receive ten to twenty calls each month from constituents, these are usually particularistic complaints or requests (fix my street, don't rezone my neighborhood, silence those barking dogs, please perform a marriage) rather than general policy views. In short, for most Arkansans, despite the abundant opportunities for local activism, the only one that is exercised is the right to vote.[31]

Since most municipal elections are held simultaneously with the general election, voter turnout is comparable to turnout in state and national elections, with only some drop-off reducing the electorate from the top to the bottom of the ballot. In special local elections, however, as on bond issues, and especially in school elections, which have been held separately from all others on the second Tuesday in March, offices and issues are regularly decided by less than 10 percent of the potential electorate. Since it is generally true that the more elite the electorate, the more likely it is to be what political scientists have termed "public-regarding," such a minuscule electorate is viewed as advantageous by concerned officials. Those few citizens with sufficient civic concern to turn out in even the most undramatic local contests are also likely to favor generous school millage rates, community improvement bonds, and tax issues. It is for this reason that Arkansas school officials, fearing they might never pass a millage increase again, have adamantly opposed all efforts to hold presidential primaries simultaneously with the March school elections. When the legislature voted in 1987 to join other southern states in a 1988 "Super Tuesday" regional presidential primary, and coopted the traditional school election date for this purpose, it also obligingly moved school elections to the third Tuesday in September.[32]

Again, the defeat of Governor Pryor's proposed Arkansas Plan, which would have sharply reduced state turnback funds to cities and counties in return for greater local authority to propose a variety of taxes to the citizenry, is illustrative. The most vocal opponents of this plan were city, county, and school officials, all of whom preferred secure and stable, albeit limited, state funds to a theoretical freedom that might have left them incapacitated. As one analysis of the Arkansas Plan's defeat concluded: "Despite the state's proud motto of 'Regnat Populus'—The People Rule— the legitimacy of governmental decisions has stemmed primarily from the popular acceptability of the leaders who make the decisions rather than from any public involvement in the decision-making process itself. The Arkansas

Plan, therefore, not only proposed novel taxation efforts, but also an unfamiliar mode of decision-making requiring unconventional amounts of
participation." That local officials had accurately estimated the willingness
of their constituents to tax themselves is suggested in a 1985 survey on the
perceived quality of community life in Arkansas. In response to a question
on the best ways to accomplish improvements, while 43 percent suggested
changing funding priorities, and 38 percent suggested increasing state
turnback to local governments, only minute percentages thought that their
community should issue municipal bonds or increase the local sales or
property tax.[33]

In summary, while there are some ways in which local politics in
Arkansas exudes egalitarianism (sheer numbers of governments and elective offices, minimal office requirements, easy availability of the initiative
and referendum, unstructured recruiting), there are more indications that
suggest democratic shortcomings: dependence on outside income limiting
local prerogatives; few genuine contests for office; high rates of volunteerism; low percentages of women and blacks; and low rates of participation by
the citizenry.

Perhaps the most important device through which local governments do
respond to and reflect the wishes of the populace comes from the mere fact
of local residency. Local office seekers are usually longtime residents of a
particular county or community who come to office with a fairly sharp sense
of local expectations about city and county services. My own survey of local
officials confirms this point. Springdale and Fayetteville are neighboring,
indeed contiguous, communities in northwest Arkansas. Fayetteville's economic activity centers on the University of Arkansas, Springdale's on
poultry and trucking industries. When Springdale aldermen were asked to
rank order what they thought their constituents wanted most from their local
government, all five respondents gave highest ranking to "Keeping costs
and taxes down; no waste, no frills." In sharp contrast, only one of the six
Fayetteville respondents gave this objective top ranking. The most popular
choice for Fayetteville was "Providing an attractive and pleasant place to
live," followed closely by "Insuring everyone equal access to government;
that everyone can be heard and treated fairly."[34]

Since most local offices are strictly part-time positions, those who serve
on city councils and quorum courts continue the commercial and other
pursuits that provide their livelihood and therefore continue to be exposed in
their everyday dealings to the wishes, suspicions, objections, and concerns
of their neighbors. Because businessmen do not want to lose customers,

professional people do not want to lose clients, and presumably nobody wishes to lose the friendship and regard of their neighbors, local officials are responsive to the popular preferences that are articulated to them.

Whether there is sufficient variation among local preferences in Arkansas to justify 75 separate county governments and nearly 500 municipal governments, each with its own expensive array of buildings and facilities, employees and equipment, few of which even approach economic self-sufficiency, is a question far beyond the scope of this chapter. As the federal government sharply reduces its assistance, however, and the state government struggles to meet statewide responsibilities, it is a question that even the staunchest advocates of grassroots governance may be forced to face in the future. And arguments that this multiplicity of governments is essential to maintaining the most democratic kind of government available to Arkansas citizens should be viewed with some skepticism.

## CHAPTER THIRTEEN

# The Politics of State Services

*Looking back over 150 years of public education gives one few hopes for optimism. All the trends nationally which work against education flourish in this state, while those which support it are weak.*

Michael Dougan, *Arkansas Gazette*, August 7, 1983

*When I was doing the report there was no question about the fact that Arkansas just jumped out as being a state that has made tremendous progress as far as education is concerned.*

C. Emily Feistritzer, quoted in *Arkansas Democrat*,
November 12, 1985

Earlier it was emphasized that for much of Arkansas's history, politics and government were often irrelevant, sometimes obstructionist, and rarely of material value to citizen well-being. The previous chapters have described some extensive changes from traditional to contemporary politics as well as many structural strengthenings of state government. Now it is time to ask, have better politics and better government resulted in better programs and services?

A sweeping and superficial response could clearly be yes. At the turn of the twentieth century, the state of Arkansas built no roads, provided almost no support to education, and maintained few public institutions other than a Neanderthal state prison and a substandard insane asylum. By the 1980s, the state was collecting and spending well over a billion dollars annually on roads, schools, a host of health and welfare institutions, and many other services. Clearly, then, better politics has produced better policy; but what may seem obvious becomes considerably less clear when additional factors are considered, as they must be.

First, what if any is the evidence that political and governmental reforms have any causal connection to public policies? Many political scientists insist that public policy is the direct outcome of certain socioeconomic factors, and therefore that Arkansas's increased spending and services are the automatic by-product of the state's increased income, urbanization, and industrialization. Other political scientists insist that, to the contrary, while the state's economic base clearly provides the resources and needs from which public policy is fashioned, factors such as voter turnout, electoral competition, interest-group strength, legislative professionalism, and gubernatorial leadership capacity have a powerful and independent mediating effect between the economic environment and public policy choices. While this controversy cannot be resolved here, it must be acknowledged.[1]

Second, what in fact is "better public policy? The health of a political system can be somewhat objectively measured by certain traditional standards of democracy: how honest and open and competitive are the elections? how attentive and informed and participatory are the citizens? how representative and responsive is the government? Measuring policy output (that is, how much does the government spend on which services) is also fairly straightforward. Assessing policy outcome (what are the ultimate results of these regulations and services on citizens' lives) is much more complicated and value-laden. Few government programs are so universally beneficial that one can say with certainty they are desirable, or that more is better. Furthermore, there is insufficient opinion data that might provide proof that government actions are or are not satisfying citizen expectations and demands.

Further complications arise when comparative considerations are factored in. Obviously, Arkansas government is a greater presence in the lives of its citizens than was once the case, but how does that measure up against the magnified needs and resources of contemporary times? And how does Arkansas's governmental effort compare with that of the other states, which have also become much more activist and interventionist regulators and service providers in recent decades?

In one recent and widely used textbook, college students are introduced to the concept of comparative state politics by a series of highly unflattering distinctions drawn between the services afforded by Arkansas as compared with those of other states. Virginia Gray, herself an ex-Arkansan, begins by contrasting the higher education services of Arkansas and California:

If you happen to grow up in the state of Arkansas, as I did, you could attend one of ten public four-year colleges or universities, all relatively undistinguished on academic or scholarly grounds. The average salary earned by Arkansas professors is near the bottom of professors' salaries in public institutions in the United States. The amount of financial aid Arkansas offers to the average needy student is even worse comparatively: it was $233 per student in 1980–81. No state offers less than that. And the situation is not getting better. Arkansas was the only state to record a net decline in state support for higher education in the year 1981–82.

This dismal scene is then contrasted with the abundance of higher educational institutions, many prestigious, in California, with well-paid faculty and generous student-aid awards.[2]

Equally sharp distinctions are drawn regarding the two states' support of elementary and secondary education, with Arkansas again in the very bottom ranks, exceeding only Mississippi in terms of teacher pay and only Georgia in terms of per pupil expenditures. While Gray points out that court decisions and a changing tax climate mean that "California may begin a slow slide in educational quality," there is "no compelling reason to predict that Arkansas will begin an ascent up the educational ladder."[3] Thus are thousands of college students given their introduction to comparative state politics, and probably their first impression of Arkansas.

As will be discussed, some of Gray's specific policy rankings have changed since 1983. Central to this chapter, however, is the question of whether the services offered by the state of Arkansas, albeit "clearly" more numerous and generous than in times past, are "better" in terms of the state's capacity and "better" in comparison to what other states now provide. By most dollar measures of state output, Arkansas ranks, as it has always ranked, in the bottom tier of states, which is natural for a state with historically low income levels. More important than this absolute measure, however, is the question of whether the gap between Arkansas and other states is widening or narrowing. If the latter is true, then the supposition that better politics and government leads to better policies, while not proven, is certainly strengthened. Since state services are impossible without state revenue, Arkansas's tax base is the best place to begin our analysis.

## RESOURCES AND REVENUES

In Arkansas's first year of operation as a state, the grand sum of revenues collected was $10,546. By 1850 state revenues had grown to $93,540, and by 1900 to $755,787. In all these years, indeed through the 1920s, the major (and always meager) source of state revenue was a property tax. There were other minor sources of state revenue: occupation and privilege taxes on such tradespeople as clock peddlers, billiard hall operators, and sewing-machine sales agents; a one-dollar poll tax on all adult males was reenacted in 1874 after a ten-year lapse; an inheritance tax was added in 1901 and a franchise tax on corporations in 1907; and the state always collected fees for certain writs and filings and copies and publications.[4]

The general property tax, however, was the heart of the state's taxation effort and the major source of local revenues as well. Property taxes were and are levied at a fixed rate in terms of mills (or $0.001) per thousand dollars of the assessed value (which may not exceed 20 percent of the actual market value) of the property. The specific millage ceilings imposed by the 1874 constitution were quickly outgrown, and a long series of constitutional amendments have established additional local purposes for which mills can be assessed, have increased some millage limits, and have abolished some ceilings entirely. Increasingly in the twentieth century, however, in Arkansas as elsewhere, the property tax came to be viewed as an appropriate source for local rather than state revenues. In 1922, property taxes accounted for almost three-fourths of the state's revenue; by 1945, state property taxes were bringing in only 10 percent of state revenues; and in 1958 a constitutional amendment was adopted prohibiting any future state use of a property tax.

The automobile created not only a new demand for roads but a new source of revenue. Prompted by threats that the federal government would terminate financial aid for roads, Arkansas enacted a gasoline tax in 1921 and it, together with motor vehicle license fees, generated over half of the state's $22,135,000 income in 1930. Also in the 1920s and 1930s, Arkansas joined other states in turning to other sources of revenue: a severance tax in 1923; corporate and personal income taxes in 1929; a cigarette tax in 1929; a general sales tax in 1935; and taxes on liquor when it again became legal after the repeal of Prohibition in 1933. While the rates of most of these taxes have increased over the years, the basic tax structure now in place is that adopted fifty years ago, and it is a much more productive and elastic system than was the property tax. By 1960 total state revenues were $278,621,000;

by 1979 Arkansas had its first billion-dollar year in state revenues; and in the 1984–85 biennium, the state collected $3.004 billion and spent $2.951 billion.

By the 1980s, income and sales taxes accounted for over 90 percent of state general revenues, which largely explains why, in the inflationary 1960s and 1970s, state income increased so dramatically, 343 percent between 1966 and 1980. In this period of population growth, increased industrial and commercial activity, and inflation, the state's reliance on taxes on personal income, consumption, and corporate earnings meant guaranteed growth. Furthermore, generous federal aids (accounting for an average 34 percent of Arkansas's total income in this period) provided a vital supplement.[5]

By the mid-1980s, the combination of slowed inflation, less economic growth, and federal cutbacks meant that the relatively painless enlargement of the state revenue base was ending. Further, the tax structure itself was coming under increasing criticism, most notably from the Winthrop Rockefeller Foundation, for its increasingly regressive nature. In a series of critical reports, the foundation noted that because Arkansas, unlike many states, exempts neither food nor utilities payments from the sales tax; because the top income-tax bracket includes all incomes over $25,000 (which means that those earning $30,000 pay the same 7 percent rate as those earning $300,000); because the severance tax on natural gas is the lowest in the nation and the corporate income tax "inadequate"; and especially because of "runaway sales tax exemptions" to "narrow special interests," lower-income people were actually contributing more to state revenues than were upper-income persons. Other voices defended the exemptions and disputed these general charges of unfairness and regressivity.[6]

What could not be contested, however, is the peculiar and clearly regressive effects of Constitutional Amendment 19 on Arkansas's revenue choices. This provision, approved by 80 percent of the electorate in the depression and debt-ridden depths of 1934, prohibits any increase in any tax then in existence except by approval of the voters or by a three-fourths majority vote in the legislature. Because the individual and corporate income, beer, gasoline, cigarette, and severance taxes were all then in effect, it takes extraordinary legislative votes to increase them, and only twenty-six votes in the house, nine in the senate, to block such an increase. Because the general sales tax was not enacted until after Amendment 19, however, it offers the path of least resistance. The contemporary effects of this constitutional restraint were clearly evident in the 1983 special legislative session on education finance and reform. A sales tax increase from three cents to four cents was enacted; proposed increases in the corporate income and severance taxes had majority support but were defeated because of the extraordinary majority requirement. Similarly, Governor Dale Bumpers's attempt in 1971 to make the income tax even more progressive with a top bracket of 9 percent had a majority, but failed by two votes of getting the necessary three-fourths vote in the senate. The defeated 1980 constitution would have required a two-thirds majority on all tax increases, and efforts to secure this constitutional change by separate amendment remained a priority for some reform groups, such as Common Cause, in the 1980s. A special twenty-five-member Tax Reform Commission was appointed by Governor Clinton on June 9, 1987, and among its first recommendations was a constitutional amendment requiring a 60 percent legislative majority for the raising or lowering of any state taxes. If submitted to and passed by the voters in November 1988, the amendment will remove one major source of tax inequity in Arkansas.[7]

Tax adequacy, however, will remain a problem. Despite the spectacular revenue gains of recent decades, per capita state and local taxes in Arkansas remained among the lowest in the nation. In fact, despite the sales tax increase of 1983, in 1984 Arkansas's state and local taxes per capita of $866 were the lowest of the fifty states, indeed only 64 percent of the U.S. average of $1,356. Even using the fairer measure of taxes per $1,000 of personal income, only four states collected less than Arkansas's $97.[8]

The Advisory Commission on Intergovernmental Relations (ACIR) has provided an alternative and, its members insist, a better yardstick for measuring the tax capacity of state-local fiscal systems than the traditional reliance on absolute or per capita income measurements. Their preferred measure, the Representative Tax System (RTS), provides both absolute and relative measures of the hypothetical abilities of a state to raise revenues assuming every state applied identical tax rates to each of the twenty-six commonly used tax bases. The RTS also measures tax effort, or a state's actual tax productivity in relation to its tax capacity. According to ACIR's most recent study, based on 1983 state and local taxes, Arkansas's 1983 tax capacity was 78, or 22 percent below the national average, and its tax effort was 83, or 17 percent below the national average. The ACIR study also showed that these averages were fairly consistent from 1967 through 1983, and that while Arkansas paid higher-than-average taxes on personal income, motor fuels and vehicle registration, and certain "sinful" pursuits (tobacco, alcohol, pari-mutuel wagering), state taxes on estates, corporations, public utilities, and severance taxes were lower than average.[9]

What this and similar studies highlight is that whereas Arkansas's state tax effort ranges from somewhat below to somewhat above average on most taxes, the "effort" on property taxes can hardly be described as an effort at all. Only about one-third of Arkansas's combined state and local taxes are levied by local governments (cities, counties, school districts). Most of these are property taxes, which, in 1984, were only 41 percent of the national average property taxes, and reflected an effort only 59 percent of the national average. The deleterious effects of low property taxes on the public schools (to which 80 percent of property tax proceeds are now dedicated) will be discussed shortly. What is noteworthy here is that no thread in Arkansas politics is longer or more persistent than the underuse, misuse, and outright abuse of the property tax.[10]

The property tax's 1836 beginnings were clouded with understandable resentment that the "poor man with land not worth fifty cents an acre would be required . . . to pay the same rate of tax per acre as did the rich influential owner of bottom lands worth one hundred dollars per acre," and the very same criticism regarding the most recent property tax revisions (that they were "mangled for the benefit of big absentee landowners") persists in 1986. The complaint in 1986 by the director of the State Education Department that "there are not enough cows on the tax books in the state of Arkansas to fill up one good farm," is the same complaint heard decades previously that there apparently "wasn't a hog or sheep on a single farm in Phillips County."[11]

For nearly 150 years, a stream of state agency studies, academic analyses, legislative investigations, court decisions, journalists' exposés, citizens' complaints, and foundation reports have produced the same conclusions: property taxes have been and are inequitably assessed, blatantly evaded, and incompetently administered. When the supreme court found the entire property tax system to be unconstitutional in 1979, the immediate consequence was a constitutional amendment (59) resoundingly approved by the voters as promised salvation against dramatic tax increases. Like all previous efforts at correcting property tax problems, however, it too has "turned failure to disaster." So long as property taxes are assessed and collected by locally elected officials who fear the political consequences of raising their constituents' taxes and ignore the state law requiring late assessment penalties, and so long as Arkansas citizens continue to feel (with astonishing incorrectness) that their property taxes are as high or higher than those in other states, it cannot be otherwise; and the state will continue to assume an ever-increasing share of the state-local tax burden. The new Tax Reform Commission was directed by Governor Clinton to determine the regressiveness or progressiveness of the overall tax system, to review the tax burden and tax capacity of Arkansas as compared with other states, and to recommend revisions that would provide greater equity and fairness. Perhaps, then, significant change is coming. Fortunately for taxpayers, the state's budgetary process, that is, the process for estimating revenue and allocating expenditures, has been reformed, rationalized, and strengthened in recent decades.[12]

WHO GETS WHAT?

Although the state government has operated with a balanced budget since 1934, when Amendment 20, effectively prohibiting debt, was added to the Constitution, until 1945 there was little formal budgeting. All state taxes were earmarked by law for more than fifty separate state agencies or programs, so that "no matter how much or how little the General Assembly authorized an agency to spend, the money just kept rolling in and could not be diverted to other needs. In addition, because of the inadequate performance of some taxes and exceptionally high performance of others, certain programs received large increases while others received decreases irrespective of their ranking in the State's priorities."[13]

The Revenue Stabilization Law, proposed by Governor Ben Laney and adopted by the legislature in 1945, brought rationality to the process. Some revenues, called "special" revenues, are still dedicated for particular purposes. Gasoline taxes and motor vehicle registration and driver's license fees, for example, are exclusively used for road construction and maintenance and other services for highway users. The broad-based taxes, however, such as income and sales, were redesignated as "general" revenues for which the governor and legislature could, for the first time, determine spending priorities. The Revenue Stabilization Act also provided mechanisms to ensure spending reductions when revenues were less than estimated and to provide a steady cash flow to state agencies despite uneven periods of revenue collections throughout the year.

Arkansas has a biennial (two-year) budget with a fiscal year beginning July 1 and ending June 30. The actual budgeting process, however, begins in the spring of even-numbered years, when state agencies submit their requests to the State Office of Budget, which compiles and analyzes the requests and presents them, together with revenue projections, to the governor. The governor then holds executive budget hearings and uses that information, together with Budget Office data and recommendations, to formulate a proposed comprehensive state budget.

This proposal is submitted to the Legislative Council, a thirty-member house-senate interim committee, which holds its own budget hearings throughout the fall to discuss the impact of the governor's recommendations and make its own. When the legislature convenes, the Legislative Council's recommendations are carried forward by the Joint Budget Committee (a twenty-five-member select committee whose membership largely overlaps that of the Legislative Council), which develops and introduces the final appropriation bills. Since article 5 of the constitution requires a separate bill for each appropriation, hundreds of bills must be written by the Joint Budget Committee; and since the constitution requires a three-fourths vote on most appropriations, the same opportunities for minority maneuvering exist as with most tax increases. The precise dollar amounts in these bills are often highly controversial and prompt fierce pressure and fervent bargaining. Because these negotiations tend to be private and conclusive, however, most budget bills pass the full chambers unanimously. Some of the most heated and clever bargaining goes into fashioning the biennial amendment to the Revenue Stabilization Act, because it is this law that determines how much of an agency's appropriation is placed in Category A (based on conservative revenue estimates with a 99 percent chance of funding), in Category B (predicated on economic growth), and in Category C (predicated on spectacular growth and highly unlikely to be funded). Fortunately for serious students of Arkansas budgeting, the intricacies of this process have been elaborated elsewhere.[14]

As important as the mechanics of the process are the politics of the process, specifically the relative influence of its many participants, and here there is considerable disagreement. Until recently, Arkansas was one of the few states that did not place budgeting powers directly in the hands of the chief executive; indeed, it was the only state that placed responsibility for fiscal planning in the hands of a legislative committee, that is, the Legislative Council. Informally, during the several administrations of Governor Orval Faubus, the legislature began inviting gubernatorial budget recommendations. By 1960 all agency requests were submitted to the governor before consideration by the Legislative Council, and a 1973 law explicitly gives the governor a role in budget formulation and recommendation. Still, authorship of the crucial Revenue Stabilization Act continues to switch from governor to legislature and back again. While some observers now classify Arkansas as having an executive budget, others insist that it is still a legislative budget, and still others classify it as an executive-legislative "hybrid."[15]

As Dan Durning has accurately observed, "The Arkansas budgetary process consists of changing relationships between state agencies, the governor, and the legislature. The budgetary process can be defined only temporally—it is subject to change with a turnover of the people occupying key roles in the system." Recent Arkansas governors possessing equal formal powers have had very unequal influence: Governor Faubus's extraordinary political clout and skilled legislative leadership gave him dominance in the budget process as well; Rockefeller's political weakness and problematic legislative relations sapped his budgetary influence. Gubernatorial influence also fluctuates with the economy, periods of revenue growth permitting much more gubernatorial decision making and policy activism.[16]

Timing can be a critical factor as well. In 1978 Bill Clinton, the legislature, and the state agencies were all so certain of Clinton's November election that he took over the budget formulation process after his May Democratic gubernatorial primary victory, hired professional management consultants to assist him, made budgetary decisions the focus of his transition, and managed to inject his priorities into the process. In 1980 Frank White's general election upset of Clinton meant that the Legislative Council's fall hearings and decision-making process on what was presumably to be Clinton's budget were already well under way, and White had little opportunity to influence them, a constraining situation that Clinton in turn experienced after his rematch victory over White in 1982. Although the 1981 legislature enacted a law permitting nonincumbent governors-elect to recess the legislature for thirty days immediately after the inaugural, and this may well provide future governors with valuable additional time for budget and bill preparation, legislators informally made it clear in 1982 that this law was not intended for the use of nonneophytes like Clinton. Clearly, formal powers tell only part of the story about gubernatorial budget authority.[17]

Similarly, not all legislators are equally influential in the budget process. While membership on the Legislative Council and Joint Budget Committee confers the opportunity for influence, only a handful of this elite legislative group devotes the constant time and attention to budgetary minutiae that convert into actual power. As one close observer noted, "Power belongs to those who are always there and who work hard enough to get the knowledge." [18]

Since 1973, extensive reliance on electronic data processing to assemble and analyze budget information has increased the knowledge base of both the legislative and executive branches, and both branches have also upgraded the numbers and analytical capacities of their budgetary staffs. At present, then, there is potential power in both places, with the actual exercise of that power depending upon the interest, determination, staff, skill, and political fortunes of individual incumbents.

Considering the centrality that political scientists, political participants, and political journalists alike accord to the budget as "the single most important policy statement that a state government makes from one year to the next," it is equally important to note that the battles over state spending are fought only at the margins. A combination of numerous factors such as earmarked taxes, the prohibition against deficit spending, restricted federal funds, limited time and knowledge, and commitments to interest payments and retirement programs, massively reduce the amount of actual discretion left to decision makers. [19]

Furthermore, patterns of incrementalism mean that current expenditures will vary only slightly from past expenditures. Decision makers "generally accept the legitimacy of established programs and agree to continue the previous level of expenditure. They limit their task by considering only the increments of change proposed for the new budget and by considering the narrow range of goals embodied in the departures from established activities." Attempts in recent years to get away from the automatic acceptance of the budgetary base as given through Planning-Programming Budgeting (PPB) or Zero Base Budgeting (ZBB) seem to have done little to displace traditional incremental-style budgeting. [20]

These general propositions were recently tested, and confirmed, in Arkansas. Governor Dale Bumpers initiated a version of PPB called Management by Objective in 1972, and Governor David Pryor initiated a modified form of ZBB called the Priority Budgeting System in 1976. According to T. R. Carr's analysis in 1983, however, the Priority Budgeting System has had "a minimal impact on the outcome of the budgetary process," which is still strongly incremental in nature. He concludes that "spending levels for the functions of government are firmly entrenched in tradition" and that "increases in allocation levels by function are almost perfectly correlated to increases in state revenue." His calculations of budget allocations by function, reproduced in table 7, offer an excellent overview of contemporary state spending priorities and present highly persuasive evidence of incrementalism.[21]

It is interesting to note, however, that if the analysis had been extended backward to fiscal year 1978 and forward to fiscal year 1986, one segment of the state budget would have shown a very sizable percentage increase. General revenues allocated to education (the Public School Fund, General Education, and Higher Education) went from 64.1 percent of the budget in FY 1978 to 69.9 percent of the budget in FY 1986. Since the net general revenue for distribution increased from $690.3 million in FY 1978 to $1.427 billion in FY 1986, it is clear that the absolute as well as relative amount expended on education increased dramatically. Considering Arkansas's abysmal educational effort in times past, does this trend offer evidence that "better" politics and government do indeed produce "better" policy?[22]

EDUCATION: HAS THERE BEEN REAL IMPROVEMENT?

Any attempt to assess public policy "improvements" is highly hazardous and dangerously prone to subjectivity. The mere choice of this particular policy area among many potential others, for example, might well be attributed to authorial bias, since I, as an educator and a mother, may very well value education above other public goods and services.

For a number of reasons, however, the state's educational efforts seem to offer an excellent testing ground. First, although the details of education policy are highly dissensual, there does seem to be a general consensus that it is better to be educated than ignorant, and there is abundant evidence demonstrating close correlations between educational attainments on the one hand and higher income and occupational status, improved life chances and choices, on the other. The case for good public schools as a general value is especially compelling in a state like Arkansas, where almost the only educational opportunities available are state-supported ones: only 4 percent of Arkansas's elementary and secondary students attended private schools in the 1980s. Second, public education is one of the few policy areas where a wealth of statistics (including nonexpenditure data) has been compiled throughout the century, enabling the kind of comparative analysis, both over time and among states, that is difficult or impossible on many other issues. Third, while federal dollars have provided important assistance to state schools and thus somewhat confounded a clear picture of the

Table 7: Summary of Budget Allocations by Function as a Percentage of State Budget, Fiscal Years 1981–1985

|  | Fiscal Year | | | | |
|---|---|---|---|---|---|
|  | FY81 | FY82 | FY83 | FY84 | FY85 |
| Public schools | 45.4 | 46.0 | 46.6 | 46.2 | 46.3 |
| General education | 3.2 | 3.2 | 3.1 | 3.1 | 3.1 |
| Higher education | 18.0 | 17.8 | 17.7 | 17.5 | 17.4 |
| Human services | 17.7 | 17.6 | 17.3 | 17.1 | 16.9 |
| State general government | 7.2 | 7.1 | 6.9 | 7.6 | 7.6 |
| Public health | 2.4 | 2.4 | 2.1 | 2.0 | 2.1 |
| Police | 1.1 | 0.9 | 0.8 | 1.3 | 1.4 |
| County aid | 1.8 | 1.8 | 1.7 | 1.7 | 1.6 |
| Municipal aid | 2.4 | 2.4 | 2.4 | 2.3 | 2.2 |
| Total | 99.2 | 99.2 | 98.6 | 98.8 | 98.6 |

*Source:* T. R. Carr, "An Evaluation of the Impact of the Priority Budgeting System of Arkansas on Budget Outcomes" (Paper presented to the American Society for Public Administration, New York, April 1983), p. 12.

state's own efforts, the federal influence has been much less in this area than in other major areas (health and welfare and highways) of state spending activity. Finally, because educational expenditures consume by far the greatest portion of contemporary state budgets, we are examining a central rather than peripheral facet of contemporary public policy.

For all these reasons, then, a search for signs of significant change or nonchange in Arkansas's educational effort seems legitimate. For those who care about Arkansas and who value education, such a search is also mildly masochistic.

In 1978 a special study on school finance was commissioned by the Arkansas legislature. In what came to be known from its chief author's name as the Alexander Report, the following observation was offered: "By almost any standard the Arkansas system of education must be regarded as inadequate. Children of the state are not being offered the same opportunity to develop their individual capacities as children in other states. Stated another way, from an educational standpoint the average child in Arkansas would be much better off attending the public schools of almost any other state in the country."[23]

Perhaps the most remarkable aspect of this stunning indictment is how precisely it parallels an expert study commissioned by the legislature more than fifty years previously, in 1921: "For thousands upon thousands of children, Arkansas is providing absolutely no chance. To these children, to be born in Arkansas is a misfortune and an injustice from which they will never recover and upon which they will look back with bitterness when plunged, in adult life, into competition with children born in other states which are today providing more liberally for their children." The 1921 report included massive amounts of data, placing Arkansas at the very bottom or near bottom in terms of teacher pay, per pupil expenditures, length of school year, and percentage of those enrolled in actual attendance.[24]

Almost fifty years before the 1921 survey—that is, in the 1870s—reports estimated that only 16,000 of a potential 195,714 students were actually enrolled in public schools, that circuit superintendents were giving more attention to politics than to public education, that county collectors were pocketing sparse school funds, and that the state's inadequate supply of teachers was dwindling because of their payment in worthless scrip. And the sad saga goes back even to pre-statehood, when the territorial governor John Pope urged educational improvements on the legislature in 1833, since many families were avoiding Arkansas because of the lack of school facilities.[25]

For nearly all of Arkansas's history, then, although a few elected officials and a number of educational leaders called for reform, occasionally with success, virtually every assessment of Arkansas's educational effort against that being made in other states showed the state either dead last or close to the bottom in every measurable aspect: enrollment, attendance, facilities, teacher pay and training, course requirements and offerings, and per pupil expenditures. As angrily and aptly noted in a 1926 campaign for higher school millage rates, Arkansas was "the cellar champion of the public school league."[26]

The reasons for being so persistently on the bottom rung stem from a confluence of all the socioeconomic, political, historical, governmental, and attitudinal factors that are known to depress educational efforts and that combined with devastating impact in Arkansas. As Thomas Dye and others have demonstrated in their comparative state policy studies, the economic factor that correlates most closely with educational expenditures is wealth. Thus, Arkansas's lack of wealth, as evidenced in its very low per capita and other income measures, provides one comprehensive explanation for stingy spending on education. Urbanization and industrialization also have positive correlations with per pupil expenditures, and Arkansas began as and long remained one of America's most rural states with, until recently, a pervasively agrarian economy.[27]

The reasons for nonsupport of education differed somewhat between those in the lowlands and those in the hills. The affluent Delta planters naturally opposed serious property taxes on their extensive holdings; they needed an uneducated and immobile "peasant" class to make their estates profitable; and they could educate their own children by shipping them East, importing tutors, or establishing tuition-supported private academies. The subsistence farmers in the hills simply had no disposable income, nor could they visualize any material benefits from education in their simple way of life. Furthermore, planter and scratch farmer alike shared a common southern view that education was "private, personal, and optional" and not a public responsibility.[28]

Rurality also meant isolation. Sparsely settled and widely scattered population clusters had neither the ways nor the means to support serious schooling, and nonexistent roads prohibited efficient combination of resources. Arkansas's isolation from the outside world effectively insulated it from the public school crusades that periodically swept much of the rest of the nation, and it insulated its people from the knowlege that their schools were markedly inferior. This "pluralistic ignorance" was perpetuated by the homogeneity that is also strongly associated with minimal education efforts.[29]

The question of whether any political leadership could have overcome so many constraining forces is problematic. What is certain is that few leaders even tried and that politics as usual inhibited more than it helped educational advances. Among the funds completely squandered during the Family's long nineteenth-century reign were almost all of the proceeds from the federal land grants intended to provide a base for educational purposes. By 1850 every state except Arkansas had authorized the spending of tax monies for public schools. Isaac Murphy, the first Reconstruction governor and himself a former schoolteacher, got the first state tax for education adopted, but under the subsequent Reconstruction regime, the public school system was so polluted by patronage and corruption that "free" schools acquired an even worse reputation than they had previously, when they were associated with pauperism. The Redeemers reenacted a modest state property tax, earmarked the poll tax for educational purposes, and committed the state through the 1874 constitution to "a suitable and efficient system of free schools." What was promised with words, however, was effectively prohibited by stringent millage, taxing, and spending restraints, as well as by the decision to place property tax assessments and collections in the hands of locally elected officials. Local school board membership was sought as much to find jobs for friends and relatives and to escape having to work on the roads as to advance the schools.

Governor Jeff Davis (1901–1907), the self-styled champion of the people, expressed his belief that Arkansas schools were "almost perfect" and needed no more money; and the racist sentiments deliberately inflamed by Davis and others had severe antieducational consequences as well, resulting in black schools that were definitely separate but never equal. The 1921 survey noted, for example, that the cost of instruction per child enrolled was $17.06 for each white child and $5.61 for each black child, and that nearly three-fourths of all black enrollment was in the first four grades. In their 1930 study, Dawson and Little, after noting that "public education for the negro is receiving fairly liberal support and cooperation," went on to report that only 70 percent of enumerated black schoolchildren were actually enrolled, that 61 percent of those were in the first three grades and only 1.8 percent in high school, and that 77 percent of all black teachers had no college training whatsoever.[30]

The two-year gubernatorial term and four-year tradition meant that those few governors such as Thomas McRae (1921–25) who were passionately committed to educational uplift could not sustain the improvements they started. Proeducation governors were further stymied by malapportioned legislatures that were more sensitive to antitax and rural anticonsolidation elements than to proeducation forces.

Were the people ahead of the politicians? Without historical opinion data, this is almost impossible to determine. It seems significant, however, that in most localities voters quickly assessed themselves the maximum allowable millage rates for schools (and frequently went beyond these limits with "voluntary" taxes) and that many of the most important educational advances came from constitutional amendments and referenda initiated and/or ratified by the electorate. By the time Amendment 11, raising school millage limits from twelve to eighteen, was adopted in 1926, for example, 83 percent of the school districts had already reached that limit. And according to the longtime state education director Arch Ford, the act in 1948 that consolidated school districts having fewer than 350 students and effectively reduced the number of districts from 1,589 to 424 could only have been initiated by the people. "We never could have gotten the legislature to do it."[31]

On the other hand, widespread popular attitudes that property taxes were unfair and excessive probably helped to keep them below levels adequate for school support, and much of the populace opposed and then simply ignored compulsory attendance laws. Perhaps most important, many studies demonstrate that states with more highly educated populations support stronger educational efforts. Thus, Arkansas was trapped at the bottom ranks by a vicious cycle of factors and attitudes, including an attitude that Arkansas schools were as good as they needed to be. In a state survey taken in 1978, the year of the Alexander Report, Arkansans rated their schools higher than did citizens in the nation generally, and when asked where a possible state surplus should be spent, only 25 percent said on education, whereas 36 percent said on roads. If, as Robert Erikson has persuasively argued, "the states most likely to enact a given policy are the states where the public demand for the policy is strongest," then at least through the late 1970s, there was little reason to expect any dramatic improvements in educational policy in Arkansas.[32]

Over the course of the twentieth century, of course, there had been some progress. In 1900 the state spent $1,230,362 on elementary and secondary schools and nothing on higher education. In FY 1985, the state spent nearly a billion dollars on education ($944,156,702), including over $240 million on colleges and universities. By 1986 virtually all classroom teachers were college graduates, the schools had been officially desegregated, the number of separate school districts had been reduced from a staggering 4,903 in 1900 (and 5,112 in 1920) to a more manageable 334.[33] Had there, however, been advances in Arkansas's educational effort in relationship to its financial resources and in its standing relative to the educational effort of other states? Some statistical answers to those questions are offered in table 8.

As Arkansas's per capita income has increased, so have per pupil expenditures and teacher pay, a confirmation of the correlation between state wealth and state educational effort. Arkansas still remained very much in the bottom tier of states in 1985: forty-eighth in per capita income, forty-second in teacher pay, and forty-seventh in per pupil expenditures. The gaps between Arkansas and national norms had been noticeably narrowed, however; and on one measure, average teacher pay as a percentage of per capita income, Arkansas appeared to be making a slightly greater effort (192 percent) than was the nation generally (188 percent).[34]

In fact, in a dramatic departure from the past, a number of national education studies in 1985 pointed to Arkansas as a leader instead of a laggard. A report by the Carnegie Foundation for the Advancement of Teaching noted that "Arkansas, which ranked fiftieth in average teacher

Table 8: Educational Effort in Arkansas and the Nation, 1900–1985

|  | 1900 | 1920 | 1940 | 1960 | 1980 | 1985 |
|---|---|---|---|---|---|---|
| **Length of school term (days per year)** | | | | | | |
| Arkansas | 69 | 124 | 159 | 173 | 175 | 180 |
| United States | 132 | 162 | 175 | 178 | 178 | 180 |
| Ark. as % of U.S. | (52.3) | (77.0) | (91.0) | (97.2) | (98.3) | (100) |
| **Per pupil expenditures per ADA** | | | | | | |
| Arkansas | $6 | $20 | $29 | $207 | $1193 | $2542 |
| United States | 17 | 54 | 94 | 472 | 2445 | 3677 |
| Ark. as % of U.S. | (35.2) | (37.0) | (30.9) | (43.9) | (48.8) | (69.1) |
| **Average teacher salary** | | | | | | |
| Arkansas | $160 | $476 | $584 | $3293 | $12,546 | $19,538 |
| United States | 543 | 871 | 1441 | 5415 | 18,409 | 25,257 |
| Ark. as % of U.S. | (29.5) | (55.0) | (40.5) | (61.0) | (68.2) | (77.4) |
| **Per capita income** | | | | | | |
| Arkansas | | | $332 | $1341 | $7099 | $10,180 |
| United States | | | 693 | 2223 | 9494 | 13,451 |
| Ark. as % of U.S. | | | (47.9) | (60.3) | (74.7) | (75.7) |
| **Per pupil expenditures per ADA as percent of per capita income** | | | | | | |
| Arkansas | | | 8.7% | 15.4% | 16.8% | 24.9% |
| United States | | | 13.5% | 21.2% | 25.7% | 27.3% |
| Ark. as % of U.S. | | | (64.4) | (72.6) | (64.5) | (91.2) |
| **Average teacher pay as percent of per capita income** | | | | | | |
| Arkansas | | | 176% | 246% | 178% | 192% |
| United States | | | 208% | 244% | 194% | 188% |
| Ark. as % of U.S. | | | (84.6) | (100.8) | (91.8) | (102) |

*Source:* Length of school term, per pupil expenditures, and teacher pay figures from U.S. Bureau of the Census, *Statistical Abstract* (Washington, D.C.: Government Printing Office, various years); U.S. Office of Education, *Biennial Survey of Education in the United States* and *Statistics of State School Systems* (Washington, D.C.: Government Printing Office, various years); National Center for Education Statistics, *Digest of Education Statistics* (Washington, D.C.: Government Printing Office, various years); and *Statistical Summary for the Public Schools of Arkansas* (Little Rock: State Department of Education, various years). Per capita income from U.S. Bureau of the Census, *Historical Statistics, Colonial Times to 1957, Statistical Abstract,* and *Census of Population* (Washington, D.C.: Government Printing Office, various years); and Commerce Clearinghouse report cited in *U.S. News and World Report,* May 19, 1986, p. 13.

*Note:* ADA = average daily attendance; blank cells indicate data not measured.

salary in 1982–83, increased its average salary for teachers by 12.6 percent the following year (the highest rate of change of all the states) and by an additional 11.8 percent last year. Arkansas added teachers in both of the last two years which would tend to bring the average down since new teachers usually get less." In a comparative analysis of state responses to the changes advocated in 1983 by the National Commission on Excellence in Education, Arkansas was ranked among the top eight states in both the number and breadth of reforms adopted. Arkansas was also ranked second among the states in the percentage by which it had increased funding for higher education (a 52 percent increase from 1983 to 1985) and eighth in the percentage increase from 1975 to 1985 (190 percent).[35]

Since incremental budgeting makes it highly unlikely that current expenditures will vary more than marginally from previous expenditures, and comparative studies of state adoptions of policy innovations suggest equally strong historical traditions in nonexpenditure areas, this kind of sharp break with the past is relatively rare. What occurred is a highly fortuitous combination of long-term and short-term factors.

Arkansas's rapid increase in income, urbanization, and industrialization in the 1960s and 1970s certainly created a stronger base of those economic development factors that are positively associated with proeducation public policies. Furthermore, the rapidly diminishing opportunities for an uneducated workforce were becoming increasingly apparent with the steady shrinking of the farm sector of the economy and with a steady parade of plant closings as low-wage international competition made America's low-skill manufacturing operations noncompetitive. There were still some employers with political clout who could quietly observe in response to proeducation pleas, "Honey, I've got an investment in ignorance." Their numbers were diminishing, however, and the economic establishment throughout the South had generally begun to perceive educational improvements as an industry-attracting and profitable investment.[36]

Also by the 1980s, the Arkansas Education Association was no longer a relatively passive group of educators, often dominated by cost-conscious administrators and officials, but a highly organized, well-staffed and funded, and increasingly militant teacher interest group, ranked as one of the most powerful lobbies by the state legislature. A strong educational reform act initiated by the AEA was defeated by 56 percent of the electorate in 1980, but the campaign for its adoption, and the ongoing vociferous criticism of Arkansas's educational failings by the AEA and others began to produce some attitudinal changes among the citizenry.[37]

In sharp contrast to the 1978 survey previously cited, one 1982 survey found that 41 percent of the population was willing to be taxed more for better schools, and two other 1982 opinion studies found that Arkansans had become critical of their schools compared with those in the rest of the nation and had placed a high priority on improving them. A series of widely publicized blue-ribbon national reports warning against a "rising tide of mediocrity" in the schools apparently sharpened and deepened attitudinal changes already under way in Arkansas.[38]

The reports also provided powerful reinforcement to the work of the Education Standards Committee, established by the 1983 legislature to develop new and more rigorous standards for accreditation. Chaired by the governor's wife, Hillary Clinton, the Education Standards Committee created further consciousness-raising through public hearings held in each of the seventy-five counties and began developing a consensus on a longer school day and school year, increased high school graduation requirements and academic course offerings, an end to "social" promotions, more homework, and smaller pupil-teacher ratios. The committee's work acquired even greater visibility and urgency when the supreme court, on May 31, 1983, affirmed a lower-court decision that had declared the state's system of public school funding unconstitutional. In *DePree v. Alma School District*, the supreme court struck down the state's school funding formula on the grounds that by denying equal educational opportunity to children in poor school districts, the formula violated both the constitutional guarantee of equal protection to all citizens and its promise of a "general, suitable and efficient system of free schools."[39]

In tougher economic times, in a different attitudinal environment, and under different leadership, the response might well have been to redistribute funds from the wealthier schools to the poorer schools, thus achieving greater equity at the price of mediocrity. With the state rapidly recovering from the 1981–82 recession, with the public beginning to demand improved schools, and with Clinton no longer as tax-shy as he was in the aftermath of his 1980 defeat and 1982 reelection, however, a ripe opportunity was generated for raising more revenues and advancing education, and Clinton seized it.

While his wife continued to shape and publicize the new school standards and secured their preliminary approval by the State Board of Education, Clinton began systematically building public and legislative support for the tax increases necessary to pay for them. Using the skills and staff acquired in his previous political campaigns (opinion surveys done by professional pollsters, brochures prepared by public relations professionals, fund-raising, targeted mailings), Clinton's "campaign for educational excellence" activated and intensified an already-supportive public opinion climate and turned those opinions into demands on the state legislature for better educational funding and standards.[40]

Based on research that showed the greatest impetus for educational improvements was their perceived connection to economic development, Clinton repeatedly portrayed educational funding as a smart investment in economic prosperity, and he also appealed to state pride and chauvinism: "So many people in Arkansas have seemed to believe as long as I've been alive, that in some sort of strange way God meant us to drag up the rear of the nation's economy forever." Clinton's research and his wife's feedback from her public hearings also revealed intensely held opinions that all teachers did not deserve salary increases, in fact that some did not deserve to be in the classroom at all. Hence, Clinton made competency testing of the existing teacher corps a key part of his educational excellence program. The teacher-testing program, which may have been the keystone in coalescing public support for the program, earned Clinton the passionate enmity of the A E A. Nevertheless, by the end of the longest special session in decades, the legislature had adopted a new school-funding formula and had increased the sales tax from three cents to four cents, the first increase in twenty-six years.[41]

Insofar as Clinton succeeded in making the 1984 elections a referendum on the education standards and tax increase, their popularity was broadly confirmed. Even more tangibly, under pressure from the June 1987 deadline for meeting the new standards, voters in 85 percent of Arkansas's school districts voted to increase their local school millage rates, and attempts to weaken the standards in the 1985 legislative session were narrowly defeated. Still, by 1986, there were ominous signs that Arkansas's great leap forward was beginning to stumble.

Arkansas per capita income, which had been growing faster than the national average for two decades, had below-average growth in 1985 and 1986 as the farm crisis deepened, depression hit the oil industry, and international competition in timber and manufacturing increased. As a result of slow economic growth and further federal budget cuts, state revenues were considerably below projections. The budget-balancing requirements of the Revenue Stabilization Act necessitated a record four rounds of budget cuts before the end of fiscal year 1986, and fiscal year 1987 began with an ordered spending cutback, slicing over $15 million from the Public School Fund. Continued slow-growth projections meant that school districts in the 1986–87 school year would receive the smallest percentage increase in state aid in years, and that most districts would actually get decreased aid. The A E A predicted that the average teacher salary would increase only 1.5 percent in the 1986–87 school year, the smallest increase in ten years; and higher education suffered deeper losses through mid-year cuts than those in any other state. For the first time in fifty years, land values in the state dropped and stayed down for much of 1986, with adverse effects on property tax collections. More important, Constitutional Amendment 59, which placed lids on both personal and real property taxes to minimize the tax-increasing effects of property reappraisal, was cutting sharply into local school revenues. Unsurprisingly, in the 1986 gubernatorial primary, every Democratic and Republican candidate except Clinton advocated delaying and/or diluting the new educational standards. Indeed, the insistence by the Republican gubernatorial nominee Frank White that the standards should be delayed, and by Clinton that they should not, became a focus of the 1986 gubernatorial general election.[42]

## HAS BETTER POLITICS PRODUCED BETTER POLICY?

For a brief period in the early 1980s, Arkansas overcame the long weight of the past and jumped into the forefront of the American states on some measures of education policymaking. This thrust was made possible both by an improved economic environment and by a political system that translated these richer resources into particular public policies. As Jack M. Treadway has recently concluded with respect to the "economics versus politics" debate, "Policies cannot be pursued without resources, but neither do policies magically appear in the presence of resources. Environment matters, but so does politics."[43]

Among the political factors that facilitated this translation process were the following: an Arkansas electorate increasingly aware of its educational deficiencies and unhappy with its unflattering comparisons to other states; some political campaigns in which an issue, that is, better education, received at least as much attention as did personalities; the coming to political power of an interest group, the Arkansas Education Association, which in the process of pursuing its own interests increased both the public's and the politicians' sensitivity to education issues; the acceptance of some women in some roles (Hillary Clinton, chair of the Education Standards Committee, and Peggy Nabors, executive director of the A E A) as legitimate political leaders; a legislature that, through the sustained and specialized attention that interim committees make possible, had developed an institutional memory of Arkansas's educational inadequacies and an in-house corps of effective proeducation advocates; a serendipitous series of judicial decisions; a state press that rallied almost unanimously behind improved educational programs; and a governor with the precise political skills and personal values to give these assorted elements leadership and focus.[44]

According to Ira Sharkansky, "A highly placed, highly motivated official who perceives the needs for increased services and expenditures can be a potent force in state budgeting, despite the dampening effects of incremental budgeting," and thus, "there is room in an incremental system for occasional major change." Such, at least briefly, seems to have been the case in Arkansas. Sharkansky also noted, however, that state spending increases in spurts, with alternations between periods of relative increase and periods of stability or relative decline: "While the increment during any particular spending period may represent a relative rise or decline of a state's spending position in relation to the nation-wide-trends, that increment generally is not so large as to change the *historical* position of that state's spending in relation to others." In Arkansas's faltering 1986 economy, there was abundant evidence of the truth of this observation.[45]

The kinds of dramatic and highly unflattering distinctions traditionally drawn between Arkansas and other states are no longer so easy or accurate as was once the case, and this is true with respect to a wide spectrum of public policies. A more modernized economy and a more productive tax base have brought Arkansas within closer range of the state services offered elsewhere. A more rational budget process has offered at least marginal opportunities for decision makers to establish and pursue spending priorities. The leadership capacities of both the executive and legislative branches have been strengthened, thereby providing opportunities for policy innovations and advancements when economic circumstances are favorable and leaders so inclined. Closer communications with the non-Arkansas world have provided a more critical standard by which Arkansans can assess their own public services, and more competitive and issue-centered elections afford Arkansans more meaningful opportunities for rewarding and punishing their public servants. It seems fair to conclude, then, that better politics can produce, and occasionally has produced, better public policy.

## CHAPTER FOURTEEN

# Continuity and Change in Arkansas Politics

*Arkansas history has been the scene of a constant struggle between the forces of modernization and those of tradition.*

Michael Dougan, 1986

*Arkansas is a state poised on the edge of success—or failure.*

Almanac of American Politics, 1986

*At the ripe old age of 150 years, we stand at the crossroads.*

Governor Bill Clinton, 1986

Summarizing Arkansas politics is, as Abraham Lincoln once said of running a democracy, about as easy as shoveling fleas. For every generalization, there are obvious exceptions. Every characterization must be qualified and every label must be modified.

The 1968 election in which Arkansas voters simultaneously selected George Wallace for president, J. W. Fulbright for senator, and Winthrop Rockefeller for governor is the most frequently cited anomaly, but there are countless others. How could a state that so routinely ratified Orval Faubus's leadership as late as 1966, reject him in 1970 for Dale Bumpers, who bluntly told voters that segregation was morally wrong? Why would the same voters who enthusiastically embraced Ronald Reagan's presidential candidacy in 1984 simultaneously reject all of the Arkansas candidates for whom he personally campaigned? Why did Arkansas voters repeatedly during one recent decade signal their desire for a new constitution but resoundingly reject the products of the constitutional conventions they had authorized? Why would a state with one of the oldest and least-educated populations in America elect and reelect one of the youngest and best-educated governors in America? How could voters elect and reelect a state legislature that overwhelmingly passed a "scientific creationism" law and simultaneously elect and reelect two U.S. senators consistently rated as the South's (indeed among the nation's) most liberal?[1]

Political satirist Mark Russell drew appreciative laughs from an Arkansas audience by noting, "Show me a state that gives us William Fulbright, Wilbur Mills, Dale Bumpers and Tommy Robinson, and I'll show you a state undergoing a severe identity crisis." More seriously, Arkansas political scientists are frequently asked for explanations of these and other enigmas. Conservatives from other states, seeing in Arkansas's traditions and contemporary demographics a fertile field for conservative candidacies, are exasperated by the apparent illogic of Arkansas voters' choices. Liberals from states with presumably more progressive traditions can be equally exasperated, as the recent remarks of one North Carolina political scientist illustrate: "Y'all are supposed to be the backward ones, but you've got Clinton and Bumpers and Pryor, and we've got Jesse Helms." That Arkansas in the mid-1980s should have two officials, Dale Bumpers and Bill Clinton, being seriously discussed as presidential possibilities, when some of the larger and more prosperous states have none, arouses what might be called "politician envy" among political afficionados, along with rather broad hints that the caliber of Arkansas politicians is (a) better than its people deserve, and (b) something of a fluke.[2]

That individuals of exceptional talent have sought political office in Arkansas should not be surprising. Until very recently, there have been few other attractive outlets—no great industrial enterprises or financial empires or intellectual undertakings—for those of unusual energy and intellect. It is no more mysterious that J. William Fulbright, returning from his studies at Oxford as a Rhodes scholar, should have found politics more enticing than academia (or running the family's lumberyard and bottling plant in Fayetteville) than that Bill Clinton should opt for the political arena thirty years later. It is not difficult to imagine why Dale Bumpers, recently named the best orator in the Senate, should have tired of exercising his talents before small-town juries.[3]

What is not so apparent is why Arkansas voters should have acquiesced in these individuals' ambitions, since much more traditional, much less progressive choices, were always available. After all, despite the numerous socioeconomic changes described in previous chapters, Arkansas is still one of the poorest, most rural, and most homogeneous states in the nation.

While the economic gap between Arkansas and the rest of the nation had narrowed over the decades, in 1986, Arkansas remained forty-ninth of the fifty states in per capita income, and sixth in the nation in rurality. Although the rural farm population declined from 65 percent of the population in 1920 to only 5 percent in 1980, the rural nonfarm population constituted 43 percent of the 1980 population, a percentage nearly twice that of the nation generally. In terms of ethnic variety, Arkansas has much smaller percentages of Asian-Americans and Hispanics than does America as a whole and, as throughout its history, Arkansas remains overwhelmingly Protestant, specifically, Baptist and Methodist. The proportions of Catholics (2.5 percent of the population) and Jews (0.1 percent) are among the very smallest in the fifty states.[4]

In contrast to early in-migration patterns, when most of those coming to Arkansas moved in from nearby southern states, those coming to Arkansas in recent years are of more diverse geographic origin, a possible stimulus to progressivity (table 9). The areas with the greatest in-migration, however, have become the strongest centers of Republican, that is, conservative, voting strength. Furthermore, research suggests that much of today's in-migration represents the return of those whose families out-migrated earlier, and that, on at least some attitudinal measures, "migrants to the respective regions of the state are very similar to natives already living in the regions to which they have moved." Donald Voth, based on extensive analysis of these population movements, has concluded that "Arkansas' migration experience has been at least as much a source of continuity and stability as of change."[5]

What then is the source of what has been documented in previous chapters, and curious outsiders perceive, as Arkansas's preference in recent decades for candidates from the liberal side of the spectrum? To be specific, between 1966 and 1984, Arkansas held ten gubernatorial elections. In nine of the ten, voters showed a clear preference for the progressive candidate, the single exception being Frank White's victory over Bill Clinton in 1980 (and an important qualification being 1970, when progressive Bumpers beat progressive Rockefeller). How many states can claim such a record? Can such a string of voter decisions be a mere fluke? If, as Michael Dougan has observed, "Arkansas history has been . . . a constant struggle between the forces of modernization and those of tradition," why have the political forces of modernization been so consistently beating those of tradition?[6]

Table 9: Top Ten States of Origin of Migrants to Arkansas, 1833–1850 and 1975–1980

| *1833–50* | | *1975–80* | |
| --- | --- | --- | --- |
| *State of origin* | *% of In-Migrants* | *State of Origin* | *% of In-Migrants* |
| Tennessee | 35.8 | Texas | 12.8 |
| Alabama | 14.0 | California | 10.6 |
| Missouri | 12.3 | Illinois | 9.0 |
| Mississippi | 12.3 | Missouri | 8.2 |
| Illinois | 5.2 | Oklahoma | 6.3 |
| Kentucky | 4.9 | Tennessee | 5.0 |
| Georgia | 3.9 | Louisiana | 4.2 |
| Louisiana | 2.5 | Florida | 3.4 |
| North Carolina | 2.0 | Michigan | 3.2 |
| Texas | 1.8 | Kansas | 3.0 |

*Source:* Donald Voth, "Impact of Migration on Arkansas" (Lecture presented by Center for Arkansas and Regional Studies, Fayetteville, March 15, 1984).

One possibility, highly unflattering to the Arkansas electorate, is that in moving more slowly than most of the South toward its "natural" home in the bosom of conservative Republicanism, Arkansas is simply showing the same suspicion of novelty that has always characterized the state. In an October 1986 television portrait of Arkansas on WTBS, the narrator, Hal Holbrook, quoted the old saw about wanting to be in Arkansas if the world came to an end because it would happen in Arkansas twenty years later. Thus, just as Arkansas was slow in accepting other manifestations of modernity, like electricity and compulsory education, so the powerful tugs of both tradition and inertia have kept many actual Republicans in the Democratic camp much longer than is ideologically appropriate. According to one political participant and observer, Arkansas's rural vote remains Democratic "because tradition is important to rural people. They are looking for ways to stay with the Democratic party; they have to be run off."[7]

The problem of redirecting these traditionalists is compounded by Arkansans' longstanding resentment of outsiders. Philosophically, Arkansans may be diametrically opposed to the voting stances of Pryor and Bumpers in the Senate, but when Henry Kissinger or Jerry Falwell or

Republican cabinet members arrive to "enlighten" them, the reaction is to rally around the native against the interference of meddlesome "aliens." Pryor turned the parade of visiting Republicans supporting his 1984 opponent into a plus for himself by calling attention to their numbers and insisting that Arkansas voters were informed and independent and neither needed nor wanted outsiders trying to influence their vote. Clinton got cheers at the 1984 Democratic State Convention by digging at the campaign appearance for Woody Freeman by the former secretary of state Henry Kissinger: "I hope Mr. Kissinger tells us everything he knows about what Arkansas needs and I hope my opponent tells Mr. Kissinger everything he knows about what Arkansas needs in a utility contractor." When Rev. Jerry Falwell made a 1985 Little Rock address charging that Bumpers was "a little to the left of Ted Kennedy" but then "comes home and dupes the people," newspapers and letter writers from left to right expressed outrage. The usually mild-mannered *Northwest Arkansas Times* editorialized to Falwell, "You have insulted the people of Arkansas by implying that we are ignorant and by presuming you can 'educate' us to achieve your own ends. We'll make you a deal. You stay in Virginia and we'll stay in Arkansas and keep our senator until we decide otherwise."[8]

What this theory suggests is that Arkansas's progressivism is actually a curious by-product of its provincialism, an explanation that implies not only enormous ignorance on the part of the electorate but a degree of isolation from national political debates and communications that would be astonishing given the television set in nearly every Arkansas home.[9] Most important, it ignores the fact that this preference for progressive candidates has been consistently manifested by voters in the Democratic primary for governor since 1970. It cannot, then, be merely the lingering preference for Democrats, who today happen to be more liberal than Democratic candidates of the past.

A variation upon this theme acknowledges the powerful impact of the national media but postulates a different outcome. According to this theory, Arkansans are acutely aware of, defensive about, and unhappy with their longstanding national reputation for backwardness and provincialism. As West Virginia voters may have deliberately confounded a similar national image by selecting young, rich, Catholic John F. Kennedy in their 1960 presidential primary, so the Arkansas electorate takes a perverse pleasure in defying electoral expectations about them.[10]

A second set of rationales for Arkansas's "surprisingly" progressive political choices points to the profoundly personal nature of Arkansas politics. According to this hypothesis, Arkansas voters have not actually been voting for progress, they have been voting for Winthrop Rockefeller and Dale Bumpers and David Pryor and Bill Clinton, or at least against their most prominent opponents, and accidentally got two decades of progressivism in the bargain.

This theory has appeal because perhaps the most distinctive feature of Arkansas politics is its strong personal, indeed familial, character. All political attentives in the state begin their day with the *Arkansas Gazette* and *Arkansas Democrat*, and by 8 A.M. the statewide telephone lines are buzzing over the possible political implications in a bankruptcy announcement or divorce proceeding or social event. Democratic and Republican state conventions are like family reunions where intimacy between the party's leading lights and grassroots loyalists is easily established and sustained.

While mass-media advertising absorbs the great bulk of contemporary campaign expenditures in major races, the new technology has not displaced the need for or effectiveness of the personal touch. Annie Glenn, accompanying her husband, John, on his 1984 presidential quest to Arkansas, was amazed to find how personalized the politics were, especially that everyone she met referred to the two U.S. senators as Dale and David and to the governor as Bill. And "Dale" and "David" and "Bill" could have told her, with some chagrin, that they in turn are expected to, and do in fact, remember the names of thousands and thousands of their constituents and their occupations and ailments and children's names.[11]

Major candidates may chafe at the time necessitated by command appearances at the Gillett Coon Supper and Mount Nebo Chicken Fry, the Warren Pink Tomato Festival and the Hope Watermelon Festival, the Springdale Rodeo Parade and the Bald Knob Strawberry Festival.[12] In addition, there are scores of county rallies where the major candidates are slyly scheduled to speak last so that all the lesser-known local aspirants can take advantage of the crowds gathered to hear the featured speakers. Little of this may be cost-effective in the minds of modern campaign technocrats, but it is still the accepted, indeed essential, Arkansas way.

Furthermore, the most successful Arkansas politicians make their festival and civic club appearances and high school commencement speeches with a gusto suggesting that there is nothing else they would rather be doing. Continuing longstanding southern and Arkansas traditions, the present "Big Three" of Arkansas politics—Bumpers, Pryor, and Clinton—are all superb storytellers, who rarely use a prepared address, who quote easily and effectively from Scripture, and who can bring down the house with wry, self-deprecating humor. They have very different oratorical styles: Clinton lists debating points against invisible opponents; Pryor chats and charms; Bumpers educates and preaches. All, however, quickly establish a strong rapport with the tens of thousands of Arkansans they encounter each year, thereby building powerful insulation against challengers' suggestions that they are "too intellectual" or "too liberal" or of dubious patriotism. A 1986 analysis of the Arkansas election scene for the *Congressional Quarterly* noted, "Arkansas is not really a media state; incumbents who establish a strong personal image usually manage to withstand even the most sophisticated and well-planned efforts to defeat them."[13]

In a hilarious but highly illuminating piece on the 1984 U.S. Senate race, Paul Greenberg imagined an emissary from the Republican National Committee attempting to convince Dub and Earlene, proprietors of a South Arkansas general store, of the dangers of liberal-voting David Pryor. Their response? "Hey, does ol David *look* like a liberal to you? Does he *talk* like one? . . . Notice how he started his campaign and how this here Bethune started his? Bethune went up to Washington, D.C. to huddle with ol' Reagan and that air Republican National Committee. . . . Dave just went over to his mamma's house in Camden, Lord rest her soul, and set down on the front porch in his overhauls and allowed as how he was fixin' to run again. That can't be no liberal, it ain't even hardly a politician."[14]

The "progressivism through personalism" argument is more persuasive than the "progressivism through provincialism" argument. In predominantly one-party and therefore effectively partyless Arkansas, voters have long been accustomed, indeed have been forced, to choose between competing individuals rather than between issues and parties. What this explanation also clearly suggests, however, is that Arkansas's newfound progressivism has little rational basis and is living on borrowed time. Once candidates emerge who wed an attractive personality and an engaging speaking style to a conservative philosophy, Arkansas voters could readily abandon their very superficial attachment to progressivism.

A third possibility ascribes much greater rationality and perception to the Arkansas electorate. This is the proposition that Arkansas voters have been electing progressive candidates because Arkansas voters themselves are progressive, or at least much less conservative than they have been generally assumed to be. The views of some historians and political scientists to this effect were noted in chapter 5. Their assessment is shared by at least some contemporary Arkansas politicians. Congressman Bill Alexander, for example, suggests that although Arkansans were always forced to be fiscally cautious, they were not truly conservative. In fact, he recently stated, "Although they have been poor, they have also been progressive." Similarly, Governor Clinton has cautioned against any simple characterization of the Arkansas electorate as conservative. Certainly they have been somewhat suspicious of government and have never welcomed excessive government meddling in their lives, but Clinton also points to the fact that Arkansas was the most racially tolerant of the southern states and had strong populist strains that emphasized the obligation of government to protect individuals and families against unfair treatment by an economic elite.[15]

As noted in previous chapters, all of the nineteenth- and early twentieth-century populistic "thrusts from below" were diluted and ultimately demoralized by divide and conquer techniques that so alienated poor whites from poor blacks that their mutuality of circumstance and need could never be fashioned into an effective political force. Furthermore, until very recent decades, voters were such a small part of the citizenry that the electorate that selected and sustained inactive and inattentive state political leaders was highly unrepresentative of the people generally. Congressman Brooks Hays, in his autobiography, despaired over the fact that in 1942 he was elected to represent 325,000 people having received only 16,000 votes. In contrast, most of Arkansas's contemporary officials were elected by much larger and therefore more representative electorates, in which low-to-moderate-income white and black Arkansans were an important part of the victorious coalition.[16]

Some Arkansas analysts, like the late political scientist Jim Ranchino, place Arkansas's acceptance of progressivism much later in time. According to Ranchino,

the great middle class of voters had moved from a rather conservative, intolerant posture in 1960, toward a greater degree of tolerance and moderation in 1970. . . . Faced with the rapidly moving domestic and foreign events of the 1960's, and even faster-talking candidates, the voters sifted their way through the vocabulary of proposals and promises and consistently selected more moderate candidates than they had the decade before. . . . They became one of the most independent, flexible and free electorates in the United States. Raised on party politics and a solid dose of southern conservatism, the voters in Arkansas were controlled by neither. Their instincts became more significant than their traditions and the results were remarkably free from the biases and fears of other years.[17]

Whether present-day progressivism is the final flowering of a long tradition or a very recent development, it has clearly been consequential that, unlike the situation in many southern states, racial egalitarianism and economic activism were encouraged rather than discouraged by the state's most widely read newspaper, the *Arkansas Gazette*. The "Oldest Newspaper West of the Mississippi" has, for decades, been not just passionately (critics would say pathologically) Democratic, but ardently reformist and liberal. This position nearly cost the paper its existence during the late 1950s, when the *Gazette* championed the moderate integrationists and steadily chastised Governor Faubus and his cohorts for escalating racist sentiments. Even those who have disagreed with the paper's philosophy, however, have attempted to emulate its quality, so that throughout the state there are numerous small-town newspapers of uncommon editorial vigor and excellence. David Pryor once noted, "The major difference between Arkansas and the rest of the South has been the *Arkansas Gazette*," and word of its sale to the Gannett chain in October 1986, produced the following among many tributes: "It was a newspaper that never let the demagogues get away with it, that never apologized for its literacy, and that relished doing battle against the low-lifes and buffoons who used to dominate the state's politics. My red-headed Aunt Helen hated the "knee-jerk liberals" who ran the editorial page. But she could no more have started a day without a good cussing match with the *Gazette* than she could have ended it without a bourbon and water." The *Gazette* has not been uniformly successful in the causes and candidates it has championed. Arkansans, however, were at least exposed to an articulate voice of liberalism, and those attempting to push the state in more progressive directions had at least one influential voice backing their efforts.[18]

There is, then, the possibility that Arkansans's preference for progressive leaders in recent decades is neither a peculiar twist on its provincialism nor the accidental product of personality politics. Rather, it is the expression of at least mildly progressive impulses that were suppressed or diverted in the traditional political system but have been able to flourish in contemporary times. The 1986 elections offered some interesting tests of these various theories about the Arkansas electorate and an especially clear-cut test of the relative strength of the "forces of modernization and those of tradition."

## THE 1986 ELECTIONS AND THEIR MEANINGS

The battle for Arkansas's first four-year gubernatorial term since Reconstruction began in the primaries, which, in what has become the new Arkansas norm, produced less interest and voter turnout than did the subsequent general election. In the unusually crowded Republican primary, the former governor Frank White; Winthrop Rockefeller's lieutenant governor, Maurice "Footsie" Britt; a Fort Smith dentist, Wayne Lanier; and a Calico Rock businessman, Bobby K. Hayes, all campaigned more against incumbent Bill Clinton than against each other. All four warned of the dangers of letting Clinton linger another four years for a total of ten in the governor's office: "too much raw power"; "close to creating the most dangerous situation in government we've ever had"; "there is likelihood or possibilities of abuse." All four also, while promising not to abandon the new school standards, advocated their delay or dilution or "prioritization" until more funds could be "found" for their implementation.[19]

At age seventy-six, more than half that of the state itself, Orval Faubus again reemerged from retirement to challenge Clinton's candidacy in the Democratic primary. For obvious reasons, Faubus did not make an issue of Clinton's prospective tenure. He did, however, chime in the chorus of complaints against the rigor and timing of the school standards, "dreamed up in the head of a Rhodes Scholar." He suggested, "It is ridiculous to try and teach children calculus when they can't divide" and berated the standards as a "sneaky way to force consolidation of small school districts." Faubus typified the "forces of tradition" in technique as well as substance. While Clinton aired television commercials extolling his education and economic development programs and flew around the state for personal appearances at large public gatherings, Faubus and his driver rode from county to county, stopping at the county courthouse and local newspaper and radio offices, seeking old supporters who were often no longer there (indeed, often no longer alive). The third Democratic gubernatorial candidate, W. Dean Goldsby, the black former director of the Pulaski County Economic Opportunity Agency (under investigation by federal officials on charges of misspent funds) did little campaigning of any kind and served primarily as an electoral outlet for those, especially teachers, still steaming about Clinton's teacher-testing program but unable to vote for all that Faubus represented.[20]

Both Clinton and White got approximately 61 percent of their primary vote, but for Clinton that meant 315,397 of 520,628 cast; for White it meant getting 13,831 of 22,436 cast (a total constituting less than last-placed Goldsby got in the Democratic primary). Nine counties cast no Republican votes at all, and in only twenty-one counties were as many as 100 Republican votes cast. On election night, a dejected Faubus noted, "I'm a hindsight and I'm a has-been and I understand that as well as anybody."[21]

The third match between Clinton and White quickly deteriorated into one of the nastiest and most negative in recent Arkansas history. The advertisements of both candidates concentrated much more heavily on the alleged flaws in the other's character and competence than on their own programs and merits. There were marked differences, however, in the programs and issue appeals each presented to the electorate, which made this race another referendum between the forces of tradition and of modernization. White accused Clinton of being committed to "forced rural school consolidation," which would destroy the "lifeblood, spirit and identity" of Arkansas's small communities. He warned that the school standards would necessitate a $200 million tax increase, charged Clinton with having "diverted" money to higher education, advocated adoption of a proposed antiabortion referendum, and promised that his wife would be a "full-time first lady." Clinton said he would "go to his grave" defending the school standards, said that it would cost closer to $60 million than $200 million to finish implementing them, pled that he was "guilty as sin" of having directed more money into the state's colleges, questioned the necessity for the proposed limitation on state funding of abortions, and vehemently defended his wife's contributions to the state.[22]

In the U.S. Senate race, voters were given an even more clear-cut choice between the Republican right and the Democratic left. As in the 1984 Senate race, a parade of prominent Republicans (Vice-President George Bush, senators, cabinet members) came to Arkansas to raise money for and add luster to Asa Hutchinson's challenge to Dale Bumpers. They reminded Arkansas voters that the "national Democratic party (is) deserting them," and that a senator who "voted for the liberal Eastern establishment" and "85 to 95% of the time with ultra-liberal Ted Kennedy" could not simultaneously be representing the people of Arkansas. Although President Reagan did not personally campaign in Arkansas in 1986, he was featured in television commercials urging a vote for Hutchinson as one who believes "in my conservative values: family, jobs and economic growth."[23]

At the outset, it appeared that Bumpers might be much more vulnerable than David Pryor had been in 1984 to a conservative critique. Unlike Pryor, Bumpers had opposed both the school prayer and balance-the-budget constitutional amendments, and had cast the lone southern Senate vote against a bill limiting the power of the federal judiciary to order busing. Bumpers's frequent mentions as a presidential or vice-presidential candidate gave him more closely perceived ties to the national Democratic party; his outspoken criticism of the Strategic Defense Initiative, the MX Missile, the B-1 Bomber, and other Reagan-backed weapons (together with his wife's presidency of Peace Links) provided convenient openings for questions about his support of national security; and his voting record on abortion issues had made him a target of pro-life groups. Hutchinson, a graduate of Bob Jones University, a member of a fundamentalist church, a pro-life and scientific creationism activist, a fiscal conservative and Reagan loyalist, emphasized his philosophical differences from Bumpers and offered himself as one much more in tune with Arkansans' traditional values.

On November 4, a total of 695,487 Arkansans cast their ballots. While turnout was less than in either the 1984 presidential election or the preceding 1982 off-year election, in what has become the new tradition, a higher percentage of Arkansas's voting-age population (43 percent) than of the nation's generally (37.3 percent) got to the polls. In what has also apparently become the new Arkansas tradition, voters overwhelmingly chose "the forces of modernization" over the "forces of tradition." Clinton received 64 percent of the vote, his highest margin ever over White, and Bumpers was returned to the Senate with 62 percent of the vote, a marked improvement over his 59 percent margin in 1980. Voters also approved one constitutional amendment enlarging the jurisdiction of municipal courts, and another one permitting some kinds of revenue bonds to be issued without voter approval. They narrowly defeated a proposal giving four-year terms to all county officials in both the executive and legislative branches (the latter provision having created considerable controversy since state representatives receive only two-year terms). In the year's true cliff-hanger, the proposed "Abortion and Abortion Funding Limitation Amendment," stricken by the state supreme court from the 1984 ballot when it was titled "The Unborn Child Amendment," was defeated by 519 votes.

Do these outcomes present conclusive proof that Arkansans prefer the options of action and modernization over the options of inaction and conservatism? Of course not. Both Bumpers and Clinton, as incumbents, had powerful advantages over their challengers, not least of which were campaign chests more than double those of Hutchinson and White, skilled statewide campaign organizational networks, and all the "gratitude" that flows to those who have made appointments, secured funding, and done assorted favors for thousands of individuals and communities over many years in office. Both were sufficiently well known to so many Arkansans that charges of their having given state business to a "known cocaine trafficker" (White against Clinton) or being opposed to prayer (Hutchinson against Bumpers) had little impact, in fact may have backfired. Both Clinton and Bumpers repeatedly demonstrated the artful ability—perhaps an instinctive political gift, perhaps the skill that comes with experience—of reversing an attack to skewer the attacker. When White accused Mrs. Clinton, through her law practice, of conflicts of interest, Clinton's rebuttal commercials quickly accused White of slinging mud at one of the state's most respected women and chided White's lack of chivalry while questioning his manhood: "Remember, Frank, you're running for Governor, not for First Lady." Bumpers turned back Hutchinson's school prayer criticisms with ferocious counterclaims that Hutchinson had so little respect for the Constitution that he was walking around "with a pocketful of amendments" that would "pillage this precious document, our nation's Bible."[24]

After all the caveats and conditions, however, the fact remains that Arkansans, again in 1986, collectively expressed preferences and choices that returned those with progressive records to office, rejected appeals to fundamentalism and reaction, and continued the slow process of incrementally updating the Arkansas Constitution. Twenty years of such behavior cannot be a fluke.

Where does this leave the state's struggling Republican party? As I suggested in chapter 5, and as many political scientists predict, "actuarial odds and immigration alone give the southern Republican party a bright future." As those with the most powerful devotion to the Democratic party die and are replaced by generations who have not been raised on tales of either the Civil War or the New Deal, and as Arkansas continues to attract both retirees and those seeking work in the rapidly expanding central and northwestern metropolitan areas of the state, Republican candidates will have much greater potential electability. Many political scientists also predict that the "red-neck, black-neck" coalition—that is, the combination of the nearly monolithic black vote and the traditional rural white vote—which accounts for contemporary Democratic majorities, is too strained and unnatural an alliance to persist into the future. The fact that Democrats have held the governorship in Arkansas for fourteen of the last twenty years has given the Democrats access to the most affluent members of the state's business community, who want above all to be on the winning side. Should the Democrats lose the governorship, and with it their automatic access to the state's financial heavy-hitters, they will lose not only their most generous campaign contributors but also their ability to hold both the patricians and the plebeians in the same party.[25]

The increasingly regional nature of Arkansas voting patterns, outlined in chapter 4, was evident again in the 1986 contests. Map 9, illustrating those counties where Clinton and Bumpers exceeded and got less than their

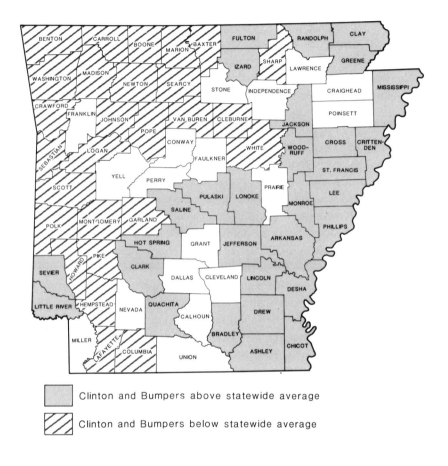

Clinton and Bumpers above statewide average

Clinton and Bumpers below statewide average

Map 9. Strongest and Weakest Counties for Clinton and Bumpers, 1986. (*Source:* Compiled from official election returns.)

statewide averages, clearly portrays the Democratic tendencies in the Delta counties and the Republican tendencies in the Ozark counties. Although both Clinton's and Bumpers's margins were such that the black vote was not decisive, it is clear from exit polls and precinct returns, as well as the lopsided margins in the Delta counties, that more than 90 percent of Arkansas's black voters supported the Democratic candidates in 1986. Underscoring the "liberalizing" impact of an expanded electorate on Arkansas politics, polls indicated that Clinton and Bumpers not only received nearly all of the black vote but were the beneficiaries of sizable gender gaps as well: 62 percent of all women voters favored Bumpers over Hutchinson, 71 percent favored Clinton over White. In traditional Arkansas politics, of course, neither women nor blacks voted.[26]

The Ozark counties returned Congressman John Paul Hammerschmidt to office with 80 percent of the vote and gave Hutchinson and White their only victories: Hutchinson won six, White won eight of these northwestern counties. Republican margins, however, were much slimmer than in previous elections. Benton County, in which more people had voted in the Republican than in the Democratic primary, supported Clinton by 58 percent. Sebastian County, which gave White 9,144 and 12,115 vote majorities in 1980 and 1982, chose White over Clinton in 1986 by only 290 votes. Bumpers recaptured five of the nine Ozark counties he had lost in 1980 and, despite his widely advertised "liberalism," fared better in these counties than did Pryor in 1984. Part of the explanation lies in the absence of a popular Republican presidential candidate at the top of the ticket in 1986, but since the governorship will henceforth be contested in the nonpresidential off-year elections, that boost to Republican voter turnout will continue to be absent in the future.

Arkansas's Urban counties continued to defy earlier political scientists' predictions of being the best breeding grounds for Republicanism. Of those described in chapter 4 as Savage and Gallagher's Urban counties, only Sebastian County went narrowly Republican. Clinton and Bumpers carried the state's most urban county, Pulaski, with 73 percent and 65 percent margins. Clinton, in fact, got two and three times the vote that White did in some of Little Rock's wealthiest neighborhoods; his strong identification with improved education has served him well with the most affluent and highly educated segments of the electorate, voters who might otherwise favor Republicans. It is also worth noting that the Democratic congressman Tommy Robinson, who lost Pulaski County to the Republican Judy Petty in

1984, carried Pulaski by 71 percent against Republican challenger Keith Hamaker in 1986.

What about the Rural Swing counties? Here, if anywhere, White's championing of the small rural schools and his other appeals to traditionalism, and Hutchinson's questioning of Bumpers's religiosity and patriotism, would seem to have had their strongest appeal. In 1986 neither Republican won any of the twenty-six counties that had provided the basis for White's upset of Clinton in 1980. That voters in these counties had still not entirely forgiven Clinton is suggested by the fact that Clinton got less than his statewide margin in seventeen of the twenty-six; that these counties still have a standing commitment to Democrats is suggested by the fact that Bumpers got more than his statewide average in nineteen of the twenty-six. The previous characterization of voters in these counties as "Populists" (according to the Maddox-Lilie typology) is broadly confirmed by their treatment of the three most contentious constitutional amendments on the 1986 ballot. The proposed antiabortion amendment got stronger support in seventeen of these twenty-six counties than it did in the state generally; the proposed extension of county officials to four-year terms fared worse in twenty of the twenty-six, and the amendment reducing voter participation in revenue bond issues fared worse in fifteen of the twenty-six. Legislated morality is somewhat more acceptable in the Rural Swing counties than in the state generally; reduced popular control over public officials and their decisions is not.

The strong support given to Reagan by Rural Swing counties in 1984 and their rebellion against Clinton in 1980 indicate that they can swing Republican when a Democrat with an unacceptable record or image is offered to them. Their "druthers," however, remain Democratic. Their 1986 voting behavior also raises doubts about the likelihood, suggested by some political scientists, that the religious right will act as a bridge for traditional southern Democrats to cross over into Republicanism. The religious right had an energetic and eloquent spokesman in Hutchinson, who was resoundingly rejected. Perhaps in other southern states this mechanism will successfully unhitch traditional Democrats, but recent opinion surveys in Arkansas indicate that efforts to exploit such appeals may backfire. In 1986 over 60 percent of surveyed Arkansans strongly agreed with the statement that "religious leaders or groups should not attempt to force their moral stands on others," and while 23 percent would be more likely to support a candidate endorsed by the Moral Majority, 36 percent would be less likely to do so. In the aftermath of the 1986 elections, state Republican leaders indicated that the religious right and prolife forces had become more of a burden than a blessing.[27]

The Arkansas Republican party has become a legitimate presence in state politics, will continue to benefit from long-range demographics, and will continue to reap the electoral rewards when a Democratic candidate is objectionable. In a remarkably harmonious postelection meeting, the Republican State Committee unanimously elected the former congressman Ed Bethune as their new chairman and outlined sensible plans for a more productive future: concentrating on grassroots development instead of victories at the top; eschewing extremism; and reattracting black Arkansans. According to Bethune, the four-year gubernatorial term would give the state Republicans a welcome breathing space in which to concentrate their organizational and electoral energies on important local and state legislative contests. In the near future, however, in most areas for most offices, the Democrats will continue to have the advantage in terms of quantity and quality of candidates, voter identification and familiarity, the traditions of the past, and the progressive preferences of the present.

## THE PAST AND THE PRESENT

In one of many colorful 1986 ceremonies marking Arkansas's 150th year of statehood, members of the seventy-fifth General Assembly gathered in the Old State House for a mock reenactment, with some fortunate modifications, of events from the First General Assembly. On December 4, 1837, during debate over a bill authorizing the use of wolf scalps to pay county taxes, the Speaker descended from his chair and stabbed the Randolph County representative to death with a Bowie knife. For the 1986 version, the Speaker read an account of the slaying, then handed a rose to the representative from Randolph County, remarking, "Thank God we're away from those kinds of actions in this day and time."[28]

One sesquicentennial "Scrooge" complained that the year-long round of contests and exhibits, parades and lectures, was a collective exercise in denying or romanticizing Arkansas's past rather than honoring it. Bob Lancaster, writing in the *Arkansas Times*, suggested that a display of the artifacts that had actually shaped the state's past would have to include not only the axe and plow and biscuit pan, but also "manacles, a noose, dueling pistols, a Klan sheet, a spittoon, a well-thumbed Bible, a bottle of Peruna, a forged poll-tax receipt, a cypress-knee lamp, a discarded automobile muffler, and a football." Perhaps so. It is true, however, that physical violence has become a rare rather than a routine part of Arkansas's political process; and this is only one of many visible and generally praiseworthy ways in which contemporary politics differs from the traditional pattern.[29]

The First General Assembly, for example, was a thoroughly male and totally white institution; the Seventy-fifth included five blacks and ten women. Those numbers are still highly disproportionate to the numbers of women and blacks in the population generally. Still, by the 1980s, almost all of the traditional white, male inner sanctums had been penetrated. Most of the women who served in the 1986 legislature, and as state treasurer and state auditor, and in other elective offices throughout the state, had gotten there on their own rather than over their husband's dead bodies. Also by 1986, women headed three of the major state agencies, had managed gubernatorial campaigns, acted as legislative floor leaders, chaired the State Highway Commission, and were being seriously discussed as future gubernatorial candidates.[30]

Blacks have made much slower progress than women in obtaining elective office, especially in eastern Arkansas. Still, a state that began the century by electing a governor (Jeff Davis) who promised subhuman treatment of black prison inmates, entered its sesquicentennial year with a black chairman of the State Board of Correction. While blacks were still much more likely than whites to be unemployed and to live in poverty, disputes between employers and employees were being resolved in 1986 by a state Workmen's Compensation Commission chaired by a black. Black and white teachers, who had not merged their professional associations until 1966, by 1986 were in one association headed by Cora McHenry, the first black woman to be the chief executive of a state affiliate of the National Education Association. During the days when Governor Faubus fashioned a political career out of resisting federal integration instructions, who could have imagined that in three decades the roles would be totally reversed? As noted in chapter 11, the Arkansas attorney general advised the federal Justice Department that Arkansas would not honor the federal government's request that the state drop its affirmative action program for the State Police Department. Considering the fanatical devotion of fans to the University of Arkansas Razorbacks, considering that the university was the last school in the Southwest Conference to give a scholarship to a black football player, and considering the former coach Lou Holtz's wry observation that a Razorback coach in Arkansas is like a state park, perhaps most amazing of all was the 1985 selection of Nolan Richardson to coach the Razorback basketball team—the first black coach of a college revenue-producing sport in the South. As Richardson himself observed, "Thank God for Arkansas." Although both women and blacks were still progressing toward rather than fully enjoying political, legal, and social equality, the state's official nickname, Land of Opportunity, was much less a travesty by 1986 than it was when officially adopted in 1953.[31]

As many of the preceding chapters have documented and explained, Arkansas politics has gone through a series of sharp and sweeping changes in the last quarter-century of its existence. Until recent decades, the hallmarks of traditional Arkansas politics were a nonparticipatory public; a corrupted and unrepresentative electoral process; absolute domination by one political party; issueless campaigns; the deliberate subordination of the black race and the systematic exclusion of women; an unresponsive, often self-serving, and frequently ineffective governing elite; and a reactionary thrust to public policy. By 1986, voter registration and participation in Arkansas occasionally exceeded national norms, elections were honest tests of a much larger and more representative electorate, general election contests in major races were much more than routine ratification of primary results, voters were offered differences of issue as well as personality, blacks and women were legitimate political participants slowly expanding their spheres of influence, and more action-oriented officials were using strengthened governing institutions to address some of Arkansas's long-neglected problems. In answer to one of the questions raised at this book's outset, these are not just changes of symbol and style but fundamental changes in structure and substance.

Arkansas politics in the 1980s continued to contain some powerful legacies from the past. Congressman Tommy Robinson, in his flamboyant, combative speech, publicity-seeking antics, self-styled championship of the common man, and warring posture toward the media that made him, was uncannily reminiscent of the governor and senator Jeff Davis. Clinton's cleverly timed 1986 television commercials, taking credit for the telephone company's refund checks, seemed suspiciously like a high-tech update of the traditional Arkansas ploy of mailing out welfare checks on election eve. Candidates now build their coalitions and campaign chests through powerful interest groups rather than powerful local machines, a method that may place more programmatic indebtedness upon contemporary candidates than did the patronage obligations of old. Furthermore, in a major diminution of political opportunity, the path to elective office has become so expensive that Arkansas has probably seen the last of the days when a total unknown, such as Dale Bumpers in 1970, could win a Democratic gubernatorial primary with expenditures of $100,000.[32]

On the other hand, it is no longer possible for one interest or individual to dry up all available campaign funds, as Witt Stephens was able to do in Senator Fulbright's behalf in the 1950s, but as the Stephens brothers found they could not do in the 1980s. The negative nature of several Arkansas campaigns in the 1970s and 1980s was a regrettable relapse to the "buckets of bile" spilled in traditional campaigns. There may be some comfort in the knowledge that negative campaigns have lost more often than they have succeeded in recent times, less comfort in the knowledge that character assassination is no longer confined to campaign trails in the South. Indeed, one native Arkansas political scientist insists that the big political story in recent years is "The Southernization of National Politics," with imagery, flamboyance, and the meaninglessness of party labels becoming the norm everywhere.[33]

Perhaps most disturbing to observers of contemporary Arkansas politics were the numerous signs that Arkansas's economy, which had been steadily expanding and flourishing along with the nation's since World War II, by the 1980s had begun to sag and slip. As was happening in the rest of the South, Arkansas was increasingly becoming a two-economy state. In the metropolitan areas, there was boom: by 1985 per capita income in Pulaski County exceeded the national average, and personal income in the Fayetteville-Springdale metropolitan area in northwestern Arkansas ranked fourth among 315 metropolitan areas in percentage growth. In much of eastern and southern Arkansas, however, and in rural areas throughout the state where the economy has been dependent upon row-crop agriculture and low-wage, low-skill manufacturing operations, there was bust. Unemployment ran at least 2 percent above the national average in the 1980s, and Arkansas per capita income, which had climbed to 77.6 percent of the national average in 1978, had slipped back to 75.6 percent of the national average in 1985. With state revenues in fiscal year 1986 having the smallest rate of growth in thirty years (except for 1968, when revenues actually declined), all of the recent advances in educational and other state services were severely threatened. To the extent that Arkansas's political progress had been made possible by Arkansas's economic vitality, there were ominous signs that the easy times were over.[34]

As the drama of the 1986 elections and the warm feelings of the sesquicentennial celebrations gave way to the unpleasant realities of a faltering economy and inadequate revenues, there were many causes for concern, but at least one major source of comfort. Probably the most persistent and damning indictment of traditional southern and Arkansas politics was that it was simply a diversionary sideshow, with no particular relevance to solving state problems. Thomas D. Clark had accurately noted, "For a vast majority of southerners playing at politics, it has been not necessarily the democratic process in action so much as a thoroughly delightful sport." Claude Fulks, writing specifically of Arkansas, despaired in 1926 that "no issues of pith and moment ever divide the State into hostile camps. Its people frequently get het up, but it is invariably over something evanescent and inconsequential. Their interest in politics is never more than a sporting interest." Robert A. Leflar, who participated in Arkansas's traditional brand of politics, emphatically agrees: "Politics mattered only on election day."[35]

By 1985 Governor Clinton, who has acknowledged that his first race for the governorship in 1978 was "a little bit like running for class president," could note in his inaugural address, "We live in a state which has too long viewed politics as sport rather than a pathway to tomorrow." Another observer, while mourning the lost "smarmy vitality" of some of the state's most outrageous past political rascals, also acknowledged: "The new breed of politicians may not be any more altruistic than the old, but they have discovered that, for the time being anyway, the best way to stay in power is to do a good job. . . . The sad truth is that good government isn't as interesting as bad government."[36]

Arkansans, who have always preferred strong individuals in politics, have come to accept the necessity for energetic leaders and an activist government as well. There are still elements of entertainment and diversion in Arkansas politics and government, but for the people, and for the politicians they can now hold accountable, there is much less sport and much more substance.

## CHAPTER FIFTEEN

# For the Future:
# Suggested Sources

*The effacing hand of time . . . cooperating with indifference and neglect, have sadly depleted the original sources of information from which this paper must be prepared.*

Jesse Turner, "The Constitution of 1836," 1911

*Some studies of southern politics have excluded the state from their universe entirely, and this writer could cite only one article in a scholarly journal dealing with Arkansas politics alone.*

Patrick F. O'Connor, "Voting Structure
in a One-Party Legislature," 1973

*At this writing, almost every aspect of Arkansas government and politics awaits our discipline's attention.*

Diane Kincaid Blair, "The Study and
Teaching of Arkansas Politics," 1980

Arkansas politics is no longer what it was, but it is not yet certain what it will be. Change, of course, is characteristic of all political systems, providing students of politics with both their greatest incentives and their gravest inhibitions. Even the most careful descriptions and insights can quickly become obsolete or inaccurate as the subject of study alters. This truism applies with particular force when the subject is Arkansas, both because the political process is still in transition from the traditional to the contemporary and because the serious study of Arkansas politics is still in its pioneering stages.

Until very recently Arkansas had one of the least studied political systems in America. Furthermore, the task of locating useful information about Arkansas government and politics was monumentally frustrating. There was no true state library; there was no authoritative bibliographic control of state publications; and there had been little systematic analysis of Arkansas's political institutions and behavior by political scientists. Fortunately, there has been dramatic improvement on all fronts in the recent past.

In 1979 the Arkansas Library Commission moved into a spacious new building on the capitol grounds in Little Rock and was reconstituted by Act 489 of the Arkansas legislature as the Arkansas State Library. Even more important from a research standpoint, section 8 of that act provided that the Arkansas State Library "shall become the official depository for State and local documents" and "shall create and maintain a State and Local Government Publications Clearinghouse." All agencies of the state and its subdivisions are required by this act to furnish copies of each of their publications to the state library, which catalogues and houses them, establishes depository arrangements with local libraries (city, county, regional, college) and, in 1981, began quarterly publication of *Arkansas Documents* (Little Rock: Arkansas State Library) together with an annual index. Not all state agencies consistently send the clearinghouse all of their publications, and staff and funding problems have slowed both the collecting and cataloguing functions. Nevertheless, the researcher who once had to stumble in a number of different directions will find that the search for official state publications has been enormously simplified.

Another light in the darkness is the increasing activity of the Arkansas Political Science Association. Established in 1973, its annual meetings have stimulated the preparation of a number of papers dealing with Arkansas government and politics. The archives of the University of Arkansas at Little Rock (UALR) Library houses these papers, and some have appeared as articles in the *Arkansas Political Science Journal*, which began annual publication in 1980.

The establishment of the University of Arkansas Press in 1980, and the increased activity of Rose and of August House publishing companies in Little Rock, have provided additional incentives and outlets for scholars and writers dealing with Arkansas subjects.

Although the researcher may still have to do some imaginative detective work and suffer the dread fear that a major source has been overlooked because nobody except its author knows that it exists, studying Arkansas politics and government is much less daunting now than it was in the recent past. Furthermore, although Arkansas documents have been unusually inaccessible, government officials and employees are usually quite accessible and cooperative. A call or note to a state agency requesting materials ordinarily produces them. If not, state legislators are glad to request desired documents for their constituents, and their requests are speedily satisfied. What follows is a selective guide to major reference materials on Arkansas government and politics.

## GENERAL REFERENCE WORKS

### Almanacs, Directories, Atlases

The single most comprehensive compilation of information on Arkansas government and politics is the *Historical Report of the Secretary of State* (Little Rock: Secretary of State). Published every ten years, the 1978 edition was issued in three data-filled volumes. Volume 1 contains the state constitution with amendments; historical rosters of elected executive officials and biographies of incumbents; brief descriptions of all state agencies, commissions, and institutions of higher education; summary election returns for major offices since their inception; legislative district maps, committees, and historical rosters; descriptions of Arkansas courts, district maps, incumbents, and historical rosters. Volume 2 briefly describes all counties (formation, county seat, population, principal products) and lists all past and present county officials. Volume 3, a 1978 innovation, contains a chronological series of descriptive historical essays on Arkansas, as well as special articles on blacks and women, and some representative political cartoons. An abbreviated one-volume sesquicentennial edition of the *Historical Report* was issued in 1986.

Since the *Historical Report* is published decennially, the best current guides to who's who in Arkansas government are the following biennial publications:

"Directory of Elected Officials," a wall poster published by the secretary of state listing names of all federal, state, district, and county officials.

*Arkansas State Directory* (North Little Rock: Heritage Publishing) lists major departments, their functions, personnel, and phone numbers.

*Directory of the——Legislature* (Little Rock: Southwestern Bell Telephone Co.) lists legislative incumbents, brief biographies, districts, and committee assignments; each directory covers one legislature.

*Guide to Arkansas Elected Officials* (Little Rock: League of Women Voters of

Arkansas) lists names, addresses, and phone numbers of federal and state executive, judicial, and legislative officials.

Another valuable comprehensive reference is *Government in Arkansas, 1983* (Little Rock: League of Women Voters of Arkansas), a carefully researched seventy-five-page overview of government institutions and their functions at state, county, and municipal levels, and a review of major constitutional provisions and of important state laws regarding elections and political parties. This handbook, now in its fourth edition, is periodically updated. Much more comprehensive, Henry M. Alexander's *Government in Arkansas* (Little Rock: Pioneer Press, 1963) was once the bible of Arkansas government but is now seriously dated.

The *Atlas of Arkansas* (Little Rock: Department of Planning, 1973) describes (with numerous maps and charts as well as narration) important physical, social, and economic characteristics of the state. Contents include land, water, and forest regions; mineral and agricultural resources; population and employment patterns; health, education, transportation, and financial data. Less comprehensive but more current is Hubert B. Stroud and Gerald T. Hanson, *Arkansas Geography* (Little Rock: Rose Publishing, 1981).

## Bibliographies and Listings

Researchers on Arkansas government and politics might well begin with the hundreds of books, articles, dissertations, and other materials referenced in this book's chapter notes. Other bibliographies, and the ways in which they supplement the sources cited in this volume, include:

Joan Ahrens and Joan Roberts, "Arkansas Reference Sources," *Arkansas Libraries* 34 (June 1977): 2–12. Organized by subject, including bibliographies and indexes, literature and folklore, government and law, U.S. government documents, business and economics, social conditions, labor, history and biography, education, agriculture and environment, maps and atlases.

Ruth Brunson, "Legal Bibliography, Arkansas Materials," September 17, 1978. A superb eleven-page guide for the nonlawyer doing research in state laws and court decisions, prepared for the Arkansas Library Association by the librarian of the UALR Law School.

Tom W. Dillard and Michael B. Dougan, compilers, *Arkansas History: A Selected Research Bibliography* (Little Rock: Department of Natural and Cultural

Heritage, 1984). Contains a fifteen-page listing of articles dealing with Arkansas politics and government from a historical perspective. Articles appearing in the *Arkansas Historical Quarterly* or *Arkansas Political Science Journal* are not included.

Each essay in *The Governors of Arkansas*, edited by Timothy P. Donovan and Willard B. Gatewood (Fayetteville: University of Arkansas Press, 1981), includes an extensive bibliographic essay on that gubernatorial era.

Norman L. Hodges, Jr., *Thirty Years on Arkansas Government 1945–1975: A Bibliographic Essay on the Political Science Literature on Arkansas State Government and Politics* (North Little Rock: Heritage Press, 1976). An exhaustive and excellent fifty-six-page survey of both original and secondary sources, including references to Arkansas in general political science literature. Hodges evaluates as well as lists, and is limited only by the paucity of worthwhile materials in the time covered.

Ruth Lindsey, *Arkansas Legal Documents*, March 1978. A six-page summary of state documents pertaining to the laws of Arkansas, prepared by the supreme court librarian for the Arkansas Library Association.

## STATE DOCUMENTS, BY SOURCE

### Legislature

The Arkansas General Assembly is woefully underdocumented. No verbatim transcript of legislative proceedings is maintained, committee meetings are not transcribed, nor are committee reports published. One copy of each issue of the *Legislative Journal* (dating from 1836) is kept in the Secretary of State's Office in the capitol, where those interested may peruse its brief synopsis of daily events. On highly controversial issues, the state's newspapers of the day may print roll-call votes. Otherwise, one must consult the original *Journal*.

The most essential guide to the legislature is the semiofficial *Arkansas Legislative Digest* (Little Rock: Legislative Reports), published daily when the legislature is in session. A loose-leaf publication, thoroughly indexed by bill number, subject, and author, it summarizes daily actions, lists new introductions with a descriptive digest, and prints verbatim those bills finally enacted. It also includes rosters, seniority rankings, biographical data, committee assignments, and seating arrangements.

The only noteworthy publications of the legislature itself are the research reports prepared for individual state legislators by the Legislative Council staff. *A Listing of Research Reports, Informational Memos, and Staff Reports* (Little Rock: Arkansas Bureau of Legislative Research) has been periodically updated since 1949. Although many of these topics are of dubious interest to the general researcher (for example, beaver control, mandatory motorcycle helmets, mosquito abatement), the topics also include general governmental issues (for example, campaign finance laws, grand juries, removal of judges, constitutional revision methods).

While not an official legislative publication, *Call the Roll*, by Representative Jerry E. Hinshaw (Little Rock: Department of Arkansas Heritage and Rose Publishing, 1986), is an excellent history of the first 150 years of the Arkansas legislature. It includes a good bibliography and some valuable appendixes: number of bills filed and enacted since 1950; proposed amendments to the constitution and their disposition; an alphabetical roster of all who served in the General Assembly from 1836 to 1985.

### Executive

The secretary of state is the official custodian of the state's legal records and also publishes many of the most important state documents. In addition to the decennial *Historical Report* and the biennial "Directory of State Officials," these publications include the following:

*Acts of Arkansas*, printed and sold after each regular session of the legislature. This book contains all laws enacted therein and is indexed. Note: *Arkansas Statutes Annotated* (Indianapolis: Bobbs-Merrill, 1947–) is the only reliable guide as to whether a law is still in effect.

*Arkansas Election Laws*, updated after each regular legislative session.

*Arkansas Register*, published monthly since August 1977. This welcome publication contains all new rules, regulations, and orders issued by most of the state's departments, agencies, and commissions; all opinions of the attorney general in their entirety; gubernatorial appointments, proclamations, and executive orders; and a calendar of upcoming official events.

*Arkansas Reports*, published at irregular intervals, contains the decisions of the Arkansas Supreme Court. Note: *Southwestern Reporter, Arkansas Cases* (St. Paul, Minn.: West Publishing) prints the same opinions, sometimes followed by concurring and/or dissenting opinions. The cases are preceded by headnotes, and unlike *Arkansas Reports*, the *Southwestern Reporter* is indexed.

*Constitution of the State of Arkansas with All Amendments*, updated periodically, and free upon request.

All of the major state departments (Corrections, Education, Highways, and so on) make annual or biennial reports to the governor, which can be obtained by contacting the department of interest. These departments and their subdivisions also issue special reports and studies from time to time.

## Judiciary

The most notable publications of the judicial branch are:

Judicial Department, *Annual Report*. Published since 1964, it describes jurisdictions of minor courts and duties of court officials and includes statistics, maps, and graphs relevant to court administration.

Supreme Court of Arkansas, *Manual of Rules and Committees*, looseleaf publication, updated annually.

SECONDARY SOURCE MATERIALS

## Newspapers, Journals, Newsletters

The state's oldest newspaper, the *Arkansas Gazette*, has been publishing since 1819, and microfilm copies exist in major libraries of the first issue to date. Most fortunately for researchers, the *Gazette* is being retroactively indexed (the years 1819 to 1887 have been completed to date), all issues have been indexed since 1964, and the quality of the *Arkansas Gazette Index* (Russellville: Arkansas Tech University Library) has steadily improved. Microfilm copies of the state's other major newspaper, the *Arkansas Democrat*, are available from October 1878 to June 1892, and from January 1898 to date but are not indexed. Since these two newspapers have frequently espoused different political philosophies, it is always wise to check both papers' coverage of any political event.

College and public libraries often have back issues of their local and regional newspapers, many of which are of excellent quality. For example, the faithful attention that Brenda Blagg of the *Springdale News* has given to local government over the years has provided scores of articles and columns analyzing the intricacies of substate operations. Useful in this respect is Robert A. Meriwether, compiler, *A Chronicle of Arkansas Newspapers*

*Published since 1922 and of the Arkansas Press Association, 1930–1972* (Little Rock: Arkansas Press Association, 1974). Excellent political pieces frequently appear in the monthly *Arkansas Times*. Furthermore, Arkansas has been blessed with some world-class cartoonists whose periodic collections are filled with political insight. See, for example, George Fisher's *Old Guard Rest Home* (1984), *All Around the Farkleberry Bush* (1967), and *Fisher's Annual Report* (1980), all available from Rose Publishing Company in Little Rock, and Jon Kennedy's *Look Back and Laugh* (Little Rock: Pioneer Press, 1978).

In addition to the articles appearing in each annual edition of the *Arkansas Political Science Journal*, the *Arkansas Historical Quarterly* frequently contains articles on past political events. Published quarterly since 1942 by the Arkansas Historical Association, its index is an excellent reference.

Several of the state's major interest groups publish monthly or periodic newsletters, which often have interesting political information, for example, *The AFL-CIO Newsletter*, the *Arkansas Educator*, and *City and Town*, the monthly publication of the Arkansas Municipal League. The Municipal League also publishes a *Handbook for Arkansas Municipal Officials*. The 1985 edition is more than 1,000 pages long and contains all statutes affecting municipal government, many court decisions interpreting those statutes, and additional information on municipal law, elections, and practices. The meeting notices sent out by the Arkansas Political Animals Club (PAC) always contain political morsels.

### Research Bureaus and Foundations

The Research and Public Service Unit (known until 1984 as the Industrial Research Extension Center, or IREC) at UALR conducts a broad range of research and advisory programs for both the public and private sectors. It also publishes regular reports on Arkansas's population and economy, some of which are described in the Statistical Information section below, as well as special studies for local governments and industrial clients. An annual checklist, *Reports and Publications* (Little Rock: Research and Public Service Unit, UALR) is a good guide to some valuable data.

The Bureau of Business and Economic Research (BBER) at the University of Arkansas at Fayetteville (UAF) has two major objectives: to develop and report measures of state and regional business economic activity, and to facilitate faculty and student research and publication in business and economics. Its publication, the *Arkansas Business and Economic Review*, has been published quarterly since 1968, is indexed biennially, and often contains useful socioeconomic data.

The Winthrop Rockefeller Foundation has periodically published studies of important public issues in Arkansas, for example, *School Property Taxation in Arkansas* (1983), *Responsible Choices in Taxation*, (1984), and *Citizens Handbook on Hazardous Substances* (1986) (Little Rock: Winthrop Rockefeller Foundation).

### *Historical Societies and Special Collections*

The Arkansas sesquicentennial in 1986 appropriately produced both an outcry about the inadequacy of good materials and texts on Arkansas history and a surge in the preparation of such. While these are working their way into print, good references are Tom Dillard and Valerie Thwing, *Researching Arkansas History, A Beginner's Guide* (Little Rock: Rose Publishing, 1979), and the Dillard and Dougan bibliography described above under General Reference Works. Even before the sesquicentennial, establishment of the Center for Arkansas and Regional Studies at the University of Arkansas at Fayetteville and the Center of Arkansas Studies at the University of Arkansas at Little Rock had begun stimulating scholarly attention to Arkansas's past with special studies, exhibits, symposia, lecture series, and occasional publications.[1]

Arkansas history has not been entirely neglected. In addition to the Arkansas Historical Association's *Arkansas Historical Quarterly*, many counties have well-established historical societies, some of which issue a regular publication.

The Arkansas History Commission has a fairly large collection for public use, including some of the papers of former governors. Special Collections at the U A F Library include the papers of Governors Orval Faubus and David Pryor; Senators Thaddeus and Hattie Caraway, J. William Fulbright, and Joseph T. Robinson; and Congressmen Oren Harris and Brooks Hays. U A F Special Collections also maintains the Arkansas Archives of Public Communication, including printed campaign materials from the 1880s to present and hundreds of audio and videotape cassettes of individual interviews, documentaries, and campaign commercials. The U A L R Archives include the papers of Governors Carl Bailey, Dale Bumpers, and Winthrop Rockefeller, the historical collection of J. N. Heiskell (who was editor of the *Arkansas Gazette* for more than seventy years), and an extensive political broadside collection containing speeches, posters, campaign documents, and paraphernalia from 1890 to present. Congressman Wilbur D. Mills's papers are at Hendrix College in Conway, Senator John L. McClellan's papers are at Ouachita Baptist University in Arkadelphia, and the University of Central Arkansas in Conway recently established its own Archives and Special Collections.

### STATISTICAL INFORMATION

A new and very welcome publication is the *Arkansas Statistical Abstract* (Little Rock: State Data Center, Research and Public Service Unit, U A L R, 1986), which is intended to be a biennial publication. Patterned after the *Statistical Abstract of the United States*, it contains nearly 500 pages of data on population and vital statistics; government expenditures and employment; income and wealth; elections; labor force, employment, and earnings; and other statistics essential for the serious study of Arkansas politics.

### *Economic and Fiscal*

In addition to the *Statistical Abstract*, the Research and Public Service Unit at U A L R publishes the following useful materials:

A *Summary of Taxes in Arkansas*, prepared after each biennial legislative session, summarizes changes in state-levied taxes as well as changes in major local government levies.

*Arkansas Personal Income Handbook* annually presents the U.S. Bureau of Economic Analysis estimates of total and per capita personal income by county and the sources of personal income by type and major industry.

*Arkansas Gross State Product* annually reviews the value of all goods and services produced in Arkansas by industrial, government, and service sectors.

The Department of Finance and Administration is another excellent source of fiscal and economic data, publishing among others: *Biennial Budget* (including sections on state revenue and state employees, appropriations enacted by the previous General Assembly and executive vetoes, and summaries of executive recommendations and legislative authorizations by agency); *Monthly Statement of Gross Tax Collections* (including general revenue receipts and a comparison with what had been forecast and with comparable receipts the preceding year).

*Demographic*

The State Data Center at U A L R is the official custodian of all U.S. Bureau of the Census data for Arkansas, which must be made available to the public. Much of the information necessary to political scientists is now compiled in the *Arkansas Statistical Abstract*. Approximately every five years, the Division of Demographic Research at U A L R issues *Arkansas Population Projections by County*, containing population projections at the county level by sex, race, and five-year age groups.

In addition, some relatively recent publications contain extensive data on specific subgroups: Arkansas Advocates for Children and Families, *Arkansas Children Have Problems* (North Little Rock: Horton Bros. Printing, 1979); Governor's Commission on the Status of Women, *The Status of Women in Arkansas* (Little Rock: Governor's Commission on the Status of Women, 1973); and Juanita Sandford, *Poverty in the Land of Opportunity* (Little Rock: Rose Publishing, 1978).

*Voting Return Information*

Voting returns are officially maintained by the secretary of state and can be inspected in that office in the capitol or in libraries where microfilm copies exist. Election results for major offices go back to 1836; detailed voting returns for statewide offices go back to 1924 and for state legislative positions to the early 1940s. Totals are tabulated by both county and precinct. The county totals are on printed sheets (which can be photocopied and mailed to researchers upon request), but precinct returns are in large books, which must be handcopied. Since 1976 the secretary of state has published primary and general election returns, by county, for all statewide races and ballot issues, plus outcomes in all district and state legislative races, in the biennial *Arkansas Elections* (Little Rock: Secretary of State). Voting returns for county and city offices are kept by the county and city clerks.

If the years are relevant to the research, also see:

*Insights.* Published by the Institute of Politics in Arkansas from 1972 to 1976; representative titles include "Voter Participation in Arkansas" (March 1973) and "The General Election: On the Decline?" (January 1974).

*Arkansas Votes 1972* and *Arkansas Votes 1974*. Also by the institute; include election data on every race above the county level for these years.

Jim Ranchino, *Faubus to Bumpers, Arkansas Votes, 1960–1970* (Arkadelphia: Action Research, 1972). Major elections plus analysis.

### Campaign Contribution Information and Public Opinion Surveys

Recent state and federal laws on campaign contributions and conflicts of interest have provided new sources of interesting information: campaign contribution reports and code of ethics filings. Since 1976, all candidates for statewide and district office have filed reports with the secretary of state on any contribution of more than $250. (Federal candidates, since 1972, have had to report contributions of more than $100.) Candidates for local office file their reports with the county clerk. These reports contain name and occupation of donor and the amount given. Since 1972, all public officials and candidates for public office have had to disclose any possible conflicts of interest (businesses in which they have financial interest, firms from which $1,500 or more was received). These reports are filed with the secretary of state, county clerk, or city clerk according to the office held or sought.

Most public opinion surveys in Arkansas are conducted by candidates who, understandably, are reluctant to share the results of these very expensive investments. In late 1985, however, the Bailey Poll (Tulsa, Okla.: Kenneth D. Bailey Research Corp.) began an Arkansas operation, with its major findings on issues and candidates periodically published in the *Arkansas Gazette*.

The Arkansas Household Research Panel of the Business College at U A F conducts a quarterly mail survey of a randomly selected sample of statewide households and has made this information available to scholars as well as to business clients. U A L R's Survey Marketing and Research Unit has periodically conducted and published some interesting surveys, including *Arkansas Attitudes on Higher Education* (1979) and *Attitudes on Arkansas, Arkansans' Attitudes toward Taxes*, and *Arkansas Public Awareness on Water Resources* (1982).

### Dissertations, Theses, and Student Research

While doctoral dissertations are centrally listed and indexed, and therefore readily accessible, master's theses are not. In 1986 the University of Central Arkansas Archives and Special Collections began quarterly publication of *The Arkansas Researcher*, which includes such useful sections as "Recent

Theses and Dissertations," "Research in Progress," and "Recent Publications of Note" (Conway: University of Central Arkansas Archives and Special Collections).

In addition, I have preserved and indexed the best undergraduate student research papers written for me in my Arkansas Politics course. On many subjects, especially interest groups and local politics, these students have occasionally had access, through relatives and family friends, to individuals who might otherwise be less obvious, and certainly less candid (Fayetteville: Political Science Department, University of Arkansas at Fayetteville).

Finally, as the references cited throughout this book should make obvious, there is much to be learned from what the political scientist Richard Fenno once described as "soaking and poking"; attending candidate rallies and party conventions; spending time in the capitol hallways when the legislature is in session; participating in campaigns; serving on study commissions; listening to coffee-shop conversation. While the lack of formal, systematic study of Arkansas's political system presents formidable research obstacles, the informality of Arkansas politics presents endless opportunities for observation and understanding.

# Notes

PREFACE

1 Governor Roane quoted in Clara B. Kennan, "The Birth of Public Schools," in Leland Duvall, ed., *Arkansas: Colony and State* (Little Rock: Rose Publishing, 1973), p. 108; Governor Davis quoted in David M. Tucker, *Arkansas: A People and Their Reputation* (Memphis, Tenn.: Memphis State University Press, 1985), p. 63.
2 G. W. Featherstonaugh, *Excursion through the Slave States* (New York: Harper and Brothers, 1844), p. 95.
3 Governor Faubus speaking on "Face the Nation," August 31, 1958.

CHAPTER I

1 Gene Lyons, " 'Rosey': He Was the Best of Us," *Newsweek*, April 9, 1984, p. 41.
2 The Central High episode is one of the most thoroughly discussed events in recent Arkansas history. A recent extensive account is Tony Freyer, *The Little Rock Crisis: A Constitutional Interpretation* (Westport, Conn.: Greenwood Press, 1984). David Wallace, "Orval Eugene Faubus," in Timothy P. Donovan and Willard B. Gatewood, Jr., eds., *The Governors of Arkansas* (Fayetteville: University of Arkansas Press, 1981), provides an excellent bibliography, pp. 283–86. For Faubus's version, see Orval E. Faubus, *Down from the Hills* (Little Rock: Pioneer Press, 1980), chaps. 11–24.
3 Little Rock public schools were closed for the 1958 school year, and not a single new industry located in Little Rock from then until 1961 (*Arkansas Democrat,*

January 10, 1982). Several analysts of recent southern politics attribute the militant segregationism of other southern governors to Faubus's example. See Jack Bass and Walter DeVries, *The Transformation of Southern Politics* (New York: New American Library, 1977), p. 90; Monroe Lee Billington, *The Political South in the Twentieth Century* (New York: Scribner, 1975), p. 122; Earl Black, *Southern Governors and Civil Rights* (Cambridge, Mass.: Harvard University Press, 1976), pp. 99, 299.

4 Bishop Turner quoted in *The Freeman* (Indianapolis), January 5, 1989; Mifflin W. Gibbs, *Shadow and Light, An Autobiography* (New York: Arno Press, 1968), pp. 126, 131, 136–39. For Little Rock's moderate racial climate, see also Freyer, *The Little Rock Crisis*, pp. 20–22.

5 NAACP director quoted in Robert A. Leflar, *The First 100 Years, Centennial History of the University of Arkansas* (Fayetteville: University of Arkansas Foundation, 1972), p. 279. Leflar provides details of the nonviolent integration of black students at the university, pp. 275–88. That some Arkansas blacks voted prior to the 1960s is noted by Boyce A. Drummond, "Arkansas Politics: A Study of a One-Party System" (Ph.D. diss., University of Chicago, 1957), p. 76, and V. O. Key, Jr., *Southern Politics* (New York: Random House, 1949), p. 639.

6 Sheriff Tommy Robinson quoted in *Arkansas Gazette*, October 31, 1981, and April 1, 1982. Paul Greenberg, "Notes on the Fringe," *Arkansas Times*, August 1984, pp. 40, 42; Senator Knox Nelson quoted in *Arkansas Gazette*, January 9, 1985.

7 It is assumed that Clinton received over 95 percent of the black vote in 1982; clearly, these 90,000 or so voters were a key part of his 78,000 vote margin. See John Brummett, "Clinton's Appeal to Blacks Rests on Record, Skill," *Arkansas Gazette*, December 6, 1982.

8 Representative Van Dalsem quoted in C. Fred Williams, S. Charles Bolton, Carl H. Moneyhon, and Leroy T. Williams, eds., *A Documentary History of Arkansas* (Fayetteville: University of Arkansas Press), p. 252. Especially since Van Dalsem's senator, Guy ("Mutt") Jones, led the successful opposition to ERA ratification, there is reason to doubt his genuine conversion to feminism.

9 Governor Pope quoted in Lonnie J. White, *Politics on the Southwestern Frontier: Arkansas Territory, 1819–1836* (Memphis, Tenn.: Memphis State University Press, 1964), p. 158. Governor McMath's caravan described in Jim Lester, *A Man for Arkansas* (Little Rock: Rose Publishing, 1976), pp. 142–43.

10 Donovan and Gatewood, *Governors of Arkansas*, pp. 20–21, 94–95. Governor Brough quoted in Williams et al., *Documentary History*, pp. 191–92.

11 For the politics surrounding the antievolution referendum, see Calvin R. Ledbet-

ter, Jr., "The Antievolution Law: Church and State in Arkansas," *Arkansas Historical Quarterly* 38 (1979): 299–327. Hereafter cited as *AHQ*.

12 Washburn quoted in Boyd W. Johnson, *The Arkansas Frontier* (n.p.: Perdue Printing, 1957), p. 9; Mencken quoted in *Arkansas Democrat*, August 3, 1921.

13 *Attitudes on Arkansas* (Little Rock: University of Arkansas at Little Rock, Center for Urban and Governmental Affairs, 1982), p. 2; "Research to Determine Strategy for Business Marketing for the State of Arkansas," prepared for the State of Arkansas by Yankelovich, Skelly and White, Inc., 1984.

14 The most thorough account of the Family's operations is Donald A. Stokes, "Public Affairs in Arkansas, 1836–50" (Ph.D. diss., University of Texas at Austin, 1966). For additional details and equally harsh assessments see A. L. Bramlett and David Y. Thomas, "1541–1865," in David Y. Thomas, ed., *Arkansas and Its People* (New York: American Historical Society, 1930), pp. 84–112; Michael B. Dougan, *Confederate Arkansas* (University: University of Alabama Press, 1982), pp. 12–22; Elsie M. Lewis, "Economic Conditions in Ante-Bellum Arkansas," *AHQ* 6 (1947): 256–74; and David Tucker, *Arkansas* (Memphis, Tenn.: Memphis State University Press, 1985), pp. 19–26.

15 Stokes, "Public Affairs," p. 448.

16 On the centrality of slavery to the statehood movement, see Calvin R. Ledbetter, Jr., "The Constitution of 1836: A New Perspective," *AHQ* 41 (1982): 215–52; White, *Politics on the Southwestern Frontier*, chap. 1; Waddy W. Moore, "Territorial Arkansas, 1819–1836," in *Historical Report of the Secretary of State, Arkansas*, vol. 3 (Little Rock: Arkansas Secretary of State, 1978), pp. 40–57. Tucker, *Arkansas*, pp. 20–21, suggests that the planters' desire for a state bank was the most powerful incentive. On the issueless nature of elections, see Harold Truman Smith, "Arkansas Politics, 1850–1861" (Master's thesis, Memphis State University, 1964), and Gene W. Boyett, "The Whigs of Arkansas, 1836–1856" (Ph.D. diss., Louisiana State University, 1972).

17 *Ballou's Pictorial*, April 7, 1955.

18 Michael B. Dougan, "Harris Flanagin," in Donovan and Gatewood, *Governors of Arkansas*, p. 35. In *Confederate Arkansas*, Dougan notes, "Though Arkansas was remote from the centers of war, the destruction, the ruin, and the hatreds were, if anything, greater than in Tennessee or Virginia" (p. 126).

19 See George H. Thompson, *Arkansas and Reconstruction* (Port Washington, N.Y.: Kennikat Press, 1976); essays on Reconstruction governors in Donovan and Gatewood, *Governors of Arkansas*, pp. 38–60; Thomas S. Staples and David Y. Thomas, "Part II—1865–1930," in Thomas, *Arkansas and Its People*, pp. 135–64.

20 The most extensive accounts of the Redeemers are Joe Segraves, "Arkansas Politics, 1874–1918" (Ph.D. diss., University of Kentucky, 1974); Garland E. Bayliss, "Public Affairs in Arkansas, 1874–1896" (Ph.D. diss., University of Texas at Austin, 1972); and Waddy W. Moore, ed., *Arkansas in the Gilded Age, 1874–1900* (Little Rock: Rose Publishing, 1976).

21 James C. Fouse and Ray Granade, "Arkansas, 1874–1900," in *Historical Report of the Secretary of State*, vol. 3, p. 140; C. Vann Woodward, *Origins of the New South, 1877–1913* (Baton Rouge: Louisiana State University Press, 1951), p. 51.

22 Harry S. Ashmore, *Arkansas: A History* (New York: Norton, 1978), pp. 124–36.

23 Quoted in Williams et al., *Documentary History*, pp. 131–32.

24 For articles on the various agrarian organizations, see Moore, *Arkansas in the Gilded Age*, pp. 3–74.

25 Essays on "Development of an Educational System," in Duvall, *Arkansas: Colony and State*, pp. 105–46.

26 Staples and Thomas, "Part II," p. 247; Jerome C. Rose, "Cedar Grove Historic Cemetery: A Study in Black American Bio-History" (Lecture given in Center for Arkansas and Regional Studies Series, Fayetteville, December 6, 1984); William Orestus Pemrose, "Political Ideas in Arkansas, 1880–1907" (Master's thesis, University of Arkansas, 1945), pp. 72–74.

27 Raymond Arsenault, *The Wild Ass of the Ozarks* (Philadelphia: Temple University Press, 1984), p. 245. Arsenault's is the most extensive account of Arkansas's most colorful and controversial governor. For other details and assessments, see John Gould Fletcher, *Arkansas* (Chapel Hill: University of North Carolina Press, 1947), pp. 287–314; Calvin R. Ledbetter, Jr., "Jeff Davis and the Politics of Combat," *AHQ* 33 (1974): 16–37; Richard L. Niswonger, "A Study in Southern Demogoguery: Jeff Davis of Arkansas," *AHQ* 39 (1980): 114–24; and Tucker, *Arkansas*, pp. 55–66.

28 Duvall, *Arkansas: Colony and State*, p. 38; Richard L. Niswonger, "Arkansas Democratic Politics" (Ph.D. diss., University of Texas at Austin, 1974) pp. 16–17, 374; Donald Holley, "Arkansas in the Great Depression," *Historical Report of the Secretary of State*, vol. 3, p. 168.

29 On roads, see Foy Lisenby, "Arkansas, 1900–1930," in *Historical Report of the Secretary of State*, vol. 3, pp. 150–51, and John L. Ferguson and J. H. Atkinson, *Historic Arkansas* (Little Rock: Arkansas History Commission, 1966), pp. 342–43.

30 Holley, "Arkansas in the Great Depression," pp. 157–74; Stephen F. Strausberg, "The Effectiveness of the New Deal in Arkansas," in Donald W. Whisenhunt, ed., *The Depression in the Southwest* (New York: Kennikat Press, 1980), pp.

102–16. What became the T V A might have been located in Arkansas but for the opposition of Sen. Joseph T. Robinson, according to Ashmore, *Arkansas*, pp. 145, 176.

31 Key, *Southern Politics*, p. 185.

32 Lester, *A Man for Arkansas*.

33 For an interesting account of socialist party activities in Arkansas and Sam Faubus's role therein, see G. Gregory Kiser, "The Socialist Party in Arkansas, 1900–1912," *AHQ* 40 (1981): 119–53. Orval Faubus, quoted in *Northwest Arkansas Times*, October 13, 1983. For an Orval Faubus bibliography, see note 2.

34 Thomas R. Dye, *Politics in States and Communities*, 5th ed. (Englewood Cliffs, N.J.: Prentice-Hall, 1985), pp. 45–46. Until the U.S. Supreme Court ordered their reapportionment on the basis of "one man, one vote" in 1962, most state legislatures had underweighted their urban, service-demanding areas and overweighted their rural areas, where political passivity was more acceptable. For an extensive discussion and bibliography, see Timothy O'Rourke, *The Impact of Reapportionment* (New Brunswick, N.J.: Transaction, 1980). Arkansas's malapportionment is discussed in chapter 9 herein.

35 The best description of Arkansas's agrarian, "colonial" economy is Duvall, *Arkansas: Colony and State*, pp. 1–104. Also see essays in Thomas, *Arkansas and Its People*, pp. 381–419. The debate between those political scientists who think economic development factors determine politics and those who argue otherwise is discussed extensively in chapter 13 herein.

CHAPTER 2

1 Josiah Shinn, *Pioneers and Makers of Arkansas* (Baltimore: Genealogical Publishing, 1967), pp. 29, 58; Rev. H. Cowles Atwater, 1857, reprinted in Margaret Ross, "Chronicles of Arkansas," no. 195, n. 299, Special Collections, Mullins Library, University of Arkansas, Fayetteville. Dr. Charles Daubery, 1837, in Ross, "Chronicles," n. 195; G. W. Featherstonaugh, *Excursion through the Slave States* (New York: Harper and Brothers, 1844), p. 92; Frederick Gerstaecker, 1838, quoted in Boyd W. Johnson, *The Arkansas Frontier* (n.p.: Perdue Printing, 1957), p. 130; C. L. Edson, "Arkansas: A Native Proletariat," *Nation*, May 2, 1933, p. 515.

2 Walter Moffatt, "Out West in Arkansas," *AHQ* 17 (1958): 33–44.

3 Robert Walz, "Migration into Arkansas, 1834–1880" (Ph.D. diss., University of Texas at Austin, 1958), p. 7.

4 A. L. Bramlett and David Y. Thomas, "Part I, 1541–1865," in David Y.

Thomas, ed., *Arkansas and Its People* (New York: American Historical Society, 1930), p. 75.

5 Walz, "Migration," pp. 55–58, 127–49.

6 Ibid., p. 246. See also Mala Daggett, ed., *Victorian Arkansans* (Little Rock: Arkansas Commemorative Commission, 1981), p. 7, who says the English were most numerous; Jonathan James Wolfe, "Background of German Immigration," *AHQ* 25 (1966): 378–84; and Wilbur Zelinsky, *The Cultural Geography of the United States* (Englewood Cliffs, N.J.: Prentice-Hall, 1973), pp. 122–23. However, four of Arkansas's nineteenth-century governors were descendants of a colony established by Germans in Virginia in 1714 according to Harry W. Readnour, "William M. Fishback," in Timothy P. Donovan and Willard B. Gatewood, eds., *The Governors of Arkansas* (Fayetteville: University of Arkansas Press, 1981), p. 91.

7 Shannon Klug Craig, "Arkansas and Foreign Immigration, 1890–1915" (Master's thesis, University of Arkansas, 1979). For Arkansas's hostility toward immigrants see Craig and especially Willard B. Gatewood, "Strangers and the Southern Eden: The South and Immigration, 1900–1920," in *Ethnic Minorities in Gulf Coast Society*, Proceedings of the Gulf Coast History and Humanities Conference, Pensacola, Fla., 1979. Religious affiliations from John L. Ferguson and J. H. Atkinson, *Historic Arkansas* (Little Rock: Arkansas History Commission, 1966), p. 205.

8 W. J. Cash, *The Mind of the South* (New York: Random House, Vintage Books, 1941), pp. 98, 140. For the relationship between social homogeneity and slow political development, see ibid., pp. 96–102, and especially John L. Sullivan, "Political Correlates of Social, Economic, and Religious Diversity in the American States," *Journal of Politics* 35 (1973): 70–84. Sullivan ranks Arkansas forty-ninth of the fifty states in terms of population diversity.

9 Orville W. Taylor, *Negro Slavery in Arkansas* (Durham, N.C.: Duke University Press, 1958); Walz, "Migration," p. 214; Ralph A. Wooster, "Notes on the Membership of the Thirteenth General Assembly of Arkansas," *AHQ* 17 (1958): 45–55; Stephen Houser, "The Arkansas Legislature," (University of Arkansas, 1983, Typescript); Gene W. Boyett, "The Whigs of Arkansas" (Ph.D. diss., Louisiana State University, 1972), pp. 113–14.

10 George H. Thompson, *Arkansas and Reconstruction* (Port Washington, N.Y.: Kennikat Press, 1976), pp. 25–28; Michael B. Dougan, *Confederate Arkansas* (University: University of Alabama Press, 1982), pp. 35–67.

11 For the "economic threshold" argument see Seymour Martin Lipset, *Political Man* (Garden City, N.Y.: Doubleday, Anchor Books, 1959), pp. 27–63.

Arkansas's post–Civil War financial status in Harry S. Ashmore, *Arkansas* (New York: Norton, 1978), p. 97.

12 Raymond Arsenault, *The Wild Ass of the Ozarks* (Philadelphia: Temple University Press, 1984), pp. 11–15, 97–109.

13 Ferguson and Atkinson, *Historic Arkansas*, pp. 41–42; *Arkansas Gazette*, February 5, 1820; Ferguson and Atkinson, *Historic Arkansas*, p. 43.

14 Brian G. Walton, "How Many Voted in Arkansas Elections before the Civil War?" *AHQ* 39 (1980): 66–75; Shinn, *Pioneers*, p. 103.

15 For colorful details on nineteenth-century Arkansas elections, see Lonnie J. White, *Politics on the Southwestern Frontier: Arkansas Territory, 1819–1836* (Memphis, Tenn.: Memphis State University Press, 1964); Boyett, "The Whigs of Arkansas." For deliberate escalation by the press of political rivalries, see Ashmore, *Arkansas*, pp. 45–47, and Fred W. Allsopp, "The Press of the State," in Thomas, *Arkansas and Its People*, pp. 563–64.

16 Daniel J. Elazar, *American Federalism: A View from the States*, 2d ed. (New York: Crowell, 1972), pp. 84–126.

17 Ibid., pp. 99–102.

18 Ibid., pp. 96–97.

19 Roy Reed, "Updating Mitch, A Hillbilly's Letter to His Great-Grandpa," *Arkansas Times*, July 1984, p. 79; Faubus, quoted in Joe Schratz, "A Little Advice from the Old Pro," *Arkansas Democrat Magazine*, January 27, 1985; Charles Morrow Wilson, *The Bodacious Ozarks* (New York: Hastings House, 1959), p. 6; family saying from Mrs. Bessie Blair of Snowball, Arkansas.

20 Shirley Abbott, *Womenfolks* (New Haven and New York: Ticknor and Fields, 1983), p. 59.

21 Ibid., p. 30.

22 For the rise of sharecropping and tenancy, see C. Vann Woodward, *Origins of the New South, 1877–1913* (Baton Rouge: Louisiana State University Press), pp. 175–204, and Joe Segraves, "Arkansas Politics, 1874–1918" (Ph.D. diss., University of Kentucky, 1973), pp. 147–97. For agrarian and populist organizations, see essays in Waddy W. Moore, ed., *Arkansas in the Gilded Age, 1874–1900* (Little Rock: Rose Publishing, 1976), pp. 3–74, and Ashmore, *Arkansas*, pp. 124–36.

23 Both Segraves, "Arkansas Politics," p. 197, and Arsenault, *Wild Ass of the Ozarks*, p. 35, suggest that an honest count might have produced a Norwood victory.

24 Both Segraves, "Arkansas Politics," and Richard L. Niswonger, "Arkansas Democratic Politics, 1896–1920" (Ph.D. diss., University of Texas at Austin,

1974), provide detailed discussions of the progressive strain in late-nineteenth-
and early twentieth-century Arkansas politics. For the lengthy struggle over
adoption of Amendment 7 and its highly confused implementation, see David Y.
Thomas, "Popular Government," in Thomas, *Arkansas and Its People*, pp. 317–
32.

25 Election outrages of 1888 in Segraves, "Arkansas Politics," pp. 183–88. Details
of the 1891 act are in John W. Graves, "Negro Disfranchisement in Arkansas,"
*AHQ* 26 (1967): 199–225. Joseph M. Kousser, "The Shaping of Southern
Politics: Suffrage Restrictions and the Establishment of the One-Party South,
1880–1910," (Ph.D. diss., Yale University, 1971), persuasively argues that
illiterate whites were the disfranchisement target as well. David M. Tucker, *Arkansas: A People and Their Reputation* (Memphis, Tenn.: Memphis State University Press, 1985), pp. 46–47, provides evidence of white resumption of power
through violence.

26 Harry S. Ashmore, *An Epitaph for Dixie* (New York: Norton, 1957), p. 52;
*Arkansas Gazette* editorial, July 22, 1892. For blacks' token position within the
state Republican party they helped establish, see James Harris Fain, "Political
Disfranchisement of the Negro in Arkansas" (Master's thesis, University of
Arkansas, 1961), and especially Tom Dillard, "To the Back of the Elephant:
Racial Conflict in the Arkansas Republican Party," *AHQ* 33 (1974): 3–15.

27 Dillard, "To the Back of the Elephant," p. 8.

28 John Gaventa, *Power and Powerlessness: Quiescence and Rebellion in an Appalachian Valley* (Urbana: University of Illinois Press, 1980).

CHAPTER 3

1 There is some doubt whether the Smith-Robinson presidential ticket actually
carried Arkansas in 1928. According to Joe N. Martin, then chairman of the
Craighead County Democratic Committee, "The word went out from Joe (Sen.
Joseph T. Robinson) that he didn't care *how* we got the votes but he was damned
if he was going to be embarrassed in his own state" (Interview with author,
Jonesboro, Ark., June 26, 1978).

2 For early nineteenth-century Arkansas voter turnout, see Brian G. Walton, "How
Many Voted in Arkansas Elections before the Civil War?" *AHQ* 39 (1980): 66–
75. For early decades of the twentieth century, see V. O. Key, Jr., *Southern
Politics* (New York: Random House, 1949), pp. 490–528, and Boyce A. Drum-
mond, "Arkansas Politics: A Study of a One-Party System" (Ph.D. diss.,
University of Chicago, 1957), pp. 60–73.

3 Key, *Southern Politics*, pp. 183, 187. There was a powerful rivalry from the

mid-1930s through the mid-1940s between Homer Adkins's "federal" faction and Carl Bailey's "state" faction, but it was based more on personal rivalries and patronage conflicts than on issues, according to Key (pp. 187–89).

4 Drummond, "Arkansas Politics," p. 231.

5 Milton Mackaye quoted in Drummond, "Arkansas Politics," p. 134; former governor quoted by Key, *Southern Politics*, p. 186; Tom Dearmore quoted by Drummond, "Arkansas Politics," p. 145.

6 W. J. Cash, *The Mind of the South* (New York: Random House, Vintage Books, 1941), p. 133.

7 Estimated campaign costs in Joseph Utley, Record Books, 1923–1943, Special Collections, University of Arkansas at Little Rock Library; Key, *Southern Politics*, pp. 465–66; Drummond, "Arkansas Politics," pp. 146–48.

8 Key, *Southern Politics*, p. 195; the federal judge Henry Woods also served as Sidney McMath's campaign manager (Interview with author, January 3, 1977). Also on local bosses, see Drummond, "Arkansas Politics," chap. 8, and Bob Lancaster's profiles of Conway County's Sheriff Marlin Hawkins in *Arkansas Gazette*, September 19, 1972, and September 20, 1972.

9 Author interviews with Robert A. Leflar, August 27, 1985; James B. Blair, June 10, 1984; Brooks Hays, July 10, 1978. For details of the 1933 contest, see Donald Holley, "Arkansas in the Great Depression," *Historical Report of the Secretary of State, Arkansas*, vol. 3 (Little Rock: Arkansas Secretary of State, 1978), pp. 171–72. When the Futrell machine switched from Sam Rorex to David Terry, one politician complained, "I've been stealing votes from Brooks all night and giving them to Sam, and now I've got to take them from Sam and give them to Dave." See Brooks Hays, *Politics Is My Parish* (Baton Rouge: Louisiana State University Press, 1981), pp. 112–14.

10 All of these practices have been experienced, observed, or confirmed by the author through interviews with practicing politicians. East Arkansas practices were described by Bill Penix, Jonesboro, Arkansas, June 23, 1978. See also Key, *Southern Politics*, pp. 458–60; Tony Freyer, *The Little Rock Crisis* (Westport, Conn.: Greenwood Press, 1984), p. 88; Jim Lester, *A Man for Arkansas* (Little Rock: Rose Publishing, 1976), p. 254.

11 See note 10. Also see Nancy Hamm, "Traditions of Newton County Politics" (University of Arkansas, 1972, Typescript); Lisa Skillman, "Analysis of Crittenden County" (University of Arkansas, 1979; Typescript); Richard E. Yates, "Arkansas: Independent and Unpredictable," in William C. Havard, ed., *The Changing Politics of the South* (Baton Rouge: Louisiana State University Press, 1972), pp. 243–45.

12 Drummond, "Arkansas Politics," p. 169; Key, *Southern Politics*, pp. 443, 184.

13 When I was first elected to the Democratic State Committee in 1972, I was as baffled by the absence of any election-winning mechanisms as other committee members were baffled by my concern.

14 Alexander Heard, *A Two-Party South* (Chapel Hill: University of North Carolina Press, 1952), pp. 96–97.

15 Jeannette Rockefeller, quoted in John Ward, *The Arkansas Rockefeller* (Baton Rouge: Louisiana State University Press, 1978), p. 16; Thomas G. Kielhorn, "Party Development and Partisan Change: An Analysis of Changing Patterns of Mass Support for the Parties in Arkansas" (Ph.D. diss., University of Illinois, 1973), p. 12. For other details on pre-Rockefeller Arkansas Republicanism, see Tom Dillard, "To the Back of the Elephant: Racial Conflict in the Arkansas Republican Party," *AHQ* 33 (1974): 3–15; Key, *Southern Politics*, pp. 296–97; Patrick F. O'Conner, "Political Party Organization in Pulaski County, Arkansas: The Democratic and Republican County Committees" (Master's thesis, University of Arkansas, 1967), pp. 175–79.

16 Key, *Southern Politics*, p. 307.

17 For a thorough discussion of the economics-versus-politics debate, see chapter 13 herein.

18 James MacGregor Burns, *Leadership* (New York: Harper and Row, 1978), p. 44.

19 Drummond, *Arkansas Politics*, p. 233; Raymond Arsenault, *The Wild Ass of the Ozarks* (Philadelphia: Temple University Press, 1984), p. 16.

20 In one week's time, Senators Long and Caraway traveled two thousand miles, visited thirty-one counties, made thirty-nine speeches, and personally addressed more than 200,000 people, many of whom as adults recall Senator Long's speech as the most consciousness-raising political experience of their lives. See Herman B. Deutsch, "Hattie and Huey," *Saturday Evening Post*, October 15, 1932, pp. 6–7, 88–90, 92, and Stuart Towns, "A Louisiana Medicine Show: The Kingfish Elects an Arkansas Senator," *AHQ* 25 (1966): 117–27. For the tactics of returning World War II veterans who challenged entrenched political machines in Arkansas, Tennessee, and Louisiana, see Lester, *A Man for Arkansas*, pp. 8–35.

21 Neal R. Peirce and Jerry Hagstrom, *The Book of America: Inside 50 States Today* (New York: Norton, 1983), p. 487; David Pryor quoted by Roy Reed, "Rockefeller Led State Out of Dark Days of Politics," *Arkansas Gazette*, July 13, 1983. The most extensive and comprehensive accounts of recent Arkansas political history are Jack Bass and Walter DeVries, *The Transformation of Southern Politics* (New York: New American Library, 1977), pp. 87–106; Dan Durning, "Arkansas: 1954 to Present," *Historical Report of the Secretary of State*, vol. 3 (Little Rock: Arkansas Secretary of State, 1978), pp. 186–202; Neil R. Peirce, *The Deep South States of America* (New York: Norton, 1972), pp. 123–61; John

Robert Starr, *Yellow Dogs and Dark Horses* (Little Rock: August House, 1987); and Yates, "Arkansas: Independent and Unpredictable," pp. 233–93.

22 See Donald Holley, "Arkansas in the Great Depression," and Stephen F. Strausberg, "The Effectiveness of the New Deal in Arkansas," in Donald F. Whisenhunt, ed., *The Depression in the Southwest* (New York: Kennikat Press, 1980), pp. 102–16.

23 State Senator Robert Harvey in an address to the Arkansas Political Science Association, Arkadelphia, February 25, 1983.

24 George Brown Tindall, *The Emergence of the New South, 1913–1945* (Baton Rouge: Louisiana State University Press, 1967), p. ix. For the impact of World War II on Arkansas, see Boyce Drummond, "Arkansas, 1910–1954," in *Historical Report of the Secretary of State, Arkansas*, vol. 3 (Little Rock: Arkansas Secretary of State, 1978), pp. 175–77; and C. Calvin Smith, *War and Wartime Changes* (Fayetteville: University of Arkansas Press, 1986).

25 Leland Duvall, *Arkansas: Colony and State* (Little Rock: Rose Publishing, 1973), pp. 10–27, 47–88. See also Harry S. Ashmore, *Arkansas: A History* (New York: Norton, 1978), pp. 162–73; and Paul Williams, "The Rise and Fall of the Great Plantations," *Arkansas Times*, July 1983, pp. 86–93.

26 Data on 1980 employment, residence, income, and poverty from U.S. Bureau of the Census, *Census of Population, 1980* (Washington, D.C.: Government Printing Office, 1982, 1983), unless otherwise indicated.

27 Governor Adkins quoted in Drummond, "Arkansas Politics," p. 83.

28 For details on the positions on racial issues of Rockefeller and Johnson, see Earl Black, *Southern Governors and Civil Rights* (Cambridge, Mass.: Harvard University Press, 1976), pp. 269–71.

29 Records of black and white poll tax purchases were maintained by the state auditor, but since the adoption in 1965 of permanent voting registration, black registration figures must be estimated. These estimates come from Donald R. Matthews and James W. Prothro, "Negro Voter Registration in the South," in Allan P. Sindler, ed., *Change in the Contemporary South* (Durham, N.C.: Duke University Press, 1963), pp. 119–49; William C. Havard, ed., *Changing Politics* (Baton Rouge: Louisiana State University Press, 1981), p. 20; Earl Black, *Southern Governors*, p. 105; and Research Department, Voter Education Project, Atlanta, Georgia, October 6, 1984.

30 For Daniel Elazar's characterizations, see chapter 2 herein.

31 According to the state auditor, twenty-four of Arkansas's seventy-five counties used voting machines by 1986. For 1974 county government reforms, see chapter 12 herein.

32 Arkansas's first radio station was WOK, Pine Bluff, 1921; its first television

station was K R T V, Little Rock, 1953. Radio jingle quoted in *Arkansas Gazette*, June 15, 1984.

33 Wright quoted in *Arkansas Democrat* and *Arkansas Gazette*, May 5, 1983; Clinton quotation from personal interview, June 30, 1986.

34 I receive many such election-eve calls from faculty colleagues and I am familiar with two races (for lieutenant governor in 1974 and for land commissioner in 1984), where insiders' preferences were decisive.

35 David Pryor quoted in *Arkansas Democrat*, November 11, 1984, and *Arkansas Gazette*, April 4, 1985. The notion of the new politics being superimposed upon the old is elaborated upon in Harold F. Bass and Andrew Westmoreland, "Parties and Campaigns in Contemporary Arkansas Politics," *Arkansas Political Science Journal* 5 (Winter 1984): 49–54.

36 For the concept of "pluralistic ignorance," coined by Floyd H. Allport in 1924, see Hubert J. O'Gorman, "Pluralistic Ignorance and White Estimates of White Support for Racial Segregation," *Public Opinion Quarterly* 39 (1975): 313–30.

## CHAPTER 4

1 For additional analysis of the 1984 presidential election in Arkansas, see Diane D. Blair, "Arkansas," in Robert P. Steed, Laurence W. Moreland, Tod A. Baker, eds., *The 1984 Presidential Election in the South* (New York: Praeger, 1986), pp. 182–207.

2 Thomas G. Kielhorn, "Party Development and Partisan Change: An Analysis of Changing Patterns of Mass Supports for the Parties in Arkansas" (Ph.D. diss., University of Illinois, 1973), pp. 16, 77. For how and why Governor McMath held Arkansas firm against the 1948 Dixiecrat revolt, see Jim Lester, *A Man for Arkansas* (Little Rock: Rose Publishing, 1976), pp. 92–127. In 1960, rumors that presidential nominee John F. Kennedy might name Senator Fulbright his secretary of state were somewhat influential in keeping Arkansas in the Democratic fold. Though Orval Faubus refused any joint billboards with Lyndon Johnson in 1964, he remained overtly loyal, as did Marion Crank to Hubert Humphrey in 1968.

3 The "Rim" distinction is used by Alexander P. Lamis, *The Two-Party South* (New York: Oxford University Press, 1984) and Louis M. Seagull, *Southern Republicanism* (New York: Wiley, 1975). "Peripheral" is used by Earl Black, *Southern Governors and Civil Rights* (Cambridge, Mass.: Harvard University Press, 1976). Barry M. Brown, "Presidential Voting Behavior in the Arkansas-Mississippi Delta," (University of Arkansas, 1978, Typescript).

4 "The most frequently advanced explanation for Rockefeller's decision to leave

the social circles of New York concerns his highly publicized and very expensive divorce from Bobo Sears Rockefeller, a divorce that reportedly cost Rockefeller six million dollars and much anguish. Rockefeller came to Arkansas to settle at the urging of a close wartime friend" (Kielhorn, "Party Development," p. 61). See also John Ward, *The Arkansas Rockefeller* (Baton Rouge: Louisiana State University Press, 1978), pp. 1–3. For industrial development figures, see "The Transformation of Arkansas," *Time*, December 2, 1966, pp. 24–28.

5 Rockefeller's "acceptance strategy" campaign is described by Kielhorn, "Party Development," pp. 76–84. Rockefeller estimated he invested more than $10 million in Republican party development activities, according to Jack Bass and Walter DeVries, *The Transformation of Southern Politics* (New York: New American Library, 1977), p. 89.

6 Rockefeller's black voter registration efforts and details of the 1966 campaign in Jim Ranchino, *Faubus to Bumpers: Arkansas Votes, 1960–70* (Arkadelphia, Ark.: Action Research, 1972), pp. 41–45, 50; Seagull, *Southern Republicanism*, pp. 130–31; Ward, *The Arkansas Rockefeller*, pp. 21–67; and Richard E. Yates, "Arkansas: Independent and Unpredictable," in William C. Havard, ed., *The Changing Politics of the South* (Baton Rouge: Louisiana State University Press, 1972), pp. 278–83.

7 For percentages of black support of Rockefeller, see Kielhorn, "Party Development," p. 103, and Bass and DeVries, *Transformation*, p. 100. According to Kielhorn, "Fully 50% of those voters supporting Rockefeller were not only identified as Democrats but, under further analysis, proved to be very loyal Democrats" (p. 272).

8 Kielhorn, "Party Development," pp. 76–84.

9 The other two governors denied their second two-year term were Thomas Terral (1925–27) and Francis Cherry (1953–55).

10 Richard E. Yates in Havard, ed., *The Changing Politics of the South*, pp. 233–93; Alexander Lamis, *The Two-Party South*, pp. 120–30.

11 C. Vann Woodward quoted in *Arkansas Times*, April 1985, p. 12; Ranchino, *Faubus to Bumpers*, p. 64.

12 For ticket-splitting, see *Arkansas Votes, 1972* (Conway, Ark.: Institute of Politics, Hendrix College, 1973), pp. 4, 6–7; Diane D. Blair and Robert L. Savage, "The 1980 Elections at the State Level, Arkansas," *Comparative State Politics Newsletter* 2 (1981): 12–13.

13 In 1980 the Republican Senate candidate got 81 percent and the successful Republican gubernatorial candidate got 108 percent of the presidential vote. In 1984 the Republican Senate and gubernatorial candidates polled 69 percent and 60 percent, respectively, of the presidential vote. For loosely correlated Republi-

can vote in the 1960s, see Seagull, *Southern Republicanism*, p. 116, and Lamis, *Two-Party South*, p. 235. For much more closely correlated Republican vote in the 1980s, see Blair, "Arkansas," pp. 197–200.

14 Donald R. Matthews and James W. Prothro, "The Concept of Party Image and the Importance for the Southern Electorate," in M. Kent Jennings and L. Harmon Ziegler, eds., *The Electoral Process* (Englewood Cliffs, N.J.: Prentice-Hall, 1966), p. 166. In 1972, Republicans ran for lieutenant governor, attorney general, and secretary of state. Since then, the only general election contests for constitutional executives have been for lieutenant governor in 1974, 1980, and 1984 and for attorney general in 1984 and 1986.

15 By 1984, Republicans held one-third or more of lower house seats in Florida, North Carolina, Tennessee, Texas, and Virginia.

16 V. O. Key, Jr., *Southern Politics* (New York: Random House, 1949), p. 187; Boyce A. Drummond, "Arkansas Politics: A Study of a One-Party System" (Ph.D. diss., University of Chicago, 1957), p. 25; Numan V. Bartley and Hugh D. Graham, *Southern Politics and the Second Reconstruction* (Baltimore: Johns Hopkins University Press, 1975), p. 50.

17 For regional voting tendencies in Democratic gubernatorial primaries in the 1950s and 1960s, see Bartley and Graham, *Second Reconstruction*, pp. 54–57, and Yates, "Arkansas," pp. 255, 259. Faubus's changing support base from the highlands to the lowlands is described and analyzed in Thomas F. Pettigrew and Ernest Q. Campbell, "Faubus and Segregation: An Analysis of Arkansas Voting," *Public Opinion Quarterly* 24 (1960): 436–47. Robert L. Savage and Richard J. Gallagher, "Politicocultural Regions in a Southern State: An Empirical Typology of Arkansas Counties," *Publius* 7 (1977): 91–105. For a test of the Savage and Gallagher hypothesis, see Fred M. Shelley and J. Clark Archer, "Political Habit, Political Culture, and the Electoral Mosaic of a Border Region," *Geographical Perspectives* 54 (1984): 7–20, who argue that Arkansas, in contrast with neighboring Kansas, Missouri, and Oklahoma, remains distinctively southern in its political behavior.

18 Robert L. Savage and Diane D. Blair, "Regionalism and Political Opinion in Arkansas: An Exploratory Survey," *Arkansas Political Science Journal* 5 (1984): 59–85.

19 Data from U.S. Bureau of the Census, *Census of Population, 1980* (Washington, D.C.: Government Printing Office, 1982, 1983), and Donald E. Voth, "Impact of Migration on Arkansas" (Lecture given in Arkansas and Regional Studies Lecture Series, Fayetteville, March 15, 1984).

20 Robert L. Savage and Diane D. Blair, analysis of results of 1982 Arkansas Household Research Panel, in authors' possession. According to my calculations

the simple correlation coefficients (Pearson's r) with percentage of natives by county are strong and positive with the Democratic vote (1976 presidential, .6636; 1980 presidential, .6665; 1984 Senate, .6636), strong and negative with the Republican vote (1960 presidential, −.7050; 1982 governor, −.5839; 1982 lieutenant governor, −.7445).

21 The influence of a large number of military retirees was suggested by the state representative Buddy Blair, quoted in John Hug, "The Rise of the Republican Party in Sebastian County," (University of Arkansas, 1981, Typescript).

22 Bill Simmons, "Voter Registration Appears to be Near 100 pct. in 2 Counties," *Arkansas Gazette*, February 8, 1986.

23 Hubert B. Stroud and Gerald T. Hanson, *Arkansas Geography* (Little Rock: Rose Publishing, 1976), pp. 27–32. For an interesting description of geographic, economic, and political distinctions between the eastern and southern lowlands in the nineteenth century, see George H. Thompson, *Arkansas and Reconstruction* (Port Washington, N.Y.: Kennikat Press, 1976), pp. 9–19.

24 Voter registration figures from Research Department, Voter Education Project, Atlanta, Ga., October 6, 1984. For the critical nature of the black vote in selected elections, see Monroe Lee Billington, *The Political South in the Twentieth Century* (New York: Scribner, 1975), p. 146; Ranchino, *Faubus to Bumpers*, pp. 45, 49–50; Ernest Dumas, "Black Vote Is the Key to Clinton's Victory," *Arkansas Gazette*, November 11, 1982; John Brummett, "Clinton's Appeal to Blacks Rests on Record, Skill," *Arkansas Gazette*, December 6, 1982; "Close Call in Arkansas Primary," *Congressional Quarterly*, May 31, 1986.

25 Billington, *Political South*, p. 77; Kielhorn, "Party Development," p. 103; Bass and DeVries, *Transformation*, p. 100. Bumpers strengthened his acceptance in the black community by refusing requests from white leaders of Lee County to shut down a federally financed medical clinic in Marianna.

26 For black disgruntlement with Democrats, see "Richardson Steps Up Attack on Clinton," *Arkansas Gazette*, May 11, 1983; "Richardson Says White May Have Done More," *Arkansas Gazette*, August 28, 1983; "Jackson's Wife Neglected," *Arkansas Gazette*, February 16, 1984. For Republican wooing efforts, see "Black Involvement Sought by GOP," *Arkansas Gazette*, January 26, 1981; "Republican Recruiter Confident," *Arkansas Gazette*, June 22, 1983; "GOP Can Draw Minority Vote," *Arkansas Gazette*, August 5, 1984. "Black GOP Leaders Vow to Weaken Blind Loyalty," *Arkansas Gazette*, December 2, 1984. Jim Johnson quoted in *Arkansas Gazette*, June 13, 1960. The correlation coefficient between the Scaife vote and the black percentage of the population was −.5165.

27 This information is from activist friends and personal experience. Also, see Bass

and DeVries, *Transformation*, pp. 101–103; "Report Shows Robinson Paid McIntosh," *Arkansas Democrat*, July 21, 1984; "Payments to Activists Reported," *Arkansas Gazette*, July 22, 1984. Bitter conflict arose between the Pryor and Clinton campaigns in 1984 regarding appropriate payments to "knockers and haulers."

28 See, for example, "NAACP Leader to Ask Censure in Endorsement," *Arkansas Gazette*, October 17, 1982, and "Power Struggle Usurping Control," *Arkansas Democrat*, March 7, 1984.

29 See T. Scott Varady, "The Changing Support Base of Senator Dale Bumpers" (University of Arkansas, 1984, Typescript).

30 Arthur English and John J. Carroll, "Political Activists in a Southern County: Some Implications for the Future" (Paper presented at the 1980 Symposium on Southern Politics, The Citadel, Charleston, S.C., March 1980), p. 5. For predictions of southern urban Republicanism, see Bernard Cosman, *Five States for Goldwater* (University: University of Alabama Press, 1966) and Donald S. Strong, *Urban Republicanism in the South* (University: Bureau of Public Administration, University of Alabama, 1960). Correlation coefficients between the percentages of county urban population and 1984 Republican vote were: Republican Presidential vote −.0650; Republican Senate vote −.3007; Republican gubernatorial −.3006. The precincts of Pleasant Valley, Seventh-Day Adventist Academy, and Second Presbyterian in Pulaski County are among many urban-affluent areas that voted Republican in the 1984 national election but voted Democratic for governor.

31 These Rural Swing counties bear some similarity to Pettigrew and Campbell's Border counties, "Faubus and Segregation," pp. 436–47. Their 1960 analysis was based on primary elections, however, and is less applicable in recent, more partisan decades. Reagan increased his vote 15 percent or more in sixteen of the twenty-six Rural Swing counties from 1980 to 1984.

32 Kielhorn, "Party Development," pp. 232–34, found that 70 percent of Wallace supporters who were interviewed were extremely "loyal" Democrats who usually voted a straight ticket and had never voted Republican for governor.

33 For the revised themes and style of the Clinton "restoration," see Diane D. Blair, "Two Transitions in Arkansas, 1978 and 1982," in Thad L. Beyle, ed., *Gubernatorial Transitions* (Durham, N.C.: Duke University Press, 1985), pp. 92–122; and Robert L. Savage and Diane D. Blair, "Constructing and Reconstructing the Image of Statecraft: The Rhetorical Challenges of Bill Clinton's Two Gubernatorial Transitions," in Keith R. Sanders, Lynda L. Kaid, and Dan Nimmo, eds., *Political Communication Yearbook 1984* (Carbondale: Southern Illinois University Press, 1985), pp. 242–61.

CHAPTER 5

1 See especially Philip E. Converse, "On the Possibility of Major Political Re-
  alignment in the South," in Angus Campbell, Philip E. Converse, Warren E.
  Miller, and Donald E. Stokes, eds., *Elections and the Political Order* (New
  York: Wiley, 1966), pp. 212–42; and Bruce A. Campbell, "Patterns of Change
  in the Partisan Loyalties of Native Southerners: 1952–1972," *Journal of Politics* 39 (1977): 730–61.

2 Paul A. Beck and Paul Lopatto, "The End of Southern Distinctiveness," in
  Laurence W. Moreland, Ted A. Baker, and Robert P. Steed, eds., *Contempo-
  rary Southern Political Attitudes and Behavior* (New York: Praeger, 1982), pp.
  160–82; Thomas G. Kielhorn, "Party Development and Partisan Change: An
  Analysis of Changing Patterns of Mass Supports for the Parties in Arkansas"
  (Ph.D. diss., University of Illinois, 1973), pp. 111–12.

3 Arkansas senatorial polls conducted throughout 1984 for Sen. David Pryor and
  graciously shared with the author; Bill Peterson, "To Southern White Youth,
  Reagan Heads the Class," *Washington Post*, May 23, 1986. According to a
  student survey by Michael Reynolds (University of Arkansas, 1984, Typescript), 80 percent of the sorority women but only 59 percent of the Independents supported Reagan.

4 For the "scorecards" given by major interest and ideological groups to the
  congressional delegation, see the biennial publication by Michael Barone and
  Grant Ujifusa, *Almanac of American Politics* (Washington, D.C.: National
  Journal). See also Ernest Dumas, "Democrats: Their Style Is Changing,"
  *Arkansas Gazette*, May 30, 1982.

5 Quotations by Jim Ray, a candidate for Washington County judge, in Steven
  Baggett, "The 1984 Elections: The Republican Challenge in Arkansas" University of Arkansas, 1984, Typescript), p. 10; Richard Earl Griffin, *Arkansas
  Gazette*, October 29, 1982. Arkansas's most prominent switcher to date is the
  former Democratic state supreme court justice Jim Johnson who, after a period
  as head of the American Independent party, ran unsuccessfully as a Republican
  for chief justice of the supreme court in 1984.

6 Key, *Southern Politics* (New York: Random House, 1949), p. 280.

7 On dual national and state party identifications, see Charles D. Hadley, "Dual
  Partisan Identification in the South," *Journal of Politics* 47 (1985): 254–68.
  According to the surveys in Kielhorn, "Party Development," in 1970 over 95
  percent of Arkansans identified with the same party at national and state levels.

8 Quotations from President Ronald Reagan, *Arkansas Democrat*, November 4,
  1984; the former postmaster general Winton Blount, *Arkansas Democrat*, Au-

gust 18, 1984; Congressman Ed Bethune, *Arkansas Gazette*, August 22, 1984. Text of television advertisement in *Arkansas Gazette*, July 20, 1984. For additional examples and analysis see Diane D. Blair, "Arkansas," in Robert P. Steed, Laurence W. Moreland, and Tod A. Baker, eds., *The 1984 Presidential Election in the South* (New York: Praeger, 1986), pp. 182–207.

9 Dewey Grantham, *The Democratic South* (Athens: University of Georgia Press, 1963); William C. Havard, "The South, A Shifting Perspective," in Havard, ed., *The Changing Politics of the South* (Baton Rouge: Louisiana State University Press, 1972), pp. 3–36; V. O. Key, Jr., *Public Opinion and American Democracy* (New York: Knopf, 1967), pp. 101–105. For contemporary findings of southern "liberalism," at least on economic issues, see chapters by Jerry Perkins, by Robert Botsch, and by Earl W. Hawkey, in Moreland, Baker, and Steed, *Contemporary Southern Political Attitudes and Behavior*; and Michael L. Mezey, "The Minds of the South," in Tod A. Baker, Robert P. Steed, and Laurence W. Moreland, eds., *Religion and Politics in the South* (New York: Praeger, 1983), pp. 5–26.

10 William S. Maddox and Stuart A. Lilie, *Beyond Liberal and Conservative: Reassessing the Political Spectrum* (Washington, D.C.: Cato Institute, 1984).

11 Ibid., pp. 68, 87, 96. In their "Ideological Orientations and State Issue Responses: Are They Related?" (Paper presented at Annual Meeting of the Southern Political Science Association, Atlanta, Ga., October 1982), Robert L. Savage and Diane D. Blair used this fourfold typology in categorizing results from a survey conducted by the University of Arkansas Household Research Panel. Respondents, however, were somewhat wealthier and considerably better educated than Arkansans generally.

12 Kielhorn, "Party Development," p. 14.

13 Sarah McCally Morehouse, *State Politics, Parties, and Policy* (New York: Holt, Rinehart and Winston, 1981), p. 71.

14 In both 1983 and 1985, bills requiring voters to register their party affiliations were defeated in the state legislature. On two previous occasions when party registration bills passed, they were vetoed by Governor Faubus in 1959 and by Governor Rockefeller in 1969. In the latter instance, the legislature overrode the veto, but the law was defeated by voters in a protest referendum.

15 Republican legislators insist there is no "discrimination" against them and that they have no particular problems passing legislation. See "Minority Party Still Has a Voice," *Arkansas Democrat*, February 11, 1985. Intimate relationships with the governor are not common, however, nor is inclusion in some of the intralegislative socializing, where many decisions are still made.

16 See Bob Wells, "White Separatist in Race Prompted Candidacy, GOP Orga-
nizer says," *Arkansas Gazette*, April 4, 1986. See also Melanie Wadkins,
"Tom Kelly, Arkansas Political Don Quixote," *Arkansas Times*, January 1979,
for a portrait of the "beer-drinking, pot-smoking" 1978 Republican U.S. Senate nominee.

17 Louis M. Seagull, *Southern Republicanism* (New York: Wiley, 1975), p. 131;
Key, *Southern Politics*, p. 277. For Arkansas political party operations from
1932 to 1956, see Boyce A. Drummond, "Arkansas Politics: A Study of a One-
Party System" (Ph.D. diss., University of Chicago, 1957). For 1960–1966, see
O'Connor, "Political Party Organization in Pulaski County."

18 Jack Bass and Walter DeVries, *The Transformation of Southern Politics* (New
York: New American Library, 1977), p. 40.

19 Arthur English and John J. Carroll, "Political Activists in a Southern County:
Some Implications for the Future" (Paper presented at the Symposium on
Southern Politics, The Citadel, Charleston, S.C., March 1980), p. 15. For
Democratic financial problems see James Scudder, "Democratic Leaders Call
for Unity, Fund-raising," *Arkansas Gazette*, June 16, 1985. For Republican
financial and leadership problems see Meredith Oakley, "Chairman of State
GOP Resigns," *Arkansas Democrat*, November 19, 1985; John Brummett,
"Small Ineffectual Arkansas GOP locks itself into a Protracted Mess,"
*Arkansas Gazette*, June 3, 1986. Quotation from David Maraniss, "Arkansas
Republican Party Is the Region's Poor Relation," *Washington Post*, May 20,
1986.

20 Harold F. Bass and Andrew Westmoreland, "Parties and Campaigns in Contemporary Arkansas Politics," *Arkansas Political Science Journal* 5 (1984): 54.

21 James L. Gibson, Cornelius P. Potter, John F. Bibby, and Robert J. Huckshorn,
"Whither the Local Parties?" *American Journal of Political Science* 29 (1985):
152.

22 Ibid., pp. 152, 154–55; the authors rank Arkansas Democrats forty-fourth,
Arkansas Republicans fortieth, in terms of local organizational strength.

23 These incentives were adapted from Frank J. Sorauf, *Party Politics in America*,
3d ed. (Boston: Little, Brown, 1976), pp. 86–96.

24 For the argument that many Arkansas businessmen are "Democrats of Expedi-
ence," fearing loss of contracts and other transactions should they openly avow
their Republican sympathies, see Deb Hilliard, "The Elephant Has Awak-
ened," *Arkansas Magazine (Arkansas Democrat)*, October 14, 1984, pp. 8–11.

25 The fact that Dale Bumpers had no previous partisan involvement is often cited
in explanation of his original electoral success. For the much greater frequency

with which party activism and electoral careers are combined in the Arkansas
Republican party, see Bass and Westmoreland, "Parties and Campaigns," pp.
41–49.

26 For the increasing importance of "purposive" incentives, see Sorauf, *Party
Politics*, p. 96, and Lewis Bowman, Dennis Ipolito, and William Ronaldson,
"Incentives for the Maintenance of Grassroots Political Activism," *Midwest
Journal of Political Science* 13 (1969): 126–39.

CHAPTER 6

1 The examples are drawn from publicly reported or personally observed events
except for the contributions by the Arkansas Motor Carriers Association, which
were described by its former president to Mark Vowell and reported in his
"Arkansas Interest Group Politics, Focusing on the AMCA and ARKPAC"
(University of Arkansas, 1984, Typescript).

2 Poultry Federation advertisement in *Arkansas Gazette*, January 22, 1985; Good
Roads advertisement in *Arkansas Gazette*, February 17, 1985.

3 See interview with John Fincher, Secretary of State's Office, in Stephen Buel,
"Biggest-spending Candidates Won 83% of Legislative Races," *Arkansas
Democrat*, January 13, 1985.

4 Fred Van Driesum, "Lobbying in a One-Party Environment: The Case of
Arkansas" (University of Arkansas, 1973, Typescript), p. 13; John Brummett,
"Highway Contractors Pledge Campaign Contributions If Candidates Will Support Tax," *Arkansas Gazette*, February 27, 1980; Larry Morse, "Donors'
Occupations Not Listed on White's Report," *Arkansas Democrat*, March 12,
1982; Ernest Dumas, "Money Counts Too Much in Politics," *Arkansas Ga-
zette*, December 17, 1982; Carol Griffee, "Both White and Clinton Receiving
19% of Chief Funds from Bankers, Investors," *Arkansas Gazette*, May 7,
1982; "Top Democrat Listed as Donor by Republicans," *Arkansas Gazette*,
April 24, 1982; Buel, "Biggest-spending Candidates"; "AP and L Political
Action Committee Contributes to 115 State Candidates," *Arkansas Gazette*,
April 26, 1986.

5 Lobbyists and their clients listed in "Registered Lobbyists—75th General Assembly," March 27, 1985, obtained from Office of Speaker.

6 Clarence Thornborough, Arkansas-Louisiana Gas, and Everett Oates, AP&L,
quoted in "ArkLa, AP&L Assistants Oppose All Lobbying Laws," *Arkansas
Gazette*, October 20, 1977; spokesmen for the Hospitality Association, Retail
Merchants Association, Medical Association, and railroads quoted in *Arkansas
Gazette*, March 6, 1985, p. 7A; Rep. Albert ("Tom") Collier quoted in "Bill to

Add Requirements on Lobbyists Dies in Panel,'' *Arkansas Gazette*, March 1, 1983.

7 On executive branch penetration generally, see Grant McConnell, *Private Power and American Democracy* (New York: Knopf, 1967), and Theodore J. Lowi, *The End of Liberalism* (New York: Norton, 1969). Arkansas data and quotation from ''Arkansas State Regulation vs. the Public Interest'' (Little Rock: Arkansas Consumer Research, 1981); and *Arkansas Democrat*, July 18, 1981.

8 See Sarah McCally Morehouse, ''Strong, Moderate, and Weak Pressure Group Systems,'' in *State Politics, Parties, and Policy* (New York: Holt, Rinehart and Winston, 1981), pp. 107–13; and L. Harmon Ziegler, ''Interest Groups in the States,'' in Virginia Gray, Herbert Jacob, and Kenneth N. Vines, eds., *Politics in the American States*, 4th ed. (Boston: Little, Brown, 1983), pp. 97–131.

9 See Neal R. Peirce and Jerry Hagstrom, *The Book of America: Inside Fifty States Today* (New York: Norton, 1983), p. 127; Boyce A. Drummond, ''Arkansas Politics: A Study of a One-Party System,'' (Ph.D. diss., University of Chicago, 1957), pp. 179–86; V. O. Key, Jr., *Southern Politics* (New York: Random House, 1949), pp. 192, 197, 338.

10 Key, *Southern Politics*, p. 477; Drummond, ''Arkansas Politics,'' pp. 179–86. For examples of the enormous influence of AP&L (including the efforts of Sen. Joseph T. Robinson, whose law firm represented AP&L, to keep TVA out of Arkansas), see Jim Lester, *A Man for Arkansas* (Little Rock: Rose Publishing, 1976), pp. 84, 170–87, 205, 209, 244; Harry Ashmore, *Arkansas: A History* (New York: Norton, 1978), pp. 145, 175–76; Jack Bass and Walter DeVries, *The Transformation of Southern Politics* (New York: New American Library, 1977), p. 93, and Richard D. Roblee and Mark Schlesinger, ''The Changing Influence of AP&L in Arkansas Politics'' (University of Arkansas, 1979, Typescript). For the influence of ArkLa, see Bill Terry, ''Witt Stephens vs. Sheffield Nelson,'' *Arkansas Times*, July 1980, pp. 55–68; ''Stephens Brothers Work for Fun, Profit,'' *Arkansas Democrat*, May 29, 1983 (reprinted from *Wall Street Journal*); and David R. Palmer, ''Country Boy Style Helped to Build Stephens Business,'' *Arkansas Gazette*, April 3, 1983.

11 Ziegler, ''Interest Groups in the States,'' p. 121.

12 Van Driesum, ''Lobbying in a One-Party Environment,'' p. 22; Rep. Lloyd George quoted in ''Soft Sell Is Secret of Lobbyists' Success,'' *Northwest Arkansas Times*, March 11, 1981.

13 The gubernatorial practice, and its demise, of firing all state employees is discussed in Diane D. Kincaid, ''Gubernatorial Appointments and Legislative Influence'' (Paper presented at the Annual Meeting of the Arkansas Political

Science Association, Eureka Springs, February 1977). Linda Garner, insurance commissioner, quoted in Jeff Thatcher, "Regulators at Technical Disadvantage," *Arkansas Democrat*, April 15, 1984. Turnover of PSC employees in Robert L. Brown, "The PSC and You," *Arkansas Times*, February 1982, p. 82.

14 Variables associated with more "integrated" (i.e., postindustrial) state economies include percentages of employed persons who are professionals, who are college graduates, and who work in finance and insurance, in addition to measures of literacy, income, and media circulation. See Morehouse, *State Politics, Parties, and Policy*, pp. 64–66, for an explanation of this measure and Arkansas's low ranking.

15 Compiled by author from "Registered Lobbyists, 75th General Assembly," March 27, 1985.

16 Lobbyists ranked in "Lobbyists Stand Out among Many Players at Arkansas General Assembly," *Arkansas Gazette*, January 13, 1985.

17 On the contemporary influence of utilities see "Registered Lobbyists Outnumber Lawmakers," *Arkansas Gazette*, February 11, 1985, and Mara Leveritt, "The Power Company: The Men and the Money behind Tommy Robinson," *Arkansas Times*, October 1984, pp. 61–73. For institutional confidence ratings, see Robert L. Savage and Diane D. Blair, "Arkansans and Their Institutions: The Question of Public Confidence Again," *Arkansas Business and Economic Review* 15 (1982): 10–14. Less than 8 percent of those surveyed had "a great deal of confidence" in either organized labor or utilities, while 50.5 percent and 47.4 percent had "hardly any confidence," respectively, in labor and utilities.

18 Drummond, "Arkansas Politics," p. 185.

19 Arthur English and John J. Carroll, *Citizen's Manual to the Arkansas General Assembly* (Little Rock: Institute of Politics and Government, 1983), p. 45. A 1979 mail survey returned by ninety-three legislators ranked the five most "successful" lobbying groups, in descending order, as Roads, Education, Banking, Cities and Counties, Industry. See Bobby Gene Pryor, "Interest Groups in the Arkansas Legislature" (University of Arkansas, 1979, Typescript). A 1985 mail survey of legislators and lobbyists rated the top five as utilities, AEA, banks, Farm Bureau, and Highway Department. See Arthur English and John J. Carroll, "Interest Groups in Arkansas: The Politics of Modified Inequality (Paper presented at the Annual Meeting of the Southern Political Science Association, Atlanta, Ga., November 1986), p. 8, table 3.

20 E. E. Schattschneider, *The Semisovereign People* (New York: Holt, Rinehart and Winston, 1960), p. 35; English and Carroll, "Interest Groups in Arkansas," p. 25.

21 For spending in the 1984 gubernatorial race, see chapter 3. Successful candidates for secretary of state and supreme court justice each spent more than $100,000 in 1984 according to "State's Candidate File Finance Reports," *Arkansas Democrat*, July 13, 1984. Costs of 1970s legislative races are cited from my own experience; 1984 figures are in Stephen Buel, "Biggest-spending Candidates," *Arkansas Democrat*, January 13, 1985. Prosecutor figures are in Bob Wells, "How Money Spent May Have Decided Race," *Arkansas Gazette*, July 15, 1984.

22 "Bill on Noting Totaled Autos Turned Down," *Arkansas Gazette*, February 2, 1985; "Money Raised to Pay Tyson's Fines," *Arkansas Gazette*, February 20, 1985.

## CHAPTER 7

1 Ralph C. Barnhart, "A New Constitution for Arkansas?" in Walter Nunn, ed., *Readings in Arkansas Government* (Little Rock: Rose Publishing, 1973), p. 5. For additional surveys of Arkansas's five constitutions see Robert A. Leflar, "A Survey of Arkansas' Constitutions," in Leland Duvall, ed., *Arkansas: Colony and State* (Little Rock: Rose Publishing, 1973), pp. 188–98; and Walter Nunn, "Arkansas' Constitutional Experience," in Robert Johnston et al., *Constitutional Revision in Arkansas: 1979–80* (Little Rock: University of Arkansas, 1980).

2 Composition of the Constitutional Convention in 1868 in Harry S. Ashmore, *Arkansas: A History* (New York: Norton, 1978), p. 92.

3 Walter Nunn, "The Negativism of the 1874 Constitution," in Nunn, *Readings in Arkansas Government*, pp. 21–25.

4 For some brief but interesting comparisons with other state constitutions, see Thomas R. Dye, *Politics in States and Communities*, 5th ed. (Englewood Cliffs, N.J.: Prentice-Hall, 1985), pp. 34–35.

5 Sponsors must get the attorney general's approval of their proposed ballot title, and the secretary of state passes upon the number and validity of signatures. For an excellent summary of the mechanics of the initiative and referendum, see League of Women Voters of Arkansas, *Government in Arkansas, '83* (Fayetteville, Ark.: League of Women Voters, 1983), pp. 19, 22–23. For all proposed amendments and action thereon, see Jerry E. Hinshaw, *Call the Roll* (Little Rock: Rose Publishing, 1987), pp. 175–79.

6 Until 1925 the Arkansas Supreme Court held that approval required a majority of all those voting in that election, an interpretation that invalidated five constitutional amendments. The court also ruled for years that the limit of three

constitutional amendment proposals applied to those submitted by the initiative as well as those submitted by the legislature. See Rod Farmer, "Direct Democracy in Arkansas, 1910–1918," *AHQ* 40 (1981): 99–118, and David Y. Thomas, "Popular Government," in David Y. Thomas, ed., *Arkansas and Its People*, (New York: American Historical Society, 1930), pp. 317–32. The other five states with a relatively easy constitutional amendment process are Arizona, Missouri, North Dakota, Oklahoma, and Oregon, according to Robert W. Meriwether, "The Amending Process," in Nunn, *Readings in Arkansas Government*, p. 55.

7 V. O. Key, Jr., *Public Opinion and American Democracy* (New York: Knopf, 1967), pp. 101–105. Farmers Union official quoted in Farmer, "Direct Democracy," pp. 104–105.

8 The three studies are Farmer, "Direct Democracy"; Thomas, "Popular Government"; and Walter Nunn, "Voting Behavior on Statewide Ballot Issues, 1964–1976" (Paper presented at the Annual Meeting of the Arkansas Political Science Association, Hot Springs, February 1976).

9 Nunn, "Voting Behavior," pp. 36–37.

10 See especially Robert A. Johnston et al., *Constitutional Revision in Arkansas: 1979–80*; Calvin R. Ledbetter, Jr., et al., *Politics in Arkansas: The Constitutional Experience* (Little Rock: Academic Press of Arkansas, 1972); Robert W. Meriwether, "The Proposed Arkansas Constitution of 1970," in Nunn, *Readings in Arkansas Government*, pp. 26–48; and Walter Nunn and Kay G. Collett, *Political Paradox: Constitutional Revision in Arkansas* (New York: National Municipal League, 1973).

11 For a complete list of group endorsements and campaign mottos, see Nunn and Collett, *Political Paradox*, pp. 133–34, 150–51.

12 Survey by Robert Johnston, cited by Nunn and Collett, *Political Paradox*, p. 174. For the adverse impact of a general election vote, see Nunn and Collett, *Political Paradox*, p. 177, Ledbetter et al., *Politics in Arkansas*, p. 191, and Meriwether, "The Proposed Arkansas Constitution of 1970," p. 48. The 1976 call for a convention did not specify the time for popular submission. Governor Pryor pushed for a special election, but the legislature resisted; the compromise result was the submission of the timing question to the voters in the 1978 general election. With little information or interest, voters opted for the 1980 general election rather than a 1979 special election.

13 For the most thorough analyses of the 1970 defeat, see Ledbetter et al., *Politics in Arkansas*, pp. 182–227; Meriwether, "The Proposed Arkansas Constitution of 1970"; and Nunn and Collett, *Political Paradox*, pp. 170–77. The best summary analysis of the 1980 defeat is Arthur English and John J. Carroll,

"Constitutional Reform in Arkansas: The 1979–1980 Convention," *National Civic Review*, May 1982, pp. 240–50, 267.

14 See "Gavels Signal End of the Assembly," *Arkansas Gazette*, March 30, 1985.

15 Three popularly initiated amendments (permitting voting machines, establishing a voter registration system, and permitting community colleges) were, however, adopted during this period.

16 For a list of these twenty-seven key recommendations, see Nunn and Collett, *Political Paradox*, pp. 29–30.

17 On the eventual adoption of many of Governor Brough's constitutional reforms, see Nunn and Collett, *Political Paradox*, p. 8.

18 On the 1985 legislative situation that produced one amendment, see Brenda Blagg, "Only One Survived the System," *Springdale News*, April 16, 1985.

19 The two most recent submissions of the four-year term proposal were within the 1970 and 1980 proposed constitutions. The last separate submission was in 1954.

20 Meriwether, "The Proposed Arkansas Constitution of 1970," p. 48.

CHAPTER 8

1 For the future expansion of gubernatorial power, see Calvin Ledbetter, Jr., "Arkansas and the Four-Year Term: Its History and Impact," *Arkansas Lawyer*, October 1985, pp. 148–52. By 1985 the governor's public relations allowance was $19,000 annually. One of the most recent and thorough comparative gubernatorial power studies is Thad L. Beyle, "Governors," in Virginia Gray, Herbert Jacob, and Kenneth N. Vines, eds., *Politics in the American States*, 4th ed. (Boston: Little, Brown, 1983), pp. 201–203, 454–59.

2 Harris polls quoted in Larry Sabato, *Goodbye to Good-time Charlie: The American Governorship Transformed*, 2d ed. (Washington, D.C.: Congressional Quarterly Press, 1983), p. 9. Quizzes and their analysis in possession of the author.

3 For general outlines and discussions of contemporary gubernatorial roles, see Beyle, "Governors," pp. 203–13; Thomas R. Dye, *Politics in States and Communities*, 5th ed. (Englewood Cliffs, N.J.: Prentice-Hall, 1985), pp. 178–80. Governor Clinton's analysis was articulated in a guest lecture to students in the author's classroom, Fayetteville, Ark., April 5, 1981. For a less systematic but very illuminating discussion of responsibilities by another contemporary governor, see "David Pryor: State Employee," *Grapevine*, October 1976.

4 For extensive analyses of Arkansas gubernatorial transitions, see Diane D. Blair, "Two Transitions in Arkansas, 1978 and 1982," in Thad Beyle, ed.,

*Gubernatorial Transitions* (Durham, N.C.: Duke University Press, 1985), pp. 92–122; and Robert L. Savage and Diane D. Blair, "Constructing and Reconstructing the Image of Statecraft: The Rhetorical Challenges of Bill Clinton's Two Gubernatorial Transitions," in Keith R. Sanders, Lynda Lee Kaid, and Dan Nimmo, eds., *Political Communication Yearbook*, 1984 (Carbondale: Southern Illinois University Press, 1985), pp. 242–61.

5 Robert Johnston and Dan Durning, "The Arkansas Governor's Role in the Policy Process, 1965–79," *Arkansas Political Science Journal* 2 (1981). According to analyses in the *Arkansas Gazette*, May 15, 1983, and April 7, 1985, 83 percent and 90 percent of Clinton's proposals were enacted in the 1983 and 1985 legislative sessions.

6 The Arkansas governor's choice of Speaker was usually honored until a backlash against Governor McMath's choice in 1953 resulted in adoption of the "pledge" system, whereby representatives select their Speaker for the following session at the preceding session, before the gubernatorial election is even held. The president pro tempore of the senate is similarly selected by advance pledges. Committee chairmanships are determined by seniority.

7 Data on vetoes were compiled from Henry M. Alexander, *Government in Arkansas* (Little Rock: Pioneer Press, 1963), p. 49, and Johnston and Durning, "The Arkansas Governor's Role," pp. 25–27. The two overrides with gubernatorial "consent" include Governor Pryor's wish to avoid a court challenge to the item veto in 1975 and Governor Clinton's feeble attempts to fight override of the 1985 gasoline tax increase.

8 John Obrecht and John Brummett, "Clinton Does Hard Lobbying for Measure," *Arkansas Gazette*, February 13, 1985. For a detailed discussion of the changing "coins of exchange" in the gubernatorial-legislative relationship, see Diane D. Kincaid, "Gubernatorial Appointments and Legislative Influence," *Public Administration Quarterly*, Winter 1984, pp. 429–40. For excellent details on how the governor's legislative aides operate, see "The Governor's Men in the Legislature," *Arkansas Democrat*, May 1, 1983.

9 Based on interviews with Governor Bumpers's legislative secretary, Bradley Jesson, January 15, 1977, and with several of Governor Clinton's aides. See also Ernest Dumas, "Free Passes Generate Annual Uproar," *Arkansas Gazette*, February 4, 1978, and Meredith Oakley, "Racing Passes or Lack of Them Angers Officials," *Arkansas Democrat*, February 10, 1980.

10 Senator Dale Bumpers in interview with author, December 30, 1976.

11 Charles Press and Kenneth VerBurg, *State and Community Governments in the Federal System* (New York: Wiley, 1979), p. 308. Governor Faubus's methods

are described in his address to the Arkansas Political Science Association, Russellville, Ark., February 23, 1985.

12 Sen. Dale Bumpers, interview with author, December 30, 1976.

13 Amendment 6, adopted in 1913 and effective in 1926, established the lieutenant governorship and eliminated the word "supreme."

14 The importance of fiscal management, supervisory control, and appointment and removal is discussed by Daniel R. Grant and H. C. Nixon, *State and Local Government in America*, 4th ed. (Boston: Allyn and Bacon, 1982), pp. 263–73.

15 For the 1971 reorganization plan and its consequences, see Ernest Dumas, "Executive Reorganization Reverses 97 Years of Traditions," in Walter Nunn, ed., *Readings in Arkansas Government* (Little Rock: Rose Publishing, 1973), pp. 140–44. For relative rankings of the governor's administrative authority, see Thad Beyle, "The Governor's Power of Organization," *State Government* 55 (1982): 79–87. On a scale of 6 to 26 possible management points, the national average was 14.76, Arkansas's governorship had 11. Survey of agency heads in Glenn Abney and Thomas Lauth, "The Governor as Chief Administrator," *Public Administration Review* 43 (1983): 40–41.

16 For the functions of these six elected executive officials, see League of Women Voters of Arkansas, *Government in Arkansas, '83* (Fayetteville, Ark.: League of Women Voters, 1983), pp. 26–27. The lieutenant governor, as president of the senate, presides over that body and may vote only to break a tie, which is a rare occurrence. See chapter 9 for the loss in 1967 of this office's legislative leadership powers. For recent examples of the attorney general's openly disagreeing with and criticizing the governor, see stories in the *Arkansas Gazette*, June 17, 1983, and February 24 and May 31, 1985, and in the *Arkansas Democrat*, February 27, 1985.

17 Sen. Jerry Bookout quoted in *Arkansas Democrat*, January 9, 1985.

18 Gov. David Pryor, interview with author, January 3, 1977.

19 The infrequent use of the cabinet as a governing device was confirmed in an interview with Betsey Wright, Governor Clinton's chief of staff, July 11, 1985. Also see Brenda Tirey, "It's Hard to Tell How Cabinet System Is Faring," *Arkansas Gazette*, January 1, 1984.

20 On state merit systems generally, see Sabato, *Goodbye to Good-time Charlie*, pp. 66–69. On Arkansas's first attempt at a merit system, proposed by a governor spending 90 percent of his time on patronage, see Donald Holley, "Carl E. Bailey: The Merit System and Arkansas Politics," *AHQ* 45 (1986): 291–320. In Arkansas, about 6,000 state employees, mostly in the Human Services Department, are covered by the Merit System Council because federal

statutes or regulations require such coverage. Most other state employees are hired under the Uniform Classification and Compensation Act of 1969 as amended. Administered by the Office of Personnel Management, there are now such merit system features as uniform job titles and pay plans between departments, state policies for holiday and sick leave, and a uniform grievance procedure.

21 Diane D. Blair, "Gubernatorial Appointment Power: Too Much of a Good Thing?" *State Government* 55 (1982): 91.

22 Ledbetter, "Arkansas and the Four-Year Term," pp. 151–52.

23 Results of 1948 study in Grant and Nixon, *State and Local Government*, p. 274. Extracted from Daniel R. Grant, "The Role of the Governor of Arkansas in Administration" (Ph.D. diss., Northwestern University, 1948).

24 On the constitutional emergency powers, see Cal Ledbetter, Jr., "The Office of Governor in Arkansas History," *AHQ* 37 (1978): 44–73. On Governor Clinton's experiences with crisis situations, see Phyllis Finton Johnston, *Bill Clinton's Public Policy for Arkansas: 1979–1980* (Little Rock: August House, 1983), pp. 70–91.

25 Leslie W. Dunbar, "The Changing Mind of the South: The Exposed Nerve," *Journal of Politics* 25 (1964): 20. Governor Clinton, classroom lecture, University of Arkansas, April 5, 1981, and speech to Arkansas AFL-CIO, *Arkansas Gazette*, June 4, 1985.

26 For the small percentage of "no-growth" advocates, see Robert L. Savage and Diane D. Blair, "Regionalism and Political Opinion in Arkansas: An Exploratory Survey," *Arkansas Political Science Journal* 5 (1984): 64, 76. The Seventy-fifth General Assembly approved Governor Clinton's complicated seventeen-bill economic development package intact and with little debate in 1985.

27 "Twelve Obstacles to Economic Development in the Land of Opportunity," Staff Report by the Winthrop Rockefeller Foundation, Little Rock, Ark., October 1982, p. 19. Robert McCord, *Arkansas Gazette*, November 27, 1984.

28 Examples collected from numerous newspaper stories. The number of proclamations cited by the secretary of state in Pam Strickland, "Governor's Proclamations Keep Constituents Smiling," *Arkansas Democrat*, December 26, 1985.

29 Thad L. Beyle and Lynn R. Muchmore, "The Governor and the Public," in Beyle and Muchmore, eds., *Being Governor: The View from the Office* (Durham, N.C.: Duke University Press, Duke Press Policy Studies, 1983), pp. 54–55.

30 Cal Ledbetter, Jr., "Jeff Davis and the Politics of Combat," *AHQ* 33 (1974): 23. On increased use of modern campaign technologies in governance, see

Larry Sabato, "Gubernatorial Politics and the New Campaign Technology," *State Government* (Summer 1980): 148–52.

31 Quotation from Jim Powell, "The Stage Is Cleared for the Next Political Drama," *Arkansas Gazette*, March 24, 1985.

32 On the reelection problems of governors responsible for tax increases, see Sabato, *Goodbye to Good-time Charlie*, pp. 105–10.

33 Governor Brough quoted in Ralph C. Barnhart, "A New Constitution for Arkansas?" in Nunn, *Readings in Arkansas Government*, p. 6. Daniel Grant, "The Role of the Arkansas Governor," n.p.

34 Governor Pryor quoted in Center for Policy Research, *Reflections on Being Governor* (Washington, D.C.: National Governor's Association, 1981), p. 169.

35 Governor Clinton, classroom lecture, University of Arkansas, April 5, 1981. See also Meredith Oakley, "Economic Plan Rides New Clinton Style," *Arkansas Democrat*, March 3, 1985.

36 Biographical data on Arkansas governors compiled from essays in Timothy P. Donovan and Willard B. Gatewood, Jr., eds., *The Governors of Arkansas* (Fayetteville: University of Arkansas Press, 1981).

37 Sabato, *Goodbye to Good-time Charlie*, pp. 20–44.

38 Speaking at a Governor's Reunion, North Little Rock, December 1, 1986, Sidney McMath recalled that in 1948, $10,000 was one of the handsomest annual salaries in the state. Quotation from Joseph Utley, *Record Books, 1923–1943*, December 7, 1923, p. 31. See chapter 3 for contemporary gubernatorial campaign costs.

39 Speaker Unruh quoted in Alan Rosenthal, *Legislative Life* (New York: Harper and Row, 1981), p. 20.

40 Cal Ledbetter and C. Fred Williams, "Arkansas Governors in the Twentieth Century: A Ranking and Analysis," *Arkansas Political Science Journal* 3 (1982): 55–58.

CHAPTER 9

1 See Walter Moffatt, "Out West in Arkansas, 1819–40," *AHQ* 17 (1958): 33–44; Donald A. Stokes, "Public Affairs in Arkansas, 1836–50" (Ph.D. diss., University of Texas at Austin, 1966); Joe Segraves, "Arkansas Politics, 1874–1918" (Ph.D. diss., University of Kentucky, 1973); William Orestus Penrose, "Political Ideas in Arkansas, 1880–1907" (Master's thesis, University of Arkansas, 1945); David Y. Thomas, ed., *Arkansas and Its People* (New York: American Historical Society, 1930); and Harry S. Ashmore, *Arkansas* (New York: Norton, 1978). In *Call the Roll: The First One Hundred Fifty Years of the Arkansas*

*Legislature* (Little Rock: Rose Publishing, 1986), Rep. Jerry E. Hinshaw attempts to paint a more positive portrait of the General Assembly but still provides more evidence of legislative failures than accomplishments.

2 See Meredith Oakley, "Old-timers Recall Colorful Legislatures Past," *Arkansas Democrat*, February 10, 1985; Phyllis Rice, "Wheels of Power Turn Smoother Now," *Northwest Arkansas Times*, April 14, 1985; and Harry Lee Williams, *Forty Years behind the Scenes in Arkansas Politics* (Little Rock: Parkin Printing and Stationery Co., 1949), pp. 83–101.

3 *The Sometime Governments* (Kansas City, Mo.: The Citizens' Conference on State Legislatures, 1973), p. 31; V. O. Key, Jr., *Southern Politics* (New York: Random House, 1949), p. 308.

4 For details on apportionment before and after federal court orders, see Donald T. Wells, "The Arkansas Legislature," in Alex B. Lacy, Jr., ed., *Power in American State Legislatures* (New Orleans: Tulane University, 1967).

5 The reform recommendations are contained in Center for State Legislative Research and Service, *Strengthening the Arkansas Legislature* (New Brunswick, N.J.: Eagleton Institute of Politics, Rutgers University, 1972).

6 Information on age and nativity calculated from *The Directory of the Arkansas Legislature*, published biennially by Southwestern Bell Company, Little Rock. Also see Donna E. Hudspeth, "Party-in-Office and Party Organization: The Arkansas Legislature and the Democratic Party" (Paper presented at Annual Meeting of Arkansas Political Science Association, Arkadelphia, February 1978).

7 Thomas, *Arkansas and Its People*, pp. 231–33; and see n. 6 above.

8 Arthur English and John J. Carroll, *Citizen's Manual to the Arkansas General Assembly* (Little Rock: Institute of Politics and Government, 1983), pp. 15–16; *Government in Arkansas '83* (Fayetteville, Ark.: League of Women Voters, 1983), p. 13; Wells, "The Arkansas Legislature," p. 11.

9 Legislators receive a $308 weekly expense allowance and one compensated trip home per week when in session, $20 per diem when in regular or special session, $60 per diem when attending committee meetings or on other official business, and they can itemize expenses up to $480 a month during the interim. They also receive life and health insurance benefits, and after ten years of service retirement benefits.

10 James D. Barber, *The Lawmakers* (New Haven, Conn.: Yale University Press, 1965), pp. 217–33; Alan Rosenthal, *Legislative Life* (New York: Harper and Row, 1981), pp. 57–60.

11 English and Carroll, *Citizen's Manual*, p. 19; Donald E. Whistler and Charles DeWitt Dunn, "Institutional Representation as Institutional Accountability in the

Arkansas General Assembly," *Arkansas Political Science Journal* 4 (1983): 50–52.

12 Rosenthal, *Legislative Life*, pp. 50, 54–55; Hudspeth, "Party-in-Office," p. 4; English and Carroll, *Citizen's Manual*, p. 18; Whistler and Dunn, "Institutional Representation," pp. 43–44.

13 Diane Kincaid Blair and Ann R. Henry, "The Family Factor in State Legislative Turnover," *Legislative Studies Quarterly* 6 (1981): 55–68; Rosenthal, *Legislative Life*, pp. 135–37.

14 Quoted in Jerry Dean, "Friends Give up Hunting to Roast Howell," *Arkansas Democrat*, November 14, 1978.

15 *Parliamentary Manual of the Senate, Permanent Rules of the House.*

16 English and Carroll, *Citizen's Manual*, p. 49; Robert McCord, "Why Arkansas Legislators Love to Legislate," *Arkansas Gazette*, February 24, 1985; Rosenthal, *Legislative Life*, pp. 256–60; Wells, "The Arkansas Legislature," p. 31.

17 Frank Triplett, "The Trivial State of the States," *Time*, May 29, 1978, p. 102. On the frequency and legal status of local acts, see Henry Alexander, *Government in Arkansas* (Little Rock: Pioneer Press, 1963), pp. 99–100.

18 English and Carroll, *Citizen's Manual*, p. 51; author's observations of many legislative sessions.

19 On the 1977 debacle, see Diane D. Blair, "David H. Pryor," in T. P. Donovan and W. B. Gatewood, Jr., eds., *The Governors of Arkansas* (Fayetteville: University of Arkansas Press, 1981), pp. 246–47; for the damage control necessitated by the 1985 regular session, see John Brummett, "Special Session to Start Monday," *Arkansas Gazette*, June 16, 1985, and "Special Session Begins," *Arkansas Gazette*, June 18, 1985. On passage of the scientific creationism law, see Brenda Tirey, "The Power in the Senate," *Arkansas Gazette*, March 15, 1981, and "Legislators Pass Creation Bill," *Arkansas Gazette*, March 18, 1981.

20 Bradley D. Jesson, classroom lecture, University of Arkansas, November 15, 1981. For some recent examples of "do nothing" bills, see "Court Reporter Bill to Cost Counties," *Arkansas Gazette*, April 19, 1981; John R. Starr, "Pension for Pals Recalls Darker Days," *Arkansas Democrat*, August 23, 1981; and discussion of HB 68 in "House Approves Bill for State Employees to Retire in 30 Years," *Arkansas Gazette*, January 23, 1985.

21 John Brummett, "Tax Exemptions Are Studied by Legislators," *Arkansas Gazette*, March 19, 1982; Meredith Oakley, "Revenue-Hungry State Losing Millions to Exemptions," *Arkansas Democrat*, March 23, 1982; Vicki F. Tynan, "Responsible Choices in Taxation," (Little Rock: Winthrop Rockefeller Foundation), p. 3.

22 Figures for 1985 calculated from the *Arkansas Legislative Digest*; comparable

figures for the senate in 1985 were 7 and 13. For similar figures for the 1975 and 1981 sessions, see Nelwyn Davis, "A Factor Analysis of Voting Blocs in the Arkansas House of Representatives, 1975" (Paper presented at Annual Meeting of Arkansas Political Science Association, Hot Springs, February 1976); and Jay Barth, "The Ladies of the House: A Study of the Voting Patterns of Female Members of the Arkansas House of Representatives" (Hendrix College, March 1985, Typescript).

23 Patrick F. O'Connor, "Voting Structure in a One-Party Legislature: The Arkansas House of Representatives over Five Sessions," (Ph.D. diss., Indiana University, 1973). See also Patrick F. O'Connor, "The Fluidity of One-Party Legislative Voting: Some Deviant Findings," *Georgia Political Science Association Journal* 7 (1979): 149–74. In a recent survey of Arkansas senators, "heeding the party position" emerged as the least important rule of the game; see Robert Johnston and Mary Storey, "The Arkansas Senate: An Overview," *Arkansas Political Science Journal* 4 (1983): 77. For legislators stating that party is an irrelevant influence, see Lisa Bickham, "Republicans Talk about Status in General Assembly," *Northwest Arkansas Times*, February 7, 1985, and "Dr. 'No' Uses His Vote in Legislature Seriously," *Arkansas Gazette*, March 18, 1985. Only one 1985 vote produced a clear-cut party division: all nine Republican representatives joined one Democrat in opposing a bill making presidential primaries compulsory for selecting national convention delegates.

24 English and Carroll, *Citizen's Manual*, p. 60; Johnston and Storey, "The Arkansas Senate," p. 79; Whistler and Dunn, "Institutional Representation," p. 54.

25 Whistler and Dunn, "Institutional Representation," pp. 46, 52.

26 Malcolm E. Jewell and Samuel C. Patterson, *The Legislative Process in the United States*, 3d ed. (New York: Random House, 1977), p. 302; student quizzes in author's possession; "AETN Viewer Survey on the Special Session" (Histecon Associates, Little Rock, June 1985), in author's possession.

27 Figures for 1927 in Thomas, *Arkansas and Its People*, p. 306; figures for 1951 quoted by the former Speaker Marion Crank (Address to Annual Meeting of Arkansas Political Science Association, Arkadelphia, February 1983); figures for 1983–85 in *State of Arkansas Biennial Budget 1983–95*, p. 16.

28 Jewell and Patterson, *The Legislative Process*, p. 117; Rosenthal, *Legislative Life*, p. 142; Sen. David Malone in interview with author, August 1, 1985. On ineffectiveness of interim committees, see Ernest Dumas, "Interim Committees Not Very Effective," *Arkansas Gazette*, November 13, 1975; Rep. John Lipton's remarks in "Legislator to Propose Having Annual Session," *Arkansas Gazette*, November 25, 1984; and "Panel Votes 'Do Pass,' " *Arkansas Gazette*, February

9, 1985, regarding defeat of an antitrespassing law that an interim committee spent eighteen months writing. On self-interested committee memberships, see John Brummett, "Change by Nelson Revealing of the Utilities Lobby's Power," *Arkansas Gazette*, March 9, 1986.

29 Johnston and Storey, "The Arkansas Senate," p. 72; Don Johnson, "Apparent Conflicts of Interest Fail to Part Legislators, Pet Project," *Arkansas Democrat*, April 14, 1985; Ernest Dumas, "It's Hard to Avoid Conflicts When a Legislator Is Also a Lobbyist," *Arkansas Gazette*, April 28, 1985.

30 Harry S. Ashmore, *An Epitaph for Dixie* (New York: Norton, 1957), p. 112. On the vagueness of Act 570 see "Senators Contend 'Conflict' Inherent in Any Legislature," *Arkansas Gazette*, April 14, 1980, and James R. Taylor, "Conflict of Interest Issue Is Clearly Uncertain," *Arkansas Democrat*, April 20, 1980. For typical press coverage of potential conflicts, see Bill Simmons, "Financial Interests of State Officials Listed," *Arkansas Democrat*, March 10, 1986, and Mel White, "The Best and Worst of the Arkansas Legislature," *Arkansas Times*, June 1982, pp. 33–38, 51–57.

31 Charles D. Dunn and Donald Whistler, "Citizen Access in the Arkansas General Assembly: Insiders and Outsiders" (Paper presented at the Annual Meeting of the Southern Political Science Association, Atlanta, Ga., November 1984); Whistler and Dunn, "Institutional Representation," p. 46.

32 Rep. David Matthews, classroom lecture, University of Arkansas, Fayetteville, November 11, 1985. On importance of colleagues as cue givers in state legislatures generally, see John C. Wahlke, Heinz Eulau, William Buchanan, Leroy C. Ferguson, *The Legislative System* (New York: Wiley, 1962), pp. 216–35. For a stunning confirmation in the Arkansas senate, see Johnston and Storey, "The Arkansas Senate," p. 79.

33 Arkansas legislator quoted in Rosenthal, *Legislative Life*, p. 79; Representative Thompson quoted in "Only Bill of Tyer Supported," *Arkansas Gazette*, March 24, 1979.

34 On the often-arbitrary exercise of power by past Speakers, see Oakley, "Old-timers Recall Colorful Legislatures Past," and Rice, "Wheels of Power Turn Smoother Now." For the transition in the senate taking away the lieutenant governor's legislative powers, see Meredith Oakley, "Senate Move Viewed in Foul Light by Republican Officer," *Arkansas Democrat*, July 20, 1980.

35 See Doug Smith, "Influence in the State Legislature: Who Wields the Power?" *Arkansas Gazette*, May 3, 1981.

36 Quotation in John Brummett, "Devotion to Jobs, Force of Personalities, Help Give Leading Legislators Influence," *Arkansas Gazette*, January 14, 1985. See also Cary Bradburn, "Howell Bears Reputation Felt Statewide," *Arkansas Dem-*

*ocrat*, October 6, 1985; and Mike Trimble, "Mad Max: Beyond Blusterdom," *Arkansas Times*, October 1985, pp. 98, 100–101, 115–18.

37 Brummett, "Devotion to Jobs"; Carol Griffee, "Pragmatism and Diplomacy Help Senator Gain Power," *Arkansas Gazette*, February 20, 1977.

38 Johnston and Storey, "The Arkansas Senate," p. 74. On time expended by Howell, Nelson, and Miller, see articles cited in nn. 36 and 37 above. Also see Doug Smith, "How to Exercise Clout," *Arkansas Gazette*, September 3, 1978, and Meredith Oakley, "Lawmaker Has His Finger in Many Committee Pies," *Arkansas Democrat*, March 3, 1980. Opposition to full-time legislature expressed by Rep. John Miller in classroom lecture, University of Arkansas, Fayetteville, October 18, 1985.

39 Whistler and Dunn, "Institutional Representation," p. 53; Johnston and Storey, "The Arkansas Senator," p. 75; author observations.

40 See Doug Smith, " 'Veto' Opinion Has Little Effect After 10 Months," *Arkansas Gazette*, July 10, 1983; for origins and development of legislative "advice" clauses and excerpts from attorney general's opinion thereon. Also see John Brummett, "Advisory Panel Violating Separation of Powers Doctrine," *Arkansas Gazette*, February 10, 1984; Steele Hays, " 'Nitpicking' Committee One of Most Powerful," *Arkansas Gazette*, October 14, 1979; and Bill Simmons, "Legislative Fingers Have Crept into Executive Pie," *Springdale News*, September 19, 1982.

41 See "Committee Says Legislature Cannot Follow Sunset Law," *Springdale News*, July 28, 1977; Ernest Dumas, "The Sunset Law," *Arkansas Gazette*, August 27, 1978; and Jerry Dean, "Legislative Trouble-shooters Afloat on Rough Seas," *Arkansas Democrat*, September 30, 1979. The repeal legislation was never transmitted to the governor and did not become law; however, the six-year period elapsed on June 30, 1983.

42 Carol Griffee, "Thompson's Son-in-law Completes First Week as 'Landfill Specialist,' " *Arkansas Gazette*, March 26, 1977; "Livestock Poultry Official Resigns," *Arkansas Gazette*, March 25, 1977; author's experience as chairman of the Governor's Commission on the Status of Women following a forum in Magnolia, Arkansas.

43 Whistler and Dunn, "Institutional Representation," p. 48.

44 Rep. David Matthews quoted in "Area Legislator Sees Need for Annual Sessions," *Springdale News*, March 31, 1985.

45 See Brenda Blagg, "Citizen Legislators Burning Out," *Springdale News*, November 27, 1983; Ernest Dumas, "Service in the Legislature Becomes Less Tolerable," *Arkansas Gazette*, November 30, 1983; and Doug Smith, "Retiring Legislators Cite Time Demands, Increased Workload," *Arkansas Gazette*, December 1, 1983.

46 A 1983 survey of seventy-two legislators conducted by the Legislative Council indicated that 56 percent thought annual sessions were "very necessary" and 27 percent thought they were "somewhat necessary." Forty-two percent favored a longer term for the speaker, 40 percent favored a longer term for the president pro tempore. See also John Brummett, "Legislator to Propose Having Annual Session," *Arkansas Gazette*, November 25, 1984, and Jonathan Runnells, "Arkansas Lawmakers May Decide to Restructure Procedures," *Arkansas Democrat*, December 30, 1984.

CHAPTER 10

1 A recent, excellent bibliographic essay on the politics of the judiciary is in Mary Cornelia Porter and G. Alan Tarr, eds., *State Supreme Courts* (Westport, Conn.: Greenwood Press, 1982), pp. 201–209. On judges' role in defeating the 1970 constitution, see Walter Nunn and Kay G. Collett, *Political Paradox, Constitutional Revision in Arkansas* (New York: National Municipal League, 1973), pp. 153–55. HB 935 of 1985 would have repealed the requirement that judges retire at age seventy or lose their retirement benefits, of direct benefit to two Little Rock judges in whose circuit the bill's sponsor practices. See Doug Smith, "Bill to Repeal Judicial Retirement Law Motivated by Desire to Aid Judges," *Arkansas Gazette*, April 10, 1985.

2 State senator quoted in Charles L. Carpenter, "A Need for Judicial Compensation, Disability, and Disciplinary Commissions," *Arkansas Lawyer*, October 1985, p. 145.

3 Calvin R. Ledbetter, Jr., "The Arkansas Supreme Court: 1958–59," (Ph.D. diss., Northwestern University, 1961), p. 142. Statistics in *Annual Report of the Judiciary of Arkansas, FY 83–84* (Little Rock: Arkansas Judicial Department, 1984), p. 22.

4 On the political supreme court of the 1920s and 1930s, see Ledbetter, "The Arkansas Supreme Court," esp. pp. 32–37. Hiram Whittington's letter in William Woodruff exhibit, Arkansas Territorial Restoration, Spring 1986. For the rough justice in Arkansas's past, see Harry S. Ashmore, *Arkansas: A History* (New York: Norton, 1978), pp. 39–42; Vernon T. Baugh, "The Administration of Criminal Justice by the Scott County Circuit Court, 1883–1939" (Master's thesis, University of Arkansas, 1941); Boyd W. Johnson, *The Arkansas Frontier* (n.p.: Perdue Printing, 1957), pp. 65–66; and Charles Morrow Wilson, *The Bodacious Ozarks* (New York: Hastings House, 1959), pp. 76–85.

5 Robert A. Leflar, "The Quality of Judges," *Indiana Law Journal* 35 (1960): 305.

6 On structure, jurisdiction, and functions of Arkansas courts, see annual issues of *Report of the Judiciary of Arkansas* (Little Rock: Arkansas Judicial Department);

"Systems Documentation, Arkansas Judicial System" (Memorandum prepared by Arkansas Court Improvement Project Staff, April 4, 1980); *Government in Arkansas '83* (Fayetteville, Ark.: League of Women Voters, 1983), pp. 36–45.

7 See John Woodruff, "NLR Judge Announces Retirement," *Arkansas Gazette*, February 15, 1986.

8 *Annual Report of the Judiciary of Arkansas, FY 83–84*, pp. 117–33.

9 Ibid., pp. 37–38.

10 *The Book of the States, 1982–83*, vol. 24, (Lexington, Ky.: Council of State Governments); Edwin H. Greenebaum, "Arkansas' Judiciary: Its History and Structure," in Walter Nunn, ed., *Readings in Arkansas Government* (Little Rock: Rose Publishing, 1973), pp. 216–23; Prof. Robert A. Leflar, interview with author, August 27, 1985. It was in 1903, by which time merged systems of law and equity courts were firmly established elsewhere in America, that the Arkansas legislature required separate courts of chancery established in every county. The immediate beneficiary was Gov. Jeff Davis, who enlarged the political base for his senate race by making all of these prized appointments.

11 James D. Gingerich, "Arkansas' New Court and Its Effect on the Arkansas Appellate System," *Arkansas Political Science Journal* 5 (1984): 34.

12 These major reform goals adapted by author from Henry Glick, "Supreme Courts in State Judicial Administration," in Porter and Tarr, *State Supreme Courts*, pp. 109–28; *The Question of State Government Capability* (Washington, D.C.: Advisory Commission on Intergovernmental Relations, 1985), pp. 183–91; and essays in Philip L. Dubois, ed., *The Politics of Judicial Reform* (Lexington, Mass.: Lexington Books, 1982).

13 Glick, "Supreme Courts," pp. 120–23.

14 Chief Justice Holt addressing county and circuit clerks, Fayetteville, Arkansas, July 24, 1985; George Bentley, "Effort under Way for Panel to Discipline, Replace and Set Pay for Judges," *Arkansas Gazette*, February 2, 1986.

15 Information on case coordinators from Chris Thomas, executive secretary, Arkansas Judicial Department, telephone interview with author, October 10, 1985; comment on Judicial Council from Robert A. Leflar, interview with author, August 27, 1985.

16 State rankings in Glick, "Supreme Courts," pp. 120–23. On Arkansas's judicial management problems, see Jacquetta Keith Alexander, "The Application of Principles and Practices of Trial Court Administration in the Circuit Court of Pulaski County, Arkansas," (M.P.A. internship paper, University of Arkansas, 1982); and James L. Elston, "Administration of the Courts in Arkansas: Challenge, Performance, and Prospects," *Arkansas Law Review* 30 (1976): 235–87. On the wide disparities in caseloads and funding resulting from judicial lobbying

of the legislature, see Jess C. Henderson, "Why Judges Must Lobby," *Spectrum*, November 26–December 9, 1986, pp. 1–3.

17 For the furor involving Circuit Judge Henry B. Means, see articles in *Arkansas Gazette*, December 1, 1976, and January 27, February 3, March 1, 2, 3, and 8, August 19, 28, and 30, and September 2, 1977. Chief Justice Holt quoted from address to Arkansas Political Science Association, North Little Rock, February 22, 1986. On the limitations of the Judicial Qualifications and Judicial Ethics committees, see Carpenter, "A Need for Judicial Compensation, Disability, and Discipline Commissions," pp. 144–45, and J. Lamar Porter, "Removal and Discipline of Judges in Arkansas," *Arkansas Law Review* 32 (1978): 545–69. On the impeachment process, see Stephen A. Smith, "Impeachment, Address, and the Removal of Judges in Arkansas: An Historical Perspective," *Arkansas Law Review* 33 (1978): 253–68.

18 Supreme Court Justice John Purtle, charged and then acquitted in 1986 of conspiracy to commit theft in an alleged arson-for-profit scheme, was the first Arkansas Supreme Court justice to be charged with a felony. See Peggy Harris, "Purtle Jury to Be Chosen," *Arkansas Gazette*, May 11, 1986. State rankings in Glick, "Supreme Courts," pp. 120–23.

19 Professionalism rankings in Henry R. Glick, and Kenneth N. Vines, *State Court Systems* (Englewood Cliffs, N.J.: Prentice-Hall, 1973), p. 60. Backlog assessment from Chris Thomas, interview with author, October 10, 1985, and *Annual Report of the Judiciary of Arkansas, FY 83–84*.

20 Experience recounted by James B. Blair, classroom lecture, University of Arkansas, Fayetteville, April 11, 1985. Excerpt from student paper, "The Power in B.," in possession of the author.

21 *Annual Report of the Judiciary of Arkansas, FY 83–84*.

22 For judicial selection methods in the fifty states, see *The Question of State Government Capability*, p. 189; *Book of the States, 1982–83*, pp. 262–68. Percentages of "elected" judges from James Anderson, Richard Murray, and Edward Farley, *Texas Politics* (New York: Harper and Row, 1971), pp. 215–16; Nicholas Henry, *Governing at the Grassroots*, 2d ed. (Englewood Cliffs, N.J.: Prentice-Hall, 1984), pp. 205–207; James Herndon, "Appointment as a Means of Initial Accession," *North Dakota Law Review* 38 (1962): 60–73; and John Paul Ryan, Allan Ashman, Bruce D. Sales, and Sandra Shane-DuBow, *American Trial Judges* (New York: Free Press, 1980), p. 122.

23 The most publicized provisions of Amendment 29 were those requiring an absolute majority rather than a plurality for primary victory, prohibiting the governor or his relatives from assuming any vacated office, and placing restrictions on nomination by party convention. The Bar Association was distressed by

Governor Futrell's appointment of C. E. Johnson as chief justice and supported this amendment along with a 1937 law prohibiting judges from participating in any campaign other than their own.

24 On September 16, 1985, the author mailed questionnaires to sixty-seven circuit and chancery judges and received fifty-nine responses. Questionnaires and tabulated responses, hereafter cited as "Judicial Questionnaire," in possession of the author.

25 The 1936, 1938, and 1958 defeats of incumbent supreme court justices are discussed in Ledbetter, "The Arkansas Supreme Court." Other data compiled by author from Arkansas election returns. On the fierce judicial lobbying for advantageous apportionment schemes, see George Bentley, "Judicial Panel Recommends Rearrangement," *Arkansas Gazette*, October 12, 1975, and Ernest Dumas, "Redistricting Plan Dropped," *Arkansas Gazette*, September 23, 1976.

26 Raymond Abramson quoted in Anthony Moser, "Lawyer Urges Judicial Reform in Wake of Traffic Judge Scam," *Arkansas Democrat*, October 31, 1985. James B. Blair, classroom lecture.

27 Judge Jameson's advertisement in *Northwest Arkansas Times*, May 25, 1980.

28 See Ernest Dumas, "The Strange World of Appellate Judgeship Elections," *Arkansas Gazette*, April 22, 1984. Twenty-six of the fifty-nine respondents to the author's questionnaire had received a judicial appointment prior to their first election; twenty of the fifty-nine had been municipal judges, and for thirteen it was the penultimate office.

29 See Stuart Nagel, "Political Party Affiliation and Judges' Decisions," *American Political Science Review* 55 (1961): 843–51; and Sidney Ulmer, "The Political Party Variable on the Michigan Supreme Court," *Journal of Public Law* 11 (1962): 352–62.

30 See, for example, "Court Candidate Blasts Opponent for Refusal to Discuss Key Issues," *Arkansas Democrat*, June 12, 1984; Bob Sanders, "Voters Must Know Views of Judicial Candidates," *Arkansas Gazette*, July 10, 1984; Stephen Buel, " 'Philosopher' Johnson Vies with 'Reformer' Holt for High Court," *Arkansas Democrat*, October 7, 1984; and "Johnson Challenges Holt to Debate," *Arkansas Democrat*, October 21, 1984. Also see "Judge Candidates," editorial, *Arkansas Democrat*, December 15, 1985.

31 See "Drop 'Gag Rules' or Bar Will Reveal Poll," *Arkansas Gazette*, April 15, 1979; "Bar Council Urges Allowing Judges to Release Survey," *Arkansas Gazette*, December 16, 1979; "Bar Policy-Making Body Votes to Keep Secret Result of Judge Ratings," *Arkansas Gazette*, January 20, 1980; and "Judges' Report Cards Come Out Unnoticed," *Arkansas Gazette*, November 18, 1984.

32 Doug Smith, "Supreme Court: Short Name Helps," *Arkansas Gazette*, October

26, 1977; interview with Leflar, who also acknowledges that Robin's chairmanship of the state Democratic party and lopsided margins in the machine counties
were influential, as was the fact that most of the young lawyers Leflar had
recruited among his former students suddenly abandoned the race to participate
in World War II.

33 The "nickname" theory is advanced by Philip L. Dubois, "The Significance of
Voting Cues in State Supreme Court Elections," *Law and Society Review* 13
(1978–79): 757–79.

34 J. Bill Becker, president of the Arkansas State AFL-CIO, telephone interview
with author, September 30, 1985.

35 Williams advertisement in *Northwest Arkansas Times*, May 25, 1980; Holt
advertisement in *Arkansas Gazette*, November 4, 1984.

36 *Arkansas Legal Directory, 1984–85* (Dallas: Legal Directories, 1984); "Judicial
Questionnaire."

37 Associate Justice Robert Dudley of the Arkansas Supreme Court, Little Rock,
Ark., interview with author, September 20, 1985.

38 Judge Hendricks quoted in Moser, "Lawyer Urges Judicial Reform."

39 For the Texas study see Charles A. Johnson, Roger C. Shaefer, and R. Neal
McKnight, "The Salience of Judicial Elections," *Social Science Quarterly* 59
(1978): 371–78; Henry R. Glick, "The Promise and the Performance of the
Missouri Plan," *University of Miami Law Review* 32 (1978): 518.

40 Judicial campaign circulars in author's possession; Razorback advertisement
used by Richard Adkisson in *Arkansas Gazette*, June 9, 1980.

41 Ledbetter, "The Arkansas Supreme Court," p. 201.

42 Quotation from Stuart S. Nagel, *Comparing Elected and Appointed Judicial
Systems* (Beverly Hills, Calif.: Sage Publications, 1973), p. 39.

43 Ann Henry and Elizabeth Crocker, "Filling the Chair: What Judicial Selection
Method Works Best?" *Arkansas Lawyer* 19 (1985): 164–71.

44 Supreme court's "efficiency" discussed in Gingerich, "Arkansas' New Court,"
p. 33.

CHAPTER 11

1 On facilities constructed under New Deal programs, see Stephen F. Strausberg,
"The Effectiveness of the New Deal in Arkansas," in Donald W. Whisenhunt,
ed., *The Depression in the Southwest* (New York: Kennikat Press, 1980), pp.
102–16; for history and economic importance of Arkansas River project, see
Charles L. Steel, "Renaissance of a River," in Leland Duvall, ed., *Arkansas:
Colony and State* (Little Rock: Rose Publishing, 1973), pp. 228–47; data on

Social Security recipients in Paul Neal and Stephen Steed, "The Green and the Gray," *Arkansas Times*, October 1985, p. 6.

2 Federal aid in early nineteenth century described in John L. Ferguson and J. H. Atkinson, *Historic Arkansas* (Little Rock: Arkansas History Commission, 1966), pp. 29, 50–55; southern role in securing early twentieth-century programs in George Brown Tindall, *The Emergence of the New South, 1913–1945* (Baton Rouge: Louisiana State University Press, 1967), pp. 14, 240–41; federal aid to Arkansas's centennial in Bob Besom, " 'Poor Folks' Celebrate Arkansas' Statehood," *Northwest Arkansas Times*, November 12, 1985.

3 R. Lawson Veasey and W. David Moody, "New Federalism: 2nd Edition," *Arkansas Political Science Journal* 4 (1983): 22–39.

4 Michael Lawson, "The Flow of Federal Funds," *Intergovernmental Perspective*, Spring/Summer 1985, pp. 18–19; Michael Barone and Grant Ujifusa, *The Almanac of American Politics, 1986* (Washington, D.C.: National Journal, 1986), p. 68; "Tax Dollars Go Back Home," *U.S. News and World Report*, February 24, 1986, p. 10; "State Climbs 3 Rungs up Ladder," *Arkansas Democrat*, April 2, 1986.

5 Morton Grodzins, *The American System: A New View of Government in the United States*, ed. Daniel J. Elazar (Chicago: Rand McNally, 1966), p. 9.

6 Ibid., pp. 171–80. The files containing Elazar's 1958 interviews are housed at the Center for the Study of Federalism, Temple University, Philadelphia.

7 Quotation from Ralph Nemir, "A Congressman's Role in Getting Federal Aid for Rural Areas," in Walter Nunn, ed., *Readings in Arkansas Government* (Little Rock: Rose Publishing, 1973), p. 302.

8 Kay Goss, Governor Clinton's Aide for Intergovernmental Relations, interview with author, Little Rock, July 11, 1985. For an excellent overview of gubernatorial responsibilities in intergovernmental relations, see Thad L. Beyle and Lynn R. Muchmore, "Governors and Intergovernmental Relations, Middlemen in the Federal System," in Beyle and Muchmore, eds., *Being Governor* (Durham, N.C.: Duke University Press, 1983), pp. 192–203.

9 A good example of intergovernmental activism by local officials is in John Woodruff, "Tax Reform, Revenues, Concern Officials at Congress of Cities," *Arkansas Gazette*, December 8, 1985.

10 An extensive analysis of the state's response to President Reagan's initiatives is Diane K. Blair and Joan Roberts, "Acquiescent Arkansas: The 1981 Response to Reaganomics and the New Federalism," in Stephen L. Schecter, ed., *The Annual Review of Federalism, 1981* (Philadelphia: Center for the Study of American Federalism, 1983), pp. 163–74. Quotation from Parris N. Glendenning and

Mavis Mann Reeves, *Pragmatic Federalism*, 2d ed. (Pacific Palisades, Calif.: Palisades Publishers, 1984), p. 63.

11 Glendenning and Reeves, *Pragmatic Federalism*, p. 63.

12 Grodzins, *The American System*, p. 173.

13 U.S. military impact in Arkansas described in Leroy Donald, "Military a Force in Arkansas Economy," *Arkansas Gazette*, February 24, 1985.

14 John Shelton Reed, *The Enduring South* (Lexington, Mass.: Heath, 1972), p. 88; Sheldon Hackney quoted by Reed, *The Enduring South*, pp. 88–89.

15 Quotation from Ernie Dean, telephone interview with author, December 6, 1985. Every Arkansas adult with whom I conversed remembers hearing this "fact" reiterated throughout their school years; and see Tim Bennett, "Center Puts World View in Classroom," *Arkansas Democrat*, February 3, 1986.

16 For one version of "The Arkansas Traveler," see Diann Sutherlin Smith, *The Arkansas Handbook* (Little Rock: Emerald City Press, 1984), pp. 44–47.

17 Senator Miller quoted in George Brown Tindall, *The Ethnic Southerners* (Baton Rouge: Louisiana State University Press, 1976), p. 219.

18 Tony Freyer, *The Little Rock Crisis: A Constitutional Interpretation* (Westport, Conn.: Greenwood Press, 1984), p. 11.

19 Jim Lester, *A Man for Arkansas* (Little Rock: Rose Publishing, 1976), p. 84.

20 For details on Governor Clinton's dealings with the federal government, see Phyllis Finton Johnston, *Bill Clinton's Public Policy for Arkansas; 1979–80* (Little Rock: August House, 1982), pp. 70–91; and Diane D. Blair, "Two Transitions in Arkansas, 1978 and 1982," in Thad Beyle, ed., *Gubernatorial Transitions* (Durham, N.C.: Duke University Press, 1985), pp. 98, 108–109, 112–14.

21 Governor Clinton quoted in Johnston, *Bill Clinton's Public Policy*, p. 73.

22 Blair, "Two Transitions in Arkansas," pp. 112–14.

23 James Powell, "Clinton Deserves Praise for Restraint," *Arkansas Gazette*, November 13, 1985; press release, Office of the Governor, September 10, 1985; George Wells, "Clinton Comment Untrue, Federal Judge Responds," *Arkansas Gazette*, September 13, 1985; Scott Van Laningham, "Clinton Defends Ads Blaming Federal Court in Settlement," *Arkansas Gazette*, September 12, 1985.

24 Quotation from Doug Smith, "Officials Resisting Request," *Arkansas Gazette*, June 1, 1985.

25 "The Bailey Arkansas Poll," November 6, 1985.

26 Legislator's remark overheard by author, who was chairman of AETN Commission, 1985–86, at hearing before Joint Interim Education Committee, May 10, 1986. Also see Meredith Oakley, "Lawmakers Cost State One Source

of Pride," *Arkansas Democrat*, August 12, 1986, and Scott Van Laningham, "Ho to Resign as Head of AETN," *Arkansas Gazette*, August 12, 1986.

27 Jim Johnson quoted in Jim Edwards, "Candidate Faults Opponents Views on Court System," *Arkansas Democrat*, October 2, 1984; Frank White, State of the State Message, February 19, 1981; Orval Faubus quoted in Joe Schratz, "A Little Advice from the Old Pro," *Arkansas Magazine*, January 27, 1985, p. 6.

28 Governor Clinton quoted in "Governor Says Pressure Building Not to Enforce New School Standards," *Arkansas Gazette*, October 22, 1984.

CHAPTER 12

1 *State and Local Roles in the Federal System* (Washington, D.C.: Advisory Commission on Intergovernmental Relations, 1981), p. 262.

2 Arkansas Constitution, Article 12, sec. 3, emphasis supplied; *State and Local Roles in the Federal System*, p. 262.

3 Municipal population figures from "Population Growth in Arkansas' Towns and Cities: 1940 to Present," *City and Town*, March 1986, pp. 4–9.

4 *1982 Census of Governments* (Washington, D.C.: U.S. Department of Commerce, 1983), vol. 3, no. 2, pp. 8–9, 31; vol. 4, pp. 4–5; Ernest Dumas, "Local Sales Tax Called City Aim," *Arkansas Gazette*, August 20, 1976.

5 John Gill speaking to the Legislative Joint Interim Committee on City and County Affairs, quoted in *Arkansas Gazette*, August 20, 1976. See John Brummett, "Running City Hall Makes Life Tough Mayors Assert," *Arkansas Gazette*, August 7, 1977, for mayors' estimates of time spent on seeking federal funds.

6 The Arkansas Plan is analyzed at length in Diane D. Kincaid, "The Arkansas Plan: Coon Dogs or Community Services," *Publius* 8 (1978): 117–33.

7 Roland L. Warren, *The Community in America* (Chicago: Rand McNally, 1963), p. 17.

8 Ibid., p. 5. The *Marshall Mountain Wave* is a wonderful weekly in which to savor the community "doings" in Canaan, Dongola, Chimes, Snowball, Archey Valley, Witts Springs, Evening Shade, and other towns.

9 O. P. Williams and C. R. Adrian, *Four Cities: A Study in Comparative Policy Making* (Philadelphia: University of Pennsylvania Press, 1963), p. 291.

10 *1982 Census of Governments*, vol. 1, p. 405.

11 The number of officials actually varied from seven to nine as the constitution authorized the combining of the offices of sheriff and assessor and the separation of the county and circuit clerkships. The male reference is used for the county judge because the 1874 constitution specified, "He shall be at least twenty-five years of age . . . a man of upright character." The male imperative was elimi-

nated by Amendment 55. Additional details on prereform and postreform county government are in Diane D. Kincaid, "Early Effects of County Reform in Arkansas" (Paper presented at the Annual Conference of the American Society for Public Administration, Baltimore, April 2, 1979).

12 To illustrate the judge's budgetary dominance, Dr. Wilma Sacks, who once headed the public health program, appeared at the Washington County's annual quorum court meeting to request a modest increase for her program. One justice of the peace inquired whether these funds would come from general revenues. "That's right," the judge responded, "right off your roads, so it can't be done" (Wilma Sacks, interview with author, March 5, 1979). See also Hugh Earnest, "Washington County Finances," in Walter Nunn, ed., *Readings in Arkansas Government* (Little Rock: Rose Publishing, 1973), pp. 488–505.

13 The opposition of county judges to reform is discussed and documented in Walter Nunn and Kay G. Collett, *Political Paradox: Constitutional Revision in Arkansas* (New York: National Municipal League, 1973), pp. 15, 63, 121, 123, 137.

14 On the importance of salary increases to the reform effort, see Charles DeWitt Dunn, "Reaction to Reform: Arkansas County Officials under Amendment 55" (Paper presented at the Annual Convention of the Arkansas Political Science Association, Conway, February 1979), p. 12.

15 The powers granted to municipalities vary with classification, but population is only a general guide to this classification. For these and other details regarding municipal structures and powers, see the excellent summary in *Government in Arkansas '83* (Fayetteville, Ark.: League of Women Voters, 1983), pp. 50–56.

16 Ibid., pp. 53–54.

17 These observations based upon the author's observation of local governments as well as discussions with many local officials over twenty years' time. For a colorful description of one of Arkansas's strongest mayors, see Jim Lynch, "Mayor Laman and the North Little Rock Budget," in Nunn, *Readings in Arkansas Government*, pp. 366–77.

18 The county judge must be at least twenty-five, and directors in a city administrator or city manager city must be at least thirty.

19 Calculated by author from Arkansas election returns.

20 For differing amounts of competition for justice of the peace before and after Amendment 55, see Charles D. Dunn, "Constitutional Reform and County Government in Arkansas: The Impact of Amendment 55 on Quorum Court Membership" (Paper presented at the Annual Meeting of the Arkansas Political Science Association, Arkadelphia, February 1978).

21 Sherrill officials quoted in "Sherrill Officials Keep Posts without Holding Elec-

tions," *Arkansas Gazette*, April 17, 1986. On the frequency of mayoral resignations, see John Brummett, "Running City Hall," *Arkansas Gazette*, August 7,
1977. See also "Cave City Mayor Resigns, Third in 21 Months," *Arkansas
Gazette*, June 14, 1978, and "Third Official in Bald Knob Resigns Office,"
*Arkansas Democrat*, July 26, 1986.

22 On the importance of recruitment practices, see Williams and Adrian, *Four
Cities*, p. 51. For the success of the Good Government Committee, see Kevin
McDaniel, "Trio Elected to City Board Gets Strong Support from West Little
Rock," *Arkansas Democrat*, November 11, 1984, and Mark Oswald, "3 Win-
ning Candidates Favored among the Business Community," *Arkansas Gazette*,
November 18, 1984. Telephone interview with the Madison County judge
Charles Whorton, Jr., January 14, 1986. Discussions at meetings of Washington
County Democratic Central Committee, of which I am a longtime member.

23 Based on responses from a mail survey of county and city legislators in Washington and Madison counties and Fayetteville and Springdale, conducted by the
author in January and February 1986, hereafter referred to as "Views of Local
Officials." Survey and responses in author's possession.

24 Joseph A. Schlesinger, Jr., *Ambition and Politics* (Chicago: Rand McNally,
1966), p. 2; W. B. Holliday quoted in Brummett, "Running City Hall."

25 By 1986 forty Arkansas mayors were women, according to Judy Bocklage,
"Women Say Role of Mayor Rough Going," *Arkansas Gazette*, July 13, 1986.
See also Guinda Reeves, "Madam Mayor, Women Take Charge in City Hall,"
*Arkansas Democrat*, March 4, 1984, and Willie Wofford, "State's Black Mayors
Serve Wide Range of Communities," *Arkansas Democrat*, September 30, 1985.

26 Dunn, "Constitutional Reform and County Government," p. 7; Laura Newman,
"Few Women Holding Administrative Posts," *Arkansas Gazette*, April 14,
1985.

27 Enrollment figures in Carol Matlack, "Tests Threat to Teachers," *Arkansas
Gazette*, January 19, 1986.

28 For many details on the difficulties blacks and women have had securing board
positions or the mayoralty in Little Rock, see James Merriweather, "Breaking
the City Board Color Barrier," *Arkansas Democrat*, April 13, 1983; Stephen
Buel, "Government of the Many by the Affluent Few?" *Arkansas-Democrat*,
June 12, 1983; Mark Oswald, "Appointments Continuing in Past Pattern,"
*Arkansas Gazette*, December 15, 1985; and Robert McCord, "The Good Ole
Boys at City Hall," *Arkansas Gazette*, January 27, 1985.

29 For the nature and outcome of recent lawsuits, see Larry Ault, "Judge Voids
Ward System in Marianna," *Arkansas Democrat*, May 17, 1986; George Wells,
"More Lawsuits Are Filed over Vote District Lines," *Arkansas Gazette*, June 8,

1986; and "Mississippi County's JP Boundaries Called Discriminatory," *Arkansas Gazette*, July 24, 1986.

30 On the background and impact of the run-off requirement, see Carol Matlack and Mark Oswald, "Two Proposals Would Change Local Elections," *Arkansas Gazette*, March 5, 1983; Ernest Dumas, "City, County Runoffs Now Required," *Arkansas Gazette*, April 3, 1983; and Marie Crawford, " 'Routine' Mayoralty Fell Shy for Chitman," *Arkansas Democrat*, March 16, 1986.

31 Fayetteville meeting described in *Northwest Arkansas Times*, August 30, 1983. Quotations from "Views of Local Officials."

32 For concept of "public regardingness," see James Q. Wilson and Edward C. Banfield, "Public Regardingness as a Value Premise in Voting Behavior," *American Political Science Review* 58 (1964): 876–87. For Arkansas school officials' attitudes toward larger electorates, see Frank Fellone, "South Gives Rise to Primary Plan," *Arkansas Democrat*, February 16, 1986.

33 Kincaid, "The Arkansas Plan," p. 132; Kenneth R. Tremblay, Jr., "Perceived Quality of Community Life," *City and Town*, April 1986, pp. 6–7.

34 Diane D. Blair, "Views of Local Officials," adapted from Williams and Adrian, *Four Cities*, pp. 185–268. According to the Williams and Adrian typology, Springdale would be classified as a "Caretaker" community, Fayetteville as combining elements of "Amenities" and "Arbiter" communities.

CHAPTER 13

1 For a brief review of this debate, see Thomas R. Dye and John Robey, " 'Politics versus Economics': Development of the Literature on Policy Determination," in Thomas R. Dye and Virginia Gray, eds., *The Determinants of Public Policy* (Lexington, Mass.: Lexington Books, 1980), pp. 3–17. For a more recent and more thorough discussion, see Jack M. Treadway, *Public Policymaking in the American States* (New York: Praeger, 1985).

2 Virginia Gray, "Politics and Policy in the American States," in V. Gray, Herbert Jacob, and Kenneth N. Vines, eds., *Politics in the American States*, 4th ed. (Boston: Little, Brown, 1983), p. 4.

3 Ibid., p. 5.

4 For historical details on Arkansas's tax system, see David Y. Thomas, "A History of Taxation in Arkansas," *Publications of the Arkansas Historical Association* (Fayetteville: Arkansas Historical Association, 1908), vol. 2, pp. 43–90; David Y. Thomas, ed., *Arkansas and Its People* (New York: American Historical Society, 1930), pp. 52–53, 103; John Gardner Lile, *The Government of Arkansas* (Columbus, Ohio: Champlin Press, 1916), pp. 112–14; *State Auditor's Reports*,

(Little Rock: Office of Auditor, 1852–1929); *Taxes in Arkansas* (Little Rock: Arkansas Public Expenditure Council, 1948); and *Financial Structure of Arkansas* (Little Rock: Arkansas League of Women Voters, 1971).

5 R. Lawson Veasey and W. David Moody, "New Federalism, 2nd Edition," *Arkansas Political Science Journal* 4 (1983): 22–39; John Brummett, "Limited Growth, Easing of Inflation, Hurting State," *Arkansas Gazette*, February 16, 1986.

6 The Rockefeller Foundation's criticisms are summarized in Vicki F. Tynan, *Responsible Choices in Taxation: A Billion Dollars in Alternatives* (Little Rock: Winthrop Rockefeller Foundation, 1983), and V. F. Tynan, *Responsible Choices in Taxation* (Little Rock: Winthrop Rockefeller Foundation, 1984). For contrary arguments, see Bob Lamb, "Why Exemptions Are Granted," *Arkansas Gazette*, September 15, 1983; Bill Sherman, "Most Tax Exemptions Are Justified," *Arkansas Gazette*, August 17, 1983; and Frank Troutman, *Taxation and Economic Development: Arkansas and Selected States* (Little Rock: Industrial and Research Center, 1983).

7 For an excellent summary of the effects of Amendment 19, see Calvin R. Ledbetter, Jr., "Arkansas Amendment 19 Is Legislative Overkill," *Arkansas Gazette*, November 16, 1983. For the 1983 tax votes, see "Severance Tax Is Defeated by Both Houses," *Arkansas Gazette*, October 3, 1983, and "Clinton's Strategy on Bill Raising Corporate Taxes Stymied by Mathematics," *Arkansas Gazette*, October 6, 1983. See Phyllis Finton Johnston, *Bill Clinton's Public Policy for Arkansas: 1979–1980)* (Little Rock: August House, 1983), pp. 60–61, for how Amendment 19 led to Clinton's fateful 1979 decision to raise vehicle license fees.

8 Commerce Clearing House report in *U.S. News and World Report*, January 27, 1986, p. 11.

9 *1983 Tax Capacity of the Fifty States* (Washington, D.C.: Advisory Commission on Intergovernmental Relations, 1986), pp. 1–11, 17, 49, 66–98.

10 Ibid., p. 89; *Significant Features of Fiscal Federalism, 1984 Edition* (Washington, D.C.: Advisory Commission on Intergovernmental Relations, 1985), p. 34; *U.S. News and World Report*, February 10, 1986, p. 11.

11 Quotations from Thomas, *Arkansas and Its People*, p. 102; Ernest Dumas, "Property Tax Proposal Gutted by Senate," *Arkansas Gazette*, March 25, 1983; Tommy Venters, director of State Education Department, quoted in "Revision of '59 Is Unlikely," *Arkansas Gazette*, January 15, 1986; and John Fletcher, *Arkansas Gazette*, September 17, 1948. On early wealth and tax discrepancies between the highlands and lowlands, see also S. Charles Bolton, Calvin Ledbet-

ter, Jr., and Gerald T. Hanson, *Arkansas Becomes a State* (Little Rock: Center for Arkansas Studies, University of Arkansas at Little Rock, 1985), p. 32.

12 Quotation from "Schools the Unfortunate Victims of Problems with Property Tax," *Arkansas Gazette*, September 11, 1983. For equally grim assessments of Amendment 59's effects, see Richard Yates, "Voters Should Learn Who Is Responsible for Amendment 59," *Arkansas Gazette*, November 12, 1985; Jonathan Runnels, "Amendment 59's Freeze Put Heat on Real Property Owner," *Arkansas Democrat*, November 24, 1985; and "Amendment 59: 1980 Supporters Are Now Hard to Find," *Northwest Arkansas Times*, December 8, 1985. Public views on property taxes from *Arkansans Attitudes toward Taxes* (Little Rock: Center for Urban and Governmental Affairs, University of Arkansas at Little Rock, 1981), p. 8. For some of the most critical studies over the decades, see "Report of Superintendent of Public Instruction," in *Report of Arkansas Bureau of Mines, Manufacturing, and Agriculture, 1899–1900*, pp. 10–11; Thomas, "A History of Taxation," pp. 43–90; Edward W. Reed, *Comparative Analysis of the Arkansas Tax System* (Fayetteville: Bureau of Business and Economic Research, University of Arkansas, December 1950), pp. 197–206; *Improving the Equity of Arkansas Taxes*, A Report to the Legislative Council by the Legislative Advisory Committee on Tax Reform, January 1, 1971; and *School Property Taxation in Arkansas* (Little Rock: Winthrop Rockefeller Foundation, 1983).

13 Bill Goodman, "Financing State Programs in Arkansas," *Arkansas Issues 83* (Little Rock: Center for Arkansas Studies, University of Arkansas at Little Rock, 1983), p. 10.

14 For detailed descriptions of the budget process, see Goodman, "Financing State Programs in Arkansas," pp. 7–14; Douglas C. Stadter, "The Arkansas Budgetary System," (M.P.A. internship paper, University of Arkansas, 1980); and Donald E. Whistler, "Budgeting in Arkansas: A Description, Reflections, and Speculations" (Paper presented at the annual Meeting of the Arkansas Political Science Association, Russellville, February 1985).

15 For the pre-1960 purely legislative budget, see Henry Alexander, *Government in Arkansas* (Little Rock: Pioneer Press, 1963), pp. 233–41. According to Robert F. Johnston and Dan Durning, "The Arkansas Governor's Role in the Policy Process, 1955–1979," *Arkansas Political Science Journal* 2 (1981): 28–29, and author interview with Janice Snead, administrator of the State Office of Budget, 1980–84, the Revenue Stabilization Act was written by the governor until 1969; by the Joint Budget Committee through the 1977 session and again in 1981; and by Governor Clinton together with key Joint Budget Committee members during

Clinton's administrations. The Advisory Commission on Intergovernmental Relations now classifies Arkansas as having an executive budget in *The Question of State Government Capability* (Washington, D.C.: ACIR, January 1985), p. 134; Goodman ("Financing State Programs," p. 7) and Stadter ("The Arkansas Budgetary System," pp. 60–62) dispute this description; Alan Rosenthal (*Legislative Life* [New York: Harper and Row, 1981], p. 207) terms it a "hybrid."

16 Dan Durning, "Budgeting in Arkansas: Agencies, Governor, and Legislature," in Walter Nunn, ed., *Readings in Arkansas Government* (Little Rock: Rose Publishing, 1973), p. 204.

17 See Diane D. Blair, "Two Transitions in Arkansas, 1978 and 1982," in Thad Beyle, ed., *Gubernatorial Transitions* (Durham, N.C.: Duke University Press, 1985), pp. 95, 97, 99–104.

18 Quotation from author interview with Janice Snead. See also Whistler, "Budgeting in Arkansas."

19 Quotation from Richard C. Elling, "State Bureaucracies," in Gray, Jacob, and Vines, *Politics in the American States*, p. 269.

20 Quotations from Ira Sharkansky, *The Politics of Taxing and Spending* (Indianapolis: Bobbs-Merrill, 1969), p. 14; Elling, "State Bureaucracies," p. 273. For the most authoritative discussion of incrementalism, see Aaron Wildavsky, *The Politics of the Budgetary Process* (Boston: Little, Brown, 1964), chap. 5. For recent confirmation of incrementalism in state spending decisions, see David Lowery, Thomas Kouda, and James Garand, "Spending in the States: A Test of Six Models," *Western Political Quarterly* 37 (1984): 48–66.

21 T. R. Carr, "An Evaluation of the Impact of the Priority Budgeting System of Arkansas on Budget Outcomes" (Paper presented at the Annual Meeting of the American Society for Public Administration, New York City, April 1983), pp. 12–13.

22 Figures calculated from *State Budget* (Little Rock: Department of Finance and Administration), relevant years, and from "Report to Taxpayers, Arkansas Legislative and Budget Highlights, Fiscal Years 1986 and 1987," (Little Rock: Department of Finance and Administration, June 1985). See also Bob Wells, "It's Over and State Is in the Black by $1 Million," *Arkansas Gazette*, July 1, 1986.

23 Kern Alexander and James Hale, "Educational Equity, Improving School Finance in Arkansas," Report to Advisory Committee of the Special School Formula Project of the Joint Interim Committee on Education, 1978, p. 11.

24 *The Public School System of Arkansas* (Washington, D.C.: U.S. Department of the Interior, Bureau of Education, October 6, 1922), repr. as "The Arkansas

Survey Report," *Journal of the Arkansas Education Association* 6 (July–October, 1922).

25 Clara B. Kennan and Evalena Berry, "The Growth of Public Schools," in Leland Duvall, ed., *Arkansas: Colony and State* (Little Rock: Rose Publishing, 1973), pp. 116–18; Lonnie J. White, *Politics on the Southwestern Frontier: Arkansas Territory, 1819–1836* (Memphis, Tenn.: Memphis State University Press, 1964), p. 158. The most extensive historical treatments of public education in Arkansas are Josiah H. Shinn, *History of Education in Arkansas*, (Washington, D.C.: U.S. Bureau of Education, 1900); Stephen B. Weeks, *History of Public School Education in Arkansas* (Washington, D.C.: U.S. Bureau of Education, 1912); and Henry C. Dial, "Historical Development of School Finance in Arkansas, 1819–1970" (Ed.D. diss., University of Arkansas, 1971). For briefer but excellent treatments see Clara B. Kennan, "The Birth of Public Schools," and Kennan and Berry, "The Growth of Public Schools," in Duvall, *Arkansas: Colony and State*, pp. 105–24; Sara Murphy, "Education," in *Arkansas: State of Transition* (Little Rock: Legal Services Corporation, 1981), pp. 43–51; and *Education in the States: Historical Development and Outlook, Arkansas* (Washington, D.C.: National Education Association, 1969).

26 Quotation from Dial, "Historical Development," p. 191. For some studies comparing Arkansas's educational "achievements" with those of other states, see *The Public School System of Arkansas*; Howard A. Dawson and Harry A. Little, *Financial and Administrative Needs of the Public Schools of Arkansas* (Little Rock: State Superintendent of Public Instruction, 1930); *Study of Local School Units in Arkansas* (Little Rock: Arkansas State Department of Education, Keith Printing, 1937); *Public Education in Arkansas: A Survey* (Little Rock: Arkansas Public Expenditure Council, 1944); Alexander and Hale, *Educational Equity*.

27 See Thomas R. Dye, *Politics, Economics, and the Public: Policy Outcomes in the American States* (Chicago: Rand McNally, 1966), pp. 74–114.

28 Stephen Weeks quoted in Dial, "Historical Development," p. 60. See also Kennan, "The Birth of Public Schools," p. 105.

29 John L. Sullivan, "Political Correlates of Social, Economic, and Religious Diversity in the United States," *Journal of Politics* 35 (1973): 70–84.

30 Jeff Davis quoted in David M. Tucker, *Arkansas: A People and Their Reputation* (Memphis, Tenn.: Memphis State University Press, 1985), p. 63; *The Public School System of Arkansas*, pp. 62–62; Dawson and Little, *Financial and Administrative Needs*, p. 21.

31 Figures for 1926 from Dial, "Historical Development," p. 180; Arch Ford quoted in Bill and Grace Harwood, *School Days, Contemporary Views on*

*Arkansas Public Education* (Little Rock: Winthrop Rockefeller Foundation, 1978), p. 85.

32 Views on property taxes in *Arkansans Attitudes toward Taxes*, p. 8; attitudes toward compulsory school attendance in Lile, *The Government of Arkansas*, p. 153; 1978 opinions in *Arkansas Attitudes on Higher Education* (Little Rock: University of Arkansas at Little Rock, Center for Urban and Governmental Affairs, 1979), pp. 4–8; Robert S. Erikson, "The Relationship between Public Opinion and State Policy," in Marilyn Gittell, ed., *State Politics and the New Federalism* (New York: Longman, 1986), p. 154.

33 Gross spending data from *Report of the Superintendent of Public Instruction* (Little Rock: Arkansas Bureau of Mines, Manufacturing, and Agriculture, 1899/1900), pp. 10–11, 183, and "Comparison of Appropriations and Funding for Selected Educational Entities, Fiscal Years 1982–1986 (Projected)," (Little Rock: Office of Budget, May 14, 1986, rev.) Number of school districts from *Statistical Summary for the Public Schools of Arkansas, 1981–83*, (Little Rock: State Department of Education, 1984), p. 35; and *The State of Education in Arkansas: A Report to the People* (Little Rock: Office of Governor, August 1986), p. 1.

34 State rankings from *U.S. News and World Report*, May 19, 1986, p. 13, and May 5, 1986, p. 13; and from C. Emily Feistritzer, *The Condition of Teaching, A State by State Analysis* (Princeton, N.J.: Carnegie Foundation for the Advancement of Teaching, 1985), p. 154.

35 Feistritzer, *The Condition of Teaching*, pp. 39–41; Doh C. Shinn and Jack R. Van Der Slik, "Legislative Efforts to Improve the Quality of Public Education in the American States: A Comparative Analysis" (Paper presented at the Annual Meeting of the American Political Science Association, New Orleans, September 1985), p. 39; Report from *The Chronicle of Higher Education*, October 30, 1985.

36 Quotation from remark to author by South Arkansas timber magnate, in Little Rock, March 1983. On the South's new emphasis on education as an industry attraction, see Christopher Connell, "Schools the New Lure for Attracting Industry," *Arkansas Gazette*, March 17, 1986.

37 The political development of the Arkansas Education Association is traced in George S. Hollowell, "The Arkansas Education Association and the General Assembly," (University of Arkansas, 1979, Typescript). According to David Davies, "Fund Commitment Lack Leads to AEA request for Legislative Session," *Arkansas Gazette*, April 6, 1986, the 17,000 member AEA had a $2.2 million budget for 1986–87. Legislative rankings of most powerful lobbies in

Arthur English and John J. Carroll, *Citizen's Manual to the Arkansas General Assembly* (Little Rock: Institute of Politics and Government, 1983), pp. 44–45.

38 For changing attitudes on public schools, see "A Report on Public Attitudes to Arkansas Louisiana Gas Company," prepared by Precision Research, Inc., Little Rock, May 31, 1983; *Attitudes on Arkansas* (Little Rock: Center for Urban and Governmental Affairs, Survey Marketing Research Unit, August 1982); Robert L. Savage and Diane D. Blair, "Regionalism and Political Opinion in Arkansas: An Exploratory Survey," *Arkansas Political Science Journal* 5 (1984), p. 80; Arkansas senatorial polls conducted for Sen. David Pryor, 1984; and "The Bailey Arkansas Poll," August–September 1985.

39 For lengthy excerpts from and analyses of this six-to-one decision, see extensive coverage in *Arkansas Democrat* and *Arkansas Gazette*, June 1, 1983.

40 An overview of the "campaign for educational excellence" is provided in Marvin E. DeBoer, "Governor Clinton and Educational Reform in Arkansas: A Study in Communication" (Paper presented at the Annual Meeting of the Arkansas Political Science Association, North Little Rock, February 1986). Additional details provided in numerous stories in *Arkansas Democrat* and *Arkansas Gazette*, March–October 1983, and from author conversations with Governor and Mrs. Clinton throughout this period.

41 Quotation from Gov. Bill Clinton, televised address, September 19, 1983. According to DeBoer, "Governor Clinton," p. 19, a survey taken in September 1983, showed 75.7 percent of respondents strongly supporting teacher testing, 11.4 percent supporting, and only 9.4 percent opposed. For the AEA's viewpoint, see John Brummett, "Deterioration of Clinton-AEA Relationship Is Nothing New," *Arkansas Gazette*, September 6, 1983.

42 On the deteriorating 1986 school finance picture, see "Education is Arkansas' Future, School Finance, 1986," (Little Rock: Arkansas Education Association, March 1986); David Davies, "Finances Big Worry of Schools," *Arkansas Gazette*, March 30, 1986, and "1.5% Pay Raise for State Teachers Predicted by AEA," *Arkansas Gazette*, August 6, 1986, and "Schools Get Bad News on Amount of State Aid," *Arkansas Gazette*, July 4, 1986 For candidate positions on school standards, see "Candidate Proposes Ranking of Standards," *Arkansas Gazette*, May 18, 1986; Pam Strickland, "White Blasts Plan to Implement Education Standards by 1987–88," *Arkansas Democrat*, August 14, 1986; and Meredith Oakley, "Clinton Vows No Dilution of Education," *Arkansas Democrat*, August 25, 1986.

43 Treadway, *Public Policymaking*, p. 178.

44 According to some observers, Hillary Clinton deserves even more credit for

education reform than does her husband. See Paul Greenberg, "Clinton on Education: 'His Finest Hour,' " *Arkansas Times*, February 1984, pp. 26–30, and Robert McCord, "Those Who Give Schools Their Vote Deserve One Themselves Election Day," *Arkansas Gazette*, May 18, 1986.

45 Sharkansky, *The Politics of Taxing and Spending*, pp. 16, 148, 151.

CHAPTER 14

1 For some analyses of the 1968 results, see chapter 4. On Senators Bumpers's and Pryor's "liberal" ratings, see Carol Matlack, "State Delegation Rated as South's Most Liberal," *Arkansas Gazette*, May 23, 1986; Damon Thompson, "Annual Ratings Tattle on Lawmakers' Mettle," *Arkansas Democrat*, January 26, 1986; and "Report Card: Who Likes Whom," *Arkansas Democrat*, October 29, 1986.

2 For a variety of non-Arkansas discussions of Bumpers or Clinton as presidential possibilities, see Martin Schram, "Hamlet of Arkansas," *Washington Post*, February 28, 1983; William Greider, "Of Virtue, Quality, and the White House," *Rolling Stone*, March 31, 1983, pp. 9–10; "New entries," *Newsweek*, November 3, 1986, p. 6. Mark Russell quoted in *Arkansas Gazette*, November 24, 1986. North Carolina political scientist's comment to author at Southern Political Science Association Meeting, Atlanta, Ga., November 1986.

3 Of seventy-three press secretaries surveyed by *USA Today*, nineteen named Bumpers the best speaker in the Senate, *Arkansas Gazette*, June 2, 1986.

4 William S. Bonner and Donald E. Voth, "The Changing Composition of the Rural Population," *Arkansas Farm Research*, July–August 1986, p. 4. *State Policy Data Book, 1986* (Alexandria, Va.: State Policy Research, 1986), tables A-14, A-16. Bernard Quinn, Herman Anderson, Martin Bradley, and Peggy Shriver, *Churches and Church Membership in the United States* (Atlanta: Glenmary Research Center, 1980), pp. 37–48.

5 Donald Voth, "Impact of Migration on Arkansas" (Lecture given in Center for Arkansas and Regional Studies Lecture Series, Fayetteville, March 15, 1984), pp. 14–15 and "Selected Reference Tables."

6 Dougan quoted in *Arkansas Gazette*, May 1, 1986.

7 Quotation by Pat Moran, former Public Service commissioner and administrative aide to Sen. Dale Bumpers, cited in Alexander P. Lamis, *The Two-Party South* (New York: Oxford University Press, 1984), p. 126.

8 Governor Clinton quoted by John Brummett, "Candidates Garner Enthusiastic Support at Democratic Convention," *Arkansas Gazette*, September 8, 1984. "Go Home!" *Northwest Arkansas Times*, January 26, 1985. See also *Arkansas*

*Democrat* poll on Falwell visit, February 21, 1985, and "Jerry and the Dupes," *Arkansas Times*, April 1985.

9 According to Arbitron ratings in November 1986, cited by Paul Johnson, "The Small Screen," *Arkansas Gazette*, January 8, 1987, almost all Arkansas households have television service, indeed more than half have more than one television set in the household, and television is viewed 44.3 hours per week.

10 For some evidence that this logic helps to explain Fulbright's long presence in the U.S. Senate, see Neal R. Peirce and Jerry Hagstrom, *The Book of America: Inside Fifty States Today* (New York: Norton, 1983), p. 489.

11 Annie Glenn's observations cited by Skip Rutherford, "Politics Is Personal in Arkansas," *Arkansas Gazette*, April 4, 1984.

12 See "The Most Likely Non-Partisan Event Where Politicians Will Show," *Newsletter of the Political Animals Club*, March 5, 1986 for a list and ranking of such events.

13 "Arkansas," *Congressional Quarterly*, October 11, 1986, p. 2404.

14 Paul Greenberg, "Bethunery and Strange Pryorities in South Arkansas," *Arkansas Times*, May 1984, p. 38. See also Stephen Buel, "Campaigning Styles Obviously Different for Pryor, Bethune," *Arkansas Democrat*, November 5, 1984.

15 Congressman Bill Alexander, class lecture, Arkansas Politics, University of Arkansas, Fayetteville, October 26, 1984. Bill Clinton, class lecture, Arkansas Politics, University of Arkansas, Fayetteville, October 12, 1981.

16 Brooks Hays, *Politics Is My Parish* (Baton Rouge: Louisiana State University Press, 1981), p. 142.

17 Jim Ranchino, *Faubus to Bumpers: Arkansas Votes, 1960–70* (Arkadelphia, Ark.: Action Research, 1972), pp. iv, 71.

18 Sen. David Pryor, interview with author, Fayetteville, Ark., April 11, 1986. Excerpt from Tim Hackler, "Gazette Is More than an Old Friend," *Arkansas Gazette*, November 17, 1986.

19.Candidate quotations from "Vote Clinton Out," *Northwest Arkansas Times*, March 28, 1986; "Britt, 66, Declares Candidacy," *Arkansas Gazette*, January 11, 1986; and "Candidate Ready to Climb Political Mountain," *Arkansas Democrat*, January 19, 1986. Candidates' positions on educational standards in Bob Wells, "Voters Get Choice of Four Republicans," *Arkansas Gazette*, May 25, 1986.

20 See Bob Wells, "The Past Ever Present for Faubus," and "Faubus Turns up Heat before Crowd at Ozark," *Arkansas Gazette*, May 18, 1986, and May 15, 1986; "Clinton, Faubus Argue School Standards' Merits," *Arkansas Gazette*, April

13, 1986; Maria Henson, "Clinton Says He's Learned from the Past," *Arkansas Gazette*, May 18, 1986; and Patrick Casey, "Clinton Rebuts Opponents' Campaign Trash," *Arkansas Democrat*, April 30, 1986.

21 Faubus quoted in *Arkansas Gazette*, May 29, 1986.

22 On the negative nature of both campaigns, see Meredith Oakley, "Negative Campaigns Tax Public Patience," *Arkansas Democrat*, October 16, 1986, and Maria Henson and Scott Van Laningham, "New Trends, Old-style Campaigning," *Arkansas Gazette*, October 26, 1986. Candidate positions and statements extracted from "Abortion Addressed by White," *Arkansas Gazette*, July 15, 1986; Pam Strickland, "New Standards Deadline to Rocket Taxes," and "Political Wives Differ on Role of First Lady," *Arkansas Democrat*, July 23, 1986, and October 19, 1986; Dan O'Mara, "White Talks about Quality Education," *Springdale News*, October 9, 1986; Maria Henson, "Clinton 'Sick and Tired' of Fund Requests," *Arkansas Gazette*, October 29, 1986; and "Clinton Keeps Silence on '65,'" *Arkansas Gazette*, November 6, 1986.

23 Vice-President Bush quoted in "Says Tide Is Turning GOP," *Arkansas Democrat*, July 2, 1986. Hutchinson's comparisons of Bumpers with Ted Kennedy in "Hutchinson Announces," *Arkansas Gazette*, January 14, 1986, and in fundraising letter dated June 9, 1986, in author's possession. President Reagan's endorsement advertisement quoted in "Hutchinson GOP Ad Gets Reagan Support," *Arkansas Democrat*, August 17, 1986.

24 Quotations from Clinton television commercial, October 1986, and from Bumpers's speech to Washington County Democratic Rally, Springdale, Ark., October 22, 1986.

25 Quotation from Ray Wolfinger and Michael G. Hagen, "Republican Prospects: Southern Comfort," *Public Opinion*, October–November 1985, p. 13. On the importance and fragility of the "red-neck, black-neck" coalition, see Lamis, *The Two-Party South*, pp. 31–43, 56, 218–24, 229–32. See also Milton Coleman, "Coalition-Building and the Color Line," *Washington Post*, May 21, 1986.

26 On 1986 black vote, see ABC exit poll cited in "Clinton Lead for Governor Came Early," *Arkansas Democrat*, November 5, 1986. In some black Little Rock precincts, such as 490, 491, and 495, Clinton and Bumpers got between 95 percent and 99 percent of the vote. In the three counties with majority black populations, Clinton and Bumpers averaged respectively 74 percent and 81 percent of the vote. Gender gap figures from ABC exit poll, cited above, and "The Bailey Arkansas Poll," October 22, 1986.

27 On the religious right as a bridge to Republicanism, see Tod A. Baker, Robert P. Steed, and Laurence W. Moreland, "The Emergence of the Religious Right and the Development of the Two-Party System in the South" (Paper presented at the

Annual Meeting of the American Political Science Association, Washington, D.C., August 1986). See also "Portrait of the Electorate," *New York Times*, November 6, 1986, p. 22, citing polls showing that 69 percent of white Fundamentalist Christians favored Republican U.S. House candidates in 1986. Arkansas opinions in "The Bailey Arkansas Poll," February 18, 1986, and October 15, 1986. Comments by Arkansas Republican leaders quoted in Bob Faulkner, "GOP Needs to Look beyond Negative, Single-Issue Thinking," *Arkansas Gazette*, November 10, 1986; Scott Van Laningham and Maria Henson, "GOP Won't be Reminiscing about Successes of '86," *Arkansas Gazette*, November 16, 1986; and Robert McCord, "Bethune Returns to Politics," *Arkansas Gazette*, November 23, 1986.

28 For the 1986 version, see Maria Henson, "Old State House Comes Back from the Future," *Arkansas Gazette*, August 19, 1986. For a thorough account and explanation of the 1837 incident, see Jerry E. Hinshaw, *Call the Roll: The First One Hundred Fifty Years of the Arkansas Legislature* (Little Rock: Department of Arkansas Heritage, Rose Publishing, 1986), pp. 20–25.

29 "Some Warm, Pretty Thoughts about the Sesquicentennial," *Arkansas Times*, February 1986, p. 126.

30 On the "widowhood" route to political power, see Diane D. Kincaid, "Over His Dead Body: A Positive Perspective on Widows in the U.S. Congress," *Western Political Quarterly* 31 (March 1978): 96–104. According to the National Women's Political Caucus, the Clinton administration ranked fourth of the fifty states in the percentage (33 percent) of women appointed to cabinet positions. See "Survey Ranks Clinton Fourth," *Arkansas Gazette*, November 30, 1986. According to the National Organization for Women, however, Arkansas ranked forty-fourth in terms of women's general economic, legal, and political equality. See "NOW Study Ranks Arkansas Sixth from Cellar," *Arkansas Democrat*, December 12, 1986.

31 On the teacher associations' merger, see John Reed, "Union of Black, White Associations More than Symbolic," *Arkansas Gazette*, November 17, 1986. On McHenry's selection, see David Davies, "New AEA Leader Seeks 'Consensus,'" *Arkansas Gazette*, November 20, 1985. On the contemporary conflict between Arkansas and the U.S. Justice Department, see Doug Smith, "Officials Resisting Request" and "Program to Remain in Effect," *Arkansas Gazette*, June 1, 1985, and June 5, 1985. On Nolan Richardson's selection, see Orville Henry, "Tulsa's Richardson Named UA Coach," *Arkansas Gazette*, April 10, 1985; John Jeansonne, "When Door Opened, Richardson Entered," *Arkansas Democrat*, April 10, 1985; and Gene Lyons, "The Winter of Nolan Richardson's Discontent," *Arkansas Times*, December 1986, pp. 33–35, 72–76.

32 For some interesting comparisons between Jeff Davis and Tommy Robinson, see Marc White, "A Comparative Analysis of Jeff Davis and Tommy Robinson" (University of Arkansas, 1984, Typescript), and Aaron Mitchell, "Tommy Robinson: A Jeff Davis Flashback for Arkansas?" (University of Arkansas, 1985, Typescript).

33 On Witt Stephens's exertions in Fulbright's behalf, see Kurt W. Tweraser, "J. W. Fulbright, Belief Systems, Models of Representation and Re-Election Strategies, 1942–1962" (Paper presented at the Annual Meeting of the Southern Political Science Association, Nashville, Tenn., November 1985). See also Doug Smith, "Is There a New Money Group?" *Arkansas Gazette*, July 11, 1978. On the Stephens' role in the 1986 gubernatorial campaign, see Maria Henson, "White Alleges Clinton Link on Securities," and "Clinton Sees Bid to 'Buy' Office," *Arkansas Gazette*, September 18, 1986, and October 10, 1986; Scott Van Laningham, "Paine, Webber, Wright Law Firm Appear Big Winners in Bond Business," *Arkansas Gazette*, October 12, 1986; and John Brummett columns, *Arkansas Gazette*, October 10, 12, 1986. John S. Jackson III, "The Southernization of National Politics" (Address at the Annual Meeting of the Arkansas Political Science Association, North Little Rock, February 1986).

34 For a good summary of Arkansas's decline relative to the national economy, see James O. Powell, "Moving Arkansas out of Its Economic Rut," *Arkansas Gazette*, December 7, 1986.

35 Thomas D. Clark, "Economic Basis of Southern Politics," *Forum* 112 (August 1949): 86. Clay Fulks, "Arkansas," *American Mercury* 8 (July 1926): 293. Robert A. Leflar, interview with author, Fayetteville, Ark., August 27, 1985.

36 Clinton quotations from class lecture, State and Local Government, University of Arkansas, Fayetteville, May 2, 1986, and Inaugural Address, January 15, 1985. Excerpt from "I Speak Arkansaw," *Arkansas Times*, November 1986, p. 22.

CHAPTER 15

1 For a vivid description of the dearth of good historical materials, see Peggy Harris, " 'Crisis' Seen in Lack of Texts, Neglect of Arkansas History," *Arkansas Gazette*, April 29, 1985.

# Index

Other volumes in the State Politics and Government series:

*Nebraska Government and Politics*
Edited by Robert D. Miewald

*Alabama Government and Politics*
By James D. Thomas and William H. Stewart